Taxation

Incorporating the Finance Act 2009

Richard Andrews BA(Hons), MSc, FCCA

Alan Combs BA, MSc, FCCA

Peter Rowes BSc(Econ), FCA, ATII

FISCAL

PUBLICATIONS

Taxation: incorporating the 2009 Finance Act – 28th Edition 2009/2010

Copyright © 2009 Fiscal Publications

For more information, contact Fiscal Publications, Unit 100, The Guildhall Edgbaston Park Road, Birmingham, B15 2TU, UK or visit: http://www.fiscalpublications.com

British Library Cataloguing-in-Publication Data
A catalogue record for this book is available from the British Library

Lecturer supplement and other materials are available from the Rowes 2009 website – see http://www.fiscalpublications.com/rowes/2009

ISBN 978-1-906201-09-8

Twenty-eighth edition 2009

Cover design by FD Design Ltd
Printed in Great Britain by Antony Rowe, Chippenham, Wiltshire

Typesetting and production by

 P. K. McBride, Southampton

Taxation

Incorporating the Finance Act 2009

28th edition 2009

Contents

Contents

Acknowledgements

The authors would like to express thanks to the following for giving permission to reproduce past examination questions and forms:

Association of Chartered Certified Accountants (ACCA)
Chartered Institute of Management Accountants (CIMA)
Chartered Institute of Taxation (CIOT)
Controller of Her Majesty's Stationery Office

Many of the questions and answers in the 28th edition are from a bank of materials compiled by Jill Webb of Leeds Metropolitan University and Dora Hancock of Birmingham City University. The use of these questions and answers is gratefully acknowledged.

Preface

Aims of the book

1.   The main aim of this book is to provide a thorough basic knowledge of taxation, covering Income Tax, Corporation Tax, Taxation of Chargeable Gains, Inheritance Tax, and Value Added Tax.

It has been written for students of the following:

Association of Chartered Certified Accountants
> Paper F6 Taxation

Certified Accounting Technicians
> Paper 9 Preparing Taxation Computations

Association of Accounting Technicians
> Unit 18 Preparing Business Taxation Computations
> Unit 19 Preparing Personal Taxation Computations

Institute of Chartered Secretaries and Administrators
> Professional Part II Corporate Administration

Association of Taxation Technicians
> All papers (introductory text)

Association of International Accountants
> Module F: Paper 16 Taxation and Tax Planning

Universities and Colleges
> Accounting and Business Studies Degrees – Taxation Modules

Approach

2.   a)   This book should provide the student with:

i) A knowledge of the basic relevant statutory law

ii)A knowledge of some of the case law developed to interpret statutory law.

It should enable the student to apply these legal principles to practical problems and prepare the necessary computations, and to understand the importance of tax planning.

b)   Each of the areas of taxation is introduced by a general principles chapter which outlines the main features of each tax. Subsequent chapters develop the principles in detail with examples.

c)   Illustrative examples form an important feature of this text. At the end of each chapter and each section (except the introductory text) there are questions with answers for student self-testing. Also provided are further questions, the answers to which are contained in a separate supplement which can be obtained direct from the publishers by lecturers recommending the manual as a course text.

This edition incorporates the provisions of the Finance Act 2009 in so far as they relate to the year 2009/10.

Richard Andrews, Alan Combs, Peter Rowes, 2009.

Abbreviations and statutes

Abbreviations

All.ER	All England Reports
BSI	Building society interest
CAA	Capital Allowances Act 2001
CFC	Controlled foreign company
CGT	Capital gains tax
CIHC	Close Investment Holding company
CRC	Commissioners for Revenue and Customs
CT	Corporation tax
CTA	Corporation Tax Act 2009
CTAP	Corporation tax accounting period
DTR	Double taxation relief
E.C.	European Community
GAAP	Generally accepted Accounting Practice
FA 2009	Finance Act 2009
IAS	International Accounting Standards
IBA	Industrial building allowance
IHT	Inheritance tax
ITA	Income Tax Act 2007ITEPA Income tax (Earnings & Pensions) Act 2003
ITTOIA	Income Tax (Trading and Other Income) Act 2005
ORI	Official rate of interest
PAYE	Pay as you earn
PRT	Petroleum revenue tax
RPI	Retail prices index
Sch.	Schedule
STC	Simons tax cases
STI	Simons tax intelligence
TA 1988	Income and Corporation Taxes Act 1988
TC	Tax cases
TCGA 1992	Taxation of Chargeable Gains Act 1992
TMA 1970	Taxes Management Act 1970
VAT	Value added tax

Statutes

Income Tax	Income Tax Act 2007
Income Tax	Income Tax (Trading and Other Income) Act 2005
Income Tax	Income Tax (Earnings & Pensions) Act 2003
Income Tax	Finance Act 2009
Corporation Tax	Corporation Tax Act 2009
Corporation Tax	Finance Act 2009
Capital Gains Tax	Taxation of Chargeable Gains Act 1992
Inheritance Tax	Inheritance Tax Act 1984
Value Added Tax	Value Added Tax Act 1994
Capital Allowances	Capital Allowances Act 2001

Summary of main changes 2009/10

Part II. Income tax

1. Personal reliefs		2009/10 £	2008/09 £
a)	Personal allowance	6,475	6,035
	Married couple's allowance	* 2,670	* 2,540
	Allowances: Aged 65–74		
	Personal allowance	9,490	9,030
	Married couple's allowance	* 6,965	*6,535
	Abatement of relief where income exceeds	22,900	21,800
	Allowances: Aged 75+		
	Personal allowance	9,640	9,180
	Married couple's allowance	* 6,965	* 6,625
	Abatement of relief where income exceeds	22,900	21,800
	Blind person's allowance	1,890	1,800

b) The allowances marked with an asterisk (*) allowed at the 10% rate are given as a deduction in computing the tax liability.

c) A gradual reduction of the personal allowance for Income Tax to nil for individuals with "adjusted net income" over £100,000 is planned for 2010/11.

2. Income tax rates	2009/10	2008/09
Starting rate - savings	10%	10%
- applicable where savings income comprises taxable income up to	£2,440	£2,320
Basic rate		
- savings	20%	20%
- non savings	20%	20%
- dividends	10%	10%
Higher rate	40%	40%
- dividends	32.5%	32.5%

An additional higher rate of 50% (42.5% for dividends) is planned for taxable income of over £150,000 for 2010/11.

3. Taxable bands

Taxable income	Band	2009/10 Rate	Tax payable on band
£	£	%	£
0 – 37,400	37,400	20	7,480

Taxable income	Band	2008/09 Rate	Tax payable on band
£	£	%	£
0 – 34,800	34,800	20	6,960

4. Class IV National Insurance

	2009/10	2008/09
Taxable band	5,715-43,875	5,435-40,040
Rate of tax	8%	8%
	above 43,875	above40,040
	1%	1%

5. Company car benefit

Car benefit is based on a % of the list price of the car graduated according to CO_2 emissions. The normal charge is 15% – 35% of the list price. For 2009/10 the normal minimum CO_2 emission is 135 grams. Cars with CO_2 emissions of up to 120 grams will be charged at 10%. Diesel engines are subject to a 3% surcharge.

6. Car fuel benefit

	2009/10
Car fuel petrol/diesel	CO_2 emissions % £16,900

7. Company van benefit   £3,000. Company van fuel benefit £500.

8. Authorised mileage rates

The statutory system of tax and NICs free mileage rates for 2009/10 are as follows:

Car and Vans	
First 10,000 miles	40p per mile
Over 10,000 miles	25p per mile
Motorcycles	24p per mile
Bicycles	20p per mile

9. National Insurance Thresholds – contracted in

	2009/10	2008/09
Weekly pay	£	£
Upper earnings limit	844.00	770.00
Upper accruals limit	770.00	n/a
Earnings threshold	110.00	105.00
Lower earnings limit	95.00	90.00

10. Official rates of interest

From 1 March 2009	4.75%
From 6 April 2007	6.25%

11. Dividends

UK dividends paid have attached to them a tax credit of 1/9 which is not recoverable by non-tax payers. The tax credit is extended to non UK resident companies for investors with a shareholding of less than 10% from 6 April 2008, and for shareholdings of 10% or more from 22 April 2009.

12. Capital allowances

a) A temporary First Year Allowance of 40% will be available on plant and machinery, in excess of the Annual Investment Allowance, that would normally be added to the general pool of plant and machinery, for the 12 months from 6 April 2009 for unincorporated taxpayers, and 1 April 2009 for companies.

b) 100% First Year Allowance is available on low emissions cars producing 110 g/km or less CO_2.

c) Capital allowances on other cars purchased from 6 April 2009 for unincorporated taxpayers, and 1 April 2009 for companies will be:

   i) 20% Writing Down Allowance for cars with CO_2 emissions of 160 g/km or less;

   ii) 10% Writing Down Allowance for cars with CO_2 emissions of more than 160 g/km.

   Cars with a private use element will need to be separated from the general and special rate pools of plant and machinery.

d) Industrial Buildings Allowance and Agricultural Buildings Allowance of 4% on cost will be restricted by one half in 2009/10.

13. Car leasing

Cars leased on or after 6 April 2009 for unincorporated taxpayers and 1 April 2009 for companies will be subject to a 15% reduction in the tax allowable expense, for cars with CO_2 emissions of more than 160 g/km.

14. Pensions

a) Limits on tax allowable contributions to pension schemes have been increased. From 6 April 2009 there is a £245,000 annual allowance (2008/09 £235,000).

A lifetime limit of £1,750,000 is set for the value of pension savings (2008/09 £1,650,000). The excess will be subject to Income Tax at 40%.

b) For taxpayers whose total annual income is £150,000 or more, special rules will apply from 22 April 2009 to prevent large additional contributions benefiting from higher rate tax relief, in anticipation of the restriction to basic rate relief in 2011/12.

15. Benchmark rates for day subsistence

HMRC has set advisory scale rates for subsistence expenses that it will accept for all employers without any taxable benefit being created. Employers may still agree a dispensation with HMRC for different rates.

16. Income Tax loss relief

Trading losses made in the tax years 2008/09 and 2009/10 by unincorporated businesses can be carried back against general income of the three previous years, against the later years first. Unlimited losses may be set against the preceding year, but a maximum of £50,000 of trading losses per loss making tax year may be carried back into the earlier two years.

17. Furnished holiday lettings

Special tax treatment for furnished holiday lettings as a trade is extended to all properties in the European Economic Area, in anticipation of the special treatment being withdrawn from 6 April 2010.

18. Individual Savings Accounts ISAs

The annual investment allowance for 2009/10 will be increased to £10,200 for taxpayers over the age of 50 (2008/09 £7,200), with a limit of £5,100 (2008/09 £3,600) in the cash ISA element.

Part III. Corporation tax

1. Rates

The rates for the financial year 2009 are as follows:

	FY 2009 - y/e 31.3.2010	FY 2008 – y/e 31.3.2009
Full rate	28%	28%
Small company rate	21%	21%
Marginal band	£300,000 - £1,500,000	£300,000 - £1,500,000

2. Corporation Tax loss relief

Trading losses made by companies in accounting periods ending in the period from 24 November 2008 to 23 November 2010 can be carried back against profits chargeable to Corporation Tax (PCTCT) of the three previous years, against the later years first. Unlimited losses may be set against the preceding 12 months accounting period, but a maximum of £50,000 of trading losses per loss making accounting period, may be carried back into the earlier two years. The £50,000 limit is shared by all companies under common control in a corporate group.

3. Corporation Tax Act 2009

Schedules and cases of income are removed, and profits arising from UK and non UK sources are amalgamated. CTA does not change the effect of the law. Minor anomalies are resolved and some extra statutory concessions and a statement of practice are included.

Part IV. Capital gains tax

Annual exemption for individuals increased to £10,100 in 2009/10 from £9,600 in 2008/09.

Part V. Inheritance tax

Rates

For chargeable transfers made on or after 6th April 2008 the IHT death rates are as follows:

On or after 6th April 2009		On or after 6th April 2008	
£	%	£	%
0 - 325,000	0	0 – 312,000	0
325,001 -	40	312,001 –	40

Part VI. Value added tax

1. Registration

Registration levels applicable from 1 May 2009.

	£
Taxable turnover in previous 12 months	68,000
Taxable turnover in next 30 days	68,000

2. Deregistration

The annual limit for deregistration is £66,000 from 1 May 2009.

3. VAT fuel rates 2009/10

Fuel scale charges are calculated on the basis of CO_2 emissions. New rates are applicable from 1 may 2009.

2009/10 CO_2 emissions	1 Month period		3 Month period	
	VAT inclusive scale charge	VAT due per car	VAT inclusive scale charge	VAT due per car
	£	£	£	£
120g/km or less	42	5.48	126	16.43
increasing in bands of 5g/km to				
235g/km or more	147	19.17	441	57.52

2008/09 CO_2 emissions	1 Month period		3 Month period	
	VAT inclusive scale charge	VAT due per car	VAT inclusive scale charge	VAT due per car
	£	£	£	£
120g/km or less	46	6.85	138	20.53
135g/km or less	69	10.28	207	30.83
increasing in bands of 5g/km to				
235g/km or more	161	23.98	483	71.94

4. Temporary VAT rate

The 15% temporary VAT rate introduced from 1 December 2008 will cease on 31 December 2009, and the standard rate from 1 January 2010 will return to 17.5%

General issues

Business Payment Support Service

Where a viable business is due to pay tax on the previous year's business profits and is likely to make a trading loss, those losses can be taken into account in agreeing the level of payments to be made. VAT, Income Tax, NI, Corporation Tax and PAYE are included. Interest will still be charged on amounts not paid on the normal due dates.

HMRC appeals procedure

From 1 April 2009 there will be appeal to an optional HMRC internal review and a two tier tribunal system: the First Tier Tribunal (Tax Chamber) and Upper Tribunal.

Part I

Introduction

1 Principles of taxation

'In this world nothing can be said to be certain, except death and taxes' Benjamin Franklin[1].

Definition of tax

1. Taxes are contributions levied on persons, property or business, for the support of national or local government[2].

Reasons for tax

2. Organised societies are said to exist because they provide greater benefits to members than living individually or in small groups[3]. Highly developed societies who use money for exchange fund the benefits by public expenditure. Some of the oldest records in history are of wealth used as a basis for raising the money for public expenditure by taxation.

3. Tax is justified by the benefits it provides. In a society that tolerates free speech public spending is subject to intense scrutiny. One reason for this may be that if benefits are not being provided to the members of society, the reason for collecting tax is lost. Adverse comments, and civil disobedience, can also result where taxation is seen as unfair.

A balanced budget

4. The amount of money raised by taxation and the amount of public expenditure will not necessarily equal each other in a particular year. A 'budget deficit' arises in a year where public expenditure is more than the amount raised by taxation. The government can fund the extra expenditure by inviting people to lend it money, in the form of government securities or investments in National Savings. Years of 'budget surplus' where taxation exceeds public expenditure would give the opportunity for government borrowings to be repaid.

Early in the history of modern Western economics 'classical' economists, such as Adam Smith, formed a view that market forces would produce the most efficient allocation of resources of labour and financial capital[4]. If there was unemployment, for example, market forces would cause wages to fall, until lower wages encouraged employers to take on more workers. It was believed the wages received by the newly employed workers would stimulate demand for more goods and services, and a virtuous circle of growth would continue until an equilibrium was reached when everyone was employed. The belief in efficient markets implied it was best for governments to intervene as little as possible in the economic choices made by people and businesses. This 'fiscal neutrality' would include running a 'balanced budget' where necessary public expenditure was financed by an equal amount of taxation.

'Keynesian' economists formed the view that equilibrium in the economy could be reached at points below full employment[5]. In times when market demand was low it would be beneficial for the government to use reflationary policies to stimulate demand, and start the cycle of growth. These policies might include[6]:

- increasing government expenditure;

- cutting direct or indirect taxation to encourage spending;

- cutting interest rates to discourage saving and encourage spending;

- allowing money supply growth.

The first two techniques are 'fiscal' policies which directly affect public expenditure and tax revenue. Applying these policies could cause a budget deficit. Keynesian economics accepts a budget deficit in years when the market economy is in recession, providing it is matched by a budget surplus in years of high growth in the market economy. The deflationary policies available to achieve budget surpluses and restrain demand would be the opposite of the reflationary policies above. Budgets should still be balanced over the long term. Applying Keynesian economics to the government's budget would involve using changes in public expenditure and taxation to affect demand for goods and services[7], and so counteract the effects of the 'boom and bust' cycles in the market economy: 'counter-cyclical demand management policies'.

The UK Treasury predicts[8] total government receipts for 2009/2010 will be £496bn and total managed expenditure will be £671bn. This is a budget deficit of £175bn, with expenditure 35% more than receipts.

In 2008/09 the Treasury predicted receipts of £575bn against expenditure of £618bn, a budget deficit of £43bn, or 7.5% excess of expenditure compared to receipts. For each of the 5 preceding years from 2003/04 onwards the budget deficit of excess of expenditure compared to receipts varied between 6.1% and 7.3%.

Desirable characteristics of taxation

5. Adam Smith[9] proposed 'Canons of Taxation' which listed desirable features for a system of taxation. These may be restated in contemporary terms as equity, certainty, convenience and efficiency.

Equity means taxes should be fair. Horizontal equity would require justice and equality of treatment, so taxpayers having similar circumstances would be treated in a similar way by the tax authorities and have similar tax liabilities. Vertical equity would mean the burden of tax fell fairly across taxpayers with different circumstances. This requires a subjective value judgement about what is fair. Adam Smith believed fairness would link tax liabilities with the taxpayer's ability to pay, so taxpayers with high income and wealth would pay more tax than those with low income and little wealth. Another possible approach to fairness would be linking the amount of a taxpayer's liability with the value of benefits from public expenditure they receive.

Certainty means taxpayers should be able to establish how taxes will result from their economic decisions such as whether to work in return for income, save or spend their wealth, or deal in assets. This would mean the tax law and regulations would need to be clearly written, and not applied retrospectively.

Convenience would minimise the taxpayers costs in complying with tax laws and regulations. A tax requiring only simple calculations by a taxpayer would satisfy the 'Canons of taxation' better than a tax requiring complex calculations based on records kept over many years.

Efficiency has two elements:

Administrative efficiency means the costs of collecting tax should be as low as possible in comparison with the revenue raised.

Economic efficiency means tax does not distort taxpayers' economic decisions, such as whether to work or take leisure, and whether to save or spend their income and wealth.

In working through this book it will be seen there are limits to which taxes in the UK achieve the ideals set out as the Canons of Taxation. Indeed some features of UK taxes are intended to influence taxpayers and have distorting effects on economic decisions. There is a current theme of encouraging spending on assets which help minimise environmental damage, and discouraging spending on vehicles with high levels of carbon dioxide emissions. Taxes with an intentional distorting effect are called 'corrective'.

Tax bases

6. What to tax? The most basic form of tax is a poll tax, where every taxpayer has an equal liability. Such a tax is widely regarded as inequitable, because it is not related to ability to pay, or to benefits consumed. A form of poll tax was used for local taxation in the UK during the 1980s and 1990s. The tax was administratively inefficient because of widespread non payment through lack of public acceptance and the impossibility of collecting tax from people without the ability to pay. The 'community charge' caused riots and the prime minister of the time was removed from office.

Major tax bases in modern economies are income, expenditure and wealth. Taxing income or expenditure recognises transactions are taking place, and so it has some relationship to ability to pay. Wealth may not be in the form of cash and so does not necessarily show an ability to pay. In the UK wealth taxes at the national level are linked to wealth being transferred by sale, gift or inheritance. The existence of a transaction increases the likelihood of cash being available to pay tax.

Direct and indirect taxes

7. Direct taxes are related to a taxpayer's circumstances, for example income or wealth. The taxpayer will in some cases be responsible for making payments of tax directly to the tax authorities. However, for some types of income including bank and building society interest and earnings from employment, income tax is deducted by the savings institution or employer before the taxpayer receives income. The institution or employer then pays the tax over to HM Revenue and Customs. This is still direct tax, as the tax is related to the taxpayer's personal circumstances.

8. Indirect taxes are charged to a taxpayer, but with the effect that the cost of the tax is suffered by another person or organisation. For example, retailers are responsible for paying Value Added Tax (VAT) to HM Revenue and Customs, but the tax is paid to the retailer by customers who actually bear the cost of the tax.

Incidence of tax

9. The 'incidence' of tax may simply be described as the person or organisation obliged to pay the tax. Indirect taxes have a different 'formal incidence', the taxpayer legally responsible for making tax payments to the tax authorities, and 'effective incidence', the person or organisation whose wealth is actually reduced by the tax. Direct taxes are more likely to have the same formal and effective incidence.

Hypothecated taxes

10. Hypothecated taxes are collected to fund a particular service. Money collected from the television licence is used to pay for the television programmes of the BBC.

Excise duties

11. Excise duties are indirect expenditure taxes on transactions for products such as alcohol, tobacco and fuel oil. They are unit taxes based on the quantity of the product. This distinguishes them from indirect taxes based on value, such as value added tax and insurance premium tax.

Withholding taxes

12. Withholding taxes are deducted from income before a taxpayer receives it. UK income tax is deducted by banks and building societies paying interest on savings accounts to individuals.

Double taxation

13. If a taxpayer receives interest or dividend income from foreign companies, withholding tax may have been deducted in the foreign country. If domestic tax is also charged in the taxpayers home country the same income has been taxed twice. Double taxation treaties between countries will arrange for some relief to be available against double taxation.

There are various possibilities for the practical workings of double taxation relief:

- income taxed in one country may be exempted from tax in another;

- withholding tax deducted in a foreign country may be deducted from the taxpayer's liability in their home country;

- the proportion of the 'underlying tax' on a foreign company's profits that relates to dividend income distributed to the home country may be deducted from the taxpayer's liability in their home country;

- the net income, after foreign tax, may be taken as the amount of income to be taxed in the home country.

Imputation system of Corporation Tax

14. A problem of double taxation arises when a company distributes dividends to shareholders. The company will pay corporation tax on its profits and gains. When dividends are received by a shareholder the profits being distributed might be taxed a second time. This is avoided for companies by excluding dividends received from their total of taxable income. Individuals can claim a tax credit based on the value of dividends received, as if tax had already been paid on that part of their income. This is the tax the individual is 'imputed' to have paid.

Evasion and Avoidance

15. Tax evasion involves breaking the law to reduce tax paid. Examples could include failing to record income, falsifying accounting records, or failing to make any returns of income, gains, or taxes collected. Tax avoidance would involve a taxpayer arranging their affairs so as to minimise the tax they legally have to pay. It has been an established principle for many years that a taxpayer should not be expected to pay more tax than they legally must. Indeed some features of the tax system depend on a taxpayer making choices in order to reduce tax liabilities, for example encouraging taxpayers to buy a car with low levels of exhaust emissions. However, a view has started to be put forward from the Treasury and HM Revenue and Customs that tax avoidance can be either 'acceptable' or 'unacceptable'. Tax avoidance schemes which are considered unacceptable tend to be complex transactions which do not reflect the economic substance of the taxpayers activities. In recent years the government has legislated against some tax avoidance, so that while the arrangements are still legal they will not be effective in saving tax.

Tax gap

16. The 'tax gap' is a term used to describe the shortage of actual tax collected, compared to the total tax which should be collected if there was no non payment through tax evasion.

'Stealth taxes'

17. Increases in taxation which are not the result of explicit changes in rates, allowances or methods of calculating tax, have come to be called 'stealth taxes' by the media.

As prices inflate the practice in recent years has been for the allowances for income which can be earned tax free, and the bands of income taxed at the various rates of income tax to rise in line with general price inflation. This means income tax remains at a similar proportion of most people's income, provided the inflation in their wages is at a similar level to general price inflation.

Some goods have increased at a much greater rate of inflation than general prices. This can unexpectedly increase the tax revenue generated by a transaction. In the UK increased tax revenue has been generated for value added tax (VAT) from increases in the cost of fuel, and for stamp duty land tax and inheritance tax from the increases in house prices. Until recently, the government would face a problem in reducing tax on transactions experiencing rapid inflation, as a reduction in tax could cause even more severe inflation in the prices of the goods. Recessionary price falls have allowed the UK government the opportunity of temporarily reducing the standard rate of VAT and increasing exemptions from stamp duty land tax.

Some UK tax limits have not been linked to inflation and the result is that over the years their real value has diminished. Greater tax liabilities are incurred from benefits in kind received by employees earning more than £8,500 a year, than on benefits received by their 'lower paid' colleagues. This limit has remained unchanged over many years to a point where all full time employees earning the minimum wage for 18 year olds are classified as earning more than £8,500, and subject to the rules for those who were once called 'higher paid'.

Timing of tax changes may have the effect of increasing tax revenues generated for a year. For the Financial Year 2007 the rate of corporation tax paid by small companies was increased from 19% to 20%. The rate of corporation tax for large companies was reduced from 30% to 28%, but not until the Financial Year 2008.

Questions without answers

1. Discuss the extent to which HM Treasury's budget deficit for 2009/10 proves the UK government is applying Keynesian economic policies.

2. Discuss the extent to which taxes on income create disincentive effects.

3. What are the advantages of an indirect tax such as VAT compared with an income tax?

References

1   Franklin, Benjamin (1789). Letter to Jean-Baptiste le Roy 13 Nov 1789, in Cohen JM & MJ, New Penguin Dictionary of Quotations, Penguin, Harmondsworth, 1992.
2   Sykes, J.B. ed. Concise Oxford Dictionary of Current English, Oxford University Press, 1976.
3   Hobbes, Thomas (1651). Leviathan, Penguin, Harmondsworth, 1968.
4   http://www.bized.co.uk/virtual/economy/library/theory/classical
5   Keynes, John Maynard (1936). General Theory of Employment Interest and Money, Prometheus Books, Amherst, New York, 1997.
6   http://www.bized.co.uk/virtual/economy/library/theory/keynesian
7   Sheehan, Brendan. Understanding Keynes' General Theory, Palgrave Macmillan, Basingstoke, 2009.
8   http://budget.treasury.gov.uk
9   Smith, Adam (1776). The Wealth of Nations, Penguin, Harmondsworth, 1999.

Part II

Income Tax

2 General principles

Introduction

1.   Income tax is a direct tax. Tax on some types of income is paid directly by the taxpayer to HM Revenue and Customs. For other types of income including bank and building society interest and earnings from employment, income tax is deducted by the savings institution or employer before the taxpayer receives income. The institution or employer then pays the tax over to HM Revenue and Customs. Income tax is the largest single source of tax revenue, planned to raise £141bn out of a total revenue of £496bn in 2009/10. In this chapter the main features of the income tax system are outlined, all of which are developed in detail in later chapters. It begins with some basic expressions. A summary of taxable income, its classification and basis of assessment is then provided. The remainder of the chapter deals with savings income, and non taxable income. A summary of tax rates, personal allowances and reliefs relating to 2009/10 is given at the end.

Basic expressions

2.   **The Income Tax Year 2009/10**

This runs from the 6th April 2009, to the 5th April 2010, and is also known as the fiscal year. Self assessment returns are made by reference to income tax years.

Tax rates Rates of income tax for an income tax year are determined annually in the Finance Act. A summary of the rates from the FA 2009 are shown at the end of this chapter.

Taxable persons Income tax is charged on the income of individuals, partners and trusts resident in the UK. Non- residents deriving any income from a UK source are also chargeable to income tax.

Taxable income Income on which income tax is payable is known as taxable income and this consists of the sum of components of income from all taxable sources, less deductions for allowable payments, and personal allowances and reliefs other than those given in terms of tax as a deduction.

Summary of taxable income 2009/10

		£	£
Components of income			
Income from employment	– salaries, wages, pensions etc		–
	– benefits treated as earnings		–
Social security income	– retirement pensions etc.		–
Income from trade profits	– business income less capital allowances		–
Savings & investment income	– dividends		–
	– bank/building society interest		–
Foreign income			–
			————
Total income			–
Allowable deductions		–	–

Net income	–
Personal allowances	–
	———
Taxable income	–

Income tax	Starting rate – 10% (savings and dividends)	–	
	Basic rate – 20% (10% dividends)	–	
	Higher rate – 40% (32.5% dividends)	–	–
		———	

Allowances and reliefs given in terms of tax		
Age related Married Couples Allowance	–	
Enterprise Investment Scheme – 20%	–	
Basic rate extension – Gift Aid, Pension contributions, V.C.Ts.	–	–
	———	

Tax liability	–
Tax suffered at source	–
	———
Tax payable	
	———

The following points should be noted at this stage:

a) The MCA in its enhanced age related form is available where one or both spouses has reached the age of 65 before 6th April 2000 and relief is given at the 10% rate.

38. Income from employment is after the deduction of any allowable expenses: income from self employment is the taxable profits of the business.

39. Savings income is, in general, subject to deduction at source of income tax at the rate of 20% (10% for dividends) and this is deemed to satisfy any basic rate liability. The higher rate of 40% (32.5% for dividends) applies for taxable incomes in excess of the starting and basic rate bands total of £37,400.

40. Income tax at the basic rate is deducted at source from Personal Pension Payments and Gift Aid payments. Relief at the higher rate of tax is given by extending the basic rate band by the gross amount of the payment. See Chapter 5.

The nature of income

3. Income is determined in accordance with the provision of the Income Tax (Earnings and Pension) Act 2003 and the Income Tax (Trading and Other Income) Act 2005.

Nature of Income	Source
Employment income, pensions income, social security income	ITEPA 2003
Income taxed as trade profits Savings and investment income Income from UK land and property Foreign income	ITTOIA 2005

A detailed analysis of each type of income is contained in later chapters.

Savings and investment income

4. The following is a summary of the tax on income from savings and investments in respect of the year 2009/10.

	Tax at source %	Higher rate tax %
Building society interest*	20	40
Bank interest*	20	40
Loan/debenture interest*	20	40
Interest on government securities*	20	40
National Savings and investments*	–	40
Dividends*	10	32.5

Notes

i)   The rate of tax deduction applicable to savings remains at 20% for income below the basic rate limit.

ii) For items marked with an asterisk there is no liability at the basic rate.

iii) The income taxed at source is grossed up for income tax purposes and any higher rate is assessed on the gross income.

iv) In the case of bank and building society interest an individual can register to receive the interest gross in appropriate circumstances.

   – Dividend income has attached to it a non-repayable tax credit of one-ninth of the dividend payment. Where tax becomes payable at a rate in excess of the basic rate then this is fixed at 32.5% of the net dividend plus the tax credit.

   – NSI interest is paid gross on the following taxable National Savings: Easy Access Account, Investment Account, Pensioners Income Bonds, Fixed Rate Savings Bonds, Capital Bonds.

   – NSI Ordinary Account interest is paid gross. The first £70 of interest is tax free, but the excess income is taxable. These accounts are becoming obsolete as they are no longer on sale, and closed to transactions.

   – Some NSI savings products are exempt from tax: Index Linked Savings Certificates, Fixed Interest Savings Certificates, Children's Bonus Bonds, ISAs, and Premium Bonds.

   – The 10% starting rate applies to savings income as well as dividends.

Basis of assessment

5. In order to ascertain an individual's taxable income for any given year of assessment, it is necessary to first identify his income with a particular income tax statute (eg ITEPA 2003 or ITTOIA 2005) and then apply the appropriate rules. All sources of income are assessed on a current years basis.

PAYE system

6. It should also be noted that a substantial proportion of all income tax on income from employment is in fact collected under what is known as the Pay As You Earn system. The main features of this system are covered in Chapter 8.

Due dates for payment – 2009/10 Year of assessment

7. Under the system for self assessment the taxpayer will automatically be required to make two payments on account and a third balancing payment to meet any outstanding tax. In respect of the year of assessment 2009/10 the position is as follows:

31st January 2010	First payment on account based on tax assessed for 2008/09. This will include tax on trade profits, investment income and property income.
31st July 2010	Second payment on account based on tax assessed for 2008/09.
31st January 2011	Final balancing payment including tax at higher rates on taxed income and capital gains tax.

For details see Chapter 3.

Non-taxable income

8. The following types of income are exempt from taxation:

a) NSI savings products exempt from tax are: Index Linked Savings Certificates, Fixed Interest Savings Certificates, Children's Bonus Bonds, and ISAs.

b) Interest and bonuses on Save As You Earn (SAYE) certified contractual savings schemes.

c) NSI Premium Bond prizes.

d) Interest on certain government securities held by non residents.

e) Job release allowances if paid within one year of normal retirement age.

f) Compensation for loss of employment up to £30,000.

g) Redundancy payments.

h) War widows' pensions.

i) Interest payable on damages for personal injury or death.

j) Gambling winnings and competition prizes.

k) Scholarship awards and other educational grants.

l) Payments for services in the armed forces relating to:

    i) wound and disability pensions

    ii) service grants, bounties and gratuities

    iii) annuities and additional pensions paid to holders of the Victoria Cross, George Cross and other gallantry awards.

m) Long service awards to employees, subject to certain limitations. (See Chapter 7.)

n) Certain social security income such as: child benefit, family income supplement, maternity benefit and grant, attendance allowance, mobility allowance. Unemployment benefit statutory sick pay and invalidity benefit are taxable.

o) Widow's payment of £1,000.

p) Up to £4,250 p.a. of gross rent received on furnished lettings in the taxpayers only or main residence.

q) Outplacement counselling.

Rates and allowances

9. Personal allowances 2009/10

	£	Relief at 10% rate
Personal allowance	6,475	
Allowances aged 65–74:		
Personal age allowance	9,490	
Married couples age allowance		6,965
Abatement income level	22,900	
Allowances aged 75–:		
Personal age allowance	9,180	
Married couples age allowance		6,965
Abatement income level	22,900	
Blind persons' allowance	1,890	

Notes

i) Married couples age related allowance is available where one or both spouses have reached the age of 65 before 6th April 2000.

Student self-testing questions

1. In 2009/10 Jules had the following income:

Income from employment (salary) - amount before tax	35,100
Building society interest - net of 20% tax	7,200

Jules' personal allowance is £6,475 and there were no payments to be treated as allowable deductions from income.

Required: How much tax is due in total and, if £7,020 was deducted under PAYE, what is the tax due?

Feedback

	Non-savings	Savings	£
Income			
Salary/ bonus	35,100		35,100
Taxed interest B Soc. 7,200 x 100/80		9,000	9,000
Total income	35,100	9,000	44,100
Personal allowance	6,475		6,475
Taxable income	28,625	9,000	37,625
Tax			
At lower rate	n/a	x 10%	0
At basic rate	28,625	x 20%	5,725
	8,775	x 20%	1,755
	37,400		
At higher rate	225	x 40%	90
	37,625		
Income tax borne on taxable income			7,570
Income tax liability			
PAYE		7,020	
Tax on interest		1,800	
			8,820
Final income tax due 31.1.2011			(1,250)

2. The following concerns the tax payable by Adam:

	2008/09	2009/10
	£	£
Total income tax payable	20,000	24,000
Tax deducted under PAYE	12,000	13,000

The income tax payable has been computed by self assessment and has been agreed by the Inspector.

Requirement: Show how the tax for 2009/10, not deducted at source, is required to be paid.

Feedback

Tax paid under self assessment 2008/09

	£
Tax payable	20,000
Less PAYE	(12,000)
Payable under self assessment	8,000

Tax paid for 2009/10

	£
Tax payable	24,000
Less PAYE	(13,000)
Payable under self assessment	11,000

Payable under self assessment

		£
Total payable		11,000
Interim payments		
31 January 2010 : 8,000 x 1/2	4,000	
31 July 2010 : 8,000 x 1/2	4,000	
		(8,000)
Balancing payment 31 January 2011		3,000

3 Administration

1. This chapter provides an outline of the administrative features of the income tax system.

Inland Revenue (branch of H.M. Revenue and Customs)

2. Income tax is administered by the Commissioners for Revenue and Customs who are responsible to the Treasury. The Inland Revenue operates in Area Offices through Inspectors of Taxes primarily responsible for the issue of Tax Returns and the assessment of income tax. Accounts Offices are concerned with the collection of assessed amounts. HMRC Enquiry Centres give an initial point of contact for taxpayers with general queries. In the case of face to face enquiries the Enquiry Centre may in fact be the Area Office, so the separation of functions is not complete. All tax prosecutions are handled by a separate department of Government called the Revenue Commissioners Prosecution Office.

Tax returns

3. The short form Self Assessment Tax Return issued in April 2009 consists of the following:

   1) The tax return headed – Short Tax Return 2009 for the Tax Year 6 April 2008 to 5 April 2009;

   2) The opportunity to request the full Tax Return where the short form is not suitable, for taxpayers with complex tax affairs.

Self-assessment

4. The following is a summary of the main administrative features of self-assessment.

   a) The 2009 full tax return consists of one main return and supplementary pages.

   b) The tax return contains a supplement for the self-calculation of the tax due or repayable.

   c) There are two key dates for the filing of tax returns.

      i) By the 31st October following the end of the tax year for those taxpayers filing a paper return.

      ii) By the 31st January following the end of the tax year for taxpayers filing online.

   d) Thus for 2009/10 the two filing dates are 31st October 2010 and 31st January 2011.

   e) Failure to file a tax return on or before 31st January 2011, in respect of 2009/10 will incur an automatic fixed penalty of £100. If the return is still outstanding 6 months after the filing date a further £100 penalty.

   f) Under self-assessment the obligation to pay tax is not linked to the issue of assessments. Instead the taxpayer is automatically required to make two payments on account and a third balancing payment to meet any tax outstanding.

   g) The first payment on account is due on the 31st January of the income tax year in question. The second payment on account is due on the 31st July following the end of the income tax year. The balancing payment is due on the 31st January following the end of the income tax year.

   h) The payments on account are contained in a Self-assessment – Statement of Account which shows the due dates for payment and contains a payslip.

i) Where the tax payable is expected to be lower in the year of assessment than in the previous year the taxpayer can make a formal claim to reduce the payments on account.

Payments on account (POA)

5. The following general points should be noted:

i) Under the Regulations taxpayers will not need to make POAs if:

a) their income tax (and national insurance contributions) liability for the preceding year – net of tax deducted at source or tax credits on dividends – is less than £500 in total; or

b) more than 80% of their income tax (and NIC) liability for the preceding year was met by deduction of tax at source or from tax credits on dividends.

ii) The most common ways of paying tax by deduction at source are through Pay As You Earn (PAYE), the sub-contractors' deduction scheme, and tax paid on interest received.

iii) Income tax and NIC liability (net of tax deducted at source and tax credits) for the preceding year will determine whether or not payments on account are needed. If they are due, they will normally be half the tax (and NIC) liability for the preceding year, net of tax deducted at source and tax credits.

iv) Where payments on account do not meet the entire tax (and NIC) liability – net of tax deducted at source and tax credits – for a tax year, a final payment will be due by 31st January after the end of the tax year. Where they exceed the final tax liability, a repayment will arise.

Interim payments on account – to be made on account of 2009/10

6. Payments on account are due in the following circumstances:

Assessment to income tax 2008/09	–	Income tax deducted at source	=	Relevant amount
Relevant amount	$>$	£500	→	POA required
Relevant amount	$>$	20% Assessment 2008/09	→	POA required

Notes

i) Income tax deducted at source includes tax credits on savings income such as dividends and building society interest. PAYE deducted at source is also included taking into consideration any deduction to be made in a future tax year and deducting amounts to be collected in respect of a previous year.

ii) Capital gains tax is excluded from the assessment to income tax and is therefore payable when the final payment is due.

iii) Property income and any savings and investment income is included in the assessment to income tax.

Example

For 2008/09 X's self-assessment return shows the following:

	£
Gross income tax liability	10,000
Gross Class IV NIC	1,030
PAYE deducted at source (relating to 2008/09)	2,570
BSI tax deducted at source	430

Calculate the interim payments to be made on account of the year 2009/10.

Solution

Relevant amount	Income tax liability		10,000
Less income tax at source	PAYE	2,570	
	Interest	430	3,000
			7,000
Class IV NIC			1,030
			8,030
Interim payment due	31st January 2010		4,015
	31st July 2010		4,015

Example

Mrs J has the following data shown on her self-assessment tax return for 2008/09

	£
Gross income tax liability	7,500
PAYE deducted at source	6,900
Tax deducted savings income	150

Calculate the interim payments to be made on account of 2009/10.

Solution

Relevant amount	Income tax liability		7,500
Less	PAYE	6,900	
	Tax credits	150	7,050
			450

As this is less than £500 no POA for 2009/10 is required.

Final payment (repayment) of tax

A final payment (or repayment) of income tax appears in the following circumstances:

<table>
<tr><td align="center">2009/10 self-assessment
tax return</td><td align="center">2008/09 self-assessment
tax return</td></tr>
</table>

Income tax liability
Class IV NIC } − POA = Final payment or repayment
Capital gains tax liability

Example

P has the following income tax and capital gain tax liabilities agreed for the year ended 5th April 2010 based on his self-assessment tax return.

	£
Trade profits & NIC	25,000
Capital gains tax	1,000

The relevant amount for 2008/09 has been agreed in the sum of £18,000 all attributable to trade profits.

Show the payments of the tax to be made in respect of the year of assessment ended 5th April 2010 and the due dates.

Solution: P's tax liability for 2009/10

		£
31st January 2009	50% × Relevant amount 2008/09 = 50% × 18,000	9,000
31st July 2010	50% × Relevant amount 2008/09 = 50% × 18,000	9,000
31st January 2011	Balance of tax due	8,000
		26,000

Note

The total tax due for 2009/10 is

Income tax	25,000
Capital gains tax	1,000
	26,000
Less Payment on account (2008/09 relevant amount)	18,000
Balance due	8,000

Surcharges on income tax

7. In addition to any interest that may arise on any tax paid late there will also be a scheme of surcharges to encourage prompt payments: the initial surcharge will be 5% of any tax unpaid after 28 days from the due date for payment. The surcharge will be 5% of any tax unpaid at that date.

Where any tax remains unpaid more than 6 months after the due date for payment, then a further surcharge of 5% of the tax due will be charged.

The surcharge will be payable in respect of any tax which is shown due in any self-assessment (whether calculated by the taxpayer or the Inland Revenue) but which is not covered by any POA or balancing payment.

Interest on under and overpayments

8.   A charge to interest will automatically arise on any tax paid late whether in respect of income tax, NIC or capital gains tax in respect of:

i)   any payment on account

ii)   any balancing item

iii)   any tax payable following an amendment to self-assessment whether made by the taxpayer or HM Revenue and Customs

iv)   any tax payable in a discovery assessment by HM Revenue and Customs.

Interest will arise from the due dates for payment to the date on which payment is finally made for payments on account and balancing payments.

For amendments to self-assessments the interest charge will run from the annual filing date for the income tax year, i.e. the 31st January following the end of the income tax year. Interest on any overpayments of tax will be paid automatically.

Example

M has the following data relating to 2008/09 and 2009/10.

		2008/09 £	2008/10 £
Relevant amount		5,000	6,000
Payments made	1 April 2009		2,500
	31 July 2009		1,500
	2 March 2010		2,000

Calculate the amounts on which interest will be charged and show the interest period.

Solution

Amount payable £	Amount paid £	Due date	Actual date	Interest period	Interest amount £
2,500	2,500	31.1.09	1.4.09	1.2.09 – 31.3.09	2,500
2,500	1,500	31.7.09	31.7.09	1.8.09 – 1.3.09	1,000
1,000	2,000	31.1.10	2.3.10	1.2.10 – 1.3.10	2,000

Notes

i)   As the first POA was late, interest will automatically be charged for the interest period shown.

ii)   As the second POA was not fully met, interest will be charged from the 1st August 2009 to the settlement date of 1st March 2010.

iii)   As the final balancing amount was not paid on the due date there will be an automatic surcharge of 5% on the balance due i.e £1,000 × 5% = £50.

HM Revenue and Customs enquiries

9. Tax inspectors may carry out an 'enquiry' into a taxpayers self assessment tax return. Such returns may be selected on a sample basis, or because the inspector has concerns about some of the information returned. The enquiry system includes both powers for the tax inspector and rights for the taxpayer. For example, the inspector may request a meeting with the taxpayer, but the taxpayer has a right to representation, and to decline to attend. The enquiry should be restricted to a specified area of investigation, and concluded within a regulated time limit.

Challenging the decisions of HM Revenue and Customs

10. Letters informing taxpayers of HMRC decisions will include information on rights to appeal. Appeals should be sent to HMRC in writing, within 30 days of the disputed decision. Some appeals may be settled by agreement with HMRC.

When agreement is not reached, HMRC may offer an internal review of the decision by another officer. The taxpayers may ask for a review if HMRC do not offer one. Whether or not a review takes place, a taxpayer may appeal to the Tribunal Service.

Tribunal service

11. The tax appeals system is a two tier tribunal system:

Most cases will be heard by the First Tier Tribunal (Tax Chamber);

The Upper Tribunal (Finance and Tax Chamber) will hear complex cases, and appeals from the First Tier Tribunal. The Upper Tribunal will be a court of record, whose decisions create binding precedents for the first tier.

Appeals from the Upper Tribunal would be to the Court of Appeal, and finally to the Supreme Court of the UK.

Penalties

12. Taxpayers are expected to take 'reasonable care' in making and keeping accurate records to enable them to provide a complete and accurate tax return. This principle applies to income tax and national insurance contributions information in the self assessment income tax return, along with return documents for other taxes. Taxpayers can demonstrate they have taken reasonable care by: keeping accurate records, confirming the correct position when they do not understand tax issues, or telling HMRC promptly about any errors discovered in tax returns after they have been sent.

Where taxpayers do not pay enough tax, and have not taken reasonable care, they may have to pay a penalty in addition to the tax due and any interest on late payment. The penalties can be reduced if the taxpayer makes an 'unprompted' disclosure of the underpayment, rather than one forced by the result of investigations by the tax authorities:

Taxpayers approach to disclosure of underpayment	Minimum penalty	Maximum penalty
Reasonable care	No penalty	No penalty
Careless unprompted	0%	30%
Careless prompted	15%	30%

Deliberate unprompted	20%	70%
Deliberate prompted	35%	70%
Deliberate and concealed unprompted	30%	100%
Deliberate and concealed prompted	50%	100%

Error or mistake relief

13. Relief can be claimed in writing against any over-assessment due to an error or mistake (including an omission) in any return or statement. The relief must be claimed within 4 years of the end of the year of assessment in which the assessment was made and is given where the return or statement was incorrect.

Student self-testing question

A has the following data relating to 2008/09 and 2009/10.

	2008/09	**2009/10**
Gross income tax liability	18,500	22,000
Capital gains tax liability	1,500	3,000
Tax credit on investment income	(1,000)	(1,500)
Total tax due	19,000	23,500

Calculate the tax payments in respect of 2009/10 and show the due dates for payments.

Solution:

	2009/10 Payments		
	Interim Payments		**Final Payment**
	31. 1. 10	**31. 7. 10**	**31. 1. 11**
1st Interim payment 50% × (18,500 − 1,000)	8,750		
2nd Interim payment 50% (18,500 − 1,000)		8,750	
Final payment (23,500 − 17,500)			6,000
	8,750	8,750	6,000

Notes

i) The interim payments are computed by reference to the tax liability for 2008/09, i.e. (18,500 − 1,000) = 17,500 excluding any capital gains tax.

ii) The final payment for 2009/10 includes the capital gains tax liability for that year, i.e. £3,000:

(22,000 + 3,000 − 1,500) = 23,500 − POA,

i.e. 23,500 − 17,500 = £6,000.

4 Personal allowances and reliefs

Introduction

1.   This chapter is concerned with the main features of the system of taxation in relation to the personal allowances and reliefs for individuals and married couples including gift aid.

List of topic headings

2.

Husbands and wives

Personal allowance

Personal age allowance

Married couple's allowance – 65 before 6 April 2000

Blind person's allowance

Death of husband or wife

Year of permanent separation and divorce

Payroll deduction scheme for charitable giving

Non-residents

Husbands and wives

3.   The main features of the system of taxation for husbands and wives are as follows.

   a)   Husband and wife are treated as separate taxpayers each completing their own tax returns and responsible for their own tax liabilities.

   b)   The income of the wife is not aggregated with that of the husband for income tax purposes.

   c)   Each spouse is entitled to the full basic rate band of income tax and the starting rate band.

   d)   Both spouses receive a personal allowance which is available for set-off against earned and unearned income. The amount of the allowance is increased for persons over 65, and again for those over 75.

   e)   The married couple's allowance was abolished from 5 April 2000 except for spouses over the age of 65 at 6 April 2000. The allowance is claimed by the husband the amount being increased where one of the spouses is over 65, and again where the spouse's age is over 75. The married couple's allowance is transferable to the wife, and can be allocated between spouses.

   f)   Each person entitled to the personal age allowance will also be entitled to the annual income limit of £22,900 for 2009/10. Married couples both eligible for the personal age allowance will therefore each be entitled to an income limit of £45,800.

   g)   The personal allowance available to an elderly wife can be used against a pension obtained as a result of her husband's contributions for national insurance.

   h)   Reliefs may be deducted from any income, to the taxpayer's best advantage, but in most cases there is no obvious benefit in utilising one source in preference to another.

   i)   Changes in the rates of personal reliefs are contained in the annual Finance Acts.

Personal allowance (PA) 2009/09 £6,475 (2008/09 £6,035)

4. This allowance is given automatically to all individuals male or female, single or married. There are higher rates of personal allowance for people over the age of 65 and these are discussed below under Section 5. The personal allowance is deducted from total income in arriving at the taxable income of each individual, and is thus given relief at the taxpayer's marginal rate of tax.

The personal allowance is not transferable.

Example

A, who is single, has a salary income from employment for 2009/10 of £55,000.

Compute his income tax liability for 2009/10

Solution: Income tax computation 2009/10

		£
Income from employment		55,000
Personal allowance		6,475
Taxable income		48,525
Tax liability	n/a @ 10%	0
	37,400 @ 20%	7,480
	11,125 @ 40%	4,450
	48,525	11,930

Note

With income from employment there would normally be some taxation already collected by way of the PAYE system which reduces the balance due accordingly. See Chapter 8.

The personal age allowance (PAA)

5.	2009/10	2008/09
Age 65–74	£9,490	£9,030
Age 75–	£9,640	£9,180

For taxpayers over the age of 65 at any time during the year of assessment a higher personal allowance is available, and there is a further additional amount for those aged 75 and over. The increased level of allowances is available even if the taxpayer dies before the specified age if he or she would have attained that age in the year of assessment.

The full amount of the PAA may be claimed where the adjusted net income is not greater than £22,900.

Adjusted net income is the taxpayers net income less the gross amount of any Gift Aid donations or pension contributions.

Where the income is greater than £22,900 then the PAA is reduced by half the excess until the basic personal allowance becomes more beneficial.

Income limits

	Minimum	Maximum
	£	£
Age 65–74	22,900	28,930
Age 75–	22,900	29,230

Age 65–74	9,490 – 1/2 (28,930 – 22,900) = £6,475
Age 75	9,640 – 1/2 (29,230 – 22,900) = £6,475

Whatever the level of income of the taxpayer, the personal allowance can never be reduced below the basic personal allowance for a person under 65, i.e. £6,475 for 2009/10.

Example

K, who is 66 and single, has income from employment in 2009/10 of £20,000 and a state retirement pension of £5,000.

Compute K's income tax liability for 2009/10.

Solution: K's Income tax computation 2009/10

	£	£
Income from employment		20,000
State Pension		5,000
Statutory total income		25,000
PAA	9,490	
Less 1/2 (25,000–22,900)	1,050	8,440
Taxable income		16,560
Tax liability:		
n/a @ 10%		0
16,560 @ 20%		3,312
16,560		
Tax		3,312

Note

The restricted age allowance of £8,440 is greater than the personal allowance of £6,475.

The married couple's age related allowance (MCA) – 10% rate relief

6.

	2009/10	2008/09
Age 65–74	n/a	£6,535
Age 75–	£6,965	£6,625
Minimum amount	£2,670	£2,540

a) The MCA is only available where one or both spouses has reached the age of 65 before the 6 April 2000. A claim for the higher level of married couple's allowance is made by the husband.

b) One of the spouses will therefore reach the age of 75 by the end of the tax year 2009/10.

c) The full amount of the allowances (i.e. PAA and MCA) is reduced by 1/2 of the excess where the husband's income exceeds £22,900. Note that the wife's income never affects the level of the MCA. Where the husband's MCA is reduced by reason of his total income it can never be reduced below the minimum allowance of £2,670 (2008/09 £2,540).

In applying the reduction in the MCA the following rules should be used:

i) First – reduce the PA until it reaches the level of the PA for people under the age of 65.

ii) Second – reduce the MCA until it reaches the level of the MCA for people under 65.

The above has the effect of preserving as late as possible any MCA which can be transferred to the spouse.

If the husband cannot use all the MCA the unused amount can be transferred to his wife.

d) The MCA is given relief at the 10% rate.

Example

Mr Z is aged 66 and his wife is aged 77. In the year 2009/10 Mr Z has employment and pension income of £24,000 and Mrs Z has employment and pension income of £26,000.

Compute the tax payable by Mr and Mrs Z for 2009/10.

Solution: Mr Z's Income tax computation 2009/10

	£	£
Employment and pension income		24,000
Reduction in total allowances		
1/2 (24,000 – 22,900) = 550		
PAA	9,490	
Less reduction	550	
PA		8,940
Taxable income		15,060
Tax liability:		
n/a @ 10%		
15,060 @ 20%		3,012
15,060		3,012
Less deduction for MCA 6,965 @ 10%		697
Tax payable		2,315

Mrs Z income tax computation 2009/10

	£	£
Employment and pension income		26,000
PAA	9,640	
Less 1/2 (26,000 – 22,900)	1,550	
		8,090
Taxable income		17,910
Tax liability: n/a @ 10%		0
17,910 @ 20%		3,582
17,910		
Tax payable		3,582

Notes

i)   The PAA of £9,640 for Mrs Z is reduced to £8,090.

ii)   The PA (or PAA) is available for set-off against both employment and savings income.

iii)   The level of Mrs Z's income has no effect on the MCAA claimed by her husband.

iv)   MCAA for 75+ is £6,965.

Blind person's allowance 2009/10 £1,890 (2008/09 £1,800)

7.   This allowance is available to any person who is on the local authority blind person's register. Where both husband and wife are blind then each can claim the allowance. If either the husband or the wife cannot fully use the amount of their blind allowance then the balance can be transferred to the other spouse. This rule applies whether or not the spouse receiving the transferred allowance is a registered blind person. A notice to transfer any unused allowance must be made in writing to the Inspector of Taxes within six years of the end of the year of assessment. This allowance is deducted from total income to arrive at taxable income, and is thus given relief at the taxpayer's marginal rate of tax.

Example

K, who is a widow aged 55, is a registered blind person. K's income for the year 2009/10 consists of the following.

	£
Widow's pension	6,000
Wages for part-time employment (gross)	14,505
(PAYE deducted £1,970)	

Compute K's income tax liability for 2009/10.

Solution: K income tax computation 2009/10

	£	£
Income from employment		14,505
Widow's pension		6,000
		20,505
Personal allowance	6,475	
Blind person's allowance	1,890	8,365
Taxable income		12,140
Tax liability		
n/a @ 10%		0
12,140 @ 20%		2,428
12,140		2,428
Less PAYE		1,970
Tax payable		458

Year of death of husband

8.   The following points should be noted under this heading:

Husband

a)   A full personal allowance is available.

b)   Total income up to the date of death less allowances and reliefs for the whole year are ascertained and any tax due is payable from the husband's estate.

Wife

a)   A full personal allowance is available.

b)   The balance of any age related MCA not used against the husband's income up to the date of his death is available for set off against widow's income.

Example

T aged 55 died on 5th October 2009. Mrs T aged 56 is employed and for the income tax year 2009/10 has the following data:

	£
Income from employment	16,000
Widow's pension	3,000

Compute the income tax liabilities of Mrs T for 2009/10.

Solution: Mrs T income tax computation 2009/10

	£	£
Income from employment		16,000
Widow's pension		3,000
		19,000
PA		6,475
Taxable income		12,525
Tax liability		
n/a @ 10% 0		
12,525 @ 20%		2,505
12,525		
Tax payable		2,505

Year of death of wife

9. In the year of the death of a wife the husband is entitled to the full amount of the enhanced married couple's allowance at the rate appropriate providing either was 65 on the 5th April 2000.

Payroll deduction scheme for charities

10. An employee can obtain income tax relief on donations to a charity from 5th April 2000 without limit. The employer is responsible for making payments to the charity, and uses the 'net pay arrangements' in computing the employees PAYE liability. See Chapter 8

Non-residents

11. A 'qualifying' non-resident can claim full personal allowances against his or her UK income.

Student self-testing question

B aged 68, a widower, looks after his mother aged 92. For the year to 5th April 2010 the following data applies:

Salary and pension income B   £23,000

Calculate the tax payable by B for 2009/10.

Solution: B income tax computation 2009/10

	£	£
Income from employment and pension		23,000
P.A.A.	9,490	
(less $\frac{1}{2}$) $\times$ (23,000 – 22,900)	50	9,440
Taxable income		13,560
Tax liability n/a @ 10%		0
13,560 @ 20%		2,712
13,560		
Tax payable		2,712

Note. PAA is £9,440 which is greater than the basic PA of £6,475.

5 Allowable payments

Introduction

1. Allowable payments reduce taxable income. The various components making up total income are reduced by allowable payments to give net income (See Chapter 2). Before the Income Tax Act 2007 'charges on income' was the term used to describe annual payments, which together with the special provisions relating to gift aid payments and interest, form the basis of this chapter. The main part of the chapter deals with the computational aspects of gift aid and the notion of 'the extended rate' method of relief at the higher rate.

Annual payments

2. These are payments which possess the quality of annual recurrence, are not voluntary transactions, and are usually supported by a legal obligation.

Annual payments are not allowable payments unless they fall within the following categories:

    a)   payments of interest;

    b)   gift aid payments to a charity;

    c)   payments made for bone fide commercial reasons in connection with the payer's trade, profession or vocation.

Gift aid for charities

3. Some of the main features are as follows:

    a)   Requirement for donors to give the charity a gift aid declaration.

    b)   Allow donors to give a gift aid declaration over the phone or over the Internet if they wish, without having to complete and sign a paper declaration.

    c)   Donors have to pay an amount of income tax whether at the basic rate or some other rate, equal to the tax deducted from their donations.

    d)   Allow donors to claim higher rate tax relief for their donations against income tax.

    e)   Relief at the higher rate is given by extending the basic rate band by the gross amount of the Gift Aid.

Computational rules for gift aid – extended basic rate band

4.   a)   **Higher rate taxpayer:** Gross the gift aid payment up by the basic rate of income tax and extend the basic rate band by that gross amount.

    b)   **Basic rate tax payer:** – Ignore in the income tax computation as relief given at source by deduction.

Example

T, who is married, has Employment income of £49,000 for 2009/10. His wife has salary income of £13,000. T makes payments of £800 net (£1,000 gross) to a registered charity by way of gift aid.

Compute the income tax liability for 2009/10 for T and Mrs T who are both aged less than 65.

Solution: Income tax computation 2009/10

	T	Mrs T
	£	£
Income from employment	49,000	13,000
Personal allowance	6,475	6,475
Taxable income	42,525	6,525
Tax liability	£	£
Income tax n/a @ 10%	0	0
37,400 / 6,525 @ 20%	7,480	1,305
1,000 @ 20%	200	
38,400		
4,125 / – @ 40%	1,650	
42,525 6,525 Tax payable	9,330	1,305

Note

The gift aid payment to the charity is allowed at all rates and the basic rate is extended to arrive at the total tax payable

i.e. 37,400 + 1,000 = 38,400. £800 x 100/80 = £1,000.

Qualifying interest payments

5.   Interest due in the UK on a loan used for any of the under-mentioned purposes is payable without deduction of income tax, and is an allowable payment against total income, and the higher rate of income tax.

   a)   To purchase plant or machinery for use in a partnership or employment.

   b)   To purchase an interest in or make a loan to a partnership, where the taxpayer would not be a limited partner.

   c)   Loans made in acquiring an interest in a co-operative enterprise as defined in section 2 of the Industrial Common Ownership Act 1976.

   d)   To pay inheritance tax. Relief is available for one year only.

   e)   To acquire ordinary shares or make loans to a close company, but not a close investment company. The borrower must, with his associates:

   i)   have a material interest in the company, i.e. more than 5% of the ordinary share capital or be entitled to more than 5% of the assets on a notional winding up; or

   ii)   if having less than a 5% interest, have worked for the greater part of his time in the management of the company.

Business loan interest

6.   Interest paid on loans for business purposes is charged as an expense of trading, and not as a separate allowable payment. This applies to bank loan or overdraft interest, providing the loan is used wholly and exclusively for the purposes of trade.

Annual payments for business purposes – patent royalties

7. Payments made by an individual for bona fide commercial reasons in connection with his or her trade, profession or vocation are eligible to be treated as allowable payments, formerly called 'charges on income'. Where an individual is trading the royalty may be treated as a trading expense deducted in the business accounts, rather than deducted under the separate rules for allowable payments.

Royalty payments made in connection with a patent used in an individual's trade are paid after deduction of basic rate income tax at source. The gross amount is allowed against the basic and higher rates of the payer.

Copyright royalties

8. Copyright royalties are paid gross without any deduction of tax.

Student self-testing question

T, who is married, has the following data relating to 2009/10.

	£
Employment earnings T	48,000
Mrs T employment earnings	8,000

On 6th April 2009 T paid £960 (net) by way of a gift aid payment to a recognised charity.

Compute the income tax liability for 2009/10 of T and Mrs T, both aged 55.

Solution: Income tax computation 2009/10

		T £	Mrs T £
Income from employment T		48,000	–
Income from employment Mrs T		–	8,000
		48,000	8,000
Personal allowance		6,475	6,475
Taxable income		41,525	1,525
Taxation liability			
n/a / n/a	@ 10%	0	0
38,600 / 1,525	@ 20%	7,720	305
2,925	@ 40%	1,170	
38,600	1,525		
Tax payable		8,890	305

Note

As the gift aid payment is allowed at the higher rate the basic rate income tax band is extended i.e. £37,400 + £1,200 = £38,600.

£960 x 100/80 = £1,200.

6 Savings and investment income

Introduction

1. This chapter is concerned with the taxation of savings income which is normally received after deduction of tax at source, and with personal investment income such as ISAs and VCTs.

    The treatment of other savings income received gross is dealt with also.

Bank/building society interest etc – 20% rate deducted at source

2. a) The rate of 20% applies to the following savings income:

    interest from banks and building societies

    interest from government securities (see 3h below)

    interest on corporate loan stocks and other securities

    purchased life annuities

    interest distributions from authorised unit trusts.

    b) Where the taxpayer is only taxable at the starting rate of 10% for investment income or the basic rate of 20%, then there will be no further liability. The deduction at source is deemed to have satisfied the full charge.

    c) For higher rate taxpayers the 40% rate applies to the gross income with due allowance for the lower rate deduction at source.

    d) Non-taxpayers who receive taxed interest will be able to claim the 20% deduction by way of repayment.

    e) Savings income (including dividends – see below) are to be treated as the top slice of an individual's taxable income, leaving out of account any termination payment relating to an office or employment.

    f) Provided application is made to the Inland Revenue then an individual resident in the UK can register with the bank or building society to receive the interest gross if he or she is not liable to income tax.

    g) A separate application to register must be made for each building society or bank account or share of joint account.

    h) If an account is for a child under 16, a parent or guardian will need to sign the registration form.

    i) The 10% starting rate band applies to savings income.

    j) In general, savings income arises on the date specified for the payment of any income

Interest paid gross

3. The following forms of investment pay interest gross:

    a) certificates of deposit and sterling or foreign currency time deposits, provided that the loan is not less than £50,000 and is repayable within five years;

    b) NSI interest is paid gross on the following taxable National Savings: Easy Access Account, Investment Account, Pensioners Income Bonds, Fixed Rate Savings Bonds, Capital Bonds;

c) NSI Ordinary Account interest is paid gross. The first £70 of interest is tax free, but the excess income is taxable.

d) general client accounts with banks and building societies operated by solicitors or estate agents;

e) accounts held at overseas branches of United Kingdom banks and building societies;

f) bank and building society accounts where the owner is not ordinarily resident in the United Kingdom and has made a declaration to that effect;

g) bank and building society accounts in the names of companies, clubs, societies and charities;

h) loans from unincorporated borrowers;

i) all holdings of government securities acquired after 5th April 1998, and any other holdings before that date provided the holder has elected to receive the interest gross.

Example

A has the following income for the year ended 5th April 2010.

Income from employment	£16,000
Building Society interest (net)	£8,000

Compute A's income tax liability for 2009/10.

Solution: A's income tax computation 2009/10

	£
Income from employment	16,000
Building Society int $\dfrac{8,000}{0.8}$	10,000
	26,000
Less PA	6,475
Taxable income	19,525
Tax liability	
n/a @ 10%	0
19,525 @ 20%	3,905
Less deducted at source	2,000
Tax payable	1,905

Note

The savings income is taxed at the rate of 20% at source and no further liability arises as A is not a higher rate payer.

Example

B has the following income for the year ended 5th April 2010.

Salary	£44,000
Building Society interest (net)	£ 8,000

Compute B's income tax liability for 2009/10.

Solution: B's income tax computation 2009/10

		£
Income from employment		44,000
Building Society interest		
£8,000 x 100/80		10,000
		54,000
Less PA		6,475
Taxable income		47,525

Tax liability		
n/a @ 10%		0
37,400 @ 20%		7,480
37,400		7,480
10,125 @ 40%		4,050
47,525		11,530
Less income tax deducted at source		
		2,000
Tax payable		9,530

Note

Savings income is deemed to be the top slice of taxable income in this example.

Dividends received from UK resident companies

4. The main features are as follows:

   a) There is a tax credit attached to each dividend received.

   b) The tax credit has been fixed at one ninth which is equivalent to a tax credit rate of 10% of the sum of the distribution and the tax credit

e.g. Dividend payment	900	
Tax credit 1/9 × 900	100	(10% × 1,000)
Gross dividend	1,000	

   c) Income chargeable under this heading is taxed at the ordinary rate of 10% and not the rate of 20%.

   d) Where tax becomes payable at a rate in excess of the basic rate it is charged at the dividend upper rate which is fixed at 32.5%.

   e) Dividend income is treated as the top slice of savings income.

   f) There are in effect five rates of income tax for 2009/10.

		%
Dividends	ordinary rate	10.0
	upper rate	32.5
Income tax	starting rate for savings income	10.0

basic rate	20.0
higher rate	40.0

- Non tax payers do not have the right to reclaim the tax credit of 10%.

- Where a married couple jointly own shares in a close company any dividends paid will be taxed in accordance with their actual ownership of the company.

Example

R, aged 50, has the following income for the year ended 5th April 2010.

Salary	£14,000
Dividend income received	£1,800

Compute R's income tax liability for 2009/10.

Solution: R's income tax liability 2009/10

	£
Income from employment	14,000
Dividends 1,800	
Tax credit 1/9 × 200	2,000
	16,000
PA	6,475
	9,525
Tax payable	
n/a @ 10%	0
7,525 @ 20%	1,505
2,000 @ 10%	200
9,525	1,705
Less tax credits on dividends	200
Tax payable	1,505

Notes

i) Dividends have a tax credit of 1/9 attached to each payment.

ii) The basic rate of tax is deemed to be satisfied.

iii) Dividend income is treated as the top slice of taxable income and taxed at the Dividend rate of 10%.

iv) The tax credit is not repayable to non-taxpayers.

Example

T, aged 50, has the following income for the year ended 5th April 2010.

Salary	£25,000
Dividend income received	£18,000

Compute T's income tax liability for 2009/10.

Solution: T's income tax liability 2009/10

		£
Income from employment		25,000
Dividends 18,000 x		
Tax credit $\frac{1}{9}$ = 2000		<u>20,000</u>
		45,000
PA		<u>6,475</u>
		<u>38,525</u>

Tax liability	
n/a @ 10%	0
18,525 @ 20%	3,705
<u>18,875</u> @ 10%	<u>1,887</u>
37,400	5,592
<u>1,125</u> @ 32.5%	<u>365</u>
<u>38,525</u>	5,957
less income tax on dividends	
	<u>2,000</u>
Tax payable	<u>3,957</u>

Note

Dividend income is taxed partly at the 10% rate £18,875 and partly at the 32.5% rate £1,125.

Individual savings accounts (ISAs)

5. The main features are summarised as follows:

   a) All income received is exempt from income tax.

   b) ISAs are classified into two categories, 'cash' and 'stocks and shares'.

   c) The annual subscription limit is £7,200 of which not more than £3,600 can be invested in cash. For 2008/09 the annual subscription limit for taxpayers aged over 50 will be £10,200, of which not more than £5,100 may be in cash. Taxpayers will be able to make use of the increased limit from 6 October 2009, but the full subscription level will apply for the tax year 2009/10, without any reduction through time apportionment.

   There is no overall lifetime limit.

   e) All PEPs held at 6 April 1999 continue to be held as PEPs outside the new savings account, but with the same tax advantages as ISAs.

   f) ISA income does not have to be recorded in the SATR and is not included as income for the purposes of the P.A.A.

Enterprise investment scheme (EIS)

6. The main features of the EIS which applies to shares issued are as follow.

a) An individual can invest up to £500,000 in any tax year and obtain relief at the 20% rate against his or her taxable income.

b) To qualify for relief the eligible shares must be held for at least three years in an unquoted trading company.

c) 50% of the amount invested by an individual between 6th April and 5th October in any year can be carried back to the previous income tax year subject to a maximum of £25,000.

d) Capital gains tax on chargeable gains arising from disposals of any assets may be deferred where such gains are invested in subscription for shares in an EIS company.

e) No limit on amount of gains that can be reinvested.

Venture capital trusts

7. The main features of this type of investment are as follow.

a) The scheme is designed to stimulate individual investment in a spread of unquoted trading companies through the mechanism of quoted venture capital trusts.

b) Individuals can invest up to a maximum of £200,000 p.a. attracting income tax relief at 30% providing the shares are held for five years.

c) Dividends received are tax free.

d) Profits on the disposal of shares within the trust are exempt from CGT.

i) Chargeable gains arising on any other asset may be rolled over into an investment in a VCT.

ii) Income tax relief holding period three years.

Miscellaneous income

8. a) **Patent royalties**. These are normally paid by deduction of basic rate income tax at source, the gross amount treated as investment income.

b) **Copyright royalties**. These are payments to authors gross without deduction of income tax at the source.

Non-taxable income

9. The following types of income are exempt from taxation.

1) Some National Savings and Investments savings products are exempt from tax: Index Linked Savings Certificates, Fixed Interest Savings Certificates, Children's Bonus Bonds, ISAs, and Premium Bonds.

2) Interest and bonuses on Save As You Earn (SAYE) certified contractual savings schemes.

3) Job release allowances if paid within one year of normal retirement age.

4) Compensation for loss of employment up to £30,000.

5) Redundancy payments.

6) War widows' pensions.

7)   Interest payable on damages for personal injury or death.

8)   Gambling winnings and competition prizes.

9)   Scholarship awards and other educational grants.

10) Payments for services in the armed forces relating to:

   a)   Wound and disability pensions

   b)   Service grants, bounties and gratuities

   c)   Annuities and additional pensions paid to holders of the Victoria Cross, George Cross and other gallantry awards.

11) The bereavement lump sum payment of £2,000.

12) Rent from the letting of part of the principal private residence up to £4,250 p.a.

13) Outplacement counselling (not limited to £30,000 redundancy level).

14) National Lottery prizes.

15) Income derived from an ISA.

Income not taxed at source

10. The following types of income are taxable at the 10%/20%/40% rates, but not subject to deduction of income tax at source.

1)   National Savings income bonds/pensioner's bonds

2)   National Savings investment account and other accounts

3)   British Government securities

4)   Deposits at non-UK branches of UK or foreign banks

5)   Deposits made by individuals not ordinarily resident in the UK

6)   Loan interest from a private individual

7)   Deposits with some off-shore building societies

8)   Bank and building society accounts where taxpayer has registered to receive interest gross.

Student self-testing questions

1.   The following information relates to the self assessment tax return of A.

Year ended 5th April 2010

	£
A salary	46,000
Taxed dividends (net)	540
Bank interest (net)	400
Gift aid to Oxfam (gross)	2,000

Calculate the income tax liability of A for 2009/10.

Solution: Income tax computation 2009/10

	£	£
Income from employment		
A salary		46,000
Income from savings		
Dividends (gross) 540/.9	600	
Bank interest 400/.80	<u>500</u>	<u>1,100</u>
		47,100
Personal allowance		<u>6,475</u>
Taxable income		<u>40,625</u>
Tax liability		
n/a @ 10%		0
37,400 @ 20%		7,480
<u>2,000</u> @ 20%		400
39,400		
<u>125</u> @40%		50
39,525		
500 @ 40%		200
<u>600</u> @ 32.5%		<u>195</u>
<u>40,625</u>		8,325
Less Income tax on savings income		<u>160</u>
Tax payable		<u>8,165</u>

Notes

i)   Income tax on savings income: dividends $1/9 \times 540 = £60$ + bank interest $\frac{1}{4} \times 400 = £100$.

ii)   The basic rate is extended by £2,000 to £39,400 to give relief for the Gift Aid at the higher rate.

2.   Emma, a 25 year-old, has business trading profits of £25,000, before paying copyright royalties for business purposes of £2,500 gross. She also receives building society interest of £6,400 (net) and pays copyright royalties of £2,500 (gross) each year. What is her income after tax for 2009/10, ignoring National Insurance?

Solution

	£	£	£
Income			
Trading income (25,000 − 2,500)	22,500		22,500
Taxed investment income BSI gross		8,000	8,000
Net Income	22,500	8,000	30,500
Personal allowance	(6,475)		(6,475)
Taxable income	16,025	8,000	24,025
Tax			
At lower rate	n/a x 10%		0
At basic rate	24,025x 20%		4,805
	24,025		
			4,805

Income tax borne on taxable income

Income tax liability

Tax paid on building society interest	(1,600)
Final income tax due 31.1.2011	3,205
Profits	22,500
Net Building society interest	6,400
	28,900
Balance of tax	3,205
Net income	25,695

3. Chris has the following income, outgoings and allowances for the year ended 5 April 2010

Business trading profits, before business related copyright	
Salary	22,975
Allowable expenses of employment	95
Taxable investment income - bank interest net	416
- building society interest net	712
Rent from UK furnished lettings	1,890
Personal allowance	6,475
Copyright royalties - (paid gross)	2,160

Requirement: Calculate Chris's tax liability for 2009/10

Solution

	Non savings £	Savings £	Total £
Income from employment			
Income from trading			
Income from property	1,890		1,890
Bank & building society interest			
Net income	32,610	1,410	34,020
Personal allowance	(6,475)		(6,475)
Taxable income	26,135	1,410	27,545
Non savings			
n/a x 10%	0		
26,135 x 20%	5,227		
Savings			
1,410 x 20%	282		
	5,509		
Tax deducted at source	(282)		
	5,227		

4. Pat has the following income for 2009/10

	£
Income from his business, before business related patent royalties	20,000
Dividends	1,944
Income from property	1,000

Pat pays patent royalties of £440 (net), and claims the personal allowance of £6,475

Requirement: Calculate Pat's income tax payable for 2009/10

How would your answers differ if Pat had £45,000 income from his business?

Solution

Pat : Income tax computation for 2009/10

	Non-saving £	Dividends £	Total £
Income			
Income from property	1,000		1,000
Income from trading			
(20,000 – (440 x 100/80))	19,450		19,450
Dividends gross		2,160	2,160
Net income	20,450	2,160	22,610
Less: personal allowances	6,475		6,475
Taxable income	13,975	2,160	16,135
Income tax			

			Non-saving
n/a	x 10%		0
13,975	x 20%		2,795
2,160	x 10%		216
16,135			
Tax borne			3,011

Add tax withheld on payment of patent royalties

550 x 20%		110
Tax liability		3,121

Less: tax credits on dividends

2,160 x 10%		216
Tax payable		2,905

Part b

Pat : Income tax computation for 2009/10

Income

Income from property	1,000		1,000
Income from trading			
(45,000 – (440 x100/80))	44,450		44,450
Dividends gross		2,160	2,160
Net income	45,450	2,160	47,610
Less: personal allowances	6,475		6,475
Taxable income	38,975	2,160	41,135

Income tax

n/a	x 10%	0
37,400	x 20%	7,480
1,575	x 40%	630
2,160	x 32.5%	702
41,135		

Tax borne	8,812
Add tax withheld on patent royalty payments	
550 x 20%	110
Tax liability	8,702
Less: tax credits on dividends	
2,160 x 10%	216
Tax payable	8,486

Questions without answers

1. Jacqui has the following income

Salary (PAYE £5,200)	26,000
Building society interest (net)	4,800
Dividends (net)	11,700
Gift aid donation (net)	700

Requirement: Calculate Jacqui's tax payable.

2. Jackie is aged 42.

Requirement: Calculate Jackie's tax position in 2009/10 if her income was:

a) trading profits of £40,500 and building society interest of £6,400 net.

b) trading profits of £2,500 and building society interest of £6,400 net.

7 Income from employment I – general aspects

Introduction

1. This chapter is concerned with the taxation of income from employment.

The major part deals with the taxation of earnings from employment and benefits treated as earnings. A summary of the benefits treated as earnings within the 'benefits code' is provided, showing in broad terms the taxation effects on employees and directors earning less than £8,500pa, and more than £8,500pa.

The legislative background is contained in the Income Tax (Earnings and Pensions) Act 2003.

Summary of taxable income

2. Tax under the ITEPA 2003 is charged in respect of the following income.

> Employment income.
>
> Pension income.
>
> Social security income.

Employment

3. a) Employment includes in particular:

    i)   any employment under a contract of service;

    ii) any employment under a contract of apprenticeship;

    iii) any employment in the service of the crown; and

    iv) any office which includes in particular any position which has an existence independent of the person who holds it and may be filled by successive holders.

    b) Employment is usually taken to be evidenced by a contract of employment or service. On the other hand a contract for services rendered is normally associated with self employment, the rewards of which are assessable as trading profits. See Fall v Hitchen 1972 49 TC 433. Hall v Lorimer 1992 CA STC 23. McManus v Griffiths CHB 1997.

    c) An office can be defined as a position with duties attached to it which do not change with the holder. It is the income of the office that is taxable. Examples of office holders are: a judge; a trustee or executor; a town clerk; a company director or secretary. An inspector of public meetings was held not to hold an office, see Edwards v Clinch HL 1981 STI.

Employment income

4. a) Earnings, in relation to employment, means:

    i)   any salary, wages or fee;

    ii) any gratuity or other profit or incidental benefit of any kind obtained by the employee if it is money or money's worth; or

    iii) anything else that constitutes an emolument of the employment.

    b) For the purposes of subsection (ii) money's worth means something that is:

    i)   of direct monetary value to the employee; or,

ii)   capable of being converted into money or something of direct monetary value to the employee.

Receipt of money earnings

5.   a)   General earnings consisting of money are to be treated as received at the earliest of the following times:

Rule 1

The time when payment is made of or on account of the earnings.

Rule 2

The time when a person becomes entitled to payment of or on account of the earnings.

Rule 3

If the employee is a director of a company and the earnings are from employment with the company (whether or not as a director), whichever is the earliest:

i)   the time when sums on account of the earnings are credited in the company's accounts or records (whether or not there is any restriction on the right to draw the sums);

ii)   if the amount of the earnings for a period is determined by the end of the period, the time when the period ends, and

iii)   if the amount of the earnings for a period is not determined until after the period has ended, the time when the amount is determined.

b)   Rule 3 applies if the employee is a director of the company at any time in the tax year in which the time mentioned falls.

c)   In this section director means:

i)   in relation to a company whose affairs are managed by a board of directors or similar body, a member of that body;

ii)   in relation to a company whose affairs are managed by a single director or similar person, that director or person, and

iii)   in relation to a company whose affairs are managed by the members themselves, a member of the company,

and includes any person in accordance with whose directions or instructions the directors of the company (as defined above) are accustomed to act.

d)   For the purposes of subsection (c) a person is not to be regarded as a person in accordance with whose directions or instructions the directors of the company are accustomed to act merely because the directors act on advice given by that person in a professional capacity.

Gifts and voluntary payments

6.   In general gifts and voluntary payments unconnected with an employment are not taxable, but see the examples noted below.

a)   Reasonable gifts made by an employer in connection with marriage or retirement are not taxable.

b)   Long service awards are not taxed providing that they are not cash; the award is in respect of not less than 20 years service; no similar payment has been made during the previous 10 years; and the cost to the employer does not exceed £50 (previously £20) for each year of service. A cash award would be taxable.

c) Benefit matches for sports personnel are not taxed providing that they are not a condition of their employment contract. See Reed v Seymour 1927 HL 11 TC 625 and Moorhouse v Doorland 1954 CA 36 TCI. However transfer signing on fees are taxable emoluments.

d) An award of £130 to a bank clerk for passing his professional examinations was held to be a non taxable gift. See Ball v Johnson 1971 47 TC 155.

e) £1,000 paid by the Football Association to each of the members of the 1966 England World Cup team was held to be a gift and not remuneration. Moore v Griffiths 1972 48 TC 338.

f) Tips of a taxi driver were held to be taxable in Calvert v Wainwright 1947 27 TC 475.

g) The Easter offerings given to a vicar in response to an appeal made by his Bishop were held to be taxable. See Cooper v Blakiston HL 1908 5 TC 347.

h) Gifts from third parties costing not more than £100 in any tax year are not taxable, by concession.

i) Payments to a footballer to join his new club were held to be taxable as emoluments under Sec 14 TA 1988 i.e. as a payment on retirement or removal from office. The inducement fee was also held to be taxable as emoluments from an employment. Shilton v Wilmhurst 1990 HL STC.

Benefits treated as earnings – Benefits Code

7. As a general rule benefits are treated as earnings in accordance with the Benefits Code. This code comprises of various sections of the ITEPA 2003, each dealing with a specific benefit e.g.,

Cars, vans and related benefits	Loans
Living accommodation	Cash equivalent benefits

Lower paid employment

8. a) The Benefits Code does not apply to an employment in relation to a tax year if:

   i) it is lower-paid employment in relation to that year, and

   ii) condition A or B is met.

   An employment is lower-paid employment in relation to a tax year if the earnings rate for the employment for the year is less than £8,500.

   b) Condition A is that the employee is not employed as a director of a company.

   c) Condition B is that the employee is employed as a director of a company but has no material interest (broadly defined as a 5% shareholding) in the company and either:

   i) the employment is as a full-time working director, or

   ii) the company is non-profit-making or is established for charitable purposes only.

   Non-profit-making means that the company does not carry on a trade and its functions do not consist wholly or mainly in the holding of investments or other property.

The taxation of benefits as earnings

9. The taxation of benefits in kind as earnings depends upon placing a value on the goods and services that are provided at less than full cost, for an employee. This is achieved as follows.

a) In respect of employees earning less than £8,500 p.a., unless provided otherwise by ITEPA, benefits are taxable if they can be converted into moneysworth, at their secondhand value. See Tenant v Smith 1892 HL 3 TC 158. and Wilkins v Rogerson 1961 39 TC 344.

Benefits which cannot be converted into moneysworth are therefore in principle not taxable, e.g. interest free loans, or the private use of a company car.

b) For directors and employees earning £8,500 or more, benefits are taxable whether or not they can be converted into moneysworth. The general charging provisions state that benefits are to be valued at the cost to the employer, or in accordance with a prescribed rate or scale e.g. private cars.

c) For directors and all employees there are prescribed scales of benefit values, or the cost to the employer is used e.g. accommodation, season tickets and transport vouchers.

d) Following the decision in Pepper v Hart HL 1992 STC 898 it appears that benefit in hand may be valued on the marginal cost principle, and not on an average cost basis.

Directors and employees earning £8,500 or more p.a.

10. The rules of the benefit code apply to directors and employees with earnings and benefits treated as earnings in total greater than £8,500 p.a.. The rules include:

a) Any employee whose total earnings, plus expenses and benefits treated as earnings is greater than £8,500 p.a.

b) Any director who has a material interest in the company i.e. is either the owner of or able to control more than 5% of the ordinary share capital of the company.

c) A full-time working director with a material interest of 5% or less in the company, if his or her total earnings and benefits treated as earnings is greater than £8,500 p.a.

Employers must complete a return (form P11D) of payments, benefits, etc. each year in respect of all directors and employees earning £8,500 or more, unless a dispensation is obtained.

In general any benefit provided for the members of the family or household of an employee are treated as if they were provided for the employee personally. The term family or household covers the employee's spouse, children and their spouses, his or her parents, servants, dependants and guests.

Dispensations

11. Where the company is able to explain to the inspector of taxes its arrangements for paying expenses and providing benefits, and satisfy them that they would all be fully covered by the expenses deduction, then it is possible to obtain a 'dispensation'. The practical effect of this is that details of the expenses covered need not be entered on the form P11D or on the employer's annual return or on the employees tax return.

The nature of the expenses covered by the dispensation depends to some extent on the particular circumstances, but they can cover:

travelling and subsistence

cost of entertaining incurred wholly and exclusively for business

subscriptions to professional bodies related to employment

telephone rentals to employees on call outside normal hours.

Benchmark rates for day subsistence

12. HMRC has introduced advisory benchmark scale rates for day subsistence, which will not give rise to taxable benefits. Employers may alternatively use dispensations agreed with HMRC. The benchmark rates are:

Five hour rate – Up to £5 may be paid where the worker has been away from his or her home or normal place of work for at least five hours, and incurred cost on a meal.

Ten hour rate - Up to £10 may be paid where the worker has been away from his or her home or normal place of work for at least ten hours, and incurred cost on a meal, or meals.

Breakfast rate (irregular early starters only) – Up to £5 may be paid where a worker leaves home earlier than usual and before 6.00 a.m. and incurs a cost on breakfast taken away from home.

Late evening meal rate (irregular late finishers only) – Up to £15 may be be paid where the employee finishes work late after 8.00 p.m. and buys a meal which he or she would usually eat at home.

Summary of benefits treated as earnings 2009/10

13 The Benefit Code	Directors and employees earning £8,500 or more	Employees earning less than £8,500
Private use of employer's car	Car and fuel benefits	Not taxable providing some business use
Private use of employer's van	Van and fuel benefits	
Mobile telephones	One phone provided to employee personally is exempt	
Accommodation (see below).	Can be wholly or partly exempt, otherwise taxed on annual value plus expenses paid	Can be wholly or partly exempt: otherwise taxed on annual value plus expenses paid
Board and lodging	Taxed on cost to the employer	Tax free unless received in cash
Industrial clothing	Tax free	Tax free
Suits and clothing	Taxed on cost to employer	Taxed on secondhand value
Medical insurance	Premiums paid by employer taxable	Exempt
Beneficial loans (see below)	Generally taxable with some exceptions	No taxable benefit
Cash vouchers, saving certificates	Full value taxable	Full value taxable
New share option schemes	Not subject to income tax, CGT on final disposal	Not subject to income tax,CGT on final disposal
Savings related share options	Not subject to income tax, CGT on final gain	Not subject to income tax, CGT on final gain

Profit sharing schemes	Limited tax free benefit	Limited tax free benefit
Subsidised meals	Tax free if generally available	Tax free if generally available
Assets loaned	20% of market value when first provided	Not taxable
Assets transferred	Taxed on net increase in value	Taxed on second-hand value
Season tickets and transport vouchers.	Taxed on cost to the employer	Taxed on cost to the employer
Private sick pay	Taxed on amount received	Taxed on amount received
Scholarships provided by reason of employment	Taxed on cost to employer	Not taxable
Employer-subsidised nursery facilities	Taxed on cost to employer	Not taxable
Loan written off	Taxed on full value	Taxed on full value
Workplace nurseries	Not taxable	Not taxable
In-house sports facilities	Not taxable	Not taxable
Overnight expenses	Up to £5 per night exempt	Not taxable
Child care	Up to £50 per week exempt	Up to £50 per week exempt

Private motor cars 2009/10 – car benefit

14.

	£	£
The benefit is calculated as follows:		
List price of car and optional accessories	X	
Less capital contribution by employee	X	
Net Value		X
Percentage of net value based on		
CO_2 emissions (per table)		X
Less reduction for unavailability		X
Less payment for private use		X
Assessable benefits		X

Notes

i)   The percentage of the net value of car is determined from the CO_2 emission table reproduced below.

ii) List price is the published price when first registered plus the list price of any optional accessories. If the car has no published price a 'notional value' will be used.

iii) Where the car is more than 15 years old at the end of the income tax year of assessment then its value, if more than £15,000 is taken to be £15,000.

iv) The maximum value of any car is limited to £80,000.

v) The benefit before private use is reduced proportionally if the car is not available for any period of 30 days or more in the year.

vi) Where the employee makes a capital contribution to the cost of the car, then, subject to a maximum of £5,000, the amount is deducted from the list price.

vii) Where an employee is required to make a capital contribution to the employer for private use of the car then this is deducted in arriving at the assessable benefit.

15. CO_2 emission table

CO_2 emissions in grams per kilometre 2009/10	% of list price Petrol
120	10%
135	15%
140	16%
145	17%
150	18%
155	19%
160	20%
165	21%
170	22%
175	23%
180	24%
185	25%
190	26%
195	27%
200	28%
205	29%
210	30%
215	31%
220	32%
225	33%
230	34%
235	35%

Notes

i) The exact CO_2 figure is always rounded down to the nearest 5 grams per kilometre (g/km). For example, CO_2 emissions of 188g/km are treated as 185g/km.

ii) The maximum charge is 35% of the list price.

iii) The rates in the above table are adjusted for cars using different fuels:

Diesel supplement 3%

Electric reduction 6%

Hybrid electric reduction 3%

Gas reduction 2%

iv) For cars with no approved CO_2 emissions, the percentage of the car's list price to be taxed is determined using the car's engine size.

One scale is for all cars registered before 1998; and another for the small number of cars registered from 1998 onwards without approved CO_2 emissions.

Engine size (cc)	Pre 1998 car	1998 or later car
0 – 1,400	15%	15%
1,401 – 2,000	22%	25%
2,001 and over	32%	35%

Example

A has a Ford petrol company car for 2009/10 with a list price of £16,000. CO_2 emission are 197g/km.

Compute the assessable car benefit for 2009/10.

Solution: Cash equivalent benefit 2009/10

List price × 27% = 16,000 × 27%	4,320

Notes

i) CO_2 emissions of 197g/km rounded down to 195g/km.

ii) Percentage for 2009/10 per table for 195g/km is 27%.

Example

K has a 5,000cc Rolls Royce company car (with no approved CO_2 emission figure) made available from 6th August 2009. The car when first registered in June 1997 had a list price of £130,000. K pays £1,000 p.a. to the company for his private use.

Compute the cash equivalent car benefit for 2009/10.

Solution: Cash equivalent benefit 2009/10

List price (restricted) £80,000 × 32%	25,600
Less reduction for period of unavailability $\dfrac{122}{365} \times 25,600$	8,557
	17,043
Less contribution by K	1,000
Assessable benefit	16,043

Notes:

i)   Period from 6.4.09 – 6.8.10 = 122 days.

ii) As the car was registered before 1998 the engine size scale rate applies at 32%, in the absence of an approved CO_2 emission figure.

iii) If the car was more than 15 years old at the end of the tax year the maximum value would be £15,000.

Private motor cars 2009/10 £16,900 – fuel benefit CO_2%

16. Fuel scale charges for employees receiving free fuel for private mileage in company cars are based on a percentage of £16,900 directly linked with the car's CO_2 emissions. The percentages for petrol and diesels ranges between 10% and 35%. There is a 3% supplement for diesels, with discounts for alternative fuelled cars.

The same percentage is used for tax and Class 1A National Insurance contributions on both car and fuel benefits.

The charge is proportionally reduced where an employee stops receiving free fuel part way through the tax year. However, opting back into free fuel in the same year will result in a full year's charge becoming payable.

Notes

i)   The petrol benefit is reduced to nil where all private petrol is paid for by the employee/director.

ii) Employers (not employees) are required to pay NIC at the main rate of 12.8% on cars provided for private use of employees earning more than £8,500 p.a. This liability is assessed on an annual basis using the car scale and fuel rates quoted above, and collected in July following the previous tax year.

iii) Where one car is used jointly by two or more employees a separate liability can arise in respect of each user.

iv) The charge is not reduced pound for pound to the extent that the employee/director makes good the fuel provided.

Example

A is employed by Beta Ltd and is provided with a 2000 cc Ford car (CO_2 emissions 240g/km) which cost £18,000 on 1st January 2004. A used the car during 2009/10 and Beta Ltd paid for all fuel, business and private. A pays £300 to the company each year for the use of the car.

Calculate the value of any car benefit for 2009/10.

Solution: A – Value of motor car benefits 2009/10

	£
Motor car benefit 35% × £18,000	6,300
Less contribution	300
	6,000
Motor fuel benefit	5,915
Total	11,915

Notes: i)   The CO_2 emission percentage for 240g/km is 35% for 2009/10.

ii) The fuel benefit is 35% × £16,900 i.e. 5,915

Vans Private use including fuel 2009/10

17. Private use of a van with a vehicle weight up to 3,500kgs is taxed in a fixed amount of £3,000.

No tax charge where employee required to take van home with no other personal use.

Where the employer provides fuel for unrestricted private use there will be a fuel charge of £500.

Pre-owned assets

18. An income tax charge will arise in respect of any benefit people get by having free or low cost enjoyment of assets they formerly owned or provided the funds to purchase. The charge will apply to both tangible and intangible assets but will not apply to the extent that:

i)   The property in question ceased to be owned before 18 March 1986;

ii) property formerly owned by a taxpayer is currently owned by their spouse;

iii) the asset in question still counts as part of the taxpayer's estate for inheritance tax purposes under the existing 'gift with reservation' rules;

iv) the property was sold by the taxpayer at an arm's length price, paid in cash: going further than the consultation document, this will not be restricted to sales between unconnected parties;

v) the taxpayer was formerly the owner of an asset only by virtue of a will or intestacy which has subsequently been varied by agreement between the beneficiaries; or

vi) any enjoyment of the property is no more than incidental, including cases where an out-and-out gift to a family, including cases where an out-and-out gift to a family member comes to benefit the donor following a change in their circumstances.

Authorised mileage allowance payments

19. There are separate rates for cars and vans, motorbikes, bicycles and for carrying passengers.

An authorised mileage allowance payment must be:-

a) paid to the employee and not to someone else for the employees advantage

b) specifically for business mileage

The rates are as follows:

Cars and vans	
First 10,000 miles	40p per mile
Over 10,000 miles	25p per mile
Motorcycles	24p per mile
Bicycles	20p per mile

Where employers pay less than the statutory rate, employees can claim tax relief on the difference. Payments made in excess of the statutory rates will be liable to tax and NICs.

Living accommodation

20. Cash equivalent value of benefits (directors and all employees)

Where any individual (i.e. with earnings above and below the £8,500 threshold) is provided with living accommodation then subject to certain exemptions noted below, he is liable to tax on the cash equivalent value of the benefit which is equal to:

Annual value + Cost of ancillary services – Employee's contribution – business use.

Annual value is the gross rating value of the property occupied, or the rent, if any, paid by the person providing the accommodation.

Cost of ancillary services is the total of any expenses incurred in providing services such as heating, lighting, rates, domestic services or gardening, and the provision of furniture.

Employee's contribution means any rent paid by an employee.

Business use means the proportion of any benefit attributable to business use.

Total exemption from annual value

An individual is not taxed on the annual value of the accommodation providing it is:

a) necessary for the proper performance of his or her duties, or

b) for the better performance of his or her duties, and in general provided for others, or

c) required for security reasons.

A full time working director with less than 5% interest in a company is eligible for the exemption under (a) and (b) but not under (c). All other directors are ineligible for any exemption.

Partial exemption from ancillary costs benefit

If an individual is exempted under any of the categories noted above, then the taxable value of all ancillary services is limited to a maximum of 10% of net assessable earnings for the year, i.e. remuneration benefits etc. (excluding ancillary benefits) less any amount paid by the employee for use of the services.

Net earnings (ignoring the benefit in question) are after deducting allowable expenses, superannuation and approved pension scheme payments and capital allowances.

Example

Q is an employee of T plc occupying a house with a gross value of £1,000, which is exempt accommodation.

The employer pays the following expenses:

	£
Heating and lighting	1,200
Gardening	800
Domestic servant's wages	500
Furniture costing	10,000

Q's salary for the year 2009/10 is £40,000 and he pays the company £300 for the use of the services.

Calculate the value of the benefit for 2009/10.

Solution: Cash equivalent value accommodation benefit 2009/10

i)	Annual value of property exempted		–
	Ancillary services:		
	Heating and lighting	1,200	
	Domestic service	500	
	Gardening	800	2,500
	Use of furniture 20% × 10,000		2,000
			4,500
	less employee contribution		300
			4,200
ii)	Q – Emoluments £40,000 × 10%		4,000
	Less contribution paid by Q		300
	Cash equivalent benefit		3,700

Notes

i) The furniture is valued as an asset loaned to an employee, at 20% of its market value when first provided, i.e. £10,000.

ii)   If Q's occupation was non exempted the value of his benefit would be the gross value plus expenses i.e. £1,000 plus £4,500 less contribution of £300 i.e. £5,200. The emolument restriction applies in this case.

Living accommodation costing more than £75,000

21. An extra taxable benefit arises where the following occurs.

a)   The cost of providing accommodation is greater than £75,000, and

b)   The living accommodation is provided for a person by reason of his office or employment, and

c)   The occupier is liable to a taxable benefit in respect of accommodation, as outlined in the previous section. If the employee is exempt from the 'annual value' charge noted above he is also exempted under this heading.

d)   The additional value is determined from:

ORI % × [cost or deemed cost – £75,000] – contribution by taxpayer

ORI %	= the official rate of interest in force on the 6th April of the year of assessment. For 2008/09 it is 4.75% (6.25% before 1 March 2009).
Cost	= cost of acquisition + cost of improvements carried out before year of assessment.
Contribution	= the amount by which any rent paid by tenant is greater than the annual value of the accommodation.

Example

J plc acquired a property in October 2006 for £250,000 which had an annual rateable value of £10,000. In May 2009 improvements costing £25,000 were incurred. On 7th April 2009, Z the marketing director, occupied the property paying a rent of £5,000 p.a. He paid £10,000 towards the original cost.

Calculate the value of the taxable benefits in kind for 2009/10.

Solution: Cash equivalent value of benefit 2009/10

	£	£
2009/10 value of accommodation benefit:		
Annual value of property	10,000	
Less rent paid	5,000	5,000
Additional value of accommodation:		
Cost of accommodation	250,000	
Less exempt amount	75,000	
	175,000	
Less 'contribution'	0	
	175,000	
4.75% × 175,000 =		8,312
		13,312

Notes

i)   The £13,312 would be benefit earnings of Z for 2009/10 chargeable to income tax.

ii)   The improvement expenditure of £25,000 will fall into the computation of the additional value for 2010/11.

iii) As the rent paid by Z is less than the gross value there is no deduction in the computation of the additional value.

iv) The official rate of interest for 2009/10 is 4.75%.

v) Where the property is not occupied throughout the year the change is pro-rated.

vi) Additional value is [175,000] × 4.75% = £8,312.

Assets other than cars – private use

22. Where assets are made available for use by directors and employees earning £8,500 or more then the annual benefit is calculated as follows.

a) Land and property (other than accommodation) is valued at a market rent.

b) Other assets e.g. a company motor cycle, are valued at 20% of the original market value or if higher, the rental paid by the employer.

Assets transferred to an employee

23. If an asset made available to a director or employee earning £8,500 or more is subsequently acquired by that person, then the assessable benefit on the acquisition is the greater of:

a) the excess of the current market price over the price paid by the employee and,

b) the excess of the market value when first provided for use by the employee, less any amounts assessed as annual benefits (at 20%) over the price paid by the employee.

When an employee buys, from his or her employer, a previously loaned computer or bicycle for its full market value no tax charge will arise on the transfer of ownership.

Beneficial loans

24. Where an individual is provided with an interest free or cheap loan then in general the benefit derived from such an arrangement is taxable. Employees earning less than £8,500 p.a. are not assessable since the benefit is not convertible into cash. The following are the main features:

a) The loan giving rise to the benefit to an employee or his or her relative must be obtained by reason of an employment.

b) The assessable amount is calculated by two methods, (see below) using the **official rate of interest** less any interest actually paid by the employee.

2009/10	4.75%	from 1 March 2009
2007/08	6.25%	to 28 February 2009

c) No benefit will arise where the interest on such a loan would normally qualify for tax relief such as: a loan for the purchase of plant or machinery for use in employment.

d) If the value of all the loans outstanding during the year does not exceed £5,000, there will be no charge.

Methods of calculation

25. I. **Average method**

a) This method averages the loan over the tax year by reference to the opening and closing balances at the beginning and end of the year (or date of creation and discharge) and applies the official rate to this amount.

b) Interest paid if any on the loan is deducted from the amount computed in (a) above to determine the amount chargeable to tax.

c) This method is applied automatically unless an election is made, either by the taxpayer or the inspector of taxes, to apply the second method.

d) Where the company's accounts year does not coincide with the tax year then it will usually be necessary to make the calculations by reference to two accounting periods.

Example

Z Ltd makes an interest free loan to R, one of its higher paid employees on the 1st October 2009 of £24,000, repayable by 8 quarterly instalments of £3,000, payable on the 1st January, April, July and October. The first payment is made on the 1st January 2010. Calculate the assessable benefit for 2009/10. The official rate is 4.75%.

Solution: Computation of interest benefit 2009/10

		£
1.10.2009	Loan granted	24,000
5.4.2010	Balance of loan outstanding	
	24,000 – 6,000	18,000
		42,000
	Average loan outstanding	
	$\dfrac{42,000}{2}$	21,000
	Period of loan	

1.10.2009–5.4.2010 = 6 months. (i.e. completed tax months)

$$\text{Interest } 4.75\% \times \frac{6}{12} \times 21,000 = \qquad 498$$

Assessable benefit 2009/10	498

26. II. Alternative method

a) Under this method the interest is calculated on the balance outstanding on a day-to-day basis, using the official rate of interest.

b) Any interest paid is deducted from the amount calculated in (a) above.

Example

Using the data relating to Z Ltd in the previous example, calculate the assessable benefit under the alternative method.

Solution: Computation of interest benefit – 2009/10

		£	£
1.10.2009	Loan granted	24,000	
1.1.2010	Loan repayment	3,000	
		21,000	
	Number of days from 1.10.2009 to 1.1.2010 = 92		
	Interest 92/365 × 4.75% × 24,000		287
1.1.2010	Balance outstanding	21,000	
1.4.2010	Loan repayment	3,000	
5.4.2010	Balance outstanding	18,000	
No. of days from	1.1.2010 to 1.4.2010 =	90	
do.	1.4.2010 to 5.4.2010 =	5	
Interest	90/365 ×4.75% × 21,000		245
	5/365 × 4.75% × 18,000		12
Assessable benefit 2009/10			544

Deductions from earnings

27. The following may be deducted in arriving at taxable earnings under the ITEPA.

a) Expenses falling within the general rule of Section 336. This states that a deduction from earnings is allowed for an amount if

   i) the employee is obliged to incur and pay it as holder of the employment and

   ii) the amount is incurred wholly and exclusively and necessary for the performance of the duties of the office or employment; for example, industrial clothing; tools of trade. Travelling expenses from home to place of business are not permitted deductions, see Ricketts v Colquhoun 1926 10 TC 118. Parikh v Sleeman 1988 STC 580; see also Elderkin v Hindmarsh 1988 STC 267. Fitzpatrick v IRC 1992 STI 456.

b) The main features of the position regarding employees' travel and subsistence are as follows.

   i) site-based employees receive tax relief for travel and subsistence costs from home to the site.

   ii) employees who have a normal place of work receive tax relief for the cost of business journeys which start from home.

   iii) employees who are seconded by their employer to a temporary place of work receive tax relief for travel and subsistence, providing there is the intention to return to the normal place of work within two years.

c) Those permitted specifically by ITEPA e.g. fees and subscriptions to professional bodies, and contributions to exempt approved pension schemes.

d) Capital allowances on plant or machinery provided by the employee in order to perform his duties may be deducted, e.g. office equipment, but not a private car.

None of the above are charges on income which can be deducted from total income. They must be deducted from employment earnings.

Employee liabilities and indemnity insurance

28. Income tax relief is available to employees and directors for payments they make to secure indemnity insurance against liability claims arising from their job or to meet uninsured work-related liabilities. Relief is also extended to situations where the employer or a third party pays the insurance which would otherwise give rise to a benefit in kind. The cost of the insurance is deducted as an expense from the earnings in the year in which the payment is made.

Relief is extended to payments made by ex-employees for periods of up to six years after the year in which employment ceases.

Employees' incidental expenses paid by employer

29. Payments by employers of certain miscellaneous personal expenses incurred by employees are exempt from income tax and NIC.

The exemption covers incidental expenses such as newspapers, telephone calls home and laundry bills incurred by employees when they stay away from home overnight on business.

Payments of up to £5.00 a night in the UK (£10.00 outside the UK) are tax free. However, if the employer pays sums greater than these limits then the whole amount becomes taxable.

Removal expenses and benefits

30. Certain payments and benefits received by reason of an employment are not to be treated as earning for income tax purposes. This applies to:

    a)   sums paid to an employee, or to a third party on behalf of an employee in respect of quantifying removal expenses, and

    b)   any qualifying removal benefit provided for the employee or to members of his or her family or household (including sons and daughters in law, servants, dependants and guests).

I)   Qualifying removal expenses comprise the following.

    1)   Expenses of disposal, i.e. legal expenses, loan redemption penalties, estate agents' or auctioneers' fees, advertising costs, disconnection charges, and rent and maintenance, etc. costs during an unoccupied period in the employee's former residence.

    2)   Expenses of acquisition i.e. legal expenses, procurement fees, survey fees, etc. relating to the acquisition by the employee of an interest in his or her new residence.

    3)   Expenses of abortive acquisition.

    4)   Expenses of transporting belongings, i.e. expenses, including insurance, temporary storage and disconnection and reconnection of appliances, connected with transporting domestic belongings of the employee and of members of his or her family or household from the former to the new residence.

    5)   Travelling and subsistence expenses (subsistence meaning food, drink and temporary accommodation).

    6)   Bridging loan expenses, i.e. interest payable by the employee on loan raised at least partly because there is a gap between the incurring of expenditure in acquiring the new residence and the receipt of the proceeds of the disposal of the former residence.

    7)   Duplicate expenses, i.e. net expenses incurred as a result of the change in the replacement of domestic goods used at the former residence but unsuitable for use at the new residence.

II)   Qualifying removal benefits consist of benefits or services corresponding to the seven headings noted above, with the restriction that the provision of a car or van for general private use is excluded from category 5 above.

The amount of the qualifying removal expenses is limited to a maximum of £8,000.

Payroll deductions for charities

31. An employee can obtain income tax relief on donations to a charity to any value. The main features of the scheme, are as follows:

    a)   Schemes are operated through charity agencies which must be approved by the Inland Revenue.

    b)   Employers are legally bound to pay the donation over to the agency charity and they may not be refunded to the employee.

    c)   Payments made by deed of covenant are not included in the scheme. However, an employee can still make a covenanted donation, subject to the normal requirements, in addition to any made under the payroll scheme.

    d)   The employer will make the deduction of the donation before PAYE is applied, in the same way that pension contributions are dealt with under the 'net pay' arrangements. The amount of the contributions made each year will not usually appear on the employee's P60.

e) National Insurance contributions at the appropriate rate are payable on the gross pay before deduction of any charitable donations.

f) Pensioners can be incorporated into the scheme provided that they are subject to PAYE.

Gift aid

32. An individual can make a single gift of any amount to a qualifying charity.

The gift is treated as if the donor had made a payment to a charity equal to the grossed up amount of the gift.

A payment of £800.00 to a charity is treated as a gross gift of

$800 \times 100/(100-20) = 800 \times 100/80 = £1,000.$

The charity can recover tax from the Inland Revenue. Higher rate tax payers can obtain relief at the higher rate on the gross amount (see Chapter 5).

Termination of employment

33. The main provisions concerned with the taxation of payments for loss of employment are contained in Part 6 Chapter 3 of the ITEPA, and these include the following:

a)
First	£30,000	exempt
Excess over	£30,000	taxed in full

b) Complete or partial exemption is available for terminal payments which relate to any foreign service.

c) General exemption applies to payments made:

   i) on the death or permanent disability of an employee

   ii) to benefits provided under a pension scheme

   iii) to terminal payments made to members of the armed forces.

d) Termination payments and benefits are taxed as income in the year in which they are actually received rather than the year of termination.

Example

N is dismissed as a director of T plc on the 1st October 2009 and receives the sum of £35,000 by way of compensation. N has no service agreement with the company.

N's other income for 2009/10 is a salary of £38,000, and bank interest of £3,200 (net).

Calculate the taxable income.

Solution: N's taxable income 2009/10

	£	£
Income from employment		38,000
Bank interest gross 3,200 x 100/80		4,000
Terminal payment	35,000	
Less exempt amount	30,000	5,000
		47,000
Personal allowance		6,475
Taxable income		40,525

Outplacement counselling

34. This involves the provision of services normally paid for by the employer, for employees who are or become redundant, to help them find new work. Expenditure will be exempt from tax whether or not it exceeds the £30,000 limit for redundancy payments.

Pension income

35. Any pension paid to a former employee is taxable as earned income on the recipient. This includes payments from company operated schemes, from schemes operated by assurance companies, and voluntary payments where there is no formal pension scheme.

If the scheme is approved by and registered with the Inland Revenue then any contributions made by the employee are deductible from taxable earnings. The company's contributions are also allowed as an expense in computing taxable profits.

Pensions paid by the state are taxable as social security income of the recipient and these include: retirement pensions, widows' pensions and service pensions.

Social security pensions

36. The following social security pensions are taxed as earned income of the recipient.

State pension	Graduated retirement pension
Industrial death benefit	Widowed mothers allowance
Widowed parents allowance	Widows pension

Social security benefits

37. The following benefits are taxable under this heading.

Job seeker's allowance

Carers allowance

Statutory maternity pay/paternity pay

Bereavement allowance but not the bereavement lump sum payment of £2,000

Statutory sick pay.

Incapacity benefit

Company share options schemes (CSOP)

38. Under these schemes, if approved, an employee is given the right to buy shares at a fixed price which will not be subject to income tax if retained for a requisite period. The main features of these schemes are as follows.

a) The price of the shares is fixed at not less than the market value, at the time the employee gets his or her option.

b) The shares must form part of the ordinary share capital of the company.

c) Employee participants in the scheme must work at least 20 hours a week for the company, and full-time working directors must work at least 25 hours a week.

d) Options are limited in value to £30,000 on the value of the shares under option.

e) There is normally no income tax liability on the grant of the option or on any increase in the value of the shares providing that the option is used at least three years and no more than ten years after the employee exercised the option.

f)   On the eventual disposal of the shares then the normal rules of capital gains tax apply.

g)   A savings-related share option scheme is also available with similar rules to those noted above.

h)   Approved schemes are not limited to quoted shares but include shares in a company which is not controlled by other companies.

Enterprise management incentive schemes (EMI)

39. The main features of these schemes are:

a)   employees are entitled to receive options with an annual value of £120,000;

b)   to be eligible employees must work for the employing company for at least 25 hours per week or, if less, for 75% of their working time;

c)   trading companies with gross assets equal to or less than £30m can participate in the scheme;

d)   there is usually no income tax liability on the grant of the option or on any increase in the value of the shares providing that the option is used at least three years and no more that ten years after the grant;

e)   on the eventual disposal of the shares then the normal rules of capital gains tax apply.

Share incentive plans (SIP)

40. Broadly, the rules for these Plans enable a company to give an employee free shares worth up to £3,000 per tax year (for which performance targets may be set) and also enable an employee to buy shares worth up to £1,500 per tax year (called 'partnership shares') by deductions from salary. The company may also give the employee up to two free shares (or further free shares) for each share he or she purchases. All shares have to be held in the Plan for specified periods to remain free of tax and national insurance. The amount of dividends on Plan shares that can be reinvested tax-free on a participant's behalf will now be £1,500 per year, replacing the more complex rules previously published. Employees and Plan trustees will be free to make their own arrangements for transferring shares.

8 Income from employment II – PAYE

Introduction

1.   The Pay As You Earn system of deducting income tax at source applies to employment income (see Chapter 7) from offices or employments such as wages, salaries, bonuses, benefits in kind and pensions. The system is operated by employers who collect the income tax on behalf of the Inland Revenue.

National Insurance contributions which are related to employees' earnings (see Chapter 17) are also collected under the PAYE system.

The system does not apply to self-employed individuals.

Taxable pay

2.   For the purposes of tax deduction pay includes the following:

   a)   salaries, wages, fees, bonuses, overtime, commissions, pensions, honoraria, etc. whether paid weekly or monthly

   b)   holiday pay

   c)   Christmas boxes in cash

   d)   terminal payments (see Chapter 7)

   e)   statutory sick pay (see Chapter 17).

In general, benefits in kind, other than cash benefits are taken into account by adjustment of the employees' coding notice (see below) rather than by being treated as pay, see 7 below.

Net pay arrangements

3.   In calculating taxable pay, the employer must deduct any contribution to a pension scheme on which the employee is entitled to relief from tax as an expense. The agreement applies only to schemes which have been approved by the Pensions Scheme Office of the Inland Revenue. The net pay scheme also applies to the payroll deduction scheme for gifts to charities.

Outline of the PAYE system

4.   In order to operate the PAYE system every employer requires the following:
   a)   code numbers for employees
   b)   tax tables
   c)   tax deduction working Sheet P11 (2009)
   d)   forms for operation of the system.

Code numbers

5.   a)   All employees, including Directors and some pensioners, are allocated a code number which is based on the personal allowances, reliefs and charges on income available to individuals, as evidenced by the information contained in their Tax Return. In appropriate cases the code number also takes into consideration other factors such as untaxed interest and tax underpaid or overpaid in previous years.

   The actual code number is equal to the sum of all allowances and reliefs, less the last digit, rounded down. Thus, a married man with no other allowances or charges is entitled to a personal allowance of £6,475 for 2009/10. The MCA is not available for 2009/10 except where either spouse is 65 before 6th April 2000.

Other income such as casual profits, property income, interest and state pensions will be included in determining the main tax code number.

b)   Some of the letters used at present after a code number are as follows:

L   Basic personal allowance

P   Personal allowance for those aged 65 – 74

V   Personal allowance for those aged 65 – 74 plus the MCAA

Y   Personal allowance for those aged 75 or over

K   An amount to be added to pay

T   This is for all other cases in which the taxpayer notifies the tax office that he or she does not wish to use one of the other letters.

c)   The following special codes are also used:

BR   This means that tax is to be deducted at the basic rate.

F   This code, followed by a number means that the tax due on a social security benefit, e.g. retirement pension, or widow's pension or allowance, is to be collected from the taxpayers earnings from employment.

NT   This means that no tax is to be deducted.

D   This code followed by a number means that the pension/benefit is more than the allowances.

OT   This code means that no allowances have been given.

Deductions from allowances in code numbers

6.   The following items may be deducted in arriving at the code number:

a)   State benefits or pension

b)   Income from property

c)   Unemployment benefit

d)   Untaxed interest

e)   Taxable expense allowances and benefits in kind

f)   Excessive basic rate adjustment where too much tax is paid at the basic rate and not enough at the higher rate

g)   Tax underpaid in earlier years

h)   Taxed investment income at the higher rate

i)   Allowance restriction. This is for allowances and reliefs at a lower rate, e.g. MCA.

j)   Under self assessment the balancing amount due may be 'coded out' up to a limit of £2,000.

K Codes

7.   'K' codes arise where there is a negative coding allowance, which usually occurs where the non-PAYE income, e.g. benefits in kind, are greater than the allowances due.

The excess is added to the taxable pay on the tax deduction sheet (P11) and taxed accordingly.

Tax tables

8. The following tables are in general use:

Pay adjustment tables.

These show the proportion of the employee's allowances, as determined by his or her code number, for each week cumulatively from 6th April to the pay date.

Taxable pay tables B, C, D – .

Tax is deducted weekly (monthly for monthly paid persons) by reference to tables which show the tax due to date when a particular code number is used. Table B shows the tax due at the basic rate and the deduction for the lower rate and Tables C and D at the higher rate of 40%.

Statutory sick pay

9. Where any amount of sick pay is paid to an employee then this is entered in Column 1d and accumulated. SSP is included in gross pay for the purposes of both deduction of income tax and National Insurance contributions. 100% of the gross amount of any SSP entered on the deduction working sheet, together with an extra amount to compensate for the employer's NIC paid in the SSP called 'NIC compensation on SSP' is deductible from the total NIC due for the period if their SSP payments for an income tax month exceed 13% of their Class I contributions for that month. See Chapter 17.

Forms for use with PAYE

10. P2 — Notice to employer of code or amended code.

P9 — Notice to employers of changed code for the coming year.

P9D — Return of expenses payments, fees, bonuses etc. for an employee to whom form P11D is not applicable.

P11D — Return of expenses payments, benefits etc. to or for directors and higher paid employees.

P14 — End of year return of pay, tax and National Insurance contributions for each employee.

P45 — Part 1. Particulars of employee leaving.

Part 2. Employee leaving – copy of employer's certificate.

Part 3. New employee – particulars of old employment.

Part 4. Retained by employee.

P11 2000 — Deduction Working Sheet.

P46 — Notice to Inland Revenue of employees without a P45.

P46 (CARS) — Details of change of cars available for private use.

P35 — Employer's annual statement, declaration and certificate.

P60 — Employer's certificate of pay and tax deductions to be given to employee at the end of the year.

Payment of tax

11. Income tax and National Insurance contributions (employer's and employee's) are due for payment to the Collector of Taxes not later than the 19th day of each month. Thus the tax and NIC due for period 8, 2009, which covers the period from 6th November to 5th December, is payable on or before the 19th December 2009.

The National Insurance payable is reduced by any statutory sick pay payments paid during the month.

Where an employer falls in arrears with his or her monthly payments of tax and National Insurance contributions deducted from employees then the Collector of Taxes can issue a notice to an employer estimating the amount unpaid. This becomes enforceable unless the estimated amount or the actual liability is paid within 7 days.

Employers whose average monthly payments to the Collector of Taxes of PAYE and NIC are less than £1,500 in total are allowed to pay quarterly. Payments will be due on the following dates: 19th July, 19th October, 19th January and 19th April. Similar arrangements apply to contractors in the construction industry.

The new limit applies to average monthly payments after taking into account Working Family Tax Credit (see Chapter 17).

Interest on late payment of tax

12. Late payments of PAYE (income tax, Class 1 and 1A NIC contributions) are charged interest at the prescribed rate.

Interest is also charged on late payments of Class IV NICs.

Late payments of monthly or quarterly PAYE within the year are not subject to an interest charge for the time being.

Bonus and commission payments

13. As a general principle taxable pay is assessed in the year in which it is paid under the rules of the ITEPA as outlined in Chapter 7.

Thus, for example, where J has a salary of £20,000 for 2008/09 and earns a commission of an additional £5,000 for that year which is only ascertained and paid in July 2009, then the commission is assessable in the tax year 2009/10.

Directors' remuneration

14. The rules of taxation under ITEPA apply to directors and all other employees. See Chapter 7.

PAYE regulations

15. Regulations for the operation of PAYE are provided under Part II of the ITEPA and embodied in The Income Tax (PAYE) Regulations 2003 (S.1 2003/2682). Where failure to operate PAYE takes place it is the employer who is primarily responsible for making good any deficit and an assessment subject to appeal may be issued for recovery. If the determined amount is not paid within 90 days then the CIR may direct that the tax should be recovered from an employee/director. This can arise where the Commissioners of Inland Revenue are of the opinion that the employee/director received his or her emoluments knowing that the employer has wilfully failed to deduct tax. In general wilful means 'with intention or deliberate' – see R v IRC Chisholm 1981 STC 253.

In R v CIR ex parte Keys and Cook 1987 QB. DT. 25.5.87 the controlling directors of a company which failed to deduct income tax under the PAYE system from their remuneration were held to be liable for that tax.

PAYE investigations

16. The main regulations enabling the Inland Revenue to undertake an audit are contained in The Income Tax (PAYE) Regulations 2003.

These provide that wherever called upon to do so by any authorised officer of the Inland Revenue, the employer must produce at his or her premises to that officer for inspection all wages sheets, deduction working sheets and other documents and records whatsoever relating to the calculation or payment of PAYE income of his employees, or to the deduction of tax from such income or to the amount of earnings related contributions payable.

End of year returns

17. At the end of the income tax year the employer must complete and return to the tax office the following forms:

> Form P35: P35SC (sub-contractors)
>
> Form P14.

The P35 is the employer's Annual Statement, Declaration and Certificate, which is signed by the employer and returned to the tax office by 19th May following the end of the income tax year.

The back of Form P35 contains a summary of the deduction card totals for the year, while the front contains a list of questions concerning payments for casual employment, expenses and Forms P11D etc. Form P14 is an end of year summary made out in respect of each employee for whom a tax deduction card has been used. This form is in triplicate and the two top copies, one marked DSS copy, must be sent to the tax office by 19th May following the end of the tax year. The third copy is the employee's P60 certificate, and shows his or her total pay and deductions for the income tax year.

An automatic penalty will arise if end of year returns (P14, P35, P38/38A) are late. The statutory deadline is the 19th May. There is a penalty of £100 per month (or part) per unit of 50 employees. Where forms P11D are required then these must be returned to the tax office before 6th June following the end of the tax year, with an initial penalty of £300.

Electronic mailing of returns

18. Large and medium sized employers, ie those with 50 or more employees must file their Forms P35 and P14 on line. Small employers, i.e. those with less than 50 employees will be required to e-file after the 2009/10 return.

Employers and self-assessment – 2009/10

19. The following is a summary of the effects of self-assessment on employers.

a) Employee forms P60 detailing pay and tax to be issued by 31st May 2009.

b) Copies of form P11D and P9D to be issued to employees by 6th July 2009.

c) Forms P14 and P35 to be sent to the Inland Revenue by 19th May 2009.

d) Forms P11D and P9D to be sent to the Inland Revenue by 6th July 2009.

e) Penalties for filing an incorrect or incomplete form P11D can amount to £300 per return.

f) Additional penalties can be imposed for failure to comply with the new regulations.

Student self-testing question

T's P60 for the year 2009/10 shows total gross pay of £30,500. He is employed as a sales manager with a salary of £12,000 p.a. for 2009/10. In addition he receives commission paid by reference to the profits shown by the company's accounts amounting to:

	£	
Year ended 31st December 2008	18,500	– paid June 2009
Year ended 31st December 2009	23,000	– paid June 2010

Tax deducted under PAYE for the year 2009/10 amounted to £5,600.

Compute the Income Tax liability for 2009/10.

Solution: Income tax computation 2009/10

			£
Income from employment			12,000
Commission paid June 2009			<u>18,500</u>
			30,500
Personal allowance			<u>6,475</u>
			24,025
	n/a	@ 10%	0
	<u>24,025</u> @ 20%		<u>4,805</u>
Tax liability	<u>24,025</u>		4,805
Less deducted by PAYE			<u>5,600</u>
Amount overpaid			<u>795</u>

9 Income from UK land and property

Introduction

1. This chapter deals with the rules applicable to UK Property income, together with computational examples.

Basis of charge

2. a) Tax is charged on the annual profits or gains arising from any business carried on for the exploitation, as a source of rents or other receipts, of any estate interest, or rights in or over land in the UK.

   Receipts in relation to land includes:

   i) any payment in respect of any licence to occupy or otherwise use any land, or in respect of the exercise of any further right over land.

   ii) rent charges, ground annuals and any other annual payments derived from land.

   b) The following are not taxed as property income, but as trade profits.

   i) Profits or gains from the occupation of any woodlands managed on a commercial basis.

   ii) Farming and agriculture.

   iii) Mines, quarries and similar concerns.

   c) Furnished accommodation is taxed as business profits, and this includes furnished holiday lettings.

   d) The letting of caravans on fixed sites and house boats on fixed moorings is chargeable as property income.

Basis of assessment

3. The basis of assessment is the annual profits or gains arising in the income tax year. It is not possible to use an 'accounts basis' of assessment.

Computation of taxable profits

4. a) All profits or gains are to be computed in accordance with the rules applicable to a trading business.

   b) Property situated in the UK is to be pooled regardless of the type of lease or whether or not it is furnished accommodation.

   c) Any business expenditure incurred in earning the profits from letting is to be deducted from the total pooled income, and is subject to the same rules for allowable expenditure as apply to trading income.

   d) Capital allowances available are given as an expense chargeable against property income so that the adjusted taxable profits are after capital allowances.

   e) As capital allowances are not generally available for plant and machinery in a let dwelling house the renewals basis or the wear and tear allowance for furnished lettings (currently 10% of annual rents less council tax) applies. Other capital allowances are available for plant and machinery e.g. as part of the office equipment used for estate management. Landlords can claim a deduction up to a maximum of £1,500 when they install loft or cavity wall insulation.

f) Interest payable in respect of a property business is allowed as a deduction in calculating the profits of the business under the same rules as apply to other expenses incurred for the purposes of the business.

g) Rental business losses must in general be carried forward and set against future profits from the same rental business. Where there are capital allowances due in respect of the business rental then that part of the loss attributable to capital allowances may be set against other income.

h) Expenses of properties which are let on uncommercial terms (for example, at a nominal rent to a relative) can only be deducted up to the amount of the rent or other receipts generated by the uncommercially let property. The excess of the expenses over the receipts from the uncommercially let property can't be deducted in the rental business and can't, therefore, create a loss.

Example

Z purchased a freehold factory site on the 6th April 2009 which he lets for an annual rental of £15,000 payable quarterly in advance. First payment due 6th April 2009 covered the period to 30th June 2009. Property expenses paid by Z for the year to 5th April 2010 amounted to £2,500 and interest paid on a loan to purchase the factory was £3,500.

Capital allowances for the 12 months to 5th April 2010 have been agreed at £2,000.

Compute Z's business income for 2009/10.

Solution: Z's property business income 2009/10

	£	£
Rents receivable		15,000
Less expenses:-		
Property expenses	2,500	
Loan interest	3,500	6,000
Adjusted profit		9,000
Less capital allowances		2,000
Taxable profits		7,000

Notes

i) The rents received are computed on an accruals basis.

ii) Property business income is normally not 'trading income'.

Lease premiums

5. One way of looking at lease premiums is to regard them as a capitalised part of future rental income which would otherwise have been received by way of annual rent. They include any sum whether payable to the immediate or a superior landlord, arising in connection with the granting of a lease, but not arising from an assignment, of an existing lease.

Under an assignment the lessee takes the position of the original lessee, with the same terms and conditions.

Where a lease is granted (but not assigned) at a premium, for a period not exceeding 50 years, then the landlord is deemed to be in receipt of a rental income equal to the premium, less an allowance of 2% of the premium for each complete year of the lease remaining, excluding the first 12 month period.

Example

B granted a lease for 24 years of his warehouse to a trader on the following terms:

A lease premium of £12,000 to be paid on 1 May 2009 and an annual rent of £7,200 from 1 May 2009.

Allowable expenditure for the year 2009/10 was £5,800.

Solution: B Property income 2009/10

	£	£
Lease premium	12,000	
Less 2% × 12,000 × (24 − 1)		
Ie 1/50 × 12,000 × 23	5,520	6,480
Annual rent 7,200 × 11/12	6,600	
	13,080	
Less allowable expenses	5,800	
Taxable profits	7,280	

In effect the lease premium is discounted by reference to its duration, and the longer the unexpired portion, the greater the discount. Thus if a lease had 49 years to run the discount would be:

$(49 − 1) × 2\%$ i.e. 96%.

The amount of the taxable premium may also be determined by use of the formula where:

$$P - \frac{P ¥ Y}{50}$$

P = amount of premium paid; Y = number of completed 12 months other than the first.

A premium on a lease for a period greater than 50 years would not be taxed as Property income. If the lease premium is paid by instalments the full amount, less the discount, is taxable in the usual way. However, if hardship can be proved the tax may be paid over a period not exceeding 8 years.

Sub-leases and assignments

6. The creation of a sub-lease out of the main or head lease for a premium would give rise to a liability, but not an assignment of that lease. Where a charge to taxation arises from the granting of a lease at a premium, and this is followed by the lessee granting a sub-lease at a premium, then any liability arising on the second occasion is reduced, as shown in the example below.

Example

J grants a lease for 20 years to M for a premium of £10,000. After occupying the premises for five years, M grants a sub-lease to another person for a period of 10 years at a premium of £6,000.

Show the computation of J's and M's liability to income tax.

Solution: Computation of J's liability

	£
Lease premium	10,000
Less 2% × 10,000 × (20 − 1) i.e. 38% × 10,000	3,800
	6,200

Computation of M's liability

	£
Lease premium	6,000
Less 2% × 6,000 × (10 − 1) i.e. 18% × 6,000	1,080
	4,920

$$4{,}920 - \frac{\text{Duration of sub lease}}{\text{Duration of head lease}} \times (\text{Income on main lease premium of J, i.e. 6,200})$$

4,920 − [10/20 × 6,200] i.e. 1,820

The amount of the lease premium assessed on M is therefore £1,820.

Lease premiums and the lessee

7.   Where the lessee makes a payment of a lease premium on the granting of a lease, then a proportion of that premium may be set against the following:

a)   any trading income, providing the premises are used for business purposes.

b)   any rental income or lease premium received from any sub lease granted by the lessee.

In effect the amount of the premium assessed as income of the lessor can be charged as an expense of trading, the taxable portion being spread over the remaining life of the lease.

Example

S is granted a lease of premises to be used for trading purposes, for a period of 20 years at an annual rent of £600 p.a. and an initial lease premium of £32,000.

	£
Lease premium	32,000
Less 2% × 32,000 × (20 − 1) i.e. 38% × 32,000	12,160
Lease premium charged on lessor	19,840

Relief available to S is $\dfrac{19840}{20}$ i.e. £992 p.a.

Furnished holiday lettings

8.   a)   The commercial letting of furnished holiday accommodation is treated as carrying on a trade.

b)   To be eligible as 'qualifying accommodation' the following requirements must be met.

i)   The accommodation must be let by the owner to a tenant who has use of the furniture.

ii)   There must be a commercial letting carried on with a view to the realisation of profit.

iii)   The accommodation must be available for commercial letting to the public generally as holiday accommodation for periods which amount in total to not less than 140 days p.a.

iv)   The periods for which the holiday accommodation is so let amount to at least 70 days.

v) For a period comprising at least 7 months (which need not be continuous, but includes the period of 70 days mentioned in (iv) above) it is not normally in the same occupation for a continuous period exceeding 31 days.

vi) Averaging may be used in determining the 70 day test in respect of all or any of the properties let by the same person. A claim to this effect must be made within two years of the end of the year of assessment or accounting period to which this is to apply.

c) Allowable expenditure deductible in computing trading income from the commercial letting of furnished holiday accommodation is the same as trade profits and accordingly the same rules of computation apply.

9. The following provisions apply to trading income from the commercial letting of holiday accommodation, as they do to trade profits.

a) Income is relevant earnings therefore eligible for personal pension plans. (See Chapter 16.)

b) Capital allowances are available on eligible expenditure. (See Chapter 13.)

c) Loss reliefs are available. (See Chapter 14.)

d) Relief for pre-trading expenditure is available. (See Chapter 14.)

e) CGT relief for business assets.

f) Lettings other than furnished holiday lettings are not treated as a trade for income tax, capital gains tax or IHT purposes.

Where a person has qualifying holiday accommodation in a year of assessment and other holiday accommodation which does not fulfil the 70 day letting test then an averaging of the whole accommodation can be made if an election is made within two years of the year of assessment.

Example

Z owns and lets holiday bungalows none of which are let to the same person for more than thirty days. In respect of 2009/10 the following information is provided about the lettings:

	Days available	Days let
Bungalow A	190	82
Bungalow B	150	48
Bungalow C	150	95
Bungalow D	135	85

Determine which of the bungalow lettings are 'qualifying accommodation'.

Solution

Bungalow D   This does not qualify as it does not satisfy the 140 day test even though its lettings are more than 70 days. It cannot be used in any averaging.

Bungalow A   This satisfies both tests.

Bungalow C   This satisfies both tests.

Bungalow B   This fails the 70 day letting test. However it can be averaged with bungalow C to qualify:

$$\frac{95 + 48}{2} = \frac{143}{2} = 71 \text{ days}$$

The income from bungalows A, B and C will therefore be treated as trading income for 2009/10.

Furnished accommodation

10. Rents from furnished accommodation are assessed as property income.

Relief for depreciation of furniture and fittings, (i.e. plant and machinery for capital allowances purposes) may be given in respect of each asset on the 'renewals method', or as an agreed 10% deduction from net rent.

Net rent is gross rent receivable less charges and services normally borne by the tenant, but in fact borne by the landlord, such as council tax, water and sewerage rates.

Capital allowances as such cannot be claimed in respect of house property. However, landlords can claim a deduction up to a maximum of £1,500 when they install loft or cavity insulation in a dwelling house which they let.

Rent a room

11. For 2009/10 householders can let rooms in their own house for £4,250 p.a. tax free provided it is furnished accommodation with the following effects.

a)   Gross rents up to £4,250 p.a. are exempt.

b)   Gross rents greater than £4,250 are taxable as follows:

   i)   pay tax on excess rent i.e. (rent − £4,250)

   ii)   pay tax on gross rents less expenses including capital allowances.

A claim must be made for the exemption not to be applied in writing within one year of the tax year to which it is to apply.

It is possible for the income to be taxed as trade profits where the taxpayer is deemed to be carrying on a trade, and provides substantial services in connection with the letting e.g. meals, cleaning, laundry, and goods and services of a similar nature.

Student self-testing questions

1.   Mrs T has a bungalow which was used for commercial letting as furnished holiday accommodation during 2009/10. The property trading profits amounted to £7,000.

She is responsible for all the organisation and management of the lettings.

Mr T has earnings income of £24,000 and taxed bank interest of £2,400 (net). Mrs T has earnings income of £10,000.

Compute T's income tax liability for 2009/10 and that of Mrs T.

Solution: Income tax computation 2009/10

	T £	Mrs T £
Earnings income T	24,000	10,000
Property income Mrs T	–	7,000
Interest (gross) 2,400 x 100/80	3,000	0
	27,000	17,000
Personal allowance	6,475	6,475
Taxable income	20,525	10,525

Tax liability

N/A / N/A	@ 10%	0	0
<u>20,525</u> / <u>10,525</u>	@ 20%	<u>4,105</u>	<u>2,105</u>
20,965 10,965		4,105	2,105
Less income tax deducted from bank interest		600	
Tax payable		<u>3,505</u>	<u>2,105</u>

2.

(a) Geta rents out a room in her house. In 2009/10 she received rent of £4,900 and paid expenses of £2,000.

Requirement: Calculate the amount of Geta's assessment on income from property for 2009/10 assuming any necessary election is made.   **(2 marks)**

(b) Raj owns three flats which he lets out.

   Flat 1. The flat was purchased on 6 September 2009 and let unfurnished from 29 September 2009. The new seven-year lease was at an annual rental of £3,500 payable on the usual quarter days. The incoming tenant was required to pay a premium of £5,000.

   Flat 2. The flat was let unfurnished at an annual rental of £4,000 on a lease which expired on 23 June 2009, the rent having been paid on the usual quarter days. The property was re-let on 30 September 2009 on the same conditions at an annual rent of £6,000.

   Flat 3. The flat was let furnished for the full year on a weekly rental of £120.

The usual quarter days are 25 March, 24 June, 29 September and 25 December.

Details of expenditure in the year ended 5 April 2010 were:

	Flat 1	Flat 2	Flat 3
	£	£	£
Insurance	400	200	600
Repairs	4,500	600	350
Water rates	-	-	400
Council tax	-	-	800

Notes

1. The amount of £400 was an annual premium

2. £4,000 was spent on UPVC double glazing on 10 September 2009 replacing leaking wooden window frames. To have replaced with wooden frames would have cost £1,200. The windows needed to be repaired to make the house habitable.

Requirement: Calculate Raj's profit from property for 2009/10.   **(8 marks)**

NB Calculations may be made to the nearest month.

(c) State how loss relief is given where the loss is in respect of property let unfurnished.

                                                                            (1 mark)

                                                            (Total: 11 marks)

Solution

(a) Geta

(i)   Ordinary basis   £

Rent   4,900

Expenses   2,000

                                                                       2,900

(ii)   Alternative basis   £

Rent   4,900

'Rent a room' limit   4,250

                                                                         650

Assessment of income from property (lower figure) £650

(b) Raj: Income from property 2009-10

		£	£	
Rent receivable	- Flat 1		1,750	(W1)
	- Flat 2		4,000	(W2)
	- Flat 3		6,240	
Premium on lease	- Flat 1		4,400	(W3)
			16,390	
Insurance	- Flat 1	233 (W4)		
	- Flats 2&3	800		
Repairs	- Flat 1	500 (W5)		
	- Flats 2&3	950		
Wear and Tear Allowance	- Flat 3	504 (W6)		
Water rates and council tax	- Flat 3	1,200	4,187	
Schedule A profit			12,203	

Working 1

6/12 x £3,500   £1,750

Working 2

3/12 x £4,000   £1,000

6/12 x £6,000   £3,000

                                                       £4,000

Working 3

Premium   £5,000

less (7-1) x 2%   600

                                                       £4,400

Working 4

7/12 x £400   £233

Working 5

As the replacement of the window frames was necessary before the flat could be let, the expenditure is deemed to be capital expenditure and not, therefore, allowable.

Working 6

The 'wear and tear' allowance is 10% of the rent less the items which are the tenant's responsibility, ie, water rates and council tax.

£6,240 – (400 + 800) = £5,040; 10% - £504

If the expenses of letting property in a tax year exceed the income from property, the excess is carried forward to be set against the first available A income from property in the future.

Question without answer

1.   Arthur owned a furnished house in a holiday resort which was available for commercial letting when not occupied by Arthur and his family.

In the tax year 2009/10 it was let for the following periods, no letting to the same person exceeded 30 days:

Month	Days
April	7
May	14
June	7
July	31
August	occupied by Arthur - 30
September	14

Apart from the above periods and two weeks in April when it was being decorated the house was available for letting throughout the tax year. The total rent received was £1,900 and the following expenditure was incurred:

	£
Insurance	250
Repairs and decorating	308
Water rates	160
Accountancy	60
Cleaning	480
Advertising	200
Interest on loan to purchase property	608
Replacement furniture	140

Arthur has also purchased two shops on the resort for unfurnished letting.

Shop 1. The annual rent was £3,000 on a lease which expired on 30 June 2009. Arthur took advantage of the shop being empty to carry out repairs and decorating. The shop was let to another tenant on a five-year lease at £4,000 per annum from 1 October 2009.

Shop 2. The shop was purchased on 10 April 2009 and required treatment to wood damaged by dry-rot before it could be let out. Arthur also undertook some normal re-decorating work before the shop was let on 1 October 2009 on a seven-year lease at an annual rental of £6,000.

A premium of £2,000 was received from the incoming tenant upon signing the lease 1 October 2009.

The rent for both shops was due in advance on the usual calendar quarter days.

The following expenditure was incurred for 2009/10:

	Shop 1	Shop 2
	£	£
Insurance	190	300
Ground rent	10	40
Repairs and decorating	3,900	5,000
Accountancy	50	50
Advertising for tenant	100	100

Notes:

(1) Includes £2,500 for re-roofing the shop following gale damage in February 2010. Because the roof had been badly maintained the insurance company refused to pay for the repair work.

(2) Includes £3,000 for remedial treatment to dry-rot damaged wood discovered when the shop was bought. The wood needed to be repaired before the shop could be let out.

Requirement: Calculate the income assessable on Arthur for 2009/10 from the house and both shops and to show how any losses would be dealt with. **(11 marks)**

(ACCA Tax Framework Pilot paper updated)

10 Income taxed as trade profits I
– general principles

Introduction

1. In this chapter the determination of business income for taxation purposes is examined. A summary of the order in which the topic is considered is given first. This is followed by an analysis of the main principles within each topic heading. Questions and answers illustrating the adjustment of profits for tax purposes appear at the end of the chapter. The basis of assessment is dealt with in the next chapter.

List of topic headings

2. Charge to tax on trade profits

The concept of trading

Capital receipts

General rules restricting deductions

Allowable expenditure

Non-allowable expenditure

Asset values for tax purposes

Adjustment of profits

Charge to tax on trade profits

3. Income derived from a business in the form of profits is chargeable to income tax where the business is conducted by an individual, either as a sole trader or in partnership with someone else. Where the business is undertaken by an incorporated person, such as a company, then corporation tax is chargeable on the profits, and not income tax.

Tax under this heading is charged on the full amount of the profits or gains arising or accruing to any person residing in the UK from any trade, profession or vocation, whether carried on in the UK or elsewhere.

Trade is defined to include any 'manufacture, adventure, or concern in the nature of trade'. All farming and market gardening in the UK are treated as carrying on a trade.

The concept of trading

4. As Lord Wilberforce pointed out in the case of Ransome v Higgs 1974 STC 539 'everyone is supposed to know what trade means so Parliament, which wrote this into the law in 1799, has wisely abstained from defining it'.

The Royal Commission on the taxation of profits and income in 1955 listed 'six badges of trade' which are generally used in determining what is an adventure in the nature of trade. These are:

a)   the subject matter of the realisation

b)   the length of the period of ownership

c)   the frequency or number of similar transactions by the same person

d)   supplementary work on or in connection with the property realised

e)   the circumstances that were responsible for the realisation

f)   motive.

5. The present day meaning must therefore be deduced from a mixture of previous legal decisions, accepted practice and the 'badges of trade'. The following is a summary of some general points.

    a)   Betting and gambling are not generally regarded as trading unless carried on by an authorised bookmaker.

    b)   The fact that a trade is illegal does not mean that it is therefore not taxable.

    c)   Where transactions are concluded within a year they may nevertheless be regarded as 'annual profits or gains'. See Martin v Lowry 1926 11 TC 297.

    d)   Isolated transactions can amount to trading if they are of a commercial nature. See Salt v Chamberlain 1979 STC 750, Wisdom v Chamberlain 1968 45 TC 92. Rutledge v CIR 1929 14 TC 490. Marson v Morton. The Times 7.8.1986. Kirkham v Williams STC 1989.

    e)   All farming and market gardening carried on in the UK are treated as carrying on a trade.

    f)   Changes in the activities of a trade may amount to the establishment of a separate trade for tax purposes. See Gordon Blair v CIR 1962 40 TC 358, DIK Transmissions (Dundee) Ltd v CIR 1980 STI 784, Cannon Industries Ltd v Edwards 1965 42 TC 625.

    g)   The commercial letting of holiday accommodation is treated as trading income. See Chapter 9.

Capital receipts

6. In general profits arising from 'capital transactions' are not treated as income for the purposes of trade profits, although they may be taxable under some other tax, such as capital gains tax. Any profit on the disposal of a fixed asset would not therefore be subject to income tax, and conversely, any loss arising would not be allowed as a business expense.

Where a person receives a sum of money which is paid under a legal obligation in return for goods or services provided in the normal course of trade, then this is clearly a trading transaction, chargeable to taxation. However, where the receipt does not arise from any contractual obligation, and the person has given nothing in return, then this may be regarded as a non-taxable receipt. Some general types of transaction are considered below.

Exchange profit and loss

In general exchange profits and losses arising from trading transactions will be chargeable to taxation whereas those relating to capital or non-trading transactions will not be chargeable.

See Imperial Tobacco of Gt Britain & Ireland Ltd v Kelly 1943 25 TC 292; Davies v The Shell Co. of China Ltd 1951 32 TC 133; Pattison v Marine Midland Bank Ltd 1983 CA STC 269. Beauchamp v FW Woolworth plc 1989 HL STC. New provisions affecting companies in effect treat all exchange gains and losses as taxable or allowable as a trading expense.

Insurance claims

On the whole, insurance compensation received in connection with damage or loss to a fixed asset is not taxable as a trading receipt. Claims under personal accident insurance, and claims relating to any loss on a current asset are generally taxable.

See Green v Gliksten J. & Son Ltd 1929 14 TC 394; Gray & Co. Ltd v Murphy 1940 23 TC 225; Keir & Cawden Ltd v CIR 1958 38 TC 23.

Compensation and voluntary payments

If these transactions arise in the ordinary course of trade then they are taxable on the recipient. If they are voluntary ex gratia payments, arising outside the domain of trading, then they are generally not taxable.

See Murray v Goodhews 1978 STC 191, CIR v Falkirk Ice Rink Ltd 1975 STC 434; Simpson v John Reynolds & Co. (Insurance) Ltd 1975 ALL.E.R 245, Poulter v Gayjon Processes Ltd 1985 STI 30.

Regional development grants

Where a regional development grant is made to a person carrying on a trade profession or vocation which would otherwise be taxable as a trading receipt then it is not a taxable receipt. Regional development grants are those made under the provisions of Part II of the Development Act 1982.

General rules restricting deductions in computing profits

7. a) In calculating the profits of a trade no deduction is allowed for items of a capital nature.

b) 1) In calculating the profits of a trade no deduction is allowed for –

a) expenses not incurred wholly and exclusively for the purposes of the trade, or

b) losses not connected with or arising out of the trade.

2) If an expense is incurred for more than one purpose, subsection (1) does not prohibit a deduction for the identifiable part or proportion of the expense which is incurred wholly and exclusively for the purposes of trade.

While an acceptable division between capital and revenue can normally be determined on sound accounting principles, it does not follow that such a treatment by itself will suffice to pass the interpretation meant by the section. Case law has supplied most of the guidance on this matter, and the words of Viscount Cave in Atherton v British Insulated and Helsby Cables Ltd 1925 10 TC 155, are the most frequently quoted:

'when an expenditure is made not only once and for all but with a view to bringing into existence an asset, or an advantage for the enduring benefit of a trade, I think that there is a very good reason for treating such expenditure as properly attributable not to revenue, but to capital'.

The following Court decisions provide some idea of the importance and range of these two sections.

1. Regent Oil Co. Ltd v Strick 1966 43 TC 1. Payments made to acquire leases were held to be capital payments.

2. IRC v Carron Co. 1968 45 TC 65. Expenditure incurred in modifying the company's charter was held to be revenue expenditure.

3. Mitchell v Noble (BW) Ltd 1927 11 TC 373. Compensation paid to a permanent director in consideration for his retirement was held to be revenue expenditure.

4. Associated Portland Cement Mfs Ltd v Kerr 1946 27 TC 103. Payments to retiring directors in consideration of covenants not to carry on similar business were held to be capital.

5. The Law Shipping Co. Ltd v IRC 1924 12 TC 103. Repair expenditure at the time of purchase of a ship, necessary to enable it to remain as a profit earning asset, was held to be capital.

6. Odeon Associated Theatres Ltd v Jones 1972 48 TC 257. Repair expenditure incurred at the time of the purchase of the cinema, not necessary to make the asset commercially viable, was held to be revenue.

7. Strong & Romsey Ltd v Woodfield 1906 5 TC 215. Damages and costs of injuries to a guest, caused by a falling chimney were held to be non revenue expenditure.

8. Smiths Potato Estates Ltd v Bolland 1948 30 TC 267. Legal and accountancy expenses of an income tax appeal were held to be non revenue expenses.

9. Morgan v Tate & Lyle Ltd 1954 35 TC 367. Expenses incurred to prevent the nationalisation of their industry were held to be allowable deductions.

10. Copeman v Flood (William) & Sons Ltd 1941 24 TC 53. Sums paid as director's remuneration are not necessarily expended wholly and exclusively for the purposes of trade.

11. ECC Quarries Ltd v Watkins 1975 STC 578. Abortive expenditure on planning permission was held to be capital expenditure.

12. Tucker v Granada Motorway Services Ltd 1979 STC 393. A sum paid to secure a change in the lease of a service station was held to be capital.

13. Garforth v Tankard Carpets Ltd 1980 STC 251. When a mortgage made to secure loans to a connected company was foreclosed, the sum paid over was held to be not allowable.

14. C.S. Robinson v Scott Bader Co. Ltd 1980 STC 241. The salary, expenses and social costs of an employee, seconded to a foreign subsidiary, were held to be allowable expenses of the parent company.

15. Dollar v Lyons 1981 STC 333. Payments made to children for work on a farm were held to be pocket money and not a trading expense.

16. Walker v Joint Credit Card Co. Ltd 1982 STI 76. Payments to a competitor to cease carrying on business were held not to be expenses of trading.

17. Whitehead v Tubbs (Elastic) Ltd 1983 STI 496. A sum of £20,000 paid to ICFC to obtain release from the terms of a loan agreement was held to be capital expenditure.

18. Watkiss v Ashford, Sparkes and Harward 1985 STC. Expenditure on partnership lunches was held to be not deductible. Annual conference costs were, however, deductible.

19. Jeffs v Ringtons Ltd 1985 STC 809. Company payments to set up a trust fund to acquire shares for the benefit of employees were held to be revenue expenditure and not capital.

20. Mackinlay v Arthur Young McClelland Moore & Co. 1988. Removal expenses of £8,658 paid to two partners were held not to be allowable in determining the firm's profits.

21. Rolfe v Wimpey Waste Management 1988 STC The company acquired land sites to be used for its waste disposal business. The annual charge to profit and loss account in respect of the amount filled was held to be capital expenditure. Decision upheld CA 1989.

22. Donald Fisher (Ealing) Ltd v Spencer STl Feb 1989. A sum received by way of compensation in connection with a rent review was held to be taxable as a trading receipt.

Allowable expenditure – a summary

8. Subject to the general principles noted above, the following is a list of the most common items of expenditure which are allowed as an expense in computing taxable trading income.

1. Cost of materials, components and goods purchased for resale.

2. Gross wages and salaries, and employer's NIC.

3. Redundancy payments.

4.   Ex gratia payments and compensation for loss of office.

5.   Pension scheme contributions to approved schemes – actually paid in year.

6.   Rent business rates and telephone.

7.   Fuel and power.

8.   Printing and stationery.

9.   Vehicle and aircraft running and maintenance expenses.

10. Repairs and renewals, see below.

11. Bad and doubtful debts, see below.

12. Travelling and accommodation expenses for business purposes, e.g. sales representatives, trade fairs and conferences.

13. Advertising and promotional expenditure.

14. Bank/loan interest.

15. Leasing payments.

16. Hire purchase interest.

17. Patent renewal fees and expenses, see below.

18. Insurance of assets, employees, goods etc.

19. Legal expenses arising from trading, such as debt collection, see below.

20. Professional charges such as audit fees and consultancy charges, but not those concerned with the acquisition of an asset.

21. Training expenditure.

22. Welfare expenditure for employees.

23. Subscriptions and donations, see below.

24. Losses and defalcations of employees, see below.

25. Penalty payments for late delivery of goods.

26. Pre-trading expenditure of a revenue nature, incurred up to seven years before trading.

27. Incidental costs of obtaining loan finance, see below.

28. Expenditure on waste disposal.

29. Gifts to educational establishments.

30. Loan relationship losses – companies only.

31. R&D expenditure – small or medium sized companies 175% of cost; - large companies 130% of cost.

Non-allowable expenditure – a summary

9.   The following is a list of the most common items of expenditure which are not generally allowed as an expense in computing trading income.

1.   Depreciation of fixed assets and losses on disposals. (But see IFA Chapter 19).

2.   Professional charges concerned with a taxation appeal.

3.   General provisions against future expenditure such as those for doubtful debts, pension schemes, furnace relinement, or for preventive maintenance.

4.   Legal expenses on the acquisition of an asset.

5. Entertainment except staff functions.

6. Losses and defalcations by directors.

7. Repairs which involve any improvement or amount to a renewal.

8. Fines for illegal acts. (except parking fines of employee)

9. Political donations.

10. Non-trading losses.

11. Penalties, interest or surcharge arising from VAT.

12. Unpaid remuneration. See below.

13. Council tax.

14. Crime related payments – blackmail or extortion.

15. Criminal bribes made in UK or overseas.

Rent paid to non-resident

10. Where net rental profits are paid to a non-resident landlord then basic rate income tax must be deducted at source from these payments and accounted for to the Inland Revenue. See Chapter 9.

Failure to so deduct does not mean that the income tax can be recouped from the future rental payments. Tenbry Investments L v Peugeot Talbot Co. Ltd 1992 STC 791.

Business entertainment and gifts

11. Expenses of this nature are not allowed unless they are incurred for the entertainment or of one's own staff, and in the latter case, this must not be incidental to the approval of any kind of hospitality to others. Where an employer bears the cost of an annual Christmas party, or similar function such as a staff dinner and dance, which is open to the staff generally, then the Revenue will not in practice seek to tax any relevant benefit in kind, where the expenditure is modest. In this context expenditure of the order of £150 per annum for each employee or guest will generally be regarded as modest, and need not be included on the form P11D. This limit does not apply to the amount allowed as a business expense.

Gifts of any kind given by way of entertainment are also disallowed except small gifts which

a) carry a prominent advertisement

b) are not food, drink or tobacco

c) do not amount in value to more than £50 per person p.a.

Gifts made to a body of persons or trust established for charitable purposes only are allowed provided that they are incurred 'wholly and exclusively' for the purposes of trade.

Repairs and renewals

12. Improvements to premises are not allowed, but repairs occasioned by normal wear and tear would be deductible. Repair is not defined but has been held to amount to 'restoration or replacement of subsidiary parts', whereas a renewal is the reconstruction of the entirety, meaning not the whole but substantially the whole. A renewal would therefore be regarded as capital expenditure and not allowed as a trading expense. As noted in the Odeon Theatre case above, repairs to newly acquired premises, necessary to make them usable, would also be disallowed.

Patent fees and expenses

13. Deduction as an expense is allowed for any fees paid or expense incurred in obtaining for the purposes of a trade:

   a)   the grant of a patent or extension of a patent period

   b)   the registration of a design or trade mark.

   Expenditure on any abandoned or rejected application for a patent is also allowable.

Bad and doubtful debts

14. Bad debts proved to be such are allowed as a deduction, and doubtful debts are also allowed in so far as they are respectively estimated to be bad. Thus a provision for specific bad debts is allowable, but not a general provision based on some overall percentage of outstanding debtors.

Where a debt is incurred outside the trading activities of the business, e.g. loans to employees written off, then any loss arising will not be allowable. This would also apply to any bad debts arising from the sale of any fixed assets.

Any bad debts recovered are treated as trading receipts in the period when received.

Pension scheme contributions

15. Sums paid to an exempt approved retirement benefits scheme are allowed as a deduction. Approved in this sense means by the Inland Revenue Savings, Pensions, Share Schemes Group which deals with the approval of all schemes. The sums must be actually paid and not just provided for, to make good any deficit in the pension scheme.

Redundancy payments/outplacement counselling

16. Payments made to employees under the Employment Rights Act 1996 are permitted deductions, and any rebates received are taxable as trading income. Payments made outside the provisions of the Act are also in general, allowed. See O'Keeffe v Southport Printers Ltd 1984 STI 381, where payments made to employees on the cessation of trade were held to be allowable.

Training costs

17. Expenditure by employers on training for new work or skills undertaken by employees about to leave or those who have already left is allowed as a trading expense if not already so treated.

Employees must undertake a qualifying course of training which must have a duration of at least one year.

Legal expenses

18. In general legal charges incurred in maintaining existing trading rights are allowable, and this would include costs of debt recovery, settling disputes, preparation of service agreements, defence of title to business property, and damages and costs arising from the normal course of trade.

As already noted, legal costs incurred in contesting an income tax appeal were held to be not allowable. However, accounting and legal expenses incurred in seeking taxation advice would normally be allowed.

Expenses concerned with the acquisition of an asset would not be allowed, but those arising in connection with the renewal of a short lease (i.e. having a life less than 50 years) are in practice permitted.

The legal costs of raising or altering any share capital of a company are disallowed, but not those relating to loan capital.

Losses and defalcations

19. Any loss not arising from the trade, or not incurred wholly and exclusively for the purposes of trade, will not be allowable as a deduction in computing taxable profits. Two categories give substance to this principle and indicate types of loss which are not deductible:

a)   Any loss not connected with or arising out of the trade, profession or vocation.

b)   Any sum recoverable under an insurance or contract of indemnity.

With regard to losses arising from the sorts of risks that are usually insured against such as fire, burglary, accident or loss of profits, then the loss sustained is allowable if arising from the trade, e.g. loss of stocks, and any compensation received must be treated as a trading receipt.

Where assets are involved then any loss arising would be of a capital nature and not allowable as a deductible expense.

Losses arising from defalcations or embezzlement by an employee would normally be allowable.

See English Crown Spelter Co. Ltd v Baker 1908 5 TC 327; Milnes v J Beam Group Ltd 1975 STC 487; Roebank Printing Co. Ltd v CIR 1928 13 TC 864; Curtis v Oldfield J & G Ltd 1925 9 TC 319.

Post-cessation expenditure

20. For payments made in connection with a trade that has been permanently discontinued, relief is available for payments made wholly and exclusively

a)   in remedying defective work done, goods supplied or services rendered

b)   in meeting legal and professional charges.

The relief is available within seven years of the discontinuance for self-employed individuals.

Relief is given primarily against an individual's total income for the year but where this is insufficient it may be set against any chargeable gains for that year.

Miscellaneous items

21. Unpaid remuneration

In calculating the profits of a trade no deduction is allowed for employees remuneration paid 9 months after the end of the period of account.

Bona fide salaries to employees and directors, including commissions and bonuses, are allowable if they are incurred for the purposes of trade. See Copeman v Flood 1941 24 TC 53.

Subscriptions and donations

Subscriptions to trade associations or other bodies for the purposes of trade would be allowable, but not those unconnected with trade, or involving entertainment of a non-deductible nature. Where the payment is for the benefit or welfare of employees it will usually be allowed, e.g. a donation to a hospital or convalescent home which is used by employees of the firm. Gifts to registered charities are allowed if made for the purposes of trade.

Where a donation is the subject of a legal contract such as a covenant or gift aid payment then it is not a business expense but a charge on the taxpayer's total income.

Employees seconded to charities

When an employer seconds an employee temporarily to a charity, then any expenditure attributable to that employment by the employer is deductible as a business expense.

Costs of loan finance

Incidental costs of obtaining loan finance (including convertible loan stock) are allowed as a deduction in computing trading income, and this includes: fees, commissions, advertising, printing and stationery, but not stamp duty.

Pre-trading expenses

Expenses incurred within seven years prior to the actual commencement of trading is allowed if the expenditure would have been allowed as a trading expense had trading taken place during that period. See Chapter 14.

Gifts to educational establishments

Where a person carrying on a trade, profession or vocation makes a gift of plant and machinery to an educational establishment, then the proceeds of sale can be treated as zero.

Capital allowances

Capital allowances are deducted from the adjusted profits for the purposes of computing income taxed as trade profits. See Chapter 13.

Mileage rates – self-employed

Self-employed persons can use the authorised mileage rates applicable to employees instead of claiming actual motor expenses and capital allowances (see Chapter 7). To be eligible the taxpayer's turnover must not exceed the current VAT level.

Urban regeneration companies

Contribution to the running cost of an URC are deductible expenses in computing taxable profits.

Asset values for tax purposes

22. Tangible fixed assets

Fixed assets such as land and buildings or plant and machinery, fixtures and fittings etc., do not usually affect the determination of taxable trading income, except where the cost of an asset is charged against income, or in so far as there is a charge for depreciation. In the former case, the cost would be disallowed as capital, whether or not capital allowances are available. With regard to the charge for depreciation, then this is not allowed as a business expense, however computed. Where leasehold property is acquired then an allowance determined by reference to any premium paid is generally available. See Chapter 8.

Intangible fixed assets

Under this heading are included goodwill, patents and trade marks, copyrights and know how. There are no special problems of valuation, and most of them give rise to a claim for capital allowances, see Chapter 13.

The rules for the tax treatment of Intangible Fixed Assets contained in Chapter 19 only apply to companies.

Long-term investments

Long-term investments held as a fixed asset do not give rise to any particular problems as they are normally non-trading assets, and any surpluses or deficits arising from annual revaluations are not brought into the computation of taxable income. Realisations would require capital gains tax consideration, however.

Where the investments are trading assets then they will be valued on the same basis as other current assets.

Current assets

Current assets held by a business for the purposes of its trade would normally be valued for accounts purposes at the lower of cost or net realisable value. The same principles are applied for taxation purposes, but there are some special factors relating to stock and work in progress.

Stock and work in progress

The following is a summary of the position with regard to the valuation of stock and WIP.

1. In the absence of statutory authority stocks should be valued at the lower of cost or market value. Market value means selling price less selling expenses, and not replacement value. See CIR v Cock Russell & Co. Ltd 1949 29 TC 287: BSC Footwear Ltd v Ridgway 1971 47 TC 495.

    Under the International Accounting Standard 2 mandatory for listed companies from 1 January 2005, inventory value will need to be shown in accounts at the lower of cost and net realisable value (NRV).

2. Consistency of method of valuation does not of itself guarantee that a correct method of valuation has been used. See BSC Footwear v Ridgway case noted above.

3. Overhead expenditure does not have to be included in the valuation of work in progress or finished stocks, however desirable this may be for accounting purposes. See Duple Motor Bodies v Ostime 1961 39 TC 537.

4. Standard cost values may be used but due allowance for variances from standard must be made where they are material.

5. In general neither the base stock method nor the LIFO method of stock valuation is an acceptable method of valuation for taxation purposes. See Partrick v Broadstone Mills Ltd 1953 35 TC 44; Minister of National Revenue v Anaconda American Brass Ltd 1956 AC.

    From 1st January 2005 the LIFO method of valuation will not be permitted for accounts of listed companies under IAS 2.

6. Where there is a change in the method of valuation from one valid basis to another, then the opening and closing stocks in the current period must be valued on the same basis. A valid basis of valuation is one which does not violate the tax statutes as interpreted by the Courts, and which is recognised by the accounting profession.

    If the charge is from one valid basis to another then the opening stock of the current period must be equal to the closing stock of the previous period. Thus if the new valuation gives rise to a surplus in that period it will be taxable, and if a deficit, a repayment can be claimed.

7. Where a trade is discontinued, then, stock must be valued at an open market price, or if sold to another trader, at realised selling price.

Where the trade is discontinued the stock must be valued on an 'arms length basis' if the purchaser and the vendor are connected persons.

8. Professional work in progress must be valued at selling price unless the realisation is uncertain at the year end. This recognises profit in the year activity takes place, applying the accruals principle.

Trading stock appropriated by traders

Where a trader takes goods from the trading stock for personal consumption or consumption by his or her household, then it must be valued at its open market realistic value.

Tax and accounting principles

23. United Kingdom tax law requires that tax computations are prepared in accordance with generally accepted accounting practice subject to any adjustment required by law. Generally accepted accounting practice is defined as being the accounting practice that is used in preparing accounts which are intended to give a 'true and fair' view. The various financial reporting standards issued by the United Kingdom Accounting Standards Board generally require that the relevant Financial Reporting Standard needs to be applied to all transactions of a reporting entity whose financial statements are intended to give a true and fair view. Since 1 January 2005 listed companies apply International Financial Reporting Standards.

Student self-testing questions

1. Hilary has been in business many years as a tile maker. Her profit and loss account for the year ended 31 March was as follows:

	Notes	£	£
Sales			900,000
Cost of sales			(553,795)
Gross profit			346,205
Less: Expenses			
Salaries and wages	1	55,000	
Rent & rates		8,500	
Motor expenses	2	12,000	
Legal expenses	3	13,000	
Advertising		5,500	
Loss on sale of fixed asset		150	
Depreciation		9,095	
Donation to Oxfam made with Gift Aid declaration (net amount paid)		50	
Employees Christmas party		1,450	
			(104,745)
Net profit			241,460

1. Salaries and wages include Hilary's salary of £12,000.

2. Motor expenses include Hilary's private use of the car amounting to 25%.

3. Legal expenses comprise the following:

Costs associated with a tax appeal	3,000
Costs associated with the renewal of a short term lease	5,000
Defending a litigation case with a customer	5,000

Requirement: Calculate Hilary's income from trading for the year.

Solution: Adjusted trading profits calculation

	£	£
Profit per financial statements		241,460
Add: disallowable expenditure		
Hilary salary	12,000	
Hilary motor expenses	3,000	
Legal costs : tax appeal	3,000	
Loss on sale of fixed asset	150	
Depreciation	9,095	
Donation to Oxfam - Gift Aid scheme applies	50	
		27,295
Income from trading		268,755

2. Mr S Eason

£

Profit and Loss Account for the year to
31 December 2009

	£	
Gross operating profit		171,000
Taxed interest received		900
		171,900
Wages and salaries	48,000	
Rent & rates	2,500	
Depreciation	1800	
Bad debts written off	120	
Provision against fall in price of raw materials	5500	
Entertainment expenses	800	
Patent royalties	1250	
Bank interest	350	
Legal expenses on acquisition of factory	300	
		60,620
Net profit		£111,280

Salaries include £22,000 paid to Mrs R Eason who worked as an employee in the business

No staff were entertained

The provision is charged because of an anticipated trade recession

Interest and patents royalties were received and paid net but are shown gross

Requirement: Compute the taxable profit from trading for the year to 31 December 2009.

Solution

Profit per accounts		111,280
Add		
Depreciation	1,800	
Provision against fall in price of raw materials (not GAAP)	5,500	
Entertainment expenses	800	
Legal expenses	300	
		8,400
		119,680
less interest received (to tax as taxed income)		900
Adjusted trading profit		118,780

Note:

Patent royalties are allowable as an expense in calculating income from trading, if wholly and exclusively for business purposes; otherwise treat as an allowable payment deducted from total income in the main income tax computation.

11 Income taxed as trade profits II – basis periods

Introduction

1. This chapter deals with the basis of assessment of income arising from any trade, profession or vocation carried on by an individual. The special rules applicable to a partnership are discussed in Chapter 15.

Part I   Business assessments

Part II   Averaging of profits for farmers, market gardeners, authors and artists.

PART I – Business assessments

2. This topic is to be covered under the following headings:

General rule

Commencement provisions

Cessation provisions

General rule

3. The general rule is that the basis period for a tax year is the period of 12 months ending with the accounting date in that tax year.

Commencement provisions

4. Where an individual starts trading the following rules apply for determining the basis of assessment.

a)   Profits of the first year are the actual profits from the date of commencement to the 5th April.

b)   Profits of the second year are normally either:

i)   profits for the 12 months ending with the accounting date in that year or

ii)   profits of the 12 months from the date of commencement.

Where the first accounting period ends in the third year of assessment then the second year will be assessed on an actual tax year basis.

c)   For subsequent years the profits are for the 12 months ending with the accounting date.

Example

T commenced trading on the 1st June 2006 with the following taxable profits.

	£
1.6.2006 – 31.5.2007	6,000
1.6.2007 – 31.5.2008	10,000
1.6.2008 – 31.5.2009	12,000

Compute the taxable profits for all years of assessment.

Solution

Year of assessment	Basis period	Assessed amount
2006/07	1.6.06 – 5.4.07 ($\frac{309}{365}$ × 6,000)	5,079
2007/08	1.6.06 – 31.5.07 (12 months to 31.5.07)	6,000
2008/09	1.6.07 – 31.5.08 (12 months to 31.5.08)	10,000
2009/10	1.6.08 – 31.5.09 (12 months to 31.5.09)	12,000

Notes

i) The second year is assessed on the profit of the 12 month accounting period ending in the second year i.e. 12 months to 30th May 2007.

ii) The second year contains an 'overlap period' where profits are taxed twice. This is the period

1 June 2006 to 5 April 2007 with overlap profit of $\frac{309}{365}$ ⬜⬜6,000 = 5,079.

iii) The amount of overlap profits is recovered on the earlier of the following:

a) a change of accounting date that results in an assessment for a period of more than 12 months or

b) the cessation of trading.

iv) Calculation should strictly be made in days and not months and fractions, although it appears that the latter will now be accepted.

v) The assessed profits less the overlap profits to be recovered are therefore equal to the actual profits (33,079 – 5,079) = 28,000.

Example

A commenced trading on the 1st May 2006 and has the following results

		£
1.5.2006 – 31.12.2007		24,000
1.1.2008 – 31.12.2008		30,000
1.1.2009 – 31.12.2009		40,000

Compute the taxable profits for all years of assessment.

Solution

Year of assessment	Basis period	Assessed amount
2006/07	1.5.06 – 5.4.07 ($\frac{340}{610}$ × 24,000)	13,377
2007/08	1.1.07 – 31.12.07 ($\frac{365}{610}$ × 24,000)	14,360
2008/09	1.1.08 – 31.12.08 (12 months to 31.12.08)	30,000
2009/10	1.1.09 – 31.12.09 (12 months to 31.12.09)	40,000

Notes

i)   The second year is assessed on the profits of the 12 months ending 31st December 2007.

ii)   The overlap period is from 1 January 2007 to 5 April 2007, with profits of $\frac{95}{610} \times 24,000 =$ 3,737.

iii)   Assessed profits less the overlap profits to be recovered are thus equal to the actual profits.

   $(13,377 + 14,360 + 30,000 + 40,000) - 3,737 = 94,000$

Example

T started business on the 1st January 2007 with first accounts for the 16 months to 30th April 2008 and thereafter:

	£
1.1.2007 – 30.4.2008	32,000
1.5.2008 – 30.4.2009	28,000

Compute the taxable profits for all years of assessment.

Solution

Year of assessment	Basis period	Assessed amount
2006/07	1.1.07 – 5.4.07 ($\frac{95}{485} \times 32,000$)	6,269
2007/08	6.4.07 – 5.4.08 ($\frac{365}{485} \times 32,000$)	24,082
2008/09	1.5.07 – 30.4.08 ($\frac{365}{485} \times 32,000$)	24,082
2009/10	1.5.08 – 30.4.09 (12 months to 30.4.09)	28,000

Notes

i)   There is no period of account ending in the second year 2007/08 therefore the actual basis applies.

ii) The overlap period is 1 May 2007 – 5 April 08 i.e. 340 days

   $\frac{340}{485} \times 32,000 = 22,433$

iii) Assessed profits less the overlap profits are thus equal to the actual profits

   $(6,269 + 24,082 + 24,082 + 28,000) - 22,433 = 60,000$

Cessation provisions

5.   The main features are as follows.

i)   The final year of assessment has a basis period from the end of the previous accounting period to the date of cessation.

ii)   Any profits from the overlap period on commencement not recouped are adjusted in the final year of assessment.

iii)   The effect of the above is that over the life of a business only its actual taxable profits will be assessed.

Example

Q commenced trading on the 1st June 2004 and ceased on the 30th April 2009 with the following results.

	£
1.6.2004 – 31.5.2005	6,000
1.6.2005 – 31.5.2006	10,000
1.6.2006 – 31.5.2007	12,000
1.6.2007 – 31.5.2008	16,000
1.6.2008 – 30.4.2009	8,000

Compute the assessment for all years.

Solution

Year of assessment	Basis period	Assessed amount
2004/05	1.6.04 – 5.4.05 ($\frac{309}{365} \times 6,000$)	5,079
2005/06	1.6.04 – 31.5.05	6,000
2006/07	1.6.05 – 31.5.06	10,000
2007/08	1.6.06 – 31.5.07	12,000
2008/09	1.6.07 – 31.5.08	16,000
2009/10	1.6.08 – 30.4.09 (8,000 – 5,079)	2,921

Notes:

i)   The overlap period is 1 June 2004 – 5 April 2005 i.e. 309 days.

$$\text{Overlap profit} = \frac{309}{365} \times 6,000 = 5,079$$

ii)   The final period of profits is from 1 June 2008 to 30 April 2009 assessed in 2009/2010 i.e. £8,000. Overlap profits of £5,079 are deducted leaving a net assessment of £2,921.

iii)   Total profits over the life of the business are £52,000 which is equal to the taxable profits assessed.

PART II – Averaging of profits – farmers and creative artists

6. Farmers market gardeners and creative artists (not companies) can claim to have their adjusted profits averaged for any two years of assessment. The main provisions are:

a) Profits of the first or last year of trading cannot be included in any claim.

b) Profits are adjusted profits after capital allowances and before loss relief.

c) Once averaged the profits become fixed for all future averaging.

d) Averaging is only available where the difference between the assessable profits of two successive years is 30% or more of the higher of the two years' profits.

Example

T, who commenced farming on the 1st January 2005, has the following adjusted profits after capital allowances:

	£
Year ended 31st December 2007	56,000
Year ended 31st December 2008	35,000
Year ended 31st December 2009	10,000

Compute the average profits for 2008/09.

Solution: Computation of average profits

		£
2007/08	assessment 31.12.07	56,000
2008/09	assessment 31.12.08	35,000

As the difference $(56,000 - 35,000) = 21,000$ is more than 30% of the higher year $(30\% \times 56,000 = 16,800)$ full averaging for both years is possible.

2007/08	$\dfrac{91,000}{2} =$	45,500
2008/09	$\dfrac{91,000}{2} =$	45,500

e) Trading losses are to be taken as nil in making the average computation. Normal claims for loss relief are not affected by the averaging process, thus a claim under Section 64 could be made after the averaging computation.

Example

V who has been in business for many years has the following adjusted results:

		£	
12 months to 31st March	2005	25,000	
12 months to 31st March	2006	15,000	
12 months to 31st March	2007	(10,000)	loss
12 months to 31st March	2008	30,000	
12 months to 31st March	2009	50,000	

Compute the assessments with and without averaging.

Solution: Assessments without averaging

		£
2004/05	12 months to 31.3.05	25,000
2005/06	12 months to 31.3.06	15,000
2006/07	12 months to 31.3.07	–
2007/08	12 months to 31.3.08	30,000
2008/09	12 months to 31.3.09	50,000
		120,000

Calculation of average profits

	Adjusted profit	Increase (decrease)	Averaged profits
2004/05 Year to 31.3.2005	25,000	(5,000)	20,000
2005/06 Year to 31.3.2006	15,000	5,000	20,000
	20,000		
Averaged profits $\dfrac{40000}{2}$	20,000		
2005/06 As averaged	20,000	–	20,000
2006/07	–	–	–
	20,000		
Averaged profits $\dfrac{20000}{2}$	10,000		

	Adjusted profit	Increase (decrease)	Averaged profits
2006/07 As averaged	10,000	—	
2007/08 Year to 31.3.2008	30,000	(10,000)	20,000
	40,000		
Averaged profits $\dfrac{40000}{2}$	20,000		
2007/08 As averaged	20,000	15,000	35,000
2008/09 Year to 31.3.2008	50,000	(15,000)	35,000
	70,000		
Averaged profits $\dfrac{70000}{2}$	35,000		
2008/09 As averaged	35,000		

	Averaged assessments	Assessments without averaging
2004/05	20,000	25,000
2005/06	20,000	15,000
2006/07	10,000	–
2007/08	35,000	30,000
2008/09	35,000	50,000
	120,000	120,000

Note

The total amount of profits is the same under both methods but the averaging has smoothed out the annual figures.

7.   A form of marginal averaging can be claimed where the difference between the two years' profits is between 25% and 30% of the highest year. This is effected by increasing the lower profit and reducing the higher profit by an amount equal to: 3 (higher profit – lower profit) – (75% × higher profit)

Student self-testing questions

1.

(i)   Hilary commenced business on 1 August 2005 and made up her first accounts for the twelve months to 31 July. Her profits adjusted for tax purposes were:

12 months ended 31 July	Adjusted profit
	£
2006	24,000
2007	40,000
2008	32,000
2009	36,000

(ii) Julia commenced business on 1 January 2007, making up her first accounts to 31 October 2007, then annually to that date. Her profits as adjusted for tax purposes were:

	£
10 months ended 31 October 2007	42,000
Year ended 31 October 2008	52,000
Year ended 31 October 2009	65,000

(iii) James began business on 1 September 2006 and made up his first accounts to 31 January 2007. His profits adjusted for tax purposes were:

	£
5 months ended 31 January 2007	24,000
Year ended 31 January 2008	60,000
Year ended 31 January 2009	72,000

(iv) Jeremy began business on the 1 February 2006 and made up his first accounts to 31 July 2007, eighteen months later. His profits adjusted for tax purposes were:

	£
Eighteen months ended 31 July 2007	56,000
Year ended 31 July 2008	40,000
Year ended 31 July 2009	45,000

Requirement: In each case calculate the assessment in the first, second and third years and any overlap profits arising.

Solution

1) Hilary

1st year	05/06	1 August '05 - 5 April '06 = 8 months	
		8/12 x 24,000	16,000
2nd year	06/07	Is there an accounting date ending in 06/07 ?	
		Yes 31/7/06	
		The accounting period is greater than or equal to 1 year and therefore the basis of assessment is 12 months to the accounting date in the 2nd tax year.	
		Year ended 31/7/06	24,000
3rd year	07/08	As there was an accounting date ending in the 2nd tax year the basis of assessment is the year ended 31/7/07	40,000
Overlap profit		1/8/05 - 5/4/06 = 8 months	16,000

2) Julia

1st year	06/07	1 Jan '07 - 5 April '07 = 3 months 3/10 x 42,000	12,600
2nd year	07/08	Is there an accounting date ending in 07/08?	42,000
		Yes 31/10/07	8,667
		The accounting date is less than 1 year therefore the basis of assessment is the first 12 months of trading	50,667
		10 months ended 31/10/07 plus Nov '07 & Dec '07	
		Assessment is therefore:	
		10 months ended 31/10/07 + 2/12 x 52,000	
3rd year	08/09	As there was an accounting date ending in the 2nd tax year the basis of assessment is the year ended 31/10/08	52,000
Overlap profits		1/1/07 - 5/4/07 :	12,600
		1/11/07 - 31/12/07 (2/12 x £52,000)	8,667
			21,267

3) James

1st year	06/07	1 September 2006 - 5 April 2007	
		= 7 months (£24,000 + (2/12 x £60,000)	34,000
2nd year	07/08	Is there an accounting date ending in 07/08?	
		Yes year ended 31/1/08	
		The accounting date is greater than or equal to 1 year after commencement therefore the basis of assessment is the year to the new accounting date	60,000
		Year ended 31/1/08	
3rd year	08/09	As there was an accounting date ending in the 2nd tax year the basis of assessment is the year ended 31/1/09	72,000
Overlap		1/2/07 - 5/4/07	10,000

4) Jeremy

1st year	05/06	1 February 2006 - 5 April 2006 2/18 x 56,000		6,222
2nd year	06/07	Is there an accounting date ending in 06/07? No		37,333
		Therefore the basis of assessment is profits from 6/4/06 - 5/4/07		
		12/18 x £56,000		
3rd year	07/08	Basis of assessment for the 3rd tax year is 12 months to the accounting date in the 3rd tax year i.e. 31 July 2007 12/18 x £56,000		37,333
	Overlap	The profits from 1 August 2006 to 5 April 2007 have been taxed in 06/07 and 07/08.		24,889
		Overlap profits are therefore £24,889 (8/18 x 56,000).		

2.   Mr E

In the spring of 2010, Mr E was considering starting a new business and had prepared a business plan. This showed that the business would commence trading on 1 July 2010, and that the pattern of profits would be:

Period to 31 December 2010	£600 per month
Twelve months to 31 December 2011	£1,200 per month
Thereafter	£2,400 per month

Mr E is considering two alternative dates on which to make up accounts each year, 31 March or 30 April.

(Note that he is not considering any other date and will not be making up accounts to 31 December.)

Required:

a)   Compute the amounts which will be assessable as income from trading for each of the first three years of assessment under each of the two above alternative accounting dates.

b)   Indicate the main advantages and disadvantages of each alternative.

5 marks

CIMA May 1998 (updated)

Solution

Accounting profits arising under the 2 proposed dates

£

31 March reference date		
1 July 2010 - 31 March 2011	(6 x £600) + (3 x £1,200)	7,200
Year ended 31 March 2012	(9 x £1,200) + (3 x £2,400)	18,000
Year ended 31 March 2013	(12 x £2,400)	28,800
30 April reference date		
10 months to 30 April 2011	(6 x £600) + (4 x £1,200)	8,400
Year ended 30 April 2012	(8 x £1,200) + (4 x £2,400)	19,200
Year ended 30 April 2013	(12 x £2,400)	28,800

Therefore based on these accounting profits the assessments of income from trading will be as follows:

31 March reference date

	Basis period	Assessable profits
		£
2010/2011	1 July 2010 - 5 April 2011	7,200
2011/2012	12 months to 31 March 2012	18,000
2012/2013	12 months to 31 March 2013	28,800
		54,000

30 April reference date

	Basis period	Calculation	Assessable profit
			£
2010/2011	1 July 2010 - 5 April 2011	9/10 x 8,400	7,560
2011/2012	1 July 2010 - 30 June 2011	8,400+(2/12 x 19,200)	11,600
2012/2013	Year ended 30 April 2012		19,200
			38,360

(b)

30 April

30 April reference date gives a lower amount of total assessable profits for the first three years of assessment. There is a greater interval between earning profits and paying taxes.

Profits in the periods 1 July 2010 to 5 April 2011 (£7,560) and 1 May 2011 to 30 June 2011 (£3,200) are being taxed twice - as 'overlap profits'

relief for overlap profits is either on cessation or a change of accounting date.

31 March

The 31 March reference date, has no 'overlap' profits

It has higher total assessable profits in early years giving rise to earlier tax liabilities on profits earned.

Hence there is a cash flow disadvantage compared to a 30 April reference date.

Questions without answers

1. Chatru commenced trading on 1 November 2005. His first accounts were made up to 30 April 2007 and thereafter to 30 April annually. He ceased trading on 31 March 2010.

    His trading results, adjusted for income tax purposes were:

	£
1.11.05-30.4.07	40,500
Year ended 30.4.08	12,000
Year ended 30.4.09	24,000
Period to 31.3.10	36,000

    Requirements:

    Calculate the assessable income for all years in question

    Calculate whether there would have been any income tax benefit in Chatru continuing to trade one extra month and making up final accounts to his normal accounting date, on the assumption that his tax-adjusted profit for April 2010 was £4,200.   **3 marks**

    Total: 11 marks

    ACCA June 1995 (updated)

2. Nan Pearson died on 30 June 2009 aged 58. She had been employed as a design engineer by Map plc, a company which specialises in the construction of motor bikes.

    The following is supplied:

(1) Nan's salary, paid on the last day of each month, was £35,000 pa from which 5% was paid to an approved staff pension fund. The company's contribution was 8%.

(2) Her other income comprised the following.

	Year ended 5 April 2009	6 April 2009 to 30 June 2009
	£	£
Interest received from a building society on a deposit account	1,264	1,280
Dividends received from UK companies including the tax credit	4,320	4,720

Arthur Pearson, Nan's husband, had been employed until his retirement in March 2005 at age 55. Since that date he undertook some self-employed bookkeeping activities and recent profits are as follows:

	£
Year to 30 April 2006	5,000
Year to 30 April 2007	4,100
Year to 30 April 2008	5,900
Year to 30 April 2009	6,700

No tax has been paid on income from trading for 2009/10

(3)   Arthur received gross interest from an NSB Investment Account (opened 1988) of £154 in 2008/09 and £130 in 2009/10. Interest was credited annually on 30 June.

The following events took place after Nan's death.

(1)   A payment of £240,000, being the sum assured on Nan's life under the Map plc's pension scheme, was paid to Arthur.

(2)   A pension of £22,980 (gross) per annum, payable on the first day of each month, was to be paid to Arthur by Map plc. The first payment was made on 1 July 2009 and a BR code was used by the company for PAYE purposes; (i.e. basic rate tax was deducted from the pension by Map plc)

Arthur used the £240,000 assurance policy receipt to acquire and furnish a small marina penthouse on 1 February 2010. He let this penthouse under a ten year lease from 1 March 2010, the incoming tenant paying a premium of £4,000. The rent of £5,500 a year is payable quarterly in advance and was received when due. Arthur incurred the following expenses in connection with the letting.

	£
Interior decorating prior to letting	790
Year's insurance of premises and contents - 1 March 2010	384
Managing agent's fee (for tenancy agreement and March 2010 management)	250

Requirement:

Prepare income tax computations for 2009/10 for

(a) Nan Pearson, showing income tax payable   **(10 marks)**

(b) Arthur Pearson, showing the final income tax position and indicating any final amounts of tax to be paid or repaid.   **(6 marks)**

(Total: 16 marks)

12 Income taxed as trade profits III – change of accounting date

Introduction

1. This chapter is concerned with the effects of a change of accounting date on the assessed income taxed as trade profits.

Main rules

2. An outline of the rules in respect of a charge of accounting date are as follows:

  a) Any change of accounting date will be ignored and assessments will be issued as if there was no change unless all of the three undermentioned circumstances apply.

    i) The first accounting period (i.e. period for which accounts are made up) ending with the new date does not exceed 18 months.

    ii) Notice of the change is given to an officer of the Board in a personal tax return on or before the day on which that return is required to be delivered.

    Either

    iii) no accounting change resulting in a change of basis period has been made in any of the previous five years of assessment;

    or

    iv) the notice in (ii) above sets out the reasons for the change and the Revenue do not, within 60 days of receiving the notice, give notice to the trader that they are not satisfied that the change is made for bona fide commercial reasons.

  b) There is a right of appeal against the Inspector's decision not to accept the change as being for commercial reasons.

  c) Obtaining a tax advantage by such a change does not appear to be a valid commercial reason for a change.

  d) Where all the conditions are satisfied, or the accounting change is made in the second or third tax year of the business, the basis period for the year of assessment is as follows.

    i) If the year is the second year of assessment of the business, the basis period is the twelve months ending with the new date in the year (unless the period from commencement of the business to the new date in the second year is less than twelve months, in which case the basis is the first twelve months of the business).

    ii) If the 'relevant period' is a period of less than twelve months, the basis period is the twelve months ending with the new date in the year.

    iii) If the 'relevant period' is a period of more than twelve months, the basis period consists of the relevant period.

  The 'relevant period' is the period beginning immediately after the end of the basis period for the preceding year and ending with the new date in the year.

	Difference between end of preceding basis period and new accounting date	Basis period
1st year	< 12 months	12 months to new A/C date
1st year	> 12 months	Period to new A/C date
2nd year	—	12 months to new A/C date

Profits for the period of overlap will need to be computed when a change of accounting date takes place.

Example

A starts in business on 1st July 2005 and produces accounts to 5th April until 2008 when a new date of 30th June 2008 is the accounting date.

		£
Accounts	1.7.05 – 5.4.06	10,000
	6.4.06 – 5.4.07	12,000
	6.4.07 – 5.4.08	15,000
	6.4.08 – 30.6.08	2,000
	1.7.08 – 30.6.09	6,000

Compute the assessments.

Solution

			£	
2005/06	1.7.05 – 5.4.06		10,000	
2006/07	12 months to 5.4.07		12,000	
2007/08	12 months to 5.4.08		15,000	
2008/09	12 months to 30.6.08			
	1.7.07 – 5.4.08 = 279 days			
	$\dfrac{279}{365} \times 15,000 =$		11,466	
	6.4.08 – 30.6.08 =		2,000	13,466
2009/10	1.7.08 – 30.6.09 =		6,000	

Notes

i) Overlap Memo

There was no overlap profit arising on the commencement of the business as a fiscal year accounting date was adopted.

Overlap relief on change of accounting date:

Overlap period 1.7.2007 – 5.4.2008

$$= \frac{279}{365} \times 15,000 = \underline{11,466}$$

Amount carried forward $\qquad \underline{11,466}$

ii) Total profit assessed less overlap relief

= £45,000 : (10,000 + 12,000 + 15,000 + 13,466 + 6,000) – 11,466.

Example

V started business on the 1st January 2005 with the following results.

6 months to 30.6.2005	20,000
12 months to 30.6.2006	40,000
12 months to 30.6.2007	50,000
18 months to 31.12.2008	75,000
12 months to 31.12.2009	60,000

Compute the assessments for all years and the overlap relief.

Solution

Years	Period		£
2004/2005	1.1.05 – 5.4.05		
	$\frac{96}{182} \times 20,000 =$		10,549
2005/2006	First 12 months trading		
	$20,000 + \frac{184}{365} \times 40,000$		
	$20,000 + 20,164$		40,164
2006/07	CY 30.6.2006		40,000
2007/08	CY 30.6.2007		50,000
2008/09	1.7.2007 – 31.12.2008		
	total for period	75,000	
	less overlap released	20,183	54,817
2009/10	CY 31.12.2009		60,000

Notes

i)   Overlap Memo

Overlap profits (1.1.05–5.4.05)+(1.7.05–31.12.05) = 280 days

$$= 10,549 + 20,164 = \qquad 30,713$$

Overlap released 1.7.07 – 31.12.08 = 549 days

$$549 - 365 = 184$$

$$\frac{184}{280} \times 30,713 = \qquad \underline{20,183}$$

Carried forward $\underline{10,530}$

ii)   Total profit assessed less overlap relief

$= £245,000 : (10,549 + 40,164 + 40,000 + 50,000 + 54,817 + 60,000) - 10,530$

Example

B has been in business for many years with the following results.

12 months to 31.12.2005	10,000
12 months to 31.12.2006	30,000
12 months to 31.12.2007	20,000
6 months to 30.6.2008	12,000
12 months to 30.6.2009	36,000

Compute the assessments for all years and the overlap relief.

Solution

Years	Period	£
2005/06	12 months to 31.12.2005	10,000
2006/07	12 months to 31.12.2006	30,000
2007/08	12 months to 31.12.2007	20,000
2008/09	12 months to 30.6.2008	
	$12,000 + \dfrac{184}{365} \times 20,000$	
	$12,000 + 10,082$	22,082
2009/10	30.6.2009	36,000

Overlap relief 1.7.07 – 31.12.07

$$\dfrac{184}{365} \times 20,000 \quad = \quad \underline{10,082}$$

Total assessed profits less overlap relief = (10,000 + 30,000 + 20,000 + 22,082 + 36,000) – 10,082 = £108,000.

Student self-testing question

A starts in business on 1st May 2004 making accounts up to 5th April each year until 2008 when a new date of 30th November 2008 is chosen as the accounting date.

Relevant accounting periods	Profits (£)
1.5.04 – 5.4.05	10,000
6.4.05 – 5.4.06	12,000
6.4.06 – 5.4.07	14,000
6.4.07 – 5.4.08	16,000
6.4.08 – 30.11.08	8,000
1.12.08 – 30.11.09	20,000

Compute the assessments for all years.

Solution

			£
2004/05	1.5.04 – 5.4.05		10,000
2005/06	12 months to 5.4.06		12,000
2006/07	12 months to 5.4.07		14,000
2007/08	12 months to 5.4.08		16,000
2008/09	12 months to 30.11.08		
	6.4.08– 30.11.08	8,000	
	1.12.07 – 5.4.08 = 126 days		
	$\dfrac{126}{365} \square\ 16,000 =$	5,523	13,523
2009/10	1.12.08 – 30.11.09 =		20,000
Overlap relief 1.12.08 – 30.11.09			5,523
Carried forward			5,523

Total profits = 85,523 – 5,523 = £80,000

Question without answer

1. X starts trading on 1st December 2005 with the following results:

	£
Period to 5th April 2006	7,000
Year to 5th April 2007	10,000
Year to 5th April 2008	15,000
6 months to 30th September 2008	8,000
Year to 30th September 2009	20,000

Compute the assessments for all years.

13 Capital allowances

Introduction

1.   The chapter is concerned with allowances available to a taxpayer in respect of capital expenditure on fixed assets. These allowances, which are called capital allowances, consist of a mixture of annual and other allowances which are available in respect of qualifying expenditure incurred under the following headings.

Plant and machinery	Industrial and commercial buildings
Conversion of premises into flats	Hotels
Agricultural buildings and works	Patent rights
Research and Development	Know how

The chapter is divided into the following main sections:

Part I	–	Plant and machinery
Part II	–	Industrial buildings and structures
Part III	–	Other assets

Examples in this chapter which cover a number of periods of account may be projected into the future. This is to avoid confusion which could result from including obsolete allowances in the workings for earlier tax years and transitional rules.

PART I – Plant and machinery – general conditions

2.   a)   Allowances are available under this heading if a person carries on a qualifying activity and incurs qualifying expenditure.

b)   Qualifying activity has the following meaning

i)   a trade, profession or vocation,

ii)   an ordinary property business,

iii)   a furnished holiday lettings business,

iv)   an overseas property business,

v)   the management of an investment company,

vi)   special leasing of plant or machinery,

vii)   an employment or office.

c)   The general rule is that expenditure is qualifying expenditure if –

i)   it is capital expenditure on the provision of plant or machinery wholly or partly for the purposes of the qualifying activity carried on by the person incurring the expenditure, and

ii)   the person incurring the expenditure owns the plant or machinery as a result of incurring it.

Qualifying expenditure

3.   a)   Plant and machinery is not defined in any tax statute and the definition most frequently referred to is perhaps that contained in a non revenue case, Yarmouth v France 1887 QBD. The case was brought under the Employers Liability Act 1880,

and consideration given as to whether or not a horse was plant and machinery. In the course of his judgement, Lindley LJ made the following statement:

'... in its ordinary sense it includes whatever apparatus is used by a business man for carrying on his business, not his stock in trade which he buys or makes for sale, but all goods and chattels, fixed or moveable, live or dead, which he keeps for permanent employment in his business.'

b) Capital expenditure on alterations to an existing building, incidental to the installation of plant, may be treated as plant and machinery, where a qualifying activity is carried on.

c) Expenditure on the thermal insulation of an industrial building.

d) Fire safety expenditure.

e) Personal security expenditure.

f) Buildings and structures – see below.

Features integral to a building

4. Features integral to a building, thermal insulation and long life assets (see section 14) comprise a 'special rate pool'. The writing down allowance is at a reduced rate compared to other items of plant and machinery. Features integral to a building are defined as: electrical systems; cold water systems; heating, ventilation, air cooling or purification systems including related floors and ceilings; lifts, escalators and moving walkways; external solar shading; active facades.

   Allowances are available both for initial expenditure and replacement. Replacement is expenditure on over 50% of the asset within a 12 month period.

Plant and machinery – buildings (to 5 April 2008 Income Tax and 31 March 2008 Corporation Tax)

5. Prior to the rules on 'features integral to a building' the following rules applied:

Plant and machinery did not include:

   a) buildings – List A

   b) fixed structures – List B

   c) interests in land.

Note The items included in list C of each table could be claimed as plant and machinery subject to the case law criteria.

List A: Buildings

1. Walls, floors, ceilings, doors, gates, shutters, windows and stairs

2. Main services, and systems, of water, electricity and gas

3. Waste disposal systems

4. Sewerage and drainage systems

5. Shafts or other structures in which lifts, hoists, escalators and moving walkways are installed

6. Fire safety systems

List B: Structures

1. Any tunnel, bridge, viaduct, aqueduct, embankment or cutting

2. Any way or hard standing, such as a pavement, road, railway or tramway, a park for vehicles or containers, or an airstrip or runway

3. Any inland navigation, including a canal or basin or a navigable river

4. Any dam, reservoir or barrage (including any sluices, gates, generators and other equipment associated with it)

5. Any dock

6. Any dike, sea wall, weir or drainage ditch

7. Any structure not within any other item in this column

List C: Assets so included, but expenditure on which is unaffected by the buildings rules

1. Electrical, cold water, gas and sewerage systems –

    a) provided mainly to meet the particular requirements of the trade, or

    b) provided mainly to serve particular machinery or plant used of the purposes of the trade

2. Space or water heating systems; powered systems of ventilation; air cooling or air purification; and any ceiling or floor comprised in such systems

3. Manufacturing or processing equipment; storage equipment, including cold rooms; display equipment; and counters, checkouts and similar equipment

4. Cookers, washing machines, dishwashers, refrigerators and similar; washbasins, sinks, baths, showers, sanitary ware and similar equipment; furniture and furnishings

5. Lifts, hoists, escalators and moving stairways

6. Sound insulation provided mainly to meet the particular requirements of the trade

7. Computer, telecommunications and surveillance systems (including their wiring or other links)

8. Refrigeration or cooling equipment

9. Sprinkler equipment and other equipment for extinguishing or containing fire; fire alarm systems

10. Burglar alarm systems

11. Any machinery (including devices for providing motive power) not within any other item in this column

12. Strong rooms in bank or building society premises; safes

13. Partition walls, where moveable and intended to be moved in the course of the trade

14. Decorative assets provided for the enjoyment of the public in the hotel, restaurant or similar trades

15. Advertising hoardings; signs, displays and similar assets

16. Alteration of land for the purpose only of installing machinery or plant

17. Provision of dry docks

18. Provision of any jetty or similar structure provided mainly to carry machinery or plant

19. Provision of pipelines

20. Provision of towers used to support floodlights

21. Provision of any reservoir incorporated into a water treatment works

22. Provision of silos used for temporary storage or on the provision of storage tanks

23. Provision of slurry pits or silage clamps

24. Provision of swimming pools, including diving boards, slides and any structure supporting them

25. Provision of fish tanks or fish ponds

26. Provision of rails, sleepers and ballast for a railway or tramway

27. Swimming pools

28. Cold stores

29. Any glass house with integral environment controls

30. Movable buildings intended to be moved in the course of the qualifying activity

Cases on plant and machinery

6. The following is a summary of some of the cases which have been concerned with the definition of plant and machinery:

1. Jarrold v Johngood & Sons Ltd 1962 CA 40 TC 681. In this case movable metal partitioning used to divide office accommodation was held to be plant.

2. Hinton v Maden & Ireland Ltd 1959 H.L. 38 TC 391. Knives and lasts which had an average life of three years, and which were used on shoe machinery, were held to be plant.

3. CIR v Barclay Curle & Co. Ltd 1969 H.L. 45 TC 221. The company constructed a dry dock, the whole cost of which, including excavation, was held to be plant.

4. Cooke v Beach Station Caravans Ltd 1974 CD 49 TC 524. The company constructed a swimming pool with an elaborate system of filtration, as one of the amenities at a caravan park. The cost, which included excavation, was held to be plant.

5. St Johns School v Ward 1974 CA 49 TC 524. A special purpose prefabricated structure, for use as a laboratory and gymnasium in a school, was held not to be plant.

6. Schofield v R & H Hall Ltd 1974 NI 49 TC 538. A grain importer built a concrete silo with gantries, conveyors and shutes, which was held to be plant.

7. Ben Odeco Ltd v Powlson 1978 CD STC 111. Interest payments made to finance expenditure on an oil rig were held not to be plant.

8. Benson v The Yard Arm Club Ltd 1978 CD STC 408. The purchase and conversion of an old ferry boat into a floating restaurant was held not to be plant.

9. Dixon v Fitchs Garage Ltd 1975 CD STC 480. A metal canopy covering the service area of a petrol filling station was held to be a shelter, and not plant.

10. Munby v Furlong 1977 CA STC 232. Books purchased by a barrister to create a library in his practice were held to be plant.

11. Hampton v Fortes Autogrill Ltd 1980 CD STC 80. A false ceiling constructed to provide cladding for electrical conduit and ventilation trunking was held not to be plant.

12. Leeds Permanent Building Society 1982 CD Decorative screens incorporating the society's name were held to be plant.

13. Van Arkadie v Sterling Coated Materials Ltd 1983. CD STC 95. Additional costs in pounds sterling, required to meet instalment payments on the purchase of plant and machinery, were held to be part of the cost.

14. Thomas v Reynolds and another 1987 CD STC 50. An inflatable dome which covered a tennis court was held to be the setting in which the tennis coaching business was carried on, and not plant or machinery.

15. Wimpey International Ltd v Warland 1988 CA Expenditure on items of decoration installed in the company's restaurants was held not to be plant or machinery.

16. Hunt v Henry Quick Ltd: King v Bridisco Ltd CHD. 1992 STC 633. The construction of mezzanine platforms in a warehouse was held to be plant and machinery.

17. Gray v Seymours Garden Centre C.H.D. 1993. The construction of a special horticultural greenhouse was held not to be plant and machinery.

18. Attwood v Anduff C.A. 1997. The expenditure on a purpose built car wash site was held not to be plant and machinery.

19. Shove v Lingfield Park C.D. 2003. Artificial all weather track was held to be part of the premises and not plant.

When capital expenditure is incurred

7. The expenditure is taken to be incurred on the date on which the obligation to pay becomes unconditional. However, if payment in whole or in part is not required until more than four months after the date on which the obligation to pay becomes unconditional, then so much of the amount as can be deferred is taken to be incurred on that date.

Example

K orders an item of plant from X plc on the following terms:

31.12.2009   plant delivered and invoiced on same date to K.

21.1.2010   due date for payment by K, being the end of the month following date of delivery.

3.2.2010   K makes payment.

The expenditure is deemed to have been incurred on 31.12.2009.

Example

L orders an item of plant from T plc costing £50,000 as follows:

31.12.2009   plant delivered and invoiced on same date.

31.1.2010   90% of invoice amount due for payment.

30.6.2010   balance of 10% due for payment.

L is deemed to have incurred the expenditure as follows:

31.12.2009   90% × £50,000 i.e. £45,000

30.6.2010   10% × £50,000 i.e. £5,000

Allowances available

8. The types of allowances which can be claimed in respect of expenditure on plant or machinery are:

annual investment allowance (AIA)

first year allowance (FYA)

enhanced capital allowances (ECA)

writing down allowance (WDA)

balancing allowance and related balancing charge (BA/BC).

Annual investment allowance (£50,000)

9. Annual investment allowance of 100% of expenditure up to £50,000 a year will be available on any category of plant and machinery other than cars, for all categories of business.

First year allowance

10. Businesses incurring expenditure in excess of the £50,000 annual investment allowance cap, which would normally be allocated to the general pool and qualify for a 20% writing down allowance in the 12 month period beginning 1 April 2009 for companies, and 6 April 2009 for unincorporated taxpayers, may instead claim a temporary 40% first year allowance.

There are exceptions where the expenditure incurred will not qualify for the temporary first year allowance: expenditure allocated to the 'special rate' pool; cars; and assets for leasing.

Enhanced capital allowances – 100% FYA Energy/water saving plant

11. Enhanced capital allowances (ECAs) are designed to encourage the use of energy efficient equipment by giving a 100% allowance on purchase. Only products included on the UK Energy Technology List approved by the Department of Environment Transport and the Regions (DETR) will qualify. These fall into thirteen categories:

combined heat and power systems;

boilers;

motors;

variable speed drives for liquid and gas movements;

lighting;

pipe insulation;

refrigeration;

thermal screens;

heat pumps

radiant and warm air heaters;

solar heaters;

energy efficient refrigeration equipment, and

compressor equipment.

The allowance which is available to all businesses is extended to assets for leasing, letting or hire purchase.

Enhanced capital allowances – 100% FYA Low emission cars

12. a)   A 100% FYA is available on the purchase of a new car if:

  i)   it is a low emission car i.e. emits not more than 110g/km of carbon dioxide, or

  ii)   it is electrically propelled.

  b)   The 100% FYA is also available for plant and machinery to refuel vehicles with natural gas or hydrogen fuel such as storage tanks, pumps, etc.

  c)   The allowance is extended to assets acquired to be leased, let or hired.

Writing down allowance – rate 20%

13. Summary of main features

  a)   A writing down allowance is available in respect of expenditure incurred in the accounting period which is the basis period.

  b)   The allowance is available whether or not the plant or machinery is in use in the basis period.

  c)   The allowance is calculated by reference to the pool of expenditure, as shown in the specimen computation below (paragraph 17).

  d)   The pool is reduced by reference to the Total Disposal Receipts (TDR) (limited to the original cost) where one of the following events occur.

  i)   The plant or machinery ceases to belong to the taxpayer.

  ii)   The taxpayer looses possession of the plant or machinery in circumstances where it is reasonable to assume that the loss is permanent.

  iii)   The plant or machinery ceases to exist as such as a result of destruction, dismantling etc.

  iv)   The plant or machinery begins to be used wholly or partly for purposes which are other than those of the trade.

  v)   The trade is permanently discontinued.

  e)   The balance remaining after deducting any proceeds of sale is written down in future years.

  f)   The taxpayer can claim any proportion of the allowance available.

  g)   If the asset has any private use then the 20% allowance is calculated in the normal way and then reduced accordingly. A separate pool is required for each asset with a private use element.

  h)   A writing down allowance is not available in the year of cessation of trading.

  i)   A writing down allowance is not available in addition to the first year allowance.

  j) Cars with CO_2 emissions of 160 g/km or less qualify for the 20% writing down allowance.

Special rate pool 10%

Assets in the special rate pool attract a writing down allowance of 10%. They are:

14.   Features integral to a building;

15.   Thermal insulation in a building;

16.   Cars with CO_2 emissions of more than 160 g/km;

17. Machinery and plant which has an expected working life when new of 25 years or more at 10% a year on the reducing balance basis.

    a)   Expenditure on long life assets which does not exceed a 'de minimis' limit is excluded from the rules.

        For companies, the de minimis limit is £100,000 a year divided by one plus the number of associated companies.

        The de minimis limit of £100,000 a year also applies to individuals and to partnerships made up of individuals provided the individual, or in the case of a partnership at least half the members, devotes substantially the whole of their time to carrying on the business.

    b)   The exclusion for expenditure below the de minimis limit does not apply to contributions to expenditure on machinery or plant, nor to expenditure on a share in machinery or plant, on machinery or plant for leasing or on machinery and plant on which allowances have been given to a previous owner at the reduced rate.

    c)   If a long life asset is sold for less than its tax written down value in order to accelerate allowances, it is treated as sold for its tax written down value.

Separate pools

18. A separate pool must be kept for the following assets:

    i)   general pool of plant and machinery;

    ii)   special rate pool;

    iii)   assets with any private use;

    iv)   short life assets where a de-pooling election is made.

Specimen computations

19. Specimen computation with FYA

		General pool	Special rate pool
Unrelieved qualifying expenditure b/fwd		-	-
Qualifying expenditure incurred		-	-
Qualifying expenditure	-		
Less: Annual Investment Allowance	(-)		
Excess of expenditure over £50,000	-		
Transfer part relating to special rate pool	(-)		-
Part eligible for temporary 40% FYA	-		
Less: Temporary First Year Allowance 40%	(-)		
Available qualifying expenditure		-	-
Less: Total disposal receipts (limited to cost)		(-)	(-)
		-	-
Less: Writing down allowances 20% or 10%		(-)	(-)

Transfer balance of expenditure after 40% FYA	(-)	-
Qualifying expenditure for 100% FYA	-	
Less: First year allowance 100%	(-)	0
Unrelieved qualifying expenditure c/fwd	-	-

Capital allowances and accounts

20. For all businesses the following provisions apply.

1) Capital allowances are available in a 'chargeable period' based on the period of accounts.

2) Capital allowances are treated as a trading expense of the businesses in the chargeable period and any balancing charge is treated as a trading receipt. This means that the trade profit for tax purposes is after the deduction of capital allowances.

3) Where the period of account is not a 12 month period the writing down allowance is contracted or expanded on a pro-rata basis. E.g.

Period of account 8 months – writing down allowance	$8/12 \times 20\%$
Period of account 15 months – writing down allowance	$15/12 \times 20\%$

4) If a company has a period of account of 18 months then this is split into one corporation tax accounting period of 12 months and one of 6 months.

5) Any FYAs, balancing allowances or charges will normally be given in the period of account in which they fall.

6) On the commencement of a new unincorporated business, in order to deal with the taxable profits of the first and second years of assessment it will be necessary first to compute the capital allowances.

Example

P started trading on the 1st May 2008 with the following results:

Adjusted profits 1.5.08 – 30.4.2009	58,000
Adjusted profits 1.5.09 – 30.4.2010	56,000
General plant and machinery purchased 1.5.2008	60,000

Compute the capital allowances available assuming 2008/09 rules continue to apply in future years, and show the taxable assessments for the years 2008/09 to 2010/11.

Solution

Capital allowances			General plant and machinery pool
1.5.2008 additions		60,000	
Annual investment allowance		(50,000)	10,000
			10,000
30.4.09 writing down allowance 20%			(2,000)
WDV 30.04.2009			8,000
30.4.2010 writing down allowance 20%			1,600
WDV 30.04.2010			6,400

Period of Account	Adjusted Profits	Capital Allowances	Taxable Profit
1.5.08 – 30.4.09	58,000	52,000	4,000
1.5.09 – 30.4.10	56,000	1,600	54,400

Assessments

2008/09 (1.5.08 – 5.4.09)	11/12 × 4,000	3,667
2009/10 (1.5.08 – 30.4.09)		4,000
2010/11 (1.5.09 – 30.4.10)		54,400

Notes

i) The overlap period is from 1.5.08 – 5.4.09, i.e. 11 months, or profits of £3,667. When the business ceases trading an adjustment in respect of this amount will be made in the final assessment.

i) Annual investment allowance is given on the first £50,000 of eligible expenditure in a year.

ii) Temporary FYA of 40% was not available for expenditure incurred on 1 May 2008.

Example

Q started trading on 1 October 2009 with first accounts for the 15 months to 31 December 2010. Capital expenditure of £100,000 on general plant and machinery was incurred on 1 October 2009. Capital expenditure of £64,000 was incurred on features integral to a building on 1 November 2009. Adjusted profits, before capital allowances, for the 15 months amounted to £90,000.

		General pool	Special rate pool
Period of account			
Capital expenditure 1.10.2009		100,000	
Annual investment allowance	50,000 x 15/12	62,500	
		37,500	
Temporary first year allowance 40%		15,000	
Capital expenditure 1.11.2009			64,000
Writing down allowance	10% x 15/12		8,000
		22,500	
Written down value carried forward		22,500	24,000

Assessments

Adjusted profits 1.10.09 – 31.12.10		90,000
Capital allowances		
(62,500 + 15,000 + 8,000)		85,500
		4,500

2009/10	1.10.09 – 5.4.10		
	4,500 x 6/15		1,800
2010/11	1.1.10 – 31.12.10		
	4,500 x 12/15		3,600

Notes

i) The capital allowances are computed for the period of account of 15 months.

ii) Capital allowances are deducted from the profits of the period of account before computing the assessments.

iii) Overlap profits are January to March 2010: 4,500 x 3/15 = £900.

iv) If the first period of account had been less than 12 months' duration the writing down allowances would have been pro-rated down.

v) First year allowances are not scaled up or down for the length of a period of account.

v) Temporary FYA of 40% is not available on features integral to a building.

21. If a private car is hired which emits more than 160 g/km of CO_2, then the hiring charge allowed as a business expense is restricted by 15%.

Example

C hires a car for £3,200 p.a. which emits 190 g/km CO_2. C uses the car 30% for private use.

Total of hire charge	3,200	
Restriction for emissions 15%	(480)	
		2,720
Restriction for private use 30%	(816)	
Allowable expense	£1,904	

Plant purchased by hire purchase

22. With this method of purchase the interest element is allowed as an expense of trading. With regard to the capital element, any capital allowances can be claimed:

a) Before the plant is brought in to use, for any instalment due.

b) When the plant is brought in to use, for all instalments outstanding, as if the whole of the balance of capital expenditure had been paid on at that date.

c) Where an HP agreement is not eventually completed after the plant has been brought into use, then an adjustment is made which claims back part of the allowance granted.

Leased plant and machinery

23. In general a lessor of plant and machinery is entitled to the full amount of capital allowances on eligible expenditure, and the rental payments of the lessee are an allowable business expense.

Separate pooling arrangements continue to apply to assets leased outside the UK other than certain ships, aircraft and containers leased in the course of UK trade.

Balancing charges and allowances: general rules

24. A balancing charge arises when the total disposal receipts (TDR) (limited to the original cost) of any poolable or non-poolable asset is greater than the amount of available qualifying expenditure (AQE) existing in the period of the sale.

Disposal value in the usual case is the amount of the proceeds of sale, or where the asset is lost or destroyed, any insurance or compensation moneys received. In other circumstances, e.g. if plant is given away, the market price is used.

Where plant or machinery is demolished giving rise to a balancing allowance or charge, the net cost of demolition can be added to the amount of unallowed expenditure at the time of the demolition.

A balancing allowance arises when the amount of available qualifying expenditure (AQE) is greater than the total disposal receipts (TDR) in the following circumstances:

a) in the terminal period when trading permanently ceases

b) when there is deemed to be a cessation of trade, see below.

Deemed cessation

25. For capital allowance purposes certain assets are treated as forming a separate trade to that of any actual trade undertaken so that on a disposal the notional trade is deemed to have ceased. This applies to the following categories:

a) assets used only partially for the purposes of a trade, e.g. a private car

b) short life assets

c) ships

d) each letting of machinery otherwise than in the course of trade

Where capital allowances are computed on the basis of a deemed trade, this is assumed to be discontinued when a disposal has to be brought into account in respect of a single item or the last item in a pool of assets.

Example

B, who has been trading for many years, has the following data relating to his year ended 31st March 2010.

		£
a)	Additions to general plant – 31.12.09	12,000
	Proceeds of sale of plant (original cost £1,500)	2,500
	Purchase of Renault car for sales manager purchased 31.1.2010	14,000
	CO_2 emissions of Renault car 180 g/km	
	Sale of Peugeot car used by sales staff (original cost £9,000)	4,500
	CO_2 emissions of Peugeot car 140 g/km	

b) At the 1st April 2009 the tax written down value of assets was:

	£
Plant and machinery	15,000
Citroen car for B (private use 30%)	7,400
CO_2 emissions of Citroen car 150 g/km	

Compute the capital allowances claimable for the AP to 31st March 2010.

Solution

	general pool £	motor car (p.u.30%) £	special rate pool £
Written down value b/f 31.3.09	15,000	7,400	
			14,000
	15,000	7,400	14,000
Proceeds of sale (1,500 + 4,500)	6,000	–	–
	9,000	7,400	14,000
Addition AIA 12,000			
AIA 100% 12,000			
WDA 31.03.10	1,800	1,480 (pu444)	1,400
WDV c/f 31.3.10	7,200	5,550	12,600

Notes

i) The proceeds of sale of the plant are limited to the original cost of £1,500.

ii) The total allowances available to B for 2009/10 are:

	£
Plant pool AIA 12,000 + WDA 1,800	13,800
Car with private use 30%	1,036
Special rate pool	1,400
	16,236

iii) Plant purchased is eligible for AIA up to £50,000 of expenditure.

iv) Notice that the car with private use forms a separate pool and the WDA is computed at the 20% rate and then restricted.

v) A car with CO_2 emissions of more than 160 g/km is entitled to a WDA of only 10%.

Plant and machinery – short life assets

26. The provisions dealing with this topic may be summarised as follows.

a) The rules apply in respect of a disposal of plant and machinery but do not apply to motor cars, ships or assets leased to non-traders, or assets required to be pooled separately.

b) Where the taxpayer expects to dispose of an item of plant or machinery at less than its tax written down value, within four years of the end of the year of acquisition, then he or she can elect to have the item extracted from the general plant pool, and a separate pool created. The plant is treated as being in use for a separate notional trade.

c) The election must be made within two years of the end of the year of acquisition.

d) Any balancing adjustment arising on the disposal is calculated separately.

e) If the item of plant or machinery is not sold or scrapped by the end of four years from the end of the year of acquisition, then its tax written down value is transferred back to the general plant pool at the beginning of the fifth year.

As a general rule, it will only be advantageous to de-pool if the proceeds of sale are less than the written down value at the date of the disposal, giving a balancing allowance.

Example

T, who has traded for many years, has an accounting year end of 31 March. On the 1 May 2005 he purchases equipment for £10,000, electing for de-pooling.

Show the computations in the following circumstances:

a) The plant is sold in the year to 31 March 2010 for £2,000.

b) The plant is sold in the year to 31 March 2010 for £5,000.

c) The equipment is not sold by the 31 March 2010.

Solution: **Capital allowances computation**

		£
2005/06	Accounting period to 31.3.2006 cost	10,000
	Writing down allowance 25%	2,500
		7,500
2006/07	Writing down allowance 25%	1,875
		5,625
2007/08	Writing down allowance 25%	1,406
		4,219
2008/09	Writing down allowance 20%	844
		3,375
2009/10	Writing down allowance 20%	675
		2,700

a) 2009/10 year to 31.3.2010.

Total disposal receipts	2,000
Written down value 2008/09 b/f	3,375
Balancing allowance	1,375

b) 2009/10 year to 31.3.2010.

Proceeds of sale	5,000
Written down value 2008/09 b/f	3,375
Balancing charge	1,625

c) As the item of plant has not been sold within four years of the end of the year of acquisition, the written down value of £2,700 must be transferred to the general plant pool.

Notes

i) Where short life assets of a similar nature are acquired in fairly large numbers e.g. small tools or returnable containers, then the cost of the assets may be aggregated and treated as one sum.

ii) Where assets used in a trade are stocked in large numbers and individual identification is possible but not readily practicable, then the computation can be based on the number of each class of asset retained. Assets falling under this heading could be calculators, amusement machines and scientific instruments, and videos.

The renewals basis

27. This is really a non-statutory method of obtaining relief on expenditure on plant and machinery, quite distinct from the capital allowance system outlined above. In fact where the renewals basis is adopted then the capital allowance system does not apply. The main points arising are:

a) The initial cost of any item of plant or machinery does not give rise to any allowances whatsoever, and no writing down allowance is available with this basis.

b) When an item is replaced then the cost of the new item, less anything received for the old one, is allowed as a deduction in computing trade profit. Any element of improvement or addition is excluded, and can only be claimed when it is replaced. Subsequent replacements are dealt with on a similar basis.

c) A change from the renewals basis to the normal capital allowance system can be made at any time, but the decision must apply to all items of plant in that class. In the year of the change, capital allowances can be claimed, irrespective of whether the expenditure is on a replacement or not.

The renewals basis effectively gives 100% relief in the year of expenditure on the replacement of an asset.

PART II – Industrial buildings and structures

28. Capital allowances are available in respect of expenditure on buildings and structures where the building or structure is in use for the purposes of a qualifying trade as defined in Table A or B below.

a) Table A: Trades which are 'Qualifying Trades'

1.	Manufacturing	A trade consisting of manufacturing goods or materials.
2.	Processing	A trade consisting of subjecting goods or materials to a process.
		This includes maintaining or repairing goods or materials.
		Maintaining or repairing goods or materials is not a qualifying trade if:
		a) the goods or materials are employed in a trade or undertaking,
		b) the maintenance or repair is carried out by the person employing the goods or materials, and
		c) the trade or undertaking is not itself a qualifying trade.
3.	Storage	A trade consisting of storing goods or materials:
		a) which are to be used in the manufacture of other goods or materials,
		b) which are to be subjected, in the course of a trade, to a process,

		c) which, having been manufactured or produced or subjected, in the course of a trade, to a process, have not yet been delivered to any purchaser, or
		d) on their arrival in the United Kingdom from a place outside the United Kingdom.
4.	Agricultural contracting	A trade consisting of: a) ploughing or cultivating land occupied by another, b) carrying out any other agricultural operation on land occupied by another, or c) forestry. For this purpose 'crops' includes vegetable produce.
5.	Working foreign plantations	A trade consisting of working land outside the United Kingdom used for: a) growing and harvesting crops, b) husbandry, or c) threshing another's crops. For this purpose 'crops' includes vegetable produce and 'harvesting crops' includes the collection of vegetable produce (however effected).
6.	Fishing	A trade consisting of catching or taking fish or shellfish.
7.	Mineral extraction	A trade consisting of working a source of mineral deposits. 'Mineral deposits' includes any natural deposits capable of being lifted or extracted from the earth, and for this purpose geothermal energy is to be treated as a natural deposit. 'Source of mineral deposits' includes a mine, an oil well and a source of geothermal energy.

Table B includes electricity, water, hydraulic power, sewerage and transport undertakings where a trade is carried on.

b) The expression 'building or structure' is not defined, and in general, an extension or addition to a building is treated as if it were a separate building. A structure embraces such things as: walls, bridges, culverts, tunnels, roads, aircraft runways, and factory car parks. Costs of site preparation are included in the cost of a building.

c) Expenditure on the acquisition of land or rights over land is to be excluded from the cost of any industrial building or structure.

d) Where the taxpayer carrying on a qualifying trade provides a building or structure for the welfare of workers employed in that trade, e.g. a canteen, and it is used for that purpose, then such a building is deemed to be an industrial building.

e) Where only a part of a building is used for a qualifying trade then only that part will rank as an industrial building.

f) A sports pavilion used by a trader for the welfare of his or her employees is treated as an industrial building whether or not the trade is a qualifying trade.

g) Even where a qualifying trade is being carried on, an industrial building does not include any building or structure in use as, or part of, a dwelling house, retail shop, showroom, hotel or office. However, where 25% or less of the cost of the whole building, excluding any land cost, is attributable to the cost of such premises, then the whole building is treated as an industrial one.

h) For details of expenditure on plant and machinery to be treated as a building or structure, see Part I above.

Cases on industrial buildings

29. a) CIR v Lambhill Ironworks Ltd 1950 31 TC 93. A drawing office used by an engineering firm for workshop plans, although separate from the main workshop, was held to be an industrial building.

b) Saxone Lilley & Skinner (Holdings) Ltd v CIR 1967 HL 44 TC 22. A warehouse used for the storage of shoes, of which one third was manufactured by a group company, was held to be an industrial building.

c) Abbott Laboratories Ltd v Carmody 1963 CD 44 TC 569. An administrative unit which cost less than 10% of the whole was held to be a separate building, and thus not an industrial one.

d) Buckingham v Securitas Properties Ltd 1980 STC 166. A building used for the purposes of wage packeting, and coin and note storage, was held not to be an industrial building, as the coins and notes were currency and not goods or materials.

e) Copol Clothing Co. Ltd v Hindmarch 1982 STI 69. A warehouse used to store imported goods was held not to be an industrial building, as it was not located near to a port or airport.

f) Girobank plc v Clarke 1998 STI. The activities in a data processing centre did not amount to a subjection of goods to a process and thus expenditure on the building did not qualify for IBA.

Allowances available

30. The following allowances are available in respect of industrial buildings:

Initial allowance	–	20% of expenditure (1.11.92 – 31.10.1993).
Writing down allowances	–	4% of expenditure, restricted to 50% of 4% for 2009/10 (2% for expenditure prior to 7.11.62).

An industrial building erected after the 6th November 1962 is deemed to have a maximum life of 25 years from the date when first used as an industrial building. After that period no allowance of any kind is available. For buildings erected prior to that date the maximum life is 50 years.

Writing down allowance

31. a) A writing down allowance of 4% p.a. is given providing that the building is in use as an industrial building at the end of the basis period. For 2009/10 the allowance is restricted to 50% of 4% in anticipation of the withdrawal of Industrial Buildings Allowance.

b) A full writing down allowance is given unless the basis period is less than 12 months, when a proportion is available.

c) Where a writing down allowance cannot be given, i.e. where the building is not being used for a qualifying trade, then a 'notional allowance' is nevertheless computed, and the life of the building is in no way affected.

Example

T is a sole trader. His accounting period is the year to 31 March 2010. He incurred the following expenditure on 1 June 2009:

	£
New factory (including land £50,000)	150,000
Drawing office	25,000
Retail shop being part of factory	23,000
	198,000

All buildings were in use for a qualifying trade at the 31st March 2010.

Solution: Capital allowances AP 31.03.2010

	£
Cost of factory	100,000
Drawing office	25,000
Retail shop	23,000
	148,000
Writing down allowance 4% × 148,000 × 50%	2,960

Notes

i) The drawing office is treated as an industrial building. The retail shop is eligible since its cost is less than 25% of the whole:

$$25\% \times 148,000 = £37,000$$

ii) The writing down allowance is a full year's amount calculated on the cost.

iii) Further additions to a shop or office could negate a claim by exceeding the 25% level.

Disposals on or after 21 March 2007

32. Disposals after 21 March 2007 do not, in general, give rise to any balancing charge or allowance. The allowances available to the purchaser of the building are based on the previous owner's cost less allowances already given. These rules are introduced in anticipation of the withdrawal of IBA. The new rules do not apply to buildings in enterprise zones.

Buildings in enterprise zones

32. Balancing adjustments are only calculated for disposals before 21 March 2007, or for buildings in enterprise zones.

a) Where the building has been used for a qualifying trade throughout the period of ownership, then a balancing adjustment arises if the proceeds of sale are greater or smaller than the 'residue of expenditure' prior to the sale.

The latter is equal to the original cost less any allowances given.

b) Where a balancing charge arises, this cannot exceed the value of the total allowances given.

c) The allowances available to a purchaser or a secondhand building are based on the residue of expenditure, plus balancing charge, minus balancing allowance, restricted where necessary to the purchase price, over the remaining tax life of the building.

Example

A, who started business on 1st January 2000, purchased an industrial building new at a cost of £100,000 on 1st July 2000. The building is sold in June 2006, six years later, after allowances of £24,000 have been claimed. The sale price was (a) £20,000 (b) £120,000. A's accounting year end is to 31st December.

Compute the balancing adjustments arising on the disposal.

Solution: Balancing adjustments AP 31.12.2006

		£	£
a)	**Balancing adjustment sale price £20,000**		
	Cost		100,000
	Less allowances ($6 \times 4\% \times 100,000$)		24,000
	Residue of expenditure prior to sale	76,000	
	Proceeds of sale	20,000	
	Balancing allowance	56,000	
b)	**Balancing adjustment sale price £120,000**		
	Residue of expenditure prior to sale	76,000	
	Proceeds of sale (limited to cost)	100,000	
	Balancing charge	24,000	

Notes

i) In the first case the purchaser would receive an annual allowance of

$$\text{Residue } 76,000 - \text{BA } 56,000 = \frac{20,000}{19} = £1,052$$

The remaining life of the building is 19 years.

ii) In the second case the annual allowance would be

$$\text{Residue } 76,000 + \text{BC} = \frac{100,000}{19} = £5,263 \text{ p.a.}$$

iii) The tax life of a building is calculated to the nearest month, in this case 30th June. The age of the building on 30th June 2006 is six years and its expired life is therefore 19 years.

Disposal after non-qualifying trade use

34. If a building has not been used for a qualifying purpose throughout the period, then a balancing adjustment on disposals before 21 March 2007 was calculated by reference to the 'adjusted cost' of the building. The latter was equal to the original cost less any proceeds of sale, adjusted for any periods of non-qualifying use.

The comparison is made between the following:

i) the actual capital allowances given (ignoring all notional allowances) and

ii) the adjusted net cost i.e.

$$(\text{original cost} - \text{proceeds of sale}) \times \frac{\text{Periods of industrial use}}{\text{Total periods of use}}$$

iii) Sale proceeds > original cost = BC equivalent to allowances given.

iv)   Sale proceeds < original cost =

    a)   BC where actual capital allowances > adjusted net cost.

    b)   BA where actual capital allowances < adjusted net cost.

Example

Q, a sole trader who started in business on 1st January 1999 and whose accounting period is to 31st December, had an industrial building constructed in December 1999 at a cost of £100,000. It was used for the first year as an industrial building then for five years as a retail warehouse. After one year's further use as an industrial building it was sold on 31st December 2006 for £60,000.

Compute the balancing adjustment arising on the sale in December 2006.

Solution

		£	£
Cost of building			100,000
Writing down allowance:			
5 years notional use	4% × 100,000 × 5	20,000	
2 years qualifying use	4% × 100,000 × 2	8,000	28,000
Residue of expenditure prior to sale		72,000	
Adjusted net cost to Q			
Cost of building in 1999			100,000
Less proceeds of sale			60,000
Net cost			40,000

Proportion of net cost attributable to the period of qualifying use.

    2/7 × 40,000 = £11,429 – adjusted net cost

Computation of balancing charge AP to 31.12.2006

		£
Net cost		40,000
Less	Proportion attributable to non-business use	
	5/7 × 40,000	28,571
Less	Capital allowances actually given	11,429
	Writing down allowances	8,000
Balancing allowance		3,429

Notes

i)   The allowances available to the purchaser would be based on the total of the residue of expenditure less the balancing allowance, restricted where necessary to the purchase price:

    Residue – Balancing allowance i.e. 72,000 – 3,429 = 68,571

    Restricted to purchase price £60,000

ii)   Where the building is sold for more than its original cost then the balancing charge is limited to the actual allowances given, which in the above example would be £8,000.

iii)   The age of the building on 31 Dec 2006 is seven years and its unexpired life is therefore 20 years.

    Writing down allowance 60,000 / 18 i.e. £3,333 p.a. available to purchaser.

Enterprise zones

35. These are areas of the country designated by the Department of the Environment, for which special provisions apply. So far as capital allowances are concerned the main features are:

a) Eligible expenditure includes the construction, extension or improvement of industrial and commercial buildings within the zone. Thus all commercial buildings, offices and hotels are included, but not dwelling houses.

b) An initial allowance of 100% is available but a reduced amount can be claimed.

c) If the building is sold within 25 years of its first use, then the normal balancing adjustments apply.

d) The allowances apply to expenditure incurred within a 10-year period beginning with the day on which the site is first designated as an enterprise zone.

PART III – Other assets

Conversion of parts of business premises into flats

36. Rates of allowance

initial allowance	100% of expenditure
writing down allowance	25%

A new scheme of 100% capital allowances was introduced for expenditure incurred from the 24th May 2001 on the renovation or conversion of vacant or underused space above shops and commercial properties in traditional shopping areas to provide flats for rent. The allowances are available where:

a) the property was built before 1980, has not more than five floors (excluding basements), and was originally constructed so that the upper floors were primarily for residential use;

b) most of the ground floors falls within certain rating categories at the time the conversion work starts (broadly retail shops, certain offices including those used for financial and professional services, and premises used for medical and health services or for providing food and drink);

c) the upper floors have either been unoccupied, or used only for storage, for at least one year before the conversion work starts;

d) apart from any extension required to provide access to the flats, the conversion takes place within the existing boundaries of the building; and

e) each new flat is self-contained, with its own external access, and has no more than four rooms (excluding the kitchen and bathroom and other small areas).

f) The rules governing the allowance code, with certain modifications and simplifications: there will be no balancing charge if a balancing event (e.g. a sale of the property, the flat ceasing to be let, or the grant of a long lease of the flat) occurs more than seven years from the time the flat is completed, and the allowance will not be transferable to a purchaser.

Renovation of business premises – disadvantaged areas

37. Initial Business Properties Renovation Allowance (BPRA) of 100% of expenditure incurred on or after 11 April 2007. The scheme allows people or companies, who own or lease property that has been vacant for a year or more in one of the designated disadvantaged areas of the UK, to claim immediate, full tax relief on their capital spending on the conversion or renovation of the property, in order to bring it back into business use.

Hotels

38. Capital allowances are also available for expenditure incurred, in respect of what is called a 'qualifying hotel'. This is a hotel which provides accommodation in a building of a permanent nature, and which complies with the following.

a) It is open for at least four months in the season, which means April to October inclusive.

b) During the time when it is open, it has at least 10 letting rooms and the accommodation offered consists wholly or mainly of letting rooms and the normal services are provided.

The following allowances are available:

Writing down allowance   4% of expenditure p.a. based on initial cost, restricted to 50% of 4% for 2009/10.

Balancing adjustments   A balancing charge or allowance can arise in similar circumstances to that for industrial buildings.

If a building ceases to be a qualifying hotel, other than by sale or destruction, for a period of two years, then a sale is deemed to take place at the end of that period, at the open market price.

Agricultural buildings and works

39. Allowances are available on capital expenditure incurred in respect of agricultural or forestry land.

Capital expenditure includes expenditure on:

construction of farmhouses, farms or forestry buildings, cottages, fences or other works such as drainage and sewerage, water and electrical installations, broiler houses and similar buildings used for the intensive rearing of livestock.

Where expenditure is on a farmhouse then not more than a third of the expenditure can qualify as an agricultural building.

To be eligible for capital allowances the person incurring the expenditure must have the 'relevant interest' which would include an owner or tenant farmer.

The agricultural or forestry land must be in the UK.

Rates of allowance

40. Expenditure incurred

Writing down allowance 4% p.a. based on cost, restricted to 50% of 4% for 2009/10.

Balancing allowance/charge subject to joint election

Example

D, the tenant of some agricultural land in the UK, has constructed a new farm building at a cost of £200,000, on 1 May 2009. D's accounting period is to 30th June 2009.

Capital allowances computation AP 30.6.2009

	£
Cost of agricultural building	200,000
Writing down allowance 4% × 200,000 x 50%	4,000
Written down value carried forward	196,000

Disposals on or after 21 March 2007

41. The writing down allowances available to the purchaser of the building are based on the original cost. Balancing events for agricultural buildings allowance are subject to the same changes as industrial buildings allowance, see paragraph 27.

Balancing events

42. A balancing charge or allowance may arise for disposals before 21 March 2007 in the following circumstances:

a) Where the 'relevant interest' is acquired by a new owner, and both elect for such treatment within two years of the end of the chargeable period.

b) In other cases e.g. where the building is destroyed or demolished or otherwise ceases to exist, if an election is made by the former owner within the two year period.

Residue of expenditure > Proceeds = Balancing allowance

Residue of expenditure < Proceeds = Balancing charge

Allowance to the new owner if election made: $\dfrac{\text{Residue of expenditure} + BC - BA}{\text{Remainder of 25 year's life}}$

If no election is made for a balancing adjustment, or for disposals after 21 March 2007 the writing down allowance based on the original cost passes to the successor.

Research and development allowance

43. Allowances for capital expenditure on research and development related to a trade carried on by a taxpayer are provided for as follows:

a) 'Research and development' means activities that fall to be treated as research and development in accordance with normal accounting practice.

b) Expenditure on research and development includes all expenditure incurred for:

i) carrying out research and development, or

ii) providing facilities for carrying out research and development.

But it does not include expenditure incurred in the acquisition of rights in research and development, or rights arising out of research and development.

c) 'Normal accounting practice' means normal accounting practice in relation to the accounts of companies incorporated in a part of the United Kingdom.

d) Capital expenditure under this heading would include buildings and plant and machinery, but not land.

e) The amount of the allowance is 100% of capital expenditure.

Balancing adjustments can arise when assets representing research and development expenditure cease to be used for such purposes and either they are sold or destroyed.

N.B The Finance Act 2000 introduced a scheme for R&D tax credits for small and medium sized companies, based on the total cost of their research and development expenditure. This has been extended to all companies, see Chapter 19.

Student self-testing questions

1. Ryan had the following expenditure on plant and machinery in the year ended 31 December 2010:

		£
6 January 2010	New plant	26,000
11 February 2010	Second hand lorry	25,000
14 February 2010	Burglar alarm system	1,500
17 July 2010	Ryan's car (30% private use)	13,000
14 August 2010	Fleet for sales team (6 cars)	60,000

CO_2 emissions of the cars were 180 g/km.

Requirement: Calculate the capital allowances available to Ryan for the year ended 31 December 2010.

Solution

Year to 31 December 2010		Special rate pool	Car 30% private
Qualifying expenditure incurred (not eligible for AIA)		60,000	13,000
Qualifying expenditure (not eligible for 100% FYA)	51,000		
Less: Annual Investment Allowance (max. £50,000)	(50,000)		
Excess of expenditure over £50,000	1,000		
	1,500		
	2,500		
Transfer part relating to special rate pool	(-)		-
Part eligible for temporary 40% FYA	2,500		
Less: Temporary First Year Allowance 40%	(1,000)		
Available qualifying expenditure		-	-
Less: Total disposal receipts (limited to cost)		(-)	(-)
		-	-
Less: Writing down allowances 20% or 10%		(6,000)	(1,300) 70% business
General pool of expenditure after 40% FYA	1,500		
Unrelieved qualifying expenditure carried forward	1,500	54,000	11,700

Allowances	Annual investment allowance	50,000
	Temporary first year allowance	1,000
	Writing down allowance 10%	6,000
	WDA 13,000 @ 10% = 1,300 x 70% business	910
		57,910

2. Tom commenced trading on 1 July 2009 and produced his first set of accounts to the period ended 30 September 2010. He purchased the following assets during this 15 month period:

		£
10 July 2009	Plant	47,500
18 July 2009	Car (private use 25%)	16,000
20 July 2009	Van	18,000
30 July 2009	Office furniture	2,000
1 August 2010	Computer equipment	5,400

CO_2 emissions of the cars were 180 g/km.

Requirement: Calculate the capital allowances available to Tom.

Solution

15 month period of account 1 July 2009 to 30 September 2010		General pool	Car 25% private
Qualifying expenditure incurred (not eligible for AIA)		-	16,000
Qualifying expenditure (not eligible for 100% FYA)	65,500		
Less: Annual Investment Allowance (£50,000 x 15/12)	(62,500)		
Excess of expenditure over £50,000	3,000		
	2,000		
	5,000		
Transfer part relating to special rate pool	(-)		-
Part eligible for temporary 40% FYA	5,000		
Less: Temporary First Year Allowance 40%	(2,000)		
Available qualifying expenditure		5,400	-
Less: Total disposal receipts (limited to cost)		(-)	(-)
		-	-
Less: Writing down allowances 20% or 10%		(1,350)	(2,000)
			75% business
Transfer to general pool of expenditure	(3,000)	3,000	
Unrelieved qualifying expenditure carried forward		7,050	14,000

Allowances	Annual investment allowance	62,500
	Temporary first year allowance	2,000
	Writing down allowance 20% x 5,400 x 15/12	1,350
	WDA 10% x 16,000 x 15/12 x 75%	1,500
		67,350

3. Jessica commenced business as a manufacturer on 1 June 2008 and purchased an industrial building for £300,000 on 4 August 2008. The cost of the building included land of £100,000 and the building also contained some offices with a cost of £20,000. Jessica made up her first accounts to 31 January 2009 and then annually to that date.

Requirement: Show the capital allowances for her first two periods of account.

Solution

1st period of account: 1st June 2008 31st January 2009

Total cost	300,000
less land	(100,000)
Cost of construction	200,000

Offices constitute 20,000/200,000 = 10% of industrial building and therefore IBAs will be given on the full £200,000

IBA at 4% x 200,000 x 75% x 8/12 = £4,000

Therefore written down value = £200,000 – 4,000 = £160,000

2nd period of account: 1st February 2009 - 31st January 2010.

IBA at 4% x £200,000 x 50% = £4,000

WDV = £160,000 - £4,000 = £156,000

Questions without answers

1. Wilton starts a trade on 1 March 2010 and has the following results before capital allowances

Period of account	Profits
1/3/10 - 31/7/11	85,000
1/8/11- 31/7/12	73,600
1/8/12 - 31/7/13	64,000

General plant is bought as follows:-

Date	Cost
1/3/10	24,000
1/12/10	18,000
1/10/11	12,000
1/2/13	4,000

On 1 May 2012 plant which cost £14,000 was sold for £8,000

Requirement: Calculate assessments on profits from trading for the first five tax years.

2. Homer started a business on 1 February 2010 and prepared accounts for the 18-month period to 31 July 2011 and then to 31 July each year. Between 1/2/10 and 31/7/12 he had the following capital expenditure and disposals.

Additions			Disposals		
1/2/10	2nd hand plant	105,000			
1/2/10	Ford car	11,000			
13/6/10	lorry	9,000			
1/10/10	photocopier	7,000			
10/11/11	Office equipment	5,000	30/11/11	Photocopier (bought 1/10/10)	9,000
15/6/12	machinery	11,000	20/6/12	Ford car (bought 1/2/10)	6,000
20/6/12	VW car	16,000			
30/6/12	new lorry	19,000	30/6/12	Lorry (bought 13/6/10)	7,000

The private use of Homer's Ford and VW cars is 40%.

CO_2 emissions of the car purchased on 1/2/06 were 190 g/km.

CO_2 emissions of the car purchased on 20/6/08 are 150 g/km.

Requirement: Calculate the maximum capital allowances available to Homer for the periods ending 31/7/11 and 31/7/12.

14 Relief for trading and capital losses

Introduction

1.   This chapter is concerned with the reliefs available to a taxpayer who incurs a trading loss and 'capital losses'. A summary of the loss reliefs available for trading businesses, forms the basis of this chapter, each of which is subsequently examined in detail with examples.

List of loss reliefs

2.

Set against total income.	Section 64 ITA 2007
Carried forward and set against future trading income from the same trade.	Section 83 ITA 2007
Losses incurred in the first four years of trading can be set against other total income of the three preceding years of assessment.	Section 72 ITA 2007
Terminal loss relief.	Section 89 ITA 2007
Relief for losses where a business is transferred to a limited company.	Section 86 ITA 2007
Relief for capital losses.	Section 131 ITA 2007
Pre-trading expenditure.	
Trading loss set against capital gains.	
Rental business losses.	

Set against 'other income' Sec 64 ITA 2007

3.   The following points should be noted:

   i)   Capital allowances are deducted in computing adjusted taxable profits.

   ii)   The current year basis of assessment applies.

   iii) Profits and losses are calculated by reference to periods of account rather than years of assessment.

   iv)   Any loss which would otherwise appear in two periods of account can only appear in the first period.

   v)   Relief against general income can be claimed in the year of the loss or the preceding year.

   vi)   Where claims are made in respect of both years the taxpayer can choose which claim should be taken in priority. Partial claims are not permitted.

   vii) Any unused loss can be carried forward under Section 83.

Example

A, who has been in business for many years, has an adjusted loss from trading for the year ended 31st December 2009 of £12,000. In respect of the year to 5th April 2009 he has the following:

	£
Trade profits year to 31.12.2008	10,000
Rental income	30,000

Compute A's income tax liability for 2008/09 on the assumption that he claims relief for the trading loss under s64 ITA 2007 in the year 2008/09.

Solution

Income tax computation 2008/09	£
Trade profits	10,000
Property income	30,000
	40,000
Section 64 loss relief 2008/09	12,000
	28,000
Personal allowance	6,035
Taxable income	21,965
Tax liability: 21,965 @ 20%	4,392

Notes

i) Personal allowances are claimed after relief for a loss so that there may be unused personal reliefs.

ii) The whole of the loss to 31st December 2009 has been used against total income of the year preceding the loss, i.e. 2008/09.

iii) The 2009/10 trade loss of £12,000 can be used in the year 2009/2010, 2008/2009 or carried forward (see section 7). For 2009/10 losses, the carry back of losses can be extended against up to £50,000 in total of trading income of 2007/08 and 2006/07 (see section 4).

Extension of trading loss carry back

4.   For trading losses of tax years 2008/09 and 2009/10 the carry back of trade losses will be extended from the current one year entitlement to three years, with the losses carried back against the later years first.

The section 64 relief against total income of the same year is unlimited.

The carry back against trading income of the two years before will be limited to £50,000 in total in respect of each loss making tax year. That is up to £50,000 of losses from 2008/09 and a further £50,000 of losses from 2009/10.

Example

An individual trader's profits losses and other income are:

2005/06	Trade profit	£80,000	Employment income £5,000
2006/07	Trade profit	£60,000	Employment income £5,000
2007/08	Trade profit	£30,000	Employment income £5,000
2008/09	Trade loss	£100,000	Employment income £5,000

The trader makes a claim under s64 ITA 2007 to set the 2008/09 loss against general income of both the year of loss (£5,000) and the previous year 2007/08 (£35,000).

The remaining part of the 2008/09 loss, up to a maximum of £50,000, is available to carry back against trading profits of 2006/07 and 2005/06 (in that order).

Loss set against:

1) £5,000 employment income of 2008/09

2) £35,000 employment income + trade profits of 2007/08

3) £50,000 trade profit of 2006/07 (cap applied)

£90,000

£10,000 available for carry forward to set against trade profits in future years.

(HMRC example)

Capital allowances

5. Capital allowances are deducted in computing trade profits, but the taxpayer does not have to claim the full allowances available in computing his or her taxable profits.

Example

T, who started in business in January 2004, has an adjusted trading profit for the 12 months to 31st December 2009 of £145, and capital allowances available of £4,000. T has property income for 2009/10 of £6,600 and no other income.

Compute T's income tax liability for 2009/10.

Solution: Income tax computation 2009/10

	£
Property income	6,600
Less Section 64 relief	(125)
	6,475
Personal allowance	6,475
Trading loss. Section 64 claim (145 – 270)	125

Note

T has claimed £270 of his capital allowances so that he does not waste his personal allowance. The balance of the capital allowance of £4,000 – £270, i.e. £3,730 can be carried forward to the pool for AP to 31.12.2010.

Tax planning considerations in making a Section 64 claim

6. The following points should be taken into consideration in deciding whether or not to make a claim for loss relief under Section 64.

a) Loss of personal allowance — This cannot be carried forward, or back.

b) Transfer of married couple's allowance spouses aged 65 at 5.4.2000 — This can all be transferred to the spouse, on a joint election, although only obtaining relief at the 10% rate.

c) Loss of personal pension plan relief (see Chapter 16) — Net relevant UK earnings are after deduction of loss relief.

d) Tax at higher rate — A claim can be made for the actual year of the loss or the preceding year.

e) Reduction in Class IV NIC — Profits for Class IV National Insurance purposes are after loss relief.

Carried forward – Section 83 ITA 2007

7. To the extent that a trading loss has not been relieved it may be carried forward and set against the first available profits of the same trade.

The loss must be set off even where this would involve a loss of personal allowances.

Example

R has taxable profits for the year to 31st December 2009 of £26,000. Trade losses brought forward under Section 83 amount to £3,105. R started in business on 1.7.2005.

Compute the income tax liability for 2009/10 of Mr R.

Solution: Income tax computation 2009/10

				£
Trade profits			26,000	
Section 83 losses b/f			3,105	22,895
Personal allowance				6,475
Taxable income				16,420
Tax Liability	n/a	@ 10%		0
	16,420	@ 20%		3,284

Losses in first four years of trading – Section 72 ITA 2007

8. The relief which is available under this section, in addition to that under Sec 64 or 83, is as follows.

a) Trading losses incurred in the first four years of assessment may be carried back and set against the total income of the taxpayer, in the previous three years of assessment.

b) The trading loss is to be calculated on the accounting year basis.

c) The loss is to be set against income of the first available year in the following order: earned income/unearned income of the claimant.

d) A claim can be made to restrict the application of relief to the claimant's income only.

e) A claim must be made within two years of the year of assessment in which the loss is incurred.

f) Where a claim is made for relief under Sec 64 and under Sec 72, then the loss cannot be apportioned between them. Butt v Haxby 1983 STC 239.

g) The set-off is against income of an earlier year before a later year, i.e. on a FIFO basis.

Example

P left his employment on the 31st December 2006 and commenced trading on the 1st January 2007 with the following results:

	£
12 months to 31.12.2007	(3,000)
12 months to 31.12.2008	(2,000)
12 months to 31.12.2009	(5,000)

Compute the losses available for set-off and show the years in which they can be utilised.

Solution

		£	£
2006/07	$1.1.07 - 5.4.07 \dfrac{95}{365} \times 3{,}000 =$		(780)
2007/08	Year ended 31.12.07	(3,000)	
	Less allocated to 2006/07	780	(2,220)
2008/09	Year ended 31.12.08		(2,000)
2009/10	Year ended 31.12.09		(5,000)

Loss relief available is as follows:

	2006/07	2007/08	2008/09	2009/10
	780	2,220	2,000	5,000
Set against total income				
2003/04	780	–	–	–
2004/05	–	2,220	–	–
2005/06	–	–	2,000	
2006/07	–	–	–	5,000

Notes

i) If the losses cannot be fully used by this process then the balance can be carried forward in the usual way under Section 83.

ii) The loss has been shown as relieved in the earliest year available.

Terminal loss relief – Section 89 ITA 2007

9. Under this section relief is available where a cessation of trading takes place, and a loss arises in the last 12 months of trading.

A terminal loss may be carried back and set against the trading profits (less capital allowances) of the three years of assessment prior to the year of assessment in which the trading ceases.

The terminal loss is made up of:

(a) The loss from 6 April to the date of cessation in the final tax year; plus

(b) The loss for the other part of the final twelve months of trading; plus

(c) Overlapped profits.

Where part (b) of the calculation shows a profit it is ignored in calculating the terminal loss.

Example

S ceased trading on 30th June 2009 with the following results:

Adjusted profits	**£**
9 months to 30.6.09	(1,500)
12 months to 30.9.08	1,200
12 months to 30.9.07	1,600

Compute the terminal loss available for relief.

Solution: Calculation of terminal loss – 12 months to 30.6.2009

		£	£
2009/10	(6.4.2009 – 30.6.2009)		
	1/3 × (1,500)	(500)	(500)
2008/09	(1.7.2008 – 5.4.2009)		
	1.10.2008 – 5.4.2009 2/3 × (1,500)	(1,000)	
	1.7.2008 – 1.10.2008 3/12 × 1,200	300	(700)
Terminal loss			(1,200)

10. Some further points on terminal losses.

   a) Capital allowances claimed including any balancing adjustments must be deducted from the assessments before terminal loss relief is applied.

   b) Normally relief under Section 64 would be claimed before any terminal loss relief, since the former is relief against total income.

   c) Terminal loss is computed after deducting capital allowances.

   d) Terminal loss is after any overlap relief brought forward.

Transfer of a business to a limited company – Section 86 ITA 2007

11. If a sole trader or partnership transfers its business to a limited company, there is a cessation of trade. Accordingly, trading losses at the date of transfer are not available for set-off against any future corporation tax profits of the new company.

However, Section 86 provides some relief where the following conditions are met.

   a) The consideration for the business consists wholly or mainly in allotted shares of the company. In this case 80% is often taken to be equivalent to 'wholly'.

   b) The shares are beneficially held by the transferor throughout the period of any year of assessment for which a claim under Section 86 is made.

   c) The company carries on the same business throughout any year for which a claim is made.

Relief is available in respect of trading losses (excluding capital allowances) from a former business which can be carried forward and they can be set against income received by the transferor from the company. The losses must be set against earned income first, e.g. directors' fees or remuneration, and then investment income, e.g. dividends.

Example

D transfers his business to a limited company on the 1st August 2009 wholly for shares.

At that date the business has trading losses of £10,000. In the year 2009/10 D receives director's remuneration of £8,000 and a net dividend of £900 from the company.

Income tax computation 2009/10

	£
Income from employment	8,000
Less Section 86 loss	8,000
Dividend income	1,000
Less Section 86 loss	1,000

Notes

i) With this example there would be trade losses to carry forward to 2010/2011 of £1,000 providing the conditions noted above prevail.

ii) In claiming the Section 86 relief for 2009/10 D has lost his personal allowances which cannot be carried forward.

iii) A claim under Section 86 in effect involves Section 83, and is subject to most of the provisions relating to that section.

Relief for capital losses – Section 131 ITA 2007

12. Under this section a loss made by an individual on the disposal of any unquoted shares can be set against his income for income tax purposes. The loss must arise from a number of shares originally subscribed for on the formation of the company, and not from an inheritance or subsequent acquisition.

The claim is similar to a claim under Section 64 ITA 2007, but takes precedence of relief under that section. The company must in general be a UK trading company at the date of the disposal. A qualifying loss can only be claimed in the following circumstances:

a) on a disposal for full market value, or

b) on a winding up, or

c) on a claim that the shares have become of negligible value.

The loss is deducted from the taxpayer's income in the year in which the disposal takes place or in the preceding year.

Example

Z and his wife have the following data relating to 2009/10.

	£
Z Income from employment	45,000
Mrs Z Income from employment	6,600
Z Building society interest (net)	8,000
Z allowable loss under Sec 131 ITA 2007 arising from shares in A Ltd	3,000

Compute the income tax liability for 2009/10 of Z and his wife.

Solution: Income tax computation 2009/10

	Z £	MRS Z £
Earned income		
Income from employment Z	45,000	–
Income from employment Mrs Z	–	6,600
	45,000	6,600
Savings income		
Building society interest (gross)	10,000	–
	55,000	6,600
Less capital loss relief Sec 131	3,000	–
	52,000	6,600
Personal allowance	6,475	6,475

Taxable income				45,525	125
Tax liability					
	n/a / n/a	@ 10 %		0	0
	37,400 / 125	@ 20%		7,480	25
	8,125 / –	@ 40%		3,250	–
	45,525	125		10,730	25
Less:income tax deducted from BSI				2,000	
Tax payable				8,730	25

Notes

i) The relief for the capital loss is deducted from the earned income of Z in the computation. If this is insufficient it is set against his unearned income.

ii) As Z is paying tax at the 40% rate it would be tax efficient to transfer some of his investments to Mrs Z, to generate additional income in her own right.

Pre-trading expenditure

13. Relief is available for expenditure incurred by a person in the seven years before he or she commences to carry on a trade.

a) The expenditure must be allowable trading expenditure which would have been deducted in computing trading profits if incurred after the commencement of trading.

b) Such expenditure is treated as a trading loss of the year of assessment in which the trade commenced, to be claimed separately from any other loss relief.

c) The relief does not apply to pre-trading purchases of stock.

d) The loss may be relieved under Section 64, 83 and 72 ITA 2007.

e) Pre-trading expenditure is treated as an expense of the trade.

Example

T purchased a secondhand bookshop for £20,000 on 6th October 2008 which was closed for renovation until 6th April 2009 when trading commenced.

Trading account for the period to 5th April 2010

	£	£
Sales		95,000
Purchases	42,000	
Less Closing stock	3,500	38,500
Gross profit		56,500
Wages	23,700	
Motor expenses	3,800	
Costs of purchase of shop	5,000	
Rent and rates	2,400	
Heat and light	6,300	
Repairs and renewals	8,000	49,200
Trading profit		7,300

Notes

i) £2,000 of the purchases were made before 6th April 2009.

ii) Private use of motor car has been agreed at 30%. All expenses incurred after 5th April 2009.

iii) Rent, rates, and heating and lighting have accrued over the period 6th October 2007 to 5th April 2009.

iv) Repairs includes £6,000 for repairs prior to 6th April 2009.

Complete T's profits chargeable to income tax for 2009/10 (ignore capital allowances).

Solution: Trade profits 2009/10

	£	£	£
Trading profit per accounts			7,300
Add back:			
Cost of purchase of shop		5,000	
Motor expenses 30% × 3,800		1,140	
Pre-trading expenses			
Repairs	6,000		
Rent and rates 1/3 × 2,400	800		
Heat and light 1/3 × 6,300	2,100	8,900	15,040
Adjusted profit			22,340
Less Pre-trading allowable expenditure			
Repairs	6,000		
Rent and rates	800		
Heat and light	2,100		8,900
Income taxed as trade profits			13,440

Notes

i) Pre-trading expenditure is treated as an expense of the business on the first day of trading.

ii) Capital allowances claimed would be deducted from the adjusted profits of £13,440 to arrive at the trade profits for the period.

Restrictions on claiming loss reliefs

14. a) A claim under Section 64 is only available to trades which are carried on with a view to profit, and on a commercial basis in year of assessment to which the claim relates.

b) Farmers and market gardeners cannot obtain relief under Section 64 if in the previous five years their business has incurred successive trade losses, unless it can be shown that the trade is being carried on with a view to profit, and there is a reasonable expectation of profits in the future.

c) Loss relief under Section 83 is available in the earliest possible years only against the profits from the same trade, and not against total income or profits from any other trade.

d) From 2008/09 Income Tax loss relief will be restricted to a maximum of £25,000 in a tax year, if an individual does not spend more than 10 hours per week on average working in the trade.

Trading losses set against capital gains

15. Where a trading loss is incurred in the year then to the extent that it has not been fully relieved under Section 64 ITA 2007, a claim for relief against any chargeable gain can be made. The amount to be claimed cannot exceed the chargeable gain for the year, before deducting the CGT exemption amount of £10,100, for 2009/10.

Example

N has the following data relating to the year 2009/10:

	£
Trade loss for year to 31.3.10	(17,000)
Chargeable gains before exemption.	12,000

In the year to 5th April 2010 N has other income of £16,000.

Compute the income tax liability for 2009/10.

Solution: Income tax computation 2009/10

	£
Taxable income	16,000
Less Section 64	16,000
	—

CGT computation 2009/10

	£
Chargeable gains	12,000
Less trading losses	1,000
	11,000
Less annual exemption	10,100
	900

Notes

i)   N's personal allowance of £6,475 would be wasted.

ii) The trading loss of £17,000 has been dealt with as follows:

	£
Section 64 2009/10	16,000
Capital gain 2009/10	1,000

iii) The CGT is chargeable at the 18% rate. For details see Chapter 31.

Rental business losses

16. 1)   The general rule is that any rental business loss is automatically carried forward and set against rental business profits of the next year.

2)   Rental business losses can only be set off against profits from the same rental business.

3)   Furnished holiday lettings are treated like a trade for loss purposes and get the same loss reliefs as trades e.g. Sections 64 and 83.

4)   Where a rental business loss is attributable to any capital allowances then all or part of that attributable loss can be set against total statutory income.

Example

K has rental income loss of £3,500 for the year 2009/10 after claiming capital allowances of £1,500.

	£
Loss relief available	1,500

Notes

    i)   The loss relief can be set against other income of 2009/10 or 2010/11.

    ii)   Loss relief is limited to the smaller of the rental business loss and the capital allowances.

5)   Where a rental business loss is incurred, which includes agricultural land, then a part of the loss attributable to the agricultural land may be set against total statutory income.

Student self-testing questions

1.   James makes up accounts annually to 31 December. His recent results have been:

Year to 31 December 2005	Profit	£40,000
Year to 31 December 2006	Profit	£42,000
Year to 31 December 2007	Profit	£48,000
Year to 31 December 2008	Loss	(£100,000)
Year to 31 December 2009	Profit	£5,000

Requirement: Show the assessments on income from trading in each of the years after any claim for loss relief.

Solution

	31.12.2005	31.12.2006	31.12.2007	31.12.2008	31.12.2009
Income from trading	40,000	42,000	48,000	Loss	5,000
S83					(2,000)
extension	(8,000)	(42,000)			
					3,000
S64			(48,000)		
Net income	32,000	0	0	0	3,000

Loss Memorandum:-

		£
2008	Loss arising	100,000
2007	S64	(48,000)
2006	extension	(42,000)
2005	extension (to max £50,000)	(8,000)
2009	S83	(2,000)

2. Clyde has the following income and expenditure

	2006/07	2007/08	2008/09	2009/10
Operating profit before royalties	24,000	23,000	2,000	42,000
Patent royalty paid (trading expense): Amount paid net of basic rate tax	17,160	17,160	17,600	17,600
	IT @ 22%	IT @ 22%	IT @ 20%	IT @ 20%
Investment income				
Amount received net of 20% tax	4,800	4,800	4,800	4,800

Requirement: Show the assessments on income from trading in each of the years after any claim for loss relief.

Solution

	2006/07	2007/08	2008/09	2009/10
Operating profit	24,000	23,000	2,000	42,000
Patent royalty expense	(22,000)	(22,000)	(22,000)	(22,000)
Income from trading	2,000	1,000	Loss	20,000
S83				(11,000)
Extension	(2,000)	(1,000)		
	0	0		9,000
Income from investments	6,000	6,000	6,000	6,000
S64			(6,000)	
Net income	6,000	6,000	0	15,000

Loss memorandum

Loss 2008/09 (2,000 – 22,000)	20,000
2008/09 S64	(6,000)
2007/08 extension	(1,000)
2006/07 extension	(2,000)
2009/10 S83	(11,000)

3. Nathaniel started trading on 1 October 2007 and prepared to 31 December of each year from 2008.

His results for the first two accounting periods were: -

15 months to 31 December 2008	Loss 23,700
Year to 31 December 2009	Loss 19,320

Prior to becoming self -employed he had the following other income: -

2004/2005	12,200
2005/2006	12,500
2006/2007	12,800
6/4/2007 to 30/9/2007	6,900

Requirement: Calculate Nathaniel's net income for 2004/2005 to 2007/2008 using all available s72 claims

Solution

Losses eligible for s72 Relief

Year	Basis period	Workings	Loss	Years for s72 claim
2007/08	1.10.07- 5.4.08	23,700 x 6/15	9,480	04/05 – 06/07
2008/09	1.1.08-31.12.08	23,700 x 12/15 - 23700 x 3/15	14,220	05/06 – 07/08
2009/10	y/e 31.12.09		19,320	06/07 - 08/09

Using all possible s72 claims, total income is

		2004/05	2005/06	2006/07	2007/08
Income from trade					0
Other income		12,200	12,500	12,800	6,900
s 72 relief	2007/08 loss	9,480			
	2008/09 loss		12,500	1,720	
	2009/10 loss			11,080	6,900
Total income		2,520	0	0	0

c/fwd loss of 1,340 for year 2009/10

Questions without answers

1. Jensen started to trade on 6/4/2008. Results were:

    Year to 5 April

2009	Profit	24,000
2010 (projected)	Profit	32,000
2011 (projected)	Profit	36,000
2012 (projected)	Profit	30,000
2013 (projected)	Loss	(56,000)

Business is expected to be profitable thereafter

Jensen also has rental income of £12,000 per annum

Outline how Jensen could get relief for the loss

Calculate the quickest way of relieving the loss

How would the situation change if Jensen ceased trading on 5/4/2013?

2. Mister Y was employed as an auditor until 1/1/2009 and on that date started in business as a commodity dealer making up accounts to 30 June each year:

Income as auditor		Results as dealer (loss)	
2005/2006	20,000	1/1/09 to 30/6/09	(6,000)
2006/2007	22,000	Year to 30/6/10	(3,000)
2007/2008	24,000	Year to 30/6/11	(2,400)
2008/2009	22,000	Year to 30/6/12	nil

Requirement: Claim relief as soon as possible

3. A business ceased on 30 September 2010. Results were

Year to 31/12/2007	4,000
Year to 31/12/2008	800
Year to 31/12/2009	600
9 months to 30/9/2010	(3,900)
Overlap profits on commencement (unrelieved)	900

Requirement: Calculate the terminal loss and show how it is relieved.

15 Partnership taxation

Introduction

1. A partnership exists where two or more persons join together for business purposes forming an association which is not a separate legal entity for taxation purposes, unlike a limited liability partnership.

The main features of partnership taxation are discussed in relation to the allocation of profits, changes in partnerships losses, and limited liability partnerships.

General provisions

2. The following provisions apply to any new partnership.

   a) For income tax purposes a partnership of two or more individuals is not treated as a separate legal entity distinct from the partners. The effect of this is that each partner is assessed individually.

   b) A partnership tax return must be completed which shows for each partner the allocation of profits as it appears in his self assessment tax return.

   c) Taxable profits of the partnership are calculated in the same way as for a sole trader so that all partnership expenses and capital allowances will be given against the profits before allocation to the partners.

   d) Profits are assessed on a current year basis with the normal basis being the period of account ending in the year of assessment. The rules for determination of taxable profits in the first two and last year of the partnership are the same as for a sole trader noted in Chapter 12.

   e) Partnership profits are allocated by reference to the partnership rules applicable in the period of account and not the year of assessment.

   f) Where there is a change in the ownership of a partnership then providing that there is at least one partner carrying on the business both before and after the change then the change does not constitute a cessation for income tax purposes.

Adjustment and allocation of profits

3. The following points arise under this heading.

   a) Partnership profits are adjusted for income tax purposes using the same principles as for a sole trader. See Chapter 10. Partners' salaries and interest on capital paid to partners during the period of account are allocated to each partner individually and the balance of profit divided in profit-sharing ratios.

   b) The adjusted partnership profit is reduced by any capital allowances on partnership assets, before any allocation is made to the partners.

Example

A and B formed a partnership in June 2004, sharing profits equally after charging interest of 10% p.a. on their fixed capital accounts of £8,000 and £5,000 respectively, and a salary for A of £5,000. Taxable profits for the year ended 31st December 2009 were £15,000.

Show the allocation of profits for 2009/10.

Solution: Partnership computation 2009/10

Adjusted profits after capital allowances year to 31st December 2009 – £15,000

Allocation of profit 2009/10

	Total £	A £	B £
Interest on capital: 10%	1,300	800	500
Salary – A	5,000	5,000	–
	6,300	5,800	500
Balance shared equally	8,700	4,350	4,350
	15,000	10,150	4,850

Notes

i)   Each partner includes his share of profit, i.e. A. £10,150 B. £4,850 in his personal self assessment tax return, being earned income to be assessed in 2009/10.

ii) All amounts shown in the partnership accounts for the year to 31st December 2009, for partners' salaries, share of profits or interest on capital, will have been added back in arriving at the taxable profit of £15,000 as shown in the partnership tax return.

Example

A and B enter into partnership on the 1st June 2005 with the following results:

	Adjusted profits £	Capital allowances £
1.6.2005 – 31.5.2006	20,000	2,000
1.6.2006 – 31.5.2007	30,000	5,000
1.6.2007 – 31.5.2008	40,000	15,000
1.6.2008 – 31.5.2009	50,000	10,000

The partners have agreed to share profits equally.

Show the partners' taxable profits for the years of assessment.

Solution

	Partnership A and B		Assessments	
			A	B
2005/06	Period of account 1.6.05 – 5.4.06	15,189	7,594	7,595
	$\dfrac{308}{365} \times (20,000 - 2,000)$			
2006/07	Period of account 1.6.05 - 31.5.06 $(20,000 - 2,000)$	18,000	9,000	9,000
2007/08	Period of account 1.6.06 - 31.5.07 $(30,000 - 5,000)$	25,000	12,500	12,500
2008/09	Period of account 1.6.07 - 31.5.08 $(40,000 - 15,000)$	25,000	12,500	12,500
2009/10	Period of account 1.6.08– 31.5.09 $(50,000 - 10,000)$	40,000	20,000	20,000

Notes

- i) The overlap period is 1.6.05 to 5.4.06 with taxable profits of £7,594/7,595 for each partner. When the partnership ceases, or a partner leaves, then the individual's final assessment will incorporate the overlap relief attributable to his share of profits.

- ii) Assessments are raised on the individuals in the partnership and not the partnership although a partnership return must be completed.

- iii) Total profits assessed = £123,189 less overlap profits £15,189 = £108,000 actual profits after capital allowances.

Changes in partnership – notional trade

4. An outline of the rules is as follows.

   a) Any change of accounting date is to be ignored and assessments are to be issued as if there was no change unless all of the three under mentioned circumstances apply.

   i) The change is made in the second or third year of the business.

   ii) The account period involving the change < 18 months, the Inland Revenue are notified of the change by the 31st January flowing the end of the year of assessment in which it is made, and the accounting date has not been changed in the previous five years.

   iii) The accounting period involving the charge < 18 months, the Inland Revenue are notified as in (ii) above and the notice contains reasons for the change and the Inspector of Taxes is satisfied that it is being made for bona fide commercial reasons.

   b) There is a right of appeal against the Inspector's decision not to accept the change as being for commercial reason.

   c) Obtaining a tax advantage by such a change does not appear to be a valid commercial reason for a change.

   d) Where the conditions are met the new basis period will be defined by reference to the new accounting date:

Difference between end of preceding basis period and new accounting date		Basis period
1st year	< 12 months	12 months to new A/C date
1st year	> 12 months	Period to new A/C date
2nd year	—	12 months to new A/C date

   Profits for the period of overlap will need to be computed when a change of accounting date takes place.

   e) On a change of partners the rules are altered so that an automatic cessation or commencement will not arise, so far as the firm is concerned, on the admission, retirement or death of a partner.

   f) No election for a continuation is required and there is an automatic continuation of the established current year basis provided at least one person is common to the partnership before and after the changes.

   g) On a change of partners each partner is treated as having a separate share of the profits (a notional trade) determined at the point of admission to and retirement from the firm.

Example

X and Y started in partnership on 1st July 2001 sharing profits equally. Their accounts are made up to 31st December each year. On 1st January 2005 Z is admitted as an equal partner, the profit ratio then becoming one third each.

Profits for the years to 31st December 2005 are as follows:

	£
1.7.2002– 31.12.2002	20,000
12 months to 31.12.03	40,000
12 months to 31.12.04	50,000
12 months to 31.12.05	60,000

Solution

			X £	Y £	Z £
2002/03 1.7.02 – 31.12.02	20,000				
1.1.02 – 5.4.02 $\frac{90}{365}$ × 40,000	9,863	29,863	14,931	14,932	–
2003/04 12 months to 31.12.03		40,000	20,000	20,000	–
2003/05 12 months to 31.12.04		50,000	25,000	25,000	–
12 months to 31.12.05					
1.1.05 – 5.4.05 $\frac{95}{365}$ × 60,000 × $\frac{1}{3}$		5,205	–	–	5,205
	55,205	25,000	25,000	5,205	
			60,000	20,000	20,000
2005/06 12 months to 31.12.05		60,000	20,000	20,000	20,000

Notes

i) When Z is admitted on 1st January 2005, there is an automatic continuation.

ii) The partners are assessed individually in respect of their shares of the profits.

iii) On Z's admission he is deemed to have started in business on 1st January 2004 and his individual overlap profit must be computed on that date. This is as follows:

   1.1.05 – 5.4.05 = 95 days

   $\frac{95}{365}$ × 60,000 (i.e. profits to 31.12.2005) × $\frac{1}{3}$ = 5,205

iv) When a partner retires, his or her due proportion of the overlap profits is adjusted in his or her final assessment.

v) Total profits assessed of £185,068 – Overlap reliefs (9,863 + 5,205) = actual profits.

vi) Overlap X and Y = 9,863 : Z 5,205

vii) **Basis periods**

	X + Y		Z
2002/03	1.7.02 – 5.4.03		–
2003/04	1.1.03 – 31.12.03		–
2004/05	1.1 .04 – 31.12.04	1.1.05 – 5.4.05	
2005/06	1.1.05 – 31.12.05		1.1.05 – 31.12.05

Example

Using the data for X, Y and Z in the above example with the following additional results:

12 months to 31.12.06	80,000
12 months to 31.12.07	90,000
12 months to 31.12.08	100,000
12 months to 31.12.09	140,000

Z leaves the partnership on the 30th September 2008.

Solution

		Total	**X**	**Y**	**Z**
2006/07 to 31.12.06		80,000	26,667	26,667	26,666
2007/08 to 31.12.07		90,000	30,000	30,000	30,000
2008/09 to 31.12.87	1.1.07 – 30.9.08				
	$\dfrac{273}{365} \times 100,000 \times \dfrac{1}{3}$	74,795	24,932	24,932	24,931
	Less overlap relief				(5,205)
	2005/06 (supra)				
	1.10.08 – 31.12.08				
	$\dfrac{92}{365} \times 100,000 \times \dfrac{1}{2}$				
	100,000 – 74,795	25,205	12,603	12,602	–
2009/10 to 31.12.09		140,000	70,000	70,000	–

Notes

i) Z's assessment for the year 2008/09 comprises:

Proportion of profits from 1st January 2007 – 30th Sept 2008 =

Less overlap relief on commencement (see previous example)	5,205
	19,726

ii) There will be an automatic continuation on the retirement of Z.

iii) **Basis periods**

	X + Y + Z	**X + Y**	**Z**
2006/07	1.1.06 – 31.12.06		
2007/08	1.1.07 – 31.12.07		
2008/09	1.1.08 – 30.09.08	1.10.08 – 31.12.08	1.1.08 – 30.09.08
2009/10		1.1.09 – 31.12.09	

Partnership taxed and untaxed income – notional business

5. a) Where a partnership receives taxed income, it is apportioned among the partners according to their traditional profit entitlement (i.e. disregarding any partners' salaries or interest on capital), and is then to be taxed on a fiscal year basis.

    b) All untaxed income of the partnership, after duly being allocated to individual partners, is treated as coming from a 'second notional business'. This second notional business commences when an individual becomes a partner and is treated as permanently discontinued only when the individual ceases to be a partner. It is to be taxed by applying the same basis period rules – including the possibility of 'overlap' profits – as apply to the principle partnership trade profits.

c) Where a partnership receives rents from subletting business accommodation, these rents can be treated as income of the primary trade (instead of forming income of a second deemed trade) in the following circumstances:

   i) the accommodation must be temporarily surplus to current business requirements;

   ii) the premises must be used partly for the business and partly let, in other words, rents from a separate property which is wholly surplus must be dealt with as property income;

   iii) the rental income must be comparatively small;

   iv) the rents must be in respect of the letting of surplus business accommodation only and not of land.

Partnership losses

6. a) Partnership losses as computed for tax purposes are apportioned between the partners in the same proportion as they share profits.

   b) Where the business as a whole makes a profit as computed for tax purposes but after allocation of prior shares (e.g. salaries) an individual partner makes a loss then this cannot be used for normal loss claim relief.

   c) For tax purposes the allocation of profit (or losses) between partners must result in a straight apportionment of the actual profits (or losses) made by the partnership. If the initial allocation using the commercial profit sharing arrangement for all the partners produces a mixture of notional profits and losses, the actual partnership profit (or loss) must be re-allocated between the profit making (or loss making) partners alone. This re-allocation is made in proportion to the notional profit (or loss) initially allocated to those partners.

   d) The loss of each partner may be dealt with as follows:

      i) Set off against his other income. Section 64.

      ii) Carried forward against his share of future partnership profits. Section 83.

      iii) Set against profits of another business in which he is a partner. Section 64.

      iv) Used in a terminal loss claim. Section 89.

      v) Used in connection with the transfer of the partnership to a limited company. Section 86.

Example

X, Y and Z have been in partnership for many years with an accounting period to 31st December.

Profits are shared equally after the provision of salaries to X and Y of £5,000.

Adjusted profits for the year ended 31st December 2009 before salaries amounted to £7,000.

Show the allocation of profits for 2009/10.

Solution: X,Y,Z partnership allocation 2009/10

	Total	X	Y	Z
Salaries	10,000	5,000	5,000	–
Balance of profit (7,000 – 10,000)	(3,000)	(1,000)	(1,000)	(1,000)
Net allocation	7,000	4,000	4,000	(1,000)

However as Z has a notional loss the actual partnership profits must be re-allocated between the profit making partners

i.e. $\dfrac{4,000}{8,000}$ or $\times \dfrac{1}{2}$ each.

In effect, Z's notional loss is allocated to X and Y proportionately, i.e. £500 each

	Total	X	Y	Z
Partnership allocation as above	7,000	4,000	4,000	(1,000)
Re-allocation	–	(500)	(500)	1,000
Net allocation	7,000	3,500	3,500	–

Student self-testing question

Mars and Venus commenced in partnership on 1 July 2007 and decided to produce their accounts to 30 June annually. On 1 January 2009, Pluto joined the partnership.

The partnership's accounts show the following adjusted profits:

	£
Year ended 30 June 2008	10,000
Year ended 30 June 2009	13,500
Year ended 30 June 2010	18,000

Requirement: Show the amounts assessable on the individual partners for all the years affected by the above information, assuming that profits are shared equally.

(11 marks)

Solution

		Mars £	Venus £	Pluto £	TOTAL £
A/c to 30 June 2008		5,000	5,000	-	10,000
A/c to 30 June 2009	6/12	3,375	3,375	-	6,750
	6/12	2,250	2,250	2,250	6,750
		5,625	5,625	2,250	13,500
A/c to 30 June 2010		6,000	6,000	6,000	18,000

Mars and Venus will both be assessed:

2007/08	£5,000 x 9/12	£3,750
2008/09	A/c to 30 June 2008	£5,000
2009/10	A/c to 30 June 2009	£5,625
2010/11	A/c to 30 June 2010	£6,000

Overlap relief on £3,750.

Pluto will be assessed:

2008/09	£2,250 x 3/6		£1,125
2009/10		£2,250	
	£6,000 x 6/12	£3,000	£5,250
2010/11	A/c to 30 June 2010		£6,000
Overlap relief on:	£1,125		
	£3,000		
	£4,125		

Question without answer

Vera and Jack commenced in business on 1 October 2005 as hotel proprietors, sharing profits equally. On 1 October 2007 their son Terry joined the partnership and from that date each of the partners was entitled to one-third of the profits. The profits of the partnership adjusted for income tax, are:

Period ended	30 June 2006	£30,000
Year ended	30 June 2007	£45,000
Year ended	30 June 2008	£50,000
Year ended	30 June 2009	£60,000

Requirement

Calculate the assessable profits on each of the partners for all relevant years from 2005/2006 to 2009/10

Calculate the overlap profits for each of the partners. (4 marks)

16 Personal investment – pensions

Introduction

1.   This chapter is concerned with the provision of personal pensions for individuals in self employment and in employment. The stakeholder pension scheme is also outlined.

Pension regime

2.   The main features of the pension regime are:

a)   **Registration**

Existing approved pension schemes will be automatically registered with the IR but new ones seeking registration will have to provide information such as:

i)   a declaration that the scheme meets certain conditions; details of the scheme and the person establishing the scheme

ii)   administration and banking details for schemes which give relief at source.

Reporting requirements during the life of the scheme include:

the scheme ceasing to be eligible for registration;

changes to the scheme since it was registered;

transfers to overseas schemes;

schemes winding up;

unauthorised payments.

Tax relief will be allowed once registration is granted.

b)   **Contribution to registered schemes – individuals**

All registered schemes will accept contributions under the Relief at Source (RAS) rules, subject to two exceptions:

i)   For existing retirement annuity policies, the insurance company may for the time being continue to collect contributions on a gross basis.

ii)   Where an employer with an 'occupational pension scheme' operates the 'net pay' arrangements in respect of all scheme members.

From April 2006, partners and other profit remunerated individuals may become members of an occupational pension scheme, but the scheme would have to operate under the RAS rules for all of its members.

The maximum allowable contribution payable by a member for each tax year will be the greater of:

£3,600 gross; or

100 percent of 'relevant UK earnings'.

'Relevant UK earnings' are defined as:

income from employment;

income chargeable derived from the carrying on or exercise of a trade, profession or vocation (whether individually or as a partner acting personally in a partnership) and patent income; or

earnings of overseas Crown employees subject to UK tax.

Unearned income does not qualify as 'relevant UK earnings'. There is no earnings cap applied to 'relevant UK earnings'.

There will be no carry forward or carry back in respect of retirement annuity / personal pension contributions.

Where an individual receives income tax relief under the RAS rules, any higher rate relief will be claimed through their self assessment tax returns in the usual way, by extending the basic rate band.

c) **Contribution to registered schemes – employers**

There is no limit to the contributions that can be paid by an employer on behalf of a scheme member provided they meet the general rules on allowable deductions (eg trade expenses) and the annual allowance provisions. Employer contributions will only be allowed for relief in the employers accounting period in which they are paid.

d) **Annual allowance**

i) The maximum amount of contribution relievable for tax purposes has been fixed for the years to 2010/11 as below

	£
2009–10	245,000
2010–11	250,000

ii) The annual allowance includes both employee and employer contributions.

iii) Employees can contribute up to 100% of the pay towards a pension scheme within the annual allowance and obtain full tax relief.

iv) Contributions in excess of the annual allowance will be taxed at the 40% rate in the year of the excess.

e) **Lifetime allowance**

A lifetime allowance has been fixed for the years to 2010–2011 as below

	£ million
2009–10	1.75
2010–11	1.80

This is the amount against which the value of an individual's prospective pension benefits will be tested prior to the due date for payment.

f) **Exceeding allowances**

Employers contributions to a defined contribution scheme in excess of the annual allowance will be taxed as income of the employee at 40%.

Employers contributions to a defined benefit scheme in a year which increase the value of benefits by more than the lifetime allowance will also be taxed as income of the employee at 40%.

g) **Unapproved schemes**

Funded and unfunded unapproved retirement schemes are redundant under the new regime and will not receive registration, unless they meet the conditions required. Instead, they will be treated as employer-financial retirement benefit schemes, and will have no tax benefits. Entitlements to 6.4.2006 will be protected, but thereafter:

i) the employer's contributions will not receive tax relief until benefits are paid to the employee;

ii) investments and capital gains will be taxable at the rate applicable to trusts, ie 40% (32.5% on dividends);

iii) payments out of such schemes will be taxed at the individual's marginal rate.

Contributions to unapproved schemes will not count towards the annual allowance, nor will the fund accrued count towards the lifetime allowance.

Stakeholder pensions

3. These schemes are intended for employees who earn between £9,500 and £18,000, who generally are not covered by private or occupational schemes. However, stakeholder pensions are not limited to individuals in that earnings range. Employers must generally offer stakeholder pensions from October 2001. Unlike occupational pension schemes, the employer has no choice about whether to provide the scheme.

Stakeholder pension contributions attract a similar tax relief to occupational pension scheme contributions, though the administration is different. Broadly, the payments are made net of tax which the scheme recovers. This means that contributions are deducted from net pay rather than gross pay, as is the case for occupational pension scheme contributions. An employer of at least five employees must offer a stakeholder pension scheme to employees. However, an employer does not have to offer the scheme to an employee who:

is under 18 years old

is within five years of retirement age

is not resident in the UK

earns less than the lower earnings limit for National Insurance (NI) purposes

has less than three months' service.

Employees must be offered the chance to join a stakeholder pension scheme within three months of starting work. They cannot be compelled to join nor can they be a member of a salary-related occupational pension scheme and a stakeholder pension scheme at the same time. However, an employee may be a member of a stakeholder pension scheme at the same time as having a personal pension or being a member of a money purchase occupational pension scheme.

An employee must be allowed to:

choose his or her own level of contributions

vary those contributions at will

make one-off payments of £10 or more

stop and start making contributions at will, without penalty.

The contribution must always be at least £10.

A stakeholder pension scheme member may contribute up to £3,600 a year to the scheme, regardless of his or her earnings. This allows those with low expenses or high unearned income to benefit. The limit is increased if the statutory limit for pension contributions gives a higher figure. This limit depends on the age of the member at the beginning of the tax year and is calculated as a percentage of net relevant earnings.

Retirement annuity relief (RAR)/personal pension plan (PPP)

4.   Where the taxpayer has net relevant earnings available for relief under an existing retirement annuity contract or personal pension plan then the following should be considered:

   a)   Retirement annuity premiums take precedence over personal pension contributions in allocating relief.

   b)   If an individual has both types of contract then the aggregate relief is limited to the PPP relief.

   c)   If the maximum payable to a PPP plus unused relief brought forward is greater than the amount paid to an RAR contract then the difference can be paid to a PPP.

Early retirement ages

5.   The Inland Revenue may permit a retirement pension to commence before the annuitant's 50th birthday, if the individual's occupation is in one in which persons automatically retire before attaining the age of 50. The latest list issued by the OPB includes the following:

Boxers 35	Footballers 35	Skiers 30
Cricketers 40	Golfers 40	Jockeys (NH) 35
Tennis players 35	Jockeys (flat) 45	Cyclists 35

N.B Under the Pensions Act 2003 early retirements are to be scrapped from 2010. Also from that date it appears that no one will be able to take retirement benefits before the age of 55.

Student self-testing question

(a)   Cecile Grand has been a self-employed antiques dealer since 1992. Her income for 2008/2009 was as follows:

	£
Income from trading	38,400
Dividends (net)	4,860
Income from property	800

The income from property is for the period 6 April 2008 to 30 June 2008. During 2008/2009 Cecile paid a personal pension contribution of £2,800 (net amount paid to pension company). Cecile's husband died on 15 June 2007 and she has not remarried. Her forecast income for 2009/10 is as follows:

	£
Adjusted profit from trading	21,750
Dividends (net)	4,320

Due to the fall in profits, Cecile will not pay a personal pension contribution during 2009/10.

Requirement:

(i)   Calculate Cecile's payments on account and balancing payment or repayment for 2009/10. You should assume that Cecile does not make a claim to reduce her payments on account. **(10 marks)**

(ii) Based on the above figures, advise Cecile of the amount of the maximum claim that she could make to reduce her payments on account for 2009/10 (2 marks)

(b) Cecile's adjusted trading profit for 2009/10 is an estimated figure based on her provisional accounts for the year ended 31 March 2010. The actual figures will not be available until 31 August 2010 because of the difficulty that Cecile has in separating antiques acquired for business purposes, from those acquired for private purposes.

Requirement:

(i) Assuming that Cecile makes the maximum claim to reduce the payments on account for 2009/10 explain the tax implications if her actual taxable income for 2009/10 is higher than the estimated figure. **(2 marks)**

(ii) Advise Cecile of the powers that the Inland Revenue have with regard to enquiring into her tax return for 2009/10 **(2 marks)**

(iii) Briefly advise Cecile of the tax implications if the Inland Revenue enquire into her tax return for 2009/10, and decide that the income from trading for the year ended 31 March 2010 is understated. **(2 marks)**

(Total 18 marks)

Solution

(a) **(i)** Cecile's payment on account will be based on her income tax and Class 4 NIC for 2008/09 as follows:

	£
Income from trading	38,400
Income from property	800
Dividends (4,860 × 100/90)	5,400
	44,600
Personal allowance	(6,035)
Taxable income	38,565
33,165 @ 20% non savings	6,633
1,635 @ 10% dividends	163
34,800	
3,500 extend basic rate band @ 10% divs	350
265 @ 32.5% divs	86
38,565	7,232
Tax suffered at source - Dividends (5,400 at 10%)	540
	6,692
Class 4 NIC (38,400 − 5,435) at 8%	2,637
	£9,329
Payments on account due 31.1.2010 - 50%	4,664
Payments on account due 31.7.2010 - 50%	4,665

Cecile's actual **tax liability for 2009/10** is as follows:

	£	£
Income from trading		21,750
Dividends (4,320 × 100/90)		4,800
		26,550
Personal allowance		6,475
Taxable income		20,075
Income tax:		
n/a @ 10%		0
15,275 @ 20%		3,055
4,800 @ 10%		480
20,075		3,535
Tax suffered at source - Dividends (4,800 at 10%)		480
		3,055
Class 4 NIC (21,750 − 5,715) at 8%		1,282
		4,337
Paid on account		9,129
Balancing refund due 31.1.11		4,792

(ii) Cecile should therefore claim to reduce her payments on account by £4,992 (9,329 − 4,337) so that £2,168 will be due on 31 January 2010, and on 31 July 2010.

(b) (i) If Cecile's payments on account are too low, then she will be charged interest. This will run from the due dates of 31 January 2010 and 31 July 2010, up to the date of payment, which will presumably be 3I January 2011. A penalty will be charged if a claim to reduce payments on account is made fraudulently or negligently.

(ii) The Inland Revenue have the right to enquire into any tax return, provided they give written notice. Enquiries may be made by reference to information in the tax return, but they may also be made on a random basis. The time limit for giving notice of an enquiry for 2009/10 returns is 31 January 2012. An enquiry after that date can normally only be made where the taxpayer has been fraudulent or negligent.

(iii) Following the completion of an enquiry, the tax return would normally be amended by the taxpayer. The additional tax liability will be due 30 days from the date of the notice of amendment Interest will be charged on the additional tax liability from 31 January 2011 (the due date for the tax return) up to the date of payment. No surcharge will be due provided that the additional tax liability is paid within 28 days of the due date. A penalty will only be charged where a tax return is filed incorrectly due to fraud or negligence.

17 National Insurance contributions and social security

Introduction

1. National Insurance is planned to contribute £98bn out of a total UK tax revenue of £496bn for 2009/10. This chapter is concerned with National Insurance and some aspects of the Social Security system under the following main headings:

Classes of contribution	Statutory sick pay	Taxable state income
Gross pay	Statutory maternity pay	Non taxable state income
Directors	Tax Credits	Class 4 contributions
Class 1 A – cars and fuel		

Note The Contributions Agency which deals with National Insurance is a branch of the Inland Revenue.

Classes of contribution

2. The classes of contribution payable to the Contributions Agency are as follows:

Class 1 All employed earners and their employers

Class 1A Employers' contributions on benefits in kind

Class 1B PAYE settlement agreements

Class 2 Self-employed persons

Class 3 Non-employed persons

Class 4 Self-employed persons, additional contribution based on 'profits'.

All employed persons and their employers must pay Class 1 contributions the weekly rates for which apply from 6th April 2009 are given below.

An employed person is someone gainfully employed either under a contract of service, or as the holder of an office as defined for income tax purposes, e.g. a company director.

A self-employed person is liable for Class 2 and Class 4 contributions. The Class 2 contribution is a flat rate payable each week. The Class 4 contribution is payable as percentage of 'profits' as determined for income tax purposes.

Class 3 contributions are voluntary contributions payable weekly at a flat rate.

Employees must be aged 16 or over before any liability to National Insurance arises.

For persons over pensionable age (men 65; women 60) the position is as follows:

i) Primary contributions (employees' NIC) are not due on earnings paid after 65th birthday for men (60th for women)

ii) Secondary contributions (employers' NICS) continue as before.

Employers' Class 1A contributions applies to all taxable benefits in kind except:

i) where Class 1 National Insurance contributions are due

ii) those covered by a dispensation

iii) those included in a PAYE settlement

iv) those provided for employees earning less than £8,500 p.a.

v) those otherwise not required to be reported through the PIID return arrangements.

Gross pay

3. Gross pay for Class 1 National Insurance purposes includes:

> Wages/salaries
>
> Bonus payments
>
> Fees
>
> Overtime pay
>
> Petrol allowances unless charged to a company account
>
> Profit-related pay
>
> Telephone where bill paid by employer. Can be limited to rental and business calls
>
> Non-cash vouchers

In general most benefits in kind (e.g. car benefits and private health care) which are taxable under income from employment for directors and employees earning more than £8,500 p.a. are now included in gross pay for National Insurance purposes.

National Insurance contributions – gross pay

4. **Class 1 Employed earners from 6th April 2009 (2008)**

£ per week earnings	Not contracted-out	Contracted-out COSR	Contracted-out COMP
Employee			
Earnings up to £110 (£105) a week – ET	Nil	Nil	Nil
Earnings between £110(£105)and £844(£770)a week	11.0%	9.4%	9.4%
Earnings over £844 (£770) a week	1.0%	1.0%	1.0%
Employer			
Earnings up to £110 (£105) a week	Nil	Nil	Nil
Earnings between £110 (£105) and £844 (£770) a week	12.8%	9.1%	11.4%
Earnings over £844 (£770) a week	12.8%	12.8%	12.8%
Rebate on earnings between £95 (£90) and £110 (£105) a week	Nil	3.7%	1.4%

Notes

i) The employee's contributions are known as Primary Class 1 contributions.

The employer's contributions are known as Secondary Class 1 contributions.

41. Separate rates apply to employers who have contracted out of the State Earnings Related Pension scheme (SERPS).

42. COSR – contracted out salary related scheme.

43. COMP – contracted out money purchase scheme.

44. LEL – employees Lower Earnings Limit, p.a. £4,940 (£4,680).

The lower earnings limit must be recorded for the employees even when no national insurance contributions are due in order to protect entitlement to benefits such as Statutory Sick Pay and Maternity Pay.

45. ET – employees Earnings Threshold, p.a. £5,715 (£5,435).

46. Upper earnings limit p.a. £43,875 (£40,040).

The contracted out rates apply to employers who are members of approved occupational pension schemes where their employees have elected to be excluded from the state earnings related scheme.

Class 1A 12.8%.

Class 2	Weekly rate £2.40 (£2.30). No liability if earnings below £5,075 (£4,825) p.a. and a certificate of exception is obtained.
Class 3	Weekly rate £12.05 (£8.10).
Class 4	See below.

Directors

5. The earnings period for employees is usually the interval at which payments are made e.g. weekly or monthly. For directors their earnings period is annual whether they are paid weekly, monthly or at other intervals.

The following rules should be noted.

i) The earnings period runs from 6th April to the following 5th April.

ii) Directors appointed before 6th April have an annual earnings period even if they cease to be directors in the course of the year.

iii) Where a director is appointed after 6th April then the earnings period is pro-rated using a 52 week period for the whole tax year.

iv) For 2009/10 the lower earnings level is £5,715.

Example

A is a Director of K Ltd and receives a salary of £50,000 in 2009/10. Compute the primary and secondary NICS payable. The company has contracted out of the state earnings related pension scheme, and operates a salary-related scheme, i.e. COSR.

Solution: A National Insurance contribution 2009/10   COSR scheme

Primary contributions – employee

			£
ET	5,715	@ 0%	–
	38,160	@ 9.4%	3,587
	43,875		
	6,125	@ 1.0%	61
	50,000		3,648

Secondary contributions – employer

	5,715	@ 0%	–
	38,160	@ 9.1%	3,472
	43,875		3,472
	6,125	@ 12.8%	557
	50,000		4,029

Note

As the earnings have already exceeded the upper earnings level there will be a further primary contribution payable for the year of 1.0% on the excess.

Class 4 contributions

6. The following are the main features of this class of contribution.

a) Contributions are calculated and collected by the Inland Revenue together with any income tax due in respect of trade profits.

b) The Class 4 liability of a husband is calculated separately from that of his wife and is assessed independently.

c) Where a partnership exists then each partner's liability is calculated separately and an assessment raised in the partnership name, as for income tax.

d) The contributions are based on the trade profits as determined in accordance with chapter 11, with the following deductions:

  i) Capital allowances (balancing charges are added)

  ii) Loss relief under Sections 64,83,89,72, ITA 2007.

  iii) Annual payments not allowed in computing trade profits incurred wholly or exclusively for the purposes of trade.

Personal reliefs and personal pension payments are not deductible.

e) The rate of contribution is 8.0% of profits in between £5,715 and £43,875 for 2009/10, plus 1% on profits above £43,875.

f) For the purposes of calculating Class 4 profits, losses allowed under Section 64 are set against trade profits of the individual. Thus any loss allowed for income tax purposes against non-trading income, can be carried forward as a Class 4 loss.

g) Where the profits of farmers are averaged the revised amounts are used for Class 4 purposes.

h) Interest on late payment of Class 4 NICS will be charged at the prevailing rate of interest.

Where an individual is both employed and self-employed then Class 1 contributions will be paid on the employment earnings and Class 2 and Class 4 (if above the minimum level) on the self-employed earnings. As the employment earnings could in some cases also give rise to an additional Class 2 and 4 liability it is possible to apply for a deferment provided this is made before the beginning of the income tax year.

Example

X has been trading for many years with an accounting year end to the 30th June. He has the following data relating to the income tax year 2009/10:

	£
Trade profits to 30.6.2009	40,000
Capital allowances	2,965
Building society interest (net)	800

Calculate the income tax and Class 4 NI liabilities for 2009/10.

Solution: X income tax computation 2009/10

£		£
Income taxed as trade profits		40,000
Less capital allowances	2,965	37,035
Building society interest (gross)		1,000

			38,035
Personal allowance			6,475
Taxable income			31,560
Tax liability	n/a @ 10%		0
	30,560 @ 20%		6,112
	1,000 @ 20%		200
	31,560		6,312
Less income tax deducted from Building society interest		200	
Tax Payable			6,112

Class 4 NIC contributions payable	
Trade profits	40,000
Less capital allowances	2,965
	37,035
(£37,035 − 5,715) = 31,320 @ 8.0%	2,505

Class 1A NIC cars and fuel

7. a) Employers are liable to pay Class 1A National Insurance contributions in respect of:

    i) a car provided for certain directors and higher paid employees (£8,500 p.a. including benefits and expenses) where it is available for private use

    i) fuel provided for private use.

    j) and all other benefits noted under section 2.

    b) The rate at which Class 1A NICs are calculated is the highest secondary Class 1 NIC applicable to the year in which the benefit is charged.

        2009/10   12.8%

Payment of the Class 1A NICs is due on or before the 19th of June following the end of the income tax year to which they relate. If a quarterly basis for paying PAYE has been claimed the Class 1A NICs are due on or before the 19th July of the following income tax year.

Directors liable for company's contributions

8. Where a company has failed to pay NICs on time and the failure appears to be attributable to fraud or neglect by one or more individuals who were officers of the company (culpable officers), the outstanding NICs may be sought from the culpable officers.

Statutory sick pay

9. Employers are responsible for paying statutory sick pay (SSP) to their employees. In general the amounts paid are subsequently recouped from National Insurance contributions paid in respect of all employees.

A brief summary of the scheme, is as follows:

    a) SSP is payable for up to 28 weeks of sickness at the undermentioned rates:

Level	Average weekly earnings	Weekly rate of SSP
Standard	£95	£79.15

    All earning at least £95 will be entitled to the standard rate.

b)   The gross amount of sick pay paid is subject to income tax under the PAYE system and to National Insurance contributions.

c)   Employers can claim full reimbursement if and to the extent that their SSP payments for an income tax month exceed 13% of their gross Class 1 contribution liability for that month.

Both employers' and employees' contributions count but not the Class 1A.

d)   Where the SSP recoverable is greater than the NI contributions due for the income tax month, the balance may be dealt with as follows:

i)   Deducted from PAYE

ii)   Carried forward to the next payment period

iii)   Reclaimed from the collector of taxes by formal application.

e)   Earnings for SSP purposes are the same as those used for National Insurance purposes.

f)   To be eligible for SSP an employee must be incapable of work for at least four calendar days in a row, including Saturdays, Sundays and Bank Holidays.

g)   Any two periods of incapacity for work (PIWs) which are separated by a period of eight weeks (56 calendar days) or less are linked together for SSP purposes.

Statutory maternity pay (SMP)

10. 1)   A woman who has been continuously employed for at least 26 weeks continuing into the 15th qualifying week (QW) before the week when the birth is due is entitled to SMP.

2)   The SMP rates are as follows:

Employment $\geq$ 26 weeks before QW

– 6 weeks at 90% of average weekly earnings, followed by

– £123.06 per week or 90% of average weekly earnings, which ever is the lesser,

up to a total of 39 weeks paid maternity leave. A mother may then take further weeks unpaid leave, giving one year in total.

3)   SMP is subject to National Insurance contributions and income tax in the same way as wages and salaries.

4)   Small employers can recover the gross amount of SMP, plus 5%, i.e. 105% as compensation for the employers' NIC, other employers can recover 92%.

5)   Recovery of SMP is made by reduction from monthly income tax and National Insurance payable.

i)   'Small employer' is one whose gross Class 1 NIC for the preceding year did not exceed £45,000.

ii)   To qualify for SMP women must be earning at least the lower earnings limit of £95 per week for 2009/10.

Statutory paternity pay

A father may take 2 weeks paid paternity leave at the lower of 90% of average weekly earnings and £123.06 per week.

Child benefit

11. Child benefit is a social security benefit paid to the person primarily responsible for caring for a child. The rate is £20.00 a week for the eldest child and £13.20 a week for each subsequent child. Child benefit is not affected by the income of the carer.

Child tax credit

12. Child tax credit consists of a family element, a child element and a disability element:

Family element	–	£545 p.a. where income below £50,000
		Reduced by 6.67p for each £1.00 above £50,000
Child element	–	£2,085 p.a. per child where income below £16,040
		Reduced by 37p for each £1.00 above £16,040

CTC is quite separate from child benefit.

Working tax credit

13. Working tax credit is for people with low incomes from employment or self employment and who:

usually work 16 hours a week or more a week,

are paid for that work, and

expect to work for at least 4 weeks

and who are:

aged 16 or over and responsible for at least one child, or

aged 16 or over and disabled, or

aged 25 or over and usually work at least 30 hours a week, or

aged 50 or over and have recently started work after receiving certain benefits for at least 6 months.

There are several elements to the WTC, in addition to the basic element, such as lone parent, couples, 30 hour work period, disability element, 50 plus element and child care element. Clearly the amount of WTC received depends on a number of factors.

For both CTC and WTC the income referred to is pre tax income and includes:

employment income

income from self employment

investment income (gross)

state/other retirement pensions

trust income

foreign income.

Claims for child tax credit and working tax credit are made to the Tax Credits offices of HM Revenue and Customs using a return of income for the family, parent or carer of any children. This separate system operates in parallel to the self assessment tax return of an individual, meaning many taxpayers submit two returns of their income each year.

Social Security income taxed as income

14. Income support payments made to unemployed people or strikers

Non-contributory retirement pension	Retirement pension
Industrial death benefit	Incapacity benefit
Statutory maternity pay	Job seekers' allowance
Widow's pension	Bereavement allowance

Note Additions for children, housing and exceptional circumstances are excluded.

Social Security income which is not taxable

15. i) Short-term benefits
      Maternity allowance
      Sickness benefit

  ii) Benefits in respect of children
      Child benefit
      Child dependency additions paid with widow's pension, widowed mother's allowance, retirement pension or invalid care allowance
      Guardian's allowance
      One parent benefit

  iii) Industrial injury benefits
      Constant attendance allowance
      Industrial injuries disablement benefit
      Pneumoconiosis, byssinosis and miscellaneous disease benefits
      Workmen's compensation supplement

  iv) War disablement benefits
      Constant attendance allowance
      Disablement pension
      Severe disablement allowance

  v) Other benefits
      Attendance allowance
      Christmas bonus
      Council tax benefit
      Disability living allowance
      Family credit
      Housing benefit
      Income support generally
      Redundancy payment
      Social fund payments
      Vaccine damage (lump sum)
      War widow's or dependant's pension
      Bereavement payment (lump sum).

Minimum earnings

16.

		2008/09		2008/09	
		LEL	ET	LEL	ET
		£	£	£	£
National Insurance	Weekly	95	110	90	105
	Yearly	4,940	5,715	4,680	5,435

LEL = Lower earnings limit. ET = Earnings threshold.

Student self testing questions

1. William Wong is the finance director of Glossy Ltd. The company runs a publishing business. The following information is available for the tax year 2009–10:

(1) William is paid director's remuneration of £2,400 per month by Glossy Ltd.

(2) In addition to his director's remuneration, William received two bonus payments from Glossy Ltd during the tax year 2009–10. The first bonus of £22,000 was paid on 30 June 2009 and was in respect of the year ended

31 December 2008. William became entitled to this bonus on 15 March 2009. The second bonus of £37,000 was paid on 31 March 2010 and was in respect of the year ended 31 December 2009. William became entitled to this second bonus on 15 March 2010.

(3) From 6 April 2009 until 31 December 2009 William used his private motor car for business purposes. During this period William drove 12,000 miles in the performance of his duties for Glossy Ltd, for which the company paid an allowance of 30 pence per mile. The relevant Inland Revenue authorised mileage rates to be used as a basis of an expense claim are 40 pence per mile for the first 10,000 miles, and 25 pence per mile thereafter.

(4) From 1 January 2010 to 5 April 2010 Glossy Ltd provided William with a diesel powered company motor car with a list price of £46,000. The motor car cost Glossy Ltd £44,500, and it has an official CO_2 emission rate of 234 g/km. Glossy Ltd also provided William with fuel for his private journeys.

(5) William was unable to drive his motor car for two weeks during February 2010 because of an accident, so Glossy Ltd provided him with a chauffeur at a total cost of £1,800.

(6) Throughout the tax year 2009–10 Glossy Ltd provided William with a television for his personal use that had originally cost £3,825.

(7) Glossy Ltd has provided William with living accommodation since 1 January 2008. The property was purchased in 1996 for £90,000, and was valued at £210,000 on 1 January 2008. It has an annual value of £10,400.

(8) Glossy Ltd pays an annual insurance premium of £680 to cover William against any liabilities that might arise in relation to his directorship.

(9) During May 2009 William spent ten nights overseas on company business. Glossy Ltd paid him a daily allowance of £10 to cover the cost of personal expenses such as telephone calls to William's family.

(10) William pays an annual professional subscription of £450 to the Institute of Finance Directors, an Inland Revenue approved professional body, and a membership fee of £800 to a golf club. He uses the golf club to entertain clients of Glossy Ltd.

(11) William has not 'contracted out' of the state earnings related pension scheme.

Required:

(a) State the rules that determine when a bonus paid to a director is treated as being received for tax purposes.

(b) Calculate William's taxable income for the tax year 2009–10.   **(15 marks)**

(c) Calculate the total amount of both Class 1 and Class 1A national insurance contributions that will have been paid by William and Glossy Ltd in respect of William's earnings and benefits for the tax year 2009–10.

(d) Advise William of the forms that Glossy Ltd must provide to him following the end of the tax year 2009–10 in respect of his earnings and benefits for that year, and state the dates by which these forms have to be provided to him.

(25 marks)

ACCA December 2005 (updated)

Solution

(a)   The earliest of:

    (1)   The date that the bonus is paid.

    (2)   The date that entitlement to the bonus arises.

    (3)   The date when the bonus is credited in the company's accounts

    (4)   The end of the period of account if the bonus relates to that period, and has been determined before the end of the period.

    (5)   The date that the bonus is determined if the period of account it relates to has already ended.

(b)   William – Taxable income computation 2009–10

Director's remuneration	(2,400 x 12)	28,800
Bonus		37,000
		65,800
Benefits		
Car benefit	4,025	
Chauffeur	1,800	
Fuel benefit	1,478	
Television	(3,825 at 20%)	765	
Living accommodation		
– Annual value	10,400	
– Additional benefit	6,412	24,880
		90,680
Expenses		
Mileage allowance	900	
Professional subscription	450	1,350
		89,330
		6,475
		£82,855

(1) The first bonus of £22,000 will have been treated as being received during 2008–09.

(2) The relevant percentage for the car benefit is 37% (15% + 19% (230 – 135 = 95/5) + 3% charge for a diesel motor car), but this is restricted to the maximum of 35%.

(3) The motor car was only available for three months of 2009–10 so the benefit is £4,025 (46,000 x 35% x 3/12). The list price must be used even though a lesser amount was actually paid.

(4) The car benefit does not cover the cost of a chauffeur, so this is an additional benefit.

(5) The fuel benefit is £1,478 (16,900 x 35% x 3/12).

(6) The living accommodation cost in excess of £75,000 so there will be an additional benefit.

(7) Since the property was purchased more then six years before first being provided to William, the benefit is based on the market value of £210,000.

(8) The additional benefit is therefore £6,412 (210,000 – 75,000 = 135,000 at 4.75%).

(9) The provision of liability insurance does not give rise to a taxable benefit, nor does the payment of the overseas allowance since it is not above the de minimis limit of £10 per night.

(10) The mileage allowance received will be tax-free, and William can make the following expense claim:

10,000 miles at 40p	4,000	
2,000 miles at 25p	500	
	4,500	
Mileage allowance		
12,000 at 30p	3,600	
	£ 900	

(11) The golf club membership is not an allowable deduction despite being used to entertain customers.

(c) NIC

Employees Class 1	(43,875 – 5,715) =	38,160 @ 11%	£4,198
	(65,800 – 43,875)=	21,925 @ 11%	£219
Employers Class 1	(65,800 – 5715) =	60,085 @ 12.8%	£7,691
Employers Class 1A		24,880 @ 12.8%	£3,184

(d)

(1) Form P60 employee's certificate of pay, income tax and NIC must be given to William by 31 May 2010.

(2) A copy of form P11D detailing expense payments and benefits in kind must be given to William by 6 July 2010.

Questions without answers

1. You are required to calculate the National Insurance contributions payable for 2009/10 by both employer and employee in the following situations.

i) Sergio is employed at an annual salary of £52,000. He is paid weekly and is not contracted out of the state pension scheme. He was provided with a 1900cc company car costing £15,000 when new, on which the business mileage was 20,000. He had use of the same vehicle for the whole of 2009/10. It was two years old. Petrol for both business and private mileage is provided by his employer. CO_2 215g/km.

ii) Antoinette is employed at an annual salary of £10,400. She is paid weekly and is not contracted out of the state pension scheme.

2. Bartholomew has been employed by Telnet TV in central London for several years as a television producer. He is 45 years old and is not contracted out of the state pension scheme. On 1st January 2002 he was provided with a company flat which has an annual value of £5,000 and was let at an annual rental of £8,500 paid for by Telnet on a five-year tenancy from the same date. The occupation of the flat was not 'job-related'.

The following information is available for the year 2009/2010:

i) His salary is £52,000.

ii) On 31 May 2009 he received a bonus of £7,615 in respect of the company's year ended 31st March 2008. The bonus for the company's year ended 31st March 2008 paid on 31st May 2010 was £10,400.

iii) A bicycle costing £400 and cycle safety equipment costing £100 were provided for Bartholomew on 6th April 2009 and were to be used mainly for travel to and from work.

iv) Telnet had an approved non-contributory pension scheme to which Telnet contributed 5% of employees' basic salary.

v) Telnet paid an annual premium of £920 for permanent health insurance for Bartholomew which would provide him with an income in the event of his not being able to continue working due to sickness or ill-health.

vi) Telnet had negotiated group membership of a nearby gymnasium. Bartholomew availed himself of this benefit paying £350 per annum compared with a normal annual membership fee of £750.

vii) Telnet paid £7,000 for utility services, decorating and repairs for the flat.

viii) On 6 December 2008 Bartholomew purchased the furniture in the flat from Telnet for £12,500 when its market value was £15,000. The furniture had cost £40,000 when provided by Telnet on 6th April 2006.

You are required to calculate:

a. the amount of tax due by on Bartholomew for 2009/10, and

b. the amount of national insurance contributions payable by Bartholomew and by Telnet in respect of Bartholomew for 2009/10. (ACCA)

3. You should assume that today's date is 15 March 2009.

Ali Patel has been employed by Box plc since 1 January 2006, and is currently paid an annual salary of £26,000. On 6 April 2009 Ali is to be temporarily relocated for a period of twelve months from Box plc's head office to one of its branch offices. He has been offered two alternative remuneration packages:

First remuneration package

(1) Ali will continue to live near Box plc's head office, and will commute on a daily basis to the branch office using his private motor car.

(2) He will be paid additional salary of £500 per month.

(3) Box plc will pay Ali an allowance of 35 pence per mile for the 1,600 miles that Ali will drive each month commuting to the branch office.

The Inland Revenue authorised mileage rates are 40 pence per mile for the first 10,000 business miles driven each year, and 25 pence per mile thereafter. Ali's additional cost of commuting for 2009–10 will be £1,800.

Second remuneration package

(1) Box plc will provide Ali with rent-free living accommodation near the branch office.

(2) The property will be rented by Box plc at a cost of £800 per month. The annual value of the property is £4,600.

(3) Ali will rent out his main residence near Box plc's head office, and this will result in income from property of £6,000 for 2009–10.

Required:

(a) **Calculate Ali's income tax liability and Class 1 national insurance contributions for 2009–10, if he:**

  (i) Accepts the first remuneration package offered by Box plc;

  (ii) Accepts the second remuneration package offered by Box plc.

(b) **Advise Ali as to which remuneration package is the most beneficial from a financial perspective. Your answer should be supported by a calculation of the amount of income, net of income tax and Class 1 national insurance contributions, which he would receive for 2003–04 under each alternative.**

(4 marks)

(15 marks)

ACCA December 2004 (updated)

End of section questions without answers

1. What "corrective" taxes, if any, might you introduce in the UK at present?

2. Do you think parents should pay more or less tax than childless individuals?

3. Evaluate the advantages, disadvantages and feasibility of replacing the taxation of income by the following: a direct expenditure tax; an annual wealth tax.

4. For the purposes of this question you should assume that today's date is 15 March 2009.

    Carol Courier is employed by Quick-Speed plc as a delivery driver, and is paid a salary of £26,000. She contributes 5% of gross salary into Quick-Speed plc's Inland Revenue approved "contracted out" occupational pension scheme.

    As an alternative to being employed, Quick-Speed plc have offered Carol the opportunity to work for the company on a self-employed basis. The details of the proposed arrangement for the year ended 5 April 2010 are as follows:

    (1) Carol will commence being self-employed on 6 April 2009.

    (2) Her income from Quick-Speed plc is expected to be £38,000.

    (3) When not working for Quick-Speed plc, Carol will be allowed to work for other clients. Her income from this work is expected to be £4,500.

    (4) Carol will lease a delivery van from Quick-Speed plc, and 100% of the mileage will be for business purposes. The cost of leasing and running the delivery van will be £4,400.

    (5) When she is unavailable Carol will have to provide a replacement driver to deliver for Quick-Speed plc. This will cost her £2,800.

    (6) Carol will contribute the equivalent of £2,000 gross into a personal pension scheme during 2009-10. This will provide her with the same benefits as the occupational pension scheme provided by Quick-Speed plc.

    Required:

    (a) Assuming that Carol does not accept the offer from Quick-Speed plc and continues to be employed by the company, calculate her income tax and Class 1 NIC liability for 2009-10. **(5 marks)**

    (b) Assuming that Carol accepts the offer to work for Quick-Speed plc on a self-employed basis from 6 April 2009 onwards, calculate her income tax, Class 2 NIC and Class 4 NIC liability for 2009-10. **(6 marks)**

    (c) Advise Carol as to whether it will be beneficial to accept the offer to work for Quick-Speed plc on a self-employed basis. Your answer should be supported by a calculation of the amount by which Carol's income for 2009-10 (net of outgoings, income tax and NIC) will increase or decrease if she accepts the offer. **(4 marks)**

    (d) Critically comment on whether Carol would be considered an employee or self-employed under current Inland Revenue policy. **(5 marks)**

    (20 marks)

    ACCA December 2002 (updated)

5.   On 30 September 2009 Mark Kett ceased trading as a marketing consultant. He had been self-employed since 1 July 2000. On 1 October 2009 Mark commenced employment as the marketing manager of Sleep-Easy plc. The company runs a hotel. The following information is available for 2009-10:

Self-employment

(1)   Mark has tax adjusted trading profits of £57,600 for the year ended 30 June 2009, and profits of £17,400 for the three month period to 30 September 2009. These figures are before taking account of capital allowances.

(2)   The tax written down values for capital allowances purposes at 1 July 2008 are as follows:

	£
General pool	43,800
Car with CO_2 emissions 180 g/km	24,900

The expensive motor car is used by Mark, and 40% of the mileage is for private purposes.

(3)   On 15 August 2008 Mark purchased office furniture for £4,450. All of the items included in the general pool were sold for £43,200 on 30 September 2009. On the cessation of trading Mark personally retained the expensive motor car. Its value on 30 September 2009 was £15,400.

(4)   Mark has unused overlap profits brought forward of £9,800.

Employment

(1)   Mark is paid a salary of £6,250 per month by Sleep-Easy plc, from which income tax of £1,890 per month has been deducted under PAYE.

(2)   During the period from 1 October 2009 to 5 April 2010 Mark used his private motor car for business purposes. He drove 10,000 miles in the performance of his duties for Sleep-Easy plc, for which the company paid an allowance of 20 pence per mile.

(3)   On 1 October 2009 Sleep-Easy plc provided Mark with an interest free loan of £80,000 so that he could purchase a new main residence.

(4)   During the period from 1 October 2009 to 5 April 2010 Mark was provided with free meals in Sleep-Easy plc's staff canteen. The total cost of these meals to the company was £1,200.

Other information

(1)   During 2009-10 Mark received dividends of £2,880 (net).

(2)   Mark's payments on account of income tax in respect of 2009-10 totalled £24,400.

Required:

(a)   Calculate Mark's income tax assessment on profits from trading for 2009-10. You should prepare separate capital allowance computations for each period of account.   **(10 marks)**

(b)   Calculate the income tax payable by Mark for 2009-10, and the balancing payment or repayment that will be due for that tax year.   **(12 marks)**

(c)   Advise Mark as to how long he must retain the records used in preparing his tax return for 2009-10, and the potential consequences of not retaining the records for the required period.   **(3 marks)**

(25 marks)

ACCA December 2002 (updated)

6. On 31 December 2009 Foo Dee resigned as an employee of Gastronomic-Food plc. The company had employed her as a chef since 1999. On 1 January 2010 Foo commenced self-employment running her own restaurant, preparing accounts to 30 September. The following information is available for 2009–10:

Employment

(1) During the period 6 April 2009 to 31 December 2009 Foo's total gross salary from her employment with Gastronomic-Food plc was £38,000. Income tax of £8,609 was deducted from this figure under PAYE.

(2) Foo used her private motor car for both business and private purposes during the period from 6 April 2009 to 31 December 2009. She received no reimbursement from Gastronomic-Food plc for any of the expenditure incurred. Foo's total mileage during this period was 15,000 miles, made up as follows:

Normal daily travel between home and permanent workplace	4,650
Travel between home and permanent workplace in order to turn off a fire alarm	120
Travel between permanent workplace and Gastronomic-Food plc's suppliers	750
Travel between home and a temporary workplace for a period of two months	3,800
Private travel	5,680
	£15,000

The relevant HM Revenue & Customs authorised mileage rates to be used as the basis of any expense claim are 40 pence per mile for the first 10,000 miles, and 25 pence per mile thereafter.

(3) On 1 October 2009 Gastronomic-Food plc paid £12,900 towards Foo's removal expenses when she was permanently relocated to a different restaurant owned by the company. The £12,900 covered the cost of disposing of Foo's old property and of acquiring her new property.

(4) Foo contributed 6% of her gross salary of £38,000 into Gastronomic-Food plc's HM Revenue & Customs' approved occupational pension scheme.

Self-employment

(1) Foo's profit and loss account for her restaurant business for the nine-month period ended 30 September 2010 is as follows:

Gross profit		128,200
Depreciation	3,500	
Motor expenses (note 2)	4,200	
Property expenses (note 3)	12,800	
Other expenses (all allowable)	50,700	71,200
Net profit		£57,000

(2) During the period 1 January 2010 to 30 September 2010 Foo drove a total of 6,000 miles, of which 2,000 were for private journeys.

(3) Foo purchased her restaurant on 1 January 2010. She lives in a flat that is situated above the restaurant, and one-quarter of the total property expenses of £12,800 relate to this flat.

(4) On 1 January 2010 Foo purchased a motor car with CO_2 emissions of 140 g/km for £15,000 (see note 2 above) and equipment for £3,600.

Other income

(1)   During the tax year 2009–10 Foo received building society interest of £640 and dividends of £360. These were the actual cash amounts received.

Other information

(1)   Foo contributed £1,600 (net) into a personal pension scheme during the period 1 January 2010 to 5 April 2010.

(2)   She did not make any payments on account of income tax in respect of the tax year 2009–10.

Required:

(a)   **Calculate Foo's tax adjusted trading profit for the nine-month period ended 30 September 2010.**   **(6 marks)**

(b)   **(i) Calculate the income tax payable by Foo for the tax year 2009–10.**

(13 marks)

(ii) Calculate Foo's balancing payment for the tax year 2009–10 and her payments on account for the tax year 2010–11, stating the relevant due dates. (Ignore national insurance contributions.)   **(3 marks)**

(c)   **Advise Foo of the consequences of not making the balancing payment for the tax year 2009–10 until 31 May 2011.**(Assume the HMRC interest rate on late paid income tax is 3.5%)   **(3 marks)**

(25 marks)
ACCA December 2006 (updated)

7. Sue Macker was made redundant from her employment on 15 March 2009. She is a vintage motor car enthusiast, and so decided to take this opportunity to indulge her hobby.

On 6 April 2009 Sue took out a bank loan of £75,000 at an annual interest rate of 10%, rented a workshop for twelve months at a rent of £400 per month, and purchased equipment at a cost of £13,500.

On 10 April 2009 Sue purchased four dilapidated vintage motor cars for £8,000 each. The restoration of the four motor cars was completed on 10 March 2010 at a cost of £12,000 per motor car. Sue immediately sold all of the motor cars for a total of £200,000.

Sue was then offered employment elsewhere in the country commencing on 6 April 2010. She therefore sold the equipment for £5,800 on 20 March 2010, and repaid the bank loan on 5 April 2010.

Because she has just been indulging her hobby, Sue believes that the disposal of the vintage motor cars during the tax year 2009–10 should be exempt from tax. She has done some research on the Internet and has discovered that whether or not she is treated as carrying on a trade will be determined according to the six following 'badges of trade':

(1) The subject matter of the transaction.

(2) The length of ownership.

(3) Frequency of similar transactions.

(4) Work done on the property.

(5) Circumstances responsible for the realisation.

(6) Motive.

Sue had no other income during the tax year 2009–10 except as indicated above.

Required:

(a) Briefly explain the meaning of each of the six 'badges of trade' listed in the question. (You are not expected to quote from decided cases.) **(3 marks)**

(b) Briefly explain why Sue is likely to be treated as carrying on a trade in respect of her vintage motor car activities. **(3 marks)**

(c) Calculate Sue's income tax liability and her Class 2 and Class 4 national insurance contributions for the tax year 2009–10, if she is treated as carrying on a trade in respect of her vintage motor car activities. (You should ignore VAT.) **(7 marks)**

(d) Explain why it would be beneficial if Sue were instead treated as not carrying on a trade in respect of her vintage motor car activities. **(2 marks)**

(15 marks)

ACCA December 2005 (updated)

8. Tony Note

Tony Note is self-employed running a music shop. His profit and loss account for the year ended 5 April 2010 is as follows:

	£	£
Gross profit		198,000
Expenses		
Depreciation	2,640	
Motor expenses (note 1)	9,800	
Professional fees (note 2)	4,680	
Repairs and renewals (note 3)	670	
Travelling and entertaining (note 4)	4,630	
Wages and salaries (note 5)	77,200	
Other expenses (note 6)	78,780	
		178,400
Net profit		19,600

Note 1 – Motor expenses
During the year ended 5 April 2010 Tony drove a total of 20,000 miles, of which 2,500 were driven when he went on holiday to Europe. The balance of the mileage is 20% for private journeys and 80% for business journeys.

Note 2 – Professional fees
The figure for professional fees consists of £920 for accountancy, £620 for personal financial planning advice, £540 for debt collection, and £2,600 for fees in connection with an unsuccessful application for planning permission to enlarge Tony's freehold music shop.

Note 3 – Repairs and renewals
The figure for repairs and renewals consists of £270 for a replacement hard drive for the shop's computer, and £400 for a new printer for this computer.

Note 4 – Travelling and entertaining
The figure for travelling and entertaining consists of £3,680 for Tony's business travelling expenses, £480 for entertaining suppliers, and £470 for entertaining employees.

Note 5 – Wages and salaries
The figure for wages and salaries includes a salary of £16,000 paid to Tony's wife. She works in the music shop as a sales assistant. The other sales assistants doing the same job are paid a salary of £12,000 p.a.

Note 6 – Other expenses
The figure for other expenses includes £75 in respect of a wedding present to an employee, £710 for Tony's health club subscription, £60 for a donation to a political party, and £180 for a trade subscription to the Guild of Musical Instrument Retailers.

Note 7 – Use of office
Tony uses one of the six rooms in his private house as an office for when he works at home. The total running costs of the house for the year ended 5 April 2010 were £4,320.

Note 8 – Private telephone
Tony uses his private telephone to make business telephone calls. The total cost of the private telephone for the year ended 5 April 2010 was £680, and 25% of this related to business telephone calls. The cost of the private telephone is not included in the profit and loss account expenses of £178,400.

Note 9 – Goods for own use
During the year ended 5 April 2010 Tony took goods out of the music shop for his personal use without paying for them, and no entry has been made in the accounts to record this. The goods cost £600, and had a selling price of £950.

Note 10 – Plant and machinery
The tax written down values for capital allowances purposes at 6 April 2009 were as follows:

	£	
General pool	9,250	
Renault motor car	15,000	CO_2 emissions 150 g/km

The Renault car is used by Tony.

Required:

(a) Calculate Tony's tax adjusted trading profit for the year ended 5 April 2010.

(16 marks)

(b) Calculate Tony's income tax liability for the tax year 2009/10. (2 marks)

(18 marks)

ACCA June 2006 (updated)

Part III

Corporation Tax

18 General principles

Introduction

1. Corporation Tax is a direct tax on the income and capital gains of companies and other corporate bodies. It is planned to raise £35bn out of total UK tax revenues of £496bn in 2009/10. In this chapter the main elements of the corporation tax system are outlined. It begins with some basic expressions and then forms of organisation liable and exempt from corporation tax are examined followed by corporation tax self assessment. The remainder of the chapter deals with the corporation tax accounting periods, and the basic rates of tax. A summary of corporation tax rates and a specimen computation are provided at the end.

2. Corporation tax as a separate form of business taxation was introduced by the FA 1965. However, an entirely new set of rules for the determination of business income was not provided, and the substance of the income tax schedular system was adroitly preserved. The Schedular system was abolished for income tax purposes on 6.4.2005 and for corporation tax purposes this year on 1st April 2009.

Basic expressions

3. Financial year
A financial year runs from the 1st April to the following 31st March, and each year is known by reference to the calendar year in which the 1st April occurs. Thus the financial year 2009 covers the period from the 1st April 2009 to the 31st March 2010. Corporation tax rates are fixed by reference to financial years.

Franked investment income
When a UK resident company makes a qualifying distribution and the recipient is another UK resident company, then the amount of the distribution with the related tax credit is known as franked investment income, by the recipient.

Profits
This is defined by the Corporation Tax Act 2009. This includes income and chargeable gains.

Deductions and reliefs
This is the total of loans, charges on income paid, group relief etc. deducted from profits.

Profits chargeable to corporation tax
This is profits less deductions and reliefs.

Mainstream liability
This is not a legal term, but is generally taken to mean the amount of corporation tax payable, after any other deductions.

Close company
This is a company which is owned or controlled by a small number of persons. Private family companies often fall into this category.

Close investment holding company
This is a close company other than one whose business consists of trading or is a member of a trading group.

Group relief
This is the term used to describe the set-off of a trade loss of one member of a group of companies against the profits of another member. The relief is also extended to members of a consortium.

Basic profits

This is the term used in the computation of the small company marginal relief and is equal to profits chargeable to corporation tax.

Dividend payments

4. For dividend payments made there is a tax credit equivalent to a tax rate of 10% of the distribution plus the tax credit attached to each distribution. For shareholders the tax credit is non-repayable.

Main organisations liable to corporation tax

5. a) Companies resident in the UK, and this includes foreign owned companies operating in the UK through resident companies.

b) State owned corporations such as the Bank of England.

c) Unincorporated associations. These are not defined, but may be taken to include any form of club or society including voluntary associations.

d) A non-resident company. See 6 below.

e) Building societies, provident societies, and insurance companies. Special rules apply to these organisations.

f) Registered friendly societies. Exemption from corporation tax can be obtained in certain circumstances.

g) Company partnerships. If a company enters into a partnership then it is charged to corporation tax in respect of its due share of the partnership profits.

Non resident companies

6. a) A company not resident in the United Kingdom is within the charge to corporation tax if, and only if, it carries on a trade in the United Kingdom through a permanent establishment in the United Kingdom.

b) If it does so, it is chargeable to corporation tax, subject to any exceptions provided for by the Corporation Tax Acts, on all profits, wherever arising, that are attributable to its permanent establishment in the United Kingdom. These profits, and these only, are the company's 'chargeable profits' for the purposes of corporation tax.

c) For the purposes of the Tax Acts a company has a permanent establishment in a territory if, and only if –

    i) it has a fixed place of business there through which the business of the company is wholly or partly carried on, or

    ii) an agent acting on behalf of the company has and habitually exercises there authority to do business on behalf of the company.

d) A fixed place of business includes:

    a place of management;

    a branch;

    an office;

    a factory;

    a workshop;

    an installation or structure for the exploration of natural resources;

a mine, an oil or gas well, a quarry or any other place of extraction of natural resources;

a building site or construction or installation project.

Main organisations exempt from corporation tax

7. a) Partnerships.

   b) Local authorities.

   c) Approved pension schemes.

   d) Charities. A charity, which is defined as 'any body of persons or trust established for charitable purposes' is exempt from corporation tax in so far as the income is applied to charitable purposes only. If a charity carries on any trade then any profits arising will be exempt providing that:

      i)   they are applied solely for the purposes of the charity, and

      ii)   either the trade is exercised out of a primary purpose of the charity, or the work is mainly carried out by the beneficiaries of the charity.

   e) Agricultural and scientific societies.

   f) The British Museum, subject to certain restrictions.

   g) The Crown.

Self assessment – CT600

8. The main features of the corporation tax self assessment (CTSA) are as follow:

   a) the payment of tax and the filing of the company tax return are separate activities;

   b) the HMRC issues a notice (form CT603) requiring the company to deliver a company tax return CT600.

   c) the return must include:

      i)   a self assessment of the tax payable for the accounting period

      ii)   claims for allowances and reliefs

      iii) supplementary pages in respect of:

             loans to participators by close companies CT600A

             controlled foreign companies relief CT600B

             group and consortium relief CT600C

             additional details where the company is a charity CT600E

             insurance companies CT600D

      Financial statements and computations must also be filed with the CT600.

   d) the company tax return is to be filed before a specified filing date which is usually 12 months from the end of the accounting period;

   e) the company can amend its tax return by giving a notice in the prescribed form to the HMRC. This cannot normally be done more than 12 months after the filing date;

   f) the HMRC can amend the tax return to correct obvious errors or omissions. This cannot be done more than nine months after the filing date and the company may, if it wishes, reject the correction;

   g) interest is automatically payable on late paid tax or on underpayments of tax;

h) penalties are automatically due if the corporation tax return is filed late. There are flat-rate and tax-related penalties depending on the extent of the delay in filing the corporation tax return:

Period of delay (months)	Penalties
1 – 3	£100
3 – 6	£200
6 – 9	£200 + 10% of tax unpaid
9 –	£200 + 20% of tax unpaid

For repeated failures to return on the due dates the fixed rate penalties are increased to £500 and £1,000.

i) Penalties are also payable for an incorrect return made fraudulently or negligently, and also when a company discovers that a return is incorrect and does not remedy the error without unreasonable delay. In such a case there is a penalty of up to the difference between the tax actually payable and the tax which would be payable on the basis of the return actually delivered.

Payments on account – main rules

9. a) Large companies are required to make quarterly instalment payments of their corporation tax liability.

b) A company is considered large for a particular corporation tax accounting period (CTAP) if its corporation tax profits, including dividends from other companies (excluding group income dividends), is more than £1.5m.

c) If there are associated companies then the £1.5m is divided by the number of associated companies plus one. Thus a parent company with 4 subsidiaries has a CT profit level of $\dfrac{1,500,000}{5}$ i.e. £300,000 per company.

d) Companies that become large during a CTAP do not have to make instalment payments provided:

i) they were not a large company in the previous CTAP, and

ii) profits chargeable to CT for that CTAP do not exceed £10.0m, reduced where appropriate by the number of associated companies in the group.

e) No company is required to make instalment payments if its own corporation tax liability for the CTAP is less than £10,000.

f) Corporation tax is payable by large companies in four quarterly instalments based on their anticipated current year's profits as follows:

Instalment	Due date
1st	6 months + 14 days after start of CTAP
2nd	9 months + 14 days after start of CTAP
3rd	14 days after end of CTAP
4th	3 months + 14 days after end of CTAP

Thus a company with a 31st March year end pays instalments on 14th October, 14th January, 14th April and 14th July following the year end.

g)   100% of the CT liability is paid by four instalments of 25% each.

h)   Groups of companies are able to pay the instalments in one payment on behalf of the group.

i)   Late payments and over payments are subject to interest which is taxable/tax deductible for corporation tax purposes.

j)   Overseas subsidiary companies must be taken into consideration in determining the number of associates.

Notes

i)   Instalments are based on the expected corporation tax liability for the current accounting period.

ii)   The final payment of 25%, due 3 months after the end of the AP, would normally be the balance of CT due for the AP.

Repayment supplement

10.   Where a repayment of corporation tax or income tax of £100 or more is made more than 12 months after the material date the amount is increased by a supplement at the appropriate rate of interest for each complete tax month from the 'relevant date' to the end of the tax month in which the repayment is made.

Material date is the normal due date for payment of corporation tax i.e. nine months after the year end.

Relevant date is:

a) if the repayment is of corporation tax paid on or after the first anniversary of the material date – the anniversary of the material date that follows the date that tax was paid.

b) in any other case – the first anniversary of the material date.

c) The repayment supplement rate is 0% from 27th January 2009.

Financial years and accounting periods

11.   Corporation tax is charged on the profits of companies for financial years, and these run from the 1st April to the following 31st March. Each financial year is known by reference to the calendar year in which the 1st April occurs, e.g.:

Financial year	Period
2008	1st April 2008 – 31st March 2009
2009	1st April 2009 – 31st March 2010

The corporation tax rates for any financial year are normally determined in the relevant Finance Act.

Corporation tax accounting periods

12. a)   A corporation tax accounting period (CTAP) is the period for which a corporation tax liability has to be computed and this can never exceed 12 months' duration.

b)   A CTAP begins in the following circumstances:

i)   when a company comes within the scope of UK corporation tax – for example, by acquiring a source of income, starting business activities or becoming resident in the UK,

ii) immediately after the end of a previous accounting period provided the company remains within the scope of corporation tax.

c) A CTAP ends when the earliest of the following events occurs.

i) The company reaches its reporting 'year' end (i.e. its accounting date), or the end of a period for which it has not made up accounts.

ii) It is twelve months since the corporation tax accounting period began.

iii) The company starts or stops trading (an accounting period ends when trading starts or stops, even if other business activities continue).

iv) The company ceases to be within the scope of corporation tax (for example, by winding up its business and selling all its income-producing assets, or in the case of non-resident companies, by ceasing to trade in the UK or to carry on mineral exploration or exploitation activities in the UK sector of the North Sea).

v) The company goes into liquidation (once a company has gone into liquidation its corporation tax accounting periods run for consecutive periods of 12 months until the completion of the winding-up).

vi) The company starts or stops being resident in the UK.

Accounting periods more than 12 months long

13. If a company's period of account has to be split into two or more accounting periods, the profits must be allocated between the various accounting periods. The following rules are applied:

i) Trading income is computed for the whole period of account, **before** deducting capital allowances or adding balancing charges. This amount is then apportioned to the various accounting periods on a time basis. Capital allowances and balancing charges are calculated for each accounting period and the above amounts are adjusted accordingly.

ii) For all income the actual income for the accounting period must be ascertained.

iii) Chargeable gains are assessable in the accounting period in which they arise.

iv) Charges on income are deducted from the total profits of the accounting period in which they are paid.

v) Where the period of account exceeds twelve months, say 15 months, it will be split into two accounting periods, one of twelve months and one of three months.

vi) Surpluses and deficits on non-trade loan relationships (See chapter 19 para 8) are allocated to accounting periods on the same basis that they would be recognised in the company's financial accounts if they were drawn up for that same period.

Example

K Ltd has regularly prepared accounts to the 31st December. With effect from the 1st January 2009 the directors decide that the year end shall be 31st March and the next set of accounts covers the period of fifteen months to the 31st March 2010.

Corporation tax accounting periods	Accounts periods
12 months to 31st December 2008	12 months to 31st December 2008

12 months to 31st December 2009	} 15 months to 31st March 2010
3 months to 31st March 2010	
12 months to 31st March 2011	12 months to 31st March 2011

Note

There will be two return periods covering the 15-month period:

12 months to 31.12.2009, 3 months to 31.3.2010.

Notice of charge to corporation tax

14.   A company must give notice to HMRC of the beginning of its first AP which brings it into the charge to corporation tax. The notice which must be in writing must be given within three months of the beginning of the AP.

The basic rates

15. There are two rates of corporation tax, a small company rate and a full or standard rate. The level of profits subject to corporation tax determines which rate applies, and in addition there is a form of marginal relief which links the various levels.

There are special rules for the determination of profits for the purposes of the small company rate and these are examined in detail in *Chapter 24*.

i)   *Small company rates*

Financial years	CT small companies rate	
	%	Band
2005 to 31.3.2006	19	0 – 300,000
2006 to 31.3.2007	19	0 – 300,000
2007 to 31.3.2008	20	0 – 300,000
2008 to 31.3.2009	21	0 – 300,000
2009 to 31.3.2010	21	0 – 300,000

ii)   *Full rates*

Financial year	Profit level	%
2005 to 31.3.2006	1,500,000	30
2006 to 31.3.2007	1,500,000	30
2007 to 31.3.2008	1,500,000	30
2008 to 31.3.2009	1,500,000	28
2009 to 31.3.2010	1,500,000	28

Changes in the basic rate

16.   Where a company's accounting period does not coincide with the corporation tax financial year, and there is a change in the rate of corporation tax, then the profits must be apportioned between the two financial years on a time basis. The profits are deemed to accrue evenly over the accounting period even though this may not reflect the actual trading experience of the company. Any apportionment must be made by reference to the number of days in the respective periods. This was the case with the change in rates from FY 2007 to FY 2008. For FY 2009 the rates have remained the same as FY 2008.

Example

D Ltd whose accounting period ended on the 30th June 2008 had profits chargeable to corporation tax of £200,000. With a corporation tax rate of 21% for the financial year 2008 and a rate of 20% for 2007 the computation would be as follows:

Profits chargeable to corporation tax	£	£
1.7.2007 to 31.3.2008 $^{274}/_{365} \times 200,000$	150,137	
1.4.2008 to 30.6.2008 $^{91}/_{365} \times 200,000$	49,863	200,000
Corporation tax payable		
Financial year to 31.3.2008 150,137 @ 20%		30,027
Financial year to 31.3.2009 49,863 @ 21%		10,471
		40,498

The small company rate applies in this case, and the rates changed w.e.f. 1st April 2008.

Corporation tax rates

17. a)

	Financial Year		
Years to 31st March	**2008**	**2009**	**2010**
Full rate	30%	28%	28%
Small company rate	20%	21%	21%
Small company fraction	1/40	7/400	7/400
Small company profit levels			
Lower relevant amount	300,000	300,000	300,000
Higher relevant amount	1,500,000	1,500,000	1,500,000

Small companies formula

$$(M - P) \times \frac{I}{P} \times (\text{a fraction})$$

b) *Effective rates for financial year 2009*

0 – 300,000	21%
300,001 – 1,500,000	29.75%
1,500,001 –	28.0%

Specimen corporation tax computation (based on FORM CT 600)

		£	£
I	INCOME		
	Trading profits		
	Adjusted profits	–	
	Less capital allowances	–	
	Trade losses brought forward	–	–
	Profits and gains from non-trading loan relationships*		
			–
	Overseas income		–
	Other Income		–
	Income from which income tax has been deducted		–
	Non-trading gains on intangible fixed assets		–
	Income from UK land and buildings		–
	Chargeable gains		–
II	PROFITS		–
III	DEDUCTIONS SPECIFICALLY FROM NON-TRADE PROFITS		–
	Non-trade loan relationship deficit		–
IV	PROFITS BEFORE OTHER DEDUCTIONS AND RELIEFS		–
V	DEDUCTIONS AND RELIEFS	–	
	Losses on unquoted shares		
	Trading losses	–	
	Management expenses	–	
	Non-trade capital allowances	–	–
	Non-trade loan deficit		–
	Profit before charges and group relief		–
	Charges paid		–
	Group relief		–
VI	PROFITS CHARGEABLE TO CORPORATION TAX		–
VII	CORPORATION TAX CHARGEABLE		
	Financial year 2009 @ 28% (21%)		–
	2008 @ 28% (21%)		–
	Total corporation tax before reliefs and set-offs in terms of tax		–

VIII RELIEFS AND SET-OFFS IN TERMS OF TAX

Marginal small companies relief _____

Double taxation relief _____

IX   NET CORPORATION TAX CHARGEABLE _____

Income tax suffered by deduction _____

X CORPORATION TAX DUE _____

Note:

* that any non-trade loan deficits suffered would firstly be automatically netted against this income before they were taken to the non trade loan deficit lines at III or V.

Student self-testing questions

1. Tina Limited has PCTCT of £2,000,000 for the year ended 30 September 2009.

Requirement

Calculate the corporation tax liability for year ended 30 September 2009.

Answer

The tax rates did not change for the FY 2009, therefore no apportionment is necessary.

1/10/2008 to 30/9/2009 £2,000,000 @ 28%	=	£560,000
Total corporation tax liability for ye 30/9/2009	=	£560,000

2. Pirate Limited, a large company, has an estimated corporation tax liability of £700,000 for the year ended 31 March 2010. The company pays instalments in line with this estimate. The final assessment to corporation tax is £1,000,000 and the remaining payment was made on the final due date.

Requirement

Calculate each of the company's corporation tax instalments and state when they will be payable. Calculate each balance upon which interest on overdue tax will be calculated and state the periods over which this interest will be charged.

Answer

	Paid	Correct payment	Balance on which interest due	Period over which interest charged
	£	£	£	£
14 October 2009	175,000	250,000	75,000	14/10/09 - 14/12/10
14 January 2010	175,000	250,000	75,000	14/1/10 - 14/12/10
14 April 2010	175,000	250,000	75,000	14/4/10 - 14/12/10
14 July 2010	175,000	250,000	75,000	14/7/10 - 14/12/10
1 January 2011	300,000	0		

19 The charge to corporation tax

Introduction

1. This chapter is concerned with the determination of corporation tax profits before deductions and reliefs, which is an important stage in the determination of profits chargeable to corporation tax, as indicated by the equations below.

The chapter begins with some basic equations which identify the main components in the corporation tax computation. The main components of profits are then summarised and the chapter concludes with two comprehensive examples of the adjustment of profits for corporation tax purposes.

Basic equations

2. Any company which is resident in the UK is chargeable to corporation tax in respect of all its profits wherever they arise. In equation form profits may be defined as follows:

Profits chargeable to corporation tax	=	Profits – deductions and reliefs
Profits	=	Income derived under the Corporation Tax Act 2009 categories
		Income from which income tax is deducted at source
		Non-trading gains on Intangible FA Non-trade loan gains (net of non-trade loan deficits, not exceeding the gains)
		Chargeable gains
Deductions and reliefs	=	Non-trade loan deficit + trade losses etc.
		Charges paid + group relief

Generally accepted Accounting Principles

3. United Kingdom tax law requires that tax computations are prepared in accordance with generally accepted accounting practice. Generally accepted accounting practice is defined as being the accounting practice that is used in preparing accounts which are intended to give a 'true and fair' view (section 836A, Taxes Act 1988). The various financial reporting standards issued by the United Kingdom/International accounting bodies generally require that the relevant financial reporting standard needs to be applied to all transactions of a reporting entity whose financial statements are intended to give a true and fair view.

The schedular system

4. The schedular system is abolished for corporation tax purposes for the FY 2009. Income is to be computed and assessed under the following headings;

Trading profits

Profits and gains from non-trading loan relationships

Overseas income

Other Income

Income from which income tax has been deducted

Non-trading gains on intangible fixed assets

Income from UK land and buildings

Chargeable gains

Trading Profits

5. The following points should be noted under this heading.

a) The general principles of deductible expenditure apply, *see Chapter 10* but any items of expenditure which are charges on income *(see Chapter 21)* are not allowed as an expense in computing trading income. Profits and losses arising from non trade loan relationships are not treated as charges on income.

b) Petroleum revenue tax is a deductible expense for corporation tax purposes.

c) Incidental costs of obtaining loan finance including acceptance credits and convertible loan stock are allowed as a deduction in computing trading income. This would include such costs as fees, commissions, advertising and printing, but not stamp duty.

d) Pre-incorporation expenses incurred up to seven years prior to the actual commencement of trading may be treated as being incurred on the first day of trading. Eligible expenditure includes all expenses which, had the company been trading would have been allowed as a trading expense such as rent, rates, wages and salaries, but not company formation expenses, stamp duties, and capital expenditure.

e) Unpaid remuneration:

   i) A deduction for remuneration in the computation of trading profits will not be allowed where they are paid more than nine months after the end of the period of account. Instead a deduction will be allowed in the period of account when they are paid.

   ii) Payment in this case means the same time as used to determine when remuneration are received by a person. *See Chapter 7.*

   iii) Where accounts are submitted with computations within the nine month period, any unpaid remuneration at that time should not be deducted in calculating the taxable profits. If the remuneration is subsequently paid before the end of the nine month period, then an adjustment can be made to the computations, if claimed within two years of the end of the period of account.

f) The computation of trading profits is after taking into consideration capital allowances *(see Chapter 20)* and trade losses brought forward *(see Chapter 23)*.

g) A company's profits are computed without any deduction in respect of dividends or other distributions.

h) Amortisation of intangible fixed assets. See 9 below.

Research and development expenditure – 175% SMEs/130% large companies

6. For the tax year 2009 - 2010 the available reliefs for qualifying research and development expenditure are up to 175% for SME's and up to 130% for large companies. The following is an outline of the rules:

a) Rates of R&D tax relief   – 175% for small or medium sized companies

      – 130% for large companies

b) Minimum threshold level of expenditure– £10,000.

c)   A company's qualifying R&D expenditure is deductible in an accounting period if:

    i)   it is allowable as a deduction in computing for tax purposes the profits for that period of a trade carried on by the company, or

    ii)   it would have been allowable as such a deduction had the company, at the time the expenditure was incurred, been carrying on a trade consisting of the activities in respect of which it was incurred.

d)   'Qualifying R&D expenditure' of a company means expenditure that meets the following conditions:

    i)   The first condition is that the expenditure is not of a capital nature.

    ii)   The second condition is that the expenditure is attributable to relevant research and development directly undertaken by the company or on its behalf.

    iii)   The third condition is that the expenditure is incurred on staffing costs, or on consumable stores (including power, fuel, water, and software w.e.f 1.4.2004.) or is qualifying expenditure on sub-contracted research and development.

    iv)   The fourth condition is that any intellectual property created as a result of the research and development to which the expenditure is attributable is, or will be, vested in the company (whether alone or with other persons)

    v)   The fifth condition is that the expenditure is not incurred by the company in carrying on activities the carrying on of which is contracted out to the company by any person.

    vi)   The sixth condition is that the expenditure is not subsidised.

e)   Where:

    i)   a company is entitled to R&D tax relief for an accounting period,

    ii)   it is carrying on a trade in that period, and

    iii)   it has qualifying R&D expenditure that is allowable as a deduction in computing for tax purposes the profits of the trade for that period, it may (on making a claim) treat that qualifying R&D expenditure as if it were an amount equal to 175%/130% of the actual amount.

Interest Income

7. The income taxable under this heading is as follows.

a)   Profits and gains arising from non-trade loan relationships.

b)   Any annuity or other annual payment which:

    i)   is payable (whether inside or outside the UK and whether annual or short) in respect of anything other than a loan relationship; or

    ii)   is not a payment chargeable under income from property and land.

Bank and building society interest normally paid gross to a company are taxed under this heading. Should a company receive interest net, i.e. with 20% rate deducted at source, the gross amount is chargeable to corporation tax.

Interest is based on the amount receivable for the accounting period.

Where income is received after deduction of income tax at source, since the gross amount is chargeable to corporation tax, then the income tax deducted at source is recoverable as follows:

a)   It can be set against any income tax payable in respect of charges on income paid or a loan relationship, e.g. debenture or loan interest.

b) If relief is not fully available under (a) then any excess may be deducted from the main corporation tax liability, or if this is exceeded, a cash repayment may be obtained. However, the offset can only be effected where the interest is actually received.

Taxed investment income must be accounted for under what is known as the 'quarterly return system' as outlined in *Chapter 21*.

Loan relationships

8. a) In general a loan relationship exists whenever there is a creditor or debtor for a debt which is regarded as a loan under general law. Thus the issue of a loan or debenture would fall within this definition, as well as other financial securities.

b) The definition in (a) above encompasses practically all Government gilt-edged securities, building society PIBS (permanent interest-bearing shares), and corporate bonds and corporate debts. Bank interest received by a trading company is taxed as a non-trading credit.

c) To give effect to the new rules there are two methods of accounting which companies are authorised to use:

    i) an accruals basis by which payments and receipts are allocated to the accounting periods in which the transaction takes place;

    ii) a market-to-market basis by which a loan relationship must be accounted for in each accounting period at a fair value.

    As a general rule, companies are allowed to follow their accounts treatment for taxation purposes.

d) Where companies enter into a loan relationship for the purposes of a trade, then all profits, losses and costs relating to the loan relationship are treated as receipts or expenses of that trade and therefore included in the calculation of its trade profits or losses.

e) Where a company enters into a loan relationship which is of a non-trade nature, i.e. it is not a loan relationship in the course of activities forming an integral part of the trade, the position is as follows:

    I   Any net income is assessed as interest income.

    II   Any net loss is dealt with as below:

    i) by offset against the company's other income and gains chargeable to corporation tax for that accounting period; or

    ii) by surrender as group relief to other United Kingdom group companies. Losses can only be surrendered to the extent that these exceed the company's taxable profits for the period *before* taking account of reliefs from other periods (for example, brought forward losses); or

    iii) by carry back on a last in first out basis against the company's previous three years' net profits arising from its loan relationship to the extent that such profits arise on a company's non-trading foreign exchange and financial instrument transactions; or

    iv) by carry forward against its future non-trading profits (including capital gains). This treatment is also extended to losses arising from non-trading foreign exchange and financial instrument transactions.

f) The rules apply to all UK companies in charge to corporation tax, including UK branches of overseas companies.

g) A company issuing corporate debt is able to obtain tax relief for interest on an accruals basis provided the interest is paid within 12 months of the accounting year end.

Intangible fixed assets

9. a) Companies (but not unincorporated businesses) are able to obtain tax refief for the cost of intangible assets/ intellectual property, in most cases based on the amortisation charge in the accounts.

Intangible assets include:

i) patents, trade marks, registered designs, copyright or design rights;

ii) database rights, computers and software licences, know how;

iii) goodwill, excluding that arising on consolidation, from the purchase of shares.

b) Expenditure on intellectual property is any expenditure incurred on the acquisition, creation, maintenance, preservation or enhancement of that property. It includes abortive expenditure and expenditure on establishing and defending title to that property. It also includes royalties paid for the use of the intellectual property. Whether or not the expenditure would have been treated as capital expenditure under the old regime is irrelevant, except that capital expenditure on tangible assets is specifically excluded.

c) The system provides that a 'tax debit' (normally an item of tax deductible expenditure) in respect of intellectual property can arise in five ways:

i) as expenditure written off as it is incurred;

ii) as amortisation of capitalised intellectual property;

iii) as a write-down following an impairment review;

iv) as a reversal of a tax credit from a previous accounting period;

v) as losses on realisation of intellectual property.

d) A tax credit can arise on the following occasions:

i) receipts recognised in the profit and loss account as they accrue;

ii) revaluations of intellectual property;

iii) credits in respect of negative goodwill;

iv) reversal of a tax debit in previous accounting periods;

v) gains on realisation of intellectual property.

e) The rules only apply to assets created or acquired after the 31st March 2002. These assets are called chargeable intangible assets. All other IFAs held by a company on the 1st April 2002 called existing assets, continue to be dealt with under the existing rules (i.e. mainly on a CGT basis) so long as the assets remain in the hands of the same 'economic family'.

f) Where the IFAs are not held for trade purposes the taxable and relievable amounts are pooled to produce a net non trading gain or loss as other income or losses.

Corporate Venturing Scheme

10. A Corporate Venturing Scheme was introduced from 1 April 2000. Under the scheme, companies can obtain 20% corporation tax relief on amounts invested in new ordinary shares in small higher-risk trading companies which are held for at least three years. A gain on disposal of such an investment can be deferred where it is reinvested in another corporate venturing investment. A loss on disposal (net of the 20% relief) can be set against income.

A proportion of the investee company's ordinary share capital must be held by individuals. The proportion is 20%.

The investing company's maximum stake in the investee company is 30%. Only ordinary share capital, and share and loan capital capable of conversion into ordinary share capital, will count towards this limit.

Only investments in unquoted companies qualify for relief, but relief will not be withdrawn if the company later becomes quoted, provided there were no arrangements in place or planned, at the time the investment was made, for seeking a listing.

Relief will not be withdrawn merely because the investee company goes into receivership.

Property income

11. Companies are charged to tax on property income in a similar manner to that which already applies to individuals. The main features of the rules are as follows:

a) Rental income and expenses are computed on an accruals basis with a deduction for expenditure being wholly and exclusively incurred for letting business.

b) Furnished lettings, holiday and non-holiday, are taxed as income from property.

c) Overseas property income remain taxed as other income but computed as income from property.

d) Profits and losses on lettings are pooled as the business is to be taxed as a single letting business.

e) Relief for interest payable and for example differences on borrowings continues to be treated on an accruals basis in accordance with the loan relationship rules.

f) The company intangible asset regime does not apply to intangible assets that bundle rights over land or buildings (i.e. typically leases, but also options): these assets have their own tax rules (see below) which did not change in 2002.

g) Capital allowances are deducted as a business expense.

Rental losses after capital allowances are relieved in the same way as management expenses, i.e. against current period total profits, surrendered as group relief or carried forward.

Lease premiums

12. One way of looking at lease premiums is to regard them as a capitalised part of future rental income which would otherwise have been received by way of annual rent. They include any sum whether payable to the immediate or a superior landlord, arising in connection with the granting of a lease, but not arising from an assignment, of an existing lease.

Under an assignment the lessee takes the position of the original lessee, with the same terms and conditions.

Where a lease is granted (but not assigned) at a premium, for a period not exceeding 50 years, then the landlord is deemed to be in receipt of a rental income equal to the premium, less an allowance of 2% of the premium for each complete year of the lease remaining, excluding the first 12 month period.

Example

B Ltd granted a lease for 24 years of its warehouse to a trader on the following terms:

A lease premium of £12,000 to be paid on 1.1.2009 and an annual rent of £1,000;

Allowable expenditure for accounting period ended 31st December 2009 was £5,800.

Corporation Tax AP 31.12.2009

	£	£
Lease premium	12,000	
Less 2% × 12,000 × (24 – 1)		
i.e. 1/50 × 12,000 × 23	5,520	6,480
Annual rent	1,000	
7,480		
Less allowable expenses		5,800
Property income		1,680

In effect the lease premium is discounted by reference to its duration, and the longer the unexpired portion, the greater the discount. Thus if a lease had 49 years to run the discount would be

$$(49 - 1) \times 2\% \text{ i.e. } 96\%.$$

The amount of the taxable premium may also be determined by use of the formula:

$$P - \frac{(P \times Y)}{50}$$

P = amount of premium paid; Y = number of completed 12 months other than the first.

Lease premiums and the lessee

13. Where the lessee makes a payment of a lease premium on the granting of a lease, then a proportion of that premium may be set against the following:

a) any trading income, providing the premises are used for business purposes.

b) any rental income or lease premium received from any sub lease granted by the lessee.

In effect the amount of the premium assessed as income of the lessor can be charged as an expense of trading, the taxable portion being spread over the remaining life of the lease.

Example

S Ltd is granted a lease of premises to be used for trading purposes, for a period of 20 years at an annual rent of £6000 p.a. and an initial lease premium of £32,000.

	£
Lease premium	32,000
Less 2% ×32,000 × (20 – 1) i.e. 38% × 32,000	12,160
Lease premium charged on lessor	19,840

Relief available to S Ltd is $\frac{19840}{20}$ i.e. £992 p.a.

Overseas income

14. Income from overseas activities is not directly covered in this text.

Capital gains tax

15. Companies are not liable to capital gains tax as such, but they are liable to corporation tax on any chargeable gains which must be computed in accordance with the appropriate rules, as outlined in *Chapters 27 to 34*.

All chargeable gains are taxed at the relevant corporation tax rate which for FY 2009 is:

Company's profits > £1,500,000	28%
Small company profits < £300,000	21%

With marginal relief where appropriate.

Example

K Ltd has corporation tax trading profits of £1,500,000 for its accounting year ended 31st March 20010, and a chargeable gain of £500,000.

Compute the corporation tax payable.

Solution: K Ltd corporation tax computation. AP to 31.3.2010

Corporation tax trading profits	1,500,000
Chargeable gain	500,000
Profits chargeable to corporation tax	2,000,000
Corporation tax @ 28%	560,000

16 Example

S plc has the following results in respect of the year ended 31st March 2010.

Compute the adjusted profits for corporation tax purposes, ignore capital allowances.

		£	£
Sales			283,165
Factory cost of sales			127,333
Factory profit		155,832	
Expenses:	General administration	37,021	
	Marketing	28,197	
	Distribution	16,031	
	Financial	22,000	103,249
			52,583
Non-sales revenue		14,723	
Profit before tax		67,306	
Corporation tax		30,000	
Profit after tax		37,306	
Dividends paid and proposed			23,000
Retained profits for the year			14,306

Additional information:

Factory cost of sales includes:

Depreciation	17,832
Partitioning works office	3,179
Repairs to new premises to make usable	1,621

General expenses include:	Legal costs of tax appeal	627
	Legal costs of share issue	175
	Stamp duty – property	1,200
	Fines on employees, motor offences	250
Marketing expenses include:	Trade debts written off	1,211
	Loan to employee written off	250
	Increase in general bad debt provision	5,000
	Increase in specific bad debt provision	1,000
	Promotional gifts, £45 each	1,800
	Advertising on TV	6,000
Financial expenses include:	Bank interest	1,100
	Bank charges	238
	Donation to political party	250
	Subscriptions to trade associations	1,250
	Redundancy payments	11,000
Non-sales revenue comprises:	Profit on sale of assets	323
	Bad debts recovered	1,700
	Agency commission	12,700

Solution: S plc adjustment of profits. Accounting period to 31st March 2010

	£	£
Retained profits per accounts		14,306
Add back items disallowed:		
Factory cost of sales:		
Depreciation	17,832	
Partitioning	3,179	
Repairs	1,621	
General administration:		
Legal expenses	627	
Legal expenses	175	
Stamp duty – property	1,200	
Marketing expenses:		
Loan to employee	250	
Including general bad debt provision	5,000	
Financial expenses:		
Donation	250	
Corporation tax	30,000	
Dividends paid and proposed	23,000	83,134
		97,440
Less profit on sale of assets		323
Adjusted trading profits		97,117

Notes to answer

1. Applications of profit are not expenses incurred in the earning of profits and accordingly the dividends and corporation tax provision have been added back. It follows that it would have been possible to commence the computation with the profits before these items, i.e. £67,306, and this is the normal procedure.

2. Depreciation £17,832 – capital allowances claimed in lieu.

3. Partitioning £3,879 – plant and machinery, see Jarrold v Johnson & Sons 1962 40 TC 681.

4. Repairs £1,621 – see Law Shipping Co. Ltd, and Odeon Theatres Ltd cases.

5. Legal expenses £627 – expenses of tax appeal not allowed.

6. Legal expenses £175 – capital expenditure not revenue.

7. Stamp duty £1,200 – capital expenditure not revenue.

8. Loan to employee £250 – non-trading debt, see Bamford v A. TA Advertising.

9. Increase in general provision for bad debts £5,000.

10. Donation to political party £250 – not an expense of trading.

11. Profit on sale of assets £323 – this is not a taxable receipt.

Student self-testing question

1. T Ltd has the following for the year ended 30th June 2009

	£	£
Sales		160,000
Cost of sales		40,000
Gross profit		120,000
Wages and salaries	42,000	
Rent and rates	4,287	
Insurance and telephone	1,721	
Repairs and renewals	35,000	
Heating and lighting	2,897	
Professional charges	3,250	
Bank interest	1,155	
Subscriptions and donations	1,200	
Directors' emoluments	22,000	
Patent renewal fees	1,000	
Bad debts	1,250	
Sales commission	5,680	
Loss on sale of assets	1,000	
Miscellaneous expenses	7,251	129,691
Trading loss		(9,691)
Other income:		
Discounts received	1,123	
Exchange surplus	12,107	
Dividends received	1,620	
Rents received less outgoings	651	15,501
Trading profit before taxation		5,810

Additional information:

Repairs and renewals:

Repairs to newly acquired premises of which £10,000 was necessary to make usable	27,000
Furnace relining – provision for future expenditure	8,000

Professional charges:

Audit and accounting	1,250
Architect's fees for new factory	1,750
Legal costs for renewal of short lease	250

Subscriptions and donations:

Donation to golf club used by staff	500
Subscriptions to trade associations	150
Gift aid payment to charity	550

Directors' emoluments:

Salaries and bonus (bonus of £10,000 paid in May 2010)	18,000
Pension scheme provisions (paid 31.8.09)	4,000

Bad debts:

Trade debts written off	250
Increase in general provision	1,000

Office party	410
Theatre tickets for foreign customers	725
Removal expenses of new managing director	850
Compensation to customers for damage from company's product	5,000
Interest on overdue VAT	266

Exchange surplus:

Profit from currency dealings arising from trade	12,107

Rents received less outgoings:

Net rents from letting part of factory	1,000
Deficit on property let to retired employee at a nominal rent	(349)

Compute the trading profits for taxation purposes for the AP to 30th June 2009.

Solution: T Ltd accounting period to 30th June 2009

	£	£
Trading profit per accounts		5,810
Add items disallowed:		
Repairs and renewals	18,000	
Professional charges	1,750	
Donation to golf club	500	
Gift aid to charity	550	
Pension provision	4,000	
Bad debt provision	1,000	
Loss on sale of asset	1,000	
Theatre tickets	725	
Interest on overdue VAT	266	
Directors' remuneration – bonus	10,000	37,791
		43,601
Less dividends received	1,620	
Rents received	651	2,271
Trading profit for taxation purposes		41,330

Notes to answer

1. Repairs to make the premises usable are not allowable. £10,000. Round sum provisions are disallowed. £8,000.

2. Architect's fees for new factory are capital expenditure.

3. Donation to golf club, although used by staff, is not welfare or sports expenditure.

4. The gift aid to the charity is not allowed as a trading expense, but is deducted as a charge on income in the computation.

5. Pension contributions are not allowed unless paid in the AP.

6. The increase in the bad debt provision is not allowed.

7. Losses on the sales of fixed assets are not trading expenses.

8. The theatre tickets are disallowed entertaining expenses.

9. Interest on overdue VAT is not allowable.

10. Dividends received are not trading income, but 'franked investment income', which is not chargeable to corporation tax.

11 Rents received are taxable under income from land and property.

12. As the exchange surplus has arisen through trading it is taxable as a trading receipt.

13. *As the directors remuneration was paid more than nine months after the year end it is not allowed until CTAP 30.6.2010.*

Questions without answers

1. Z plc has the under mentioned results for the year ended 31st March 2010.

	£	£
Trading profits		1,900,000
3½% war loan interest (gross)	1,000	
Bank deposit interest(gross)	1,500	
Building society interest (gross)	700	3,200
		1,903,200
Less allowable expenses	50,000	
Director's remuneration	25,000	
Depreciation	8,000	83,000
Profit before tax		1,820,200

Compute the profits chargeable to corporation tax and the corporation tax payable.

2. Carrot Limited, a company resident in the United Kingdom, makes up accounts annually to 30 September. The information listed below relates to Carrot Ltd's twelve month accounting period ended 30 September 2009.

INCOME	£
Trading profit (adjusted for tax)	1,120,000
Rents receivable	40,000
Building Society interest	48,000
Capital gains	148,000

Requirement: Compute the PCTCT for Carrot Ltd.

3. P Ltd's accounts for the 12 months to 31st December 2009 showed the following:

	£		£
Wages and salaries	90,500	Gross trading profit	228,100
Rent, rates and insurance	6,000	Net rents	750
Motor expenses	2,000	Profit on sale of plant	5,500
Legal expenses	2,000		
Directors' remuneration	35,000		
Audit charges	2,500		
Miscellaneous	1,300		
Depreciations	6,000		
Amortisation of Goodwill	14,000		
Net profit	75,050		
	234,350		234,350

Notes

i) Legal expenses comprise:

	£
Debt collection	600
Staff service agreements	250
Issue of debentures	1,150
	2,000

ii) Miscellaneous expenses comprise:

		£
Subscriptions		
–	trade associations	150
	political party	290
Interest on unpaid VAT		150
Staff outing		710
		1,300

iii) On 1st January 2009 the company acquired the Goodwill of a business for £140,000 which it has decided to write off over 10 years.

iv) Capital allowances for the accounting period to 31.12.2009 have been agreed at £33,230 and are deductible in computing Case I trading income.

v) Gross trading profit is arrived at after deducting £50,000 paid in December 2009 under a threat of blackmail of the chief executive.

Calculate the liability to corporation tax for the AP to 31st December 2009.

4. Valerie Limited's accounts for the 12 months to 31 December 2009 showed the following:

	£		£
Wages & salaries	140,000	Gross trading profit	328,150
Rent, rates and insurance	6,000	Net rents	1,000
Motor expenses	4,000	Capital gain on sale of plant	2,500
Miscellaneous expenses	2,000		
Director's remuneration	40,000		
Bad debts	3,650		
Audit fee	2,000		
Depreciation	5,000		
Premium on lease written off	14,000		
Net profit	115,000		

Notes:

(1)   Miscellaneous expenses comprise:

	£
Staff outing	600
Penalty on underpayment of tax	400
Wine given to customers	1,000

(2)   On the 1st July 2009 Valerie Ltd was granted the lease of additional factory premises for a period of 7 years on payment of a premium of £14,000.

(3)   Bad debts expense account comprises the following:

	£
Specific provision	2,000
Loan to an employee written off	650
Increase in general provision	1,000

Requirement: Calculate PCTCT for the accounting period to 31 December 2009.

20 Capital allowances

Introduction

1. The nature of the capital allowance system, as described in Chapter 13 in connection with income tax and business income, is essentially the same for corporation tax purposes. For the tax year 2008 - 2009, as seen earlier for unincorporated businesses, a major revision to the capital allowance system was introduced. These changes are wide ranging and include abolishing the First Year Allowance and replacing it with an Annual Investment Allowance and reducing the Writing Down Allowance from 25% to 20%. Additionally there is a difference in computing the allowances where the accounting period exceeds 12 months' duration in the case of an incorporated entity. For the FY 2009 some further changes were introduced, as outlined earlier in Chapter 13, this includes the re-introduction of a temporary First Year Allowance of 40% in certain circumstances.

Main features to 31st March 2008

2. a) Capital allowances are available in respect of qualifying expenditure incurred in an accounting period, which is the basis period.

   b) Capital allowances are deducted as an expense in arriving at the Schedule D Case I trading income. A balancing charge is treated as trading income.

   c) The pool system for plant and machinery and other assets is the same for companies as for individuals, but there is no disallowance for private use of a company asset.

   d) A writing down allowance or FYA for plant and machinery can be disclaimed by a company.

   e) If capital allowances effectively create a trading loss then they are carried forward as an integral part of the Case I loss.

   f) Where the accounting period is greater or less than 12 months' duration then the capital allowances are computed for each separate period and not 'scaled up or down' as for income tax purposes.

   g) A first year allowance is available to a qualifying company at the following rates.

Expenditure incurred	%	
2.7.1998 – –	40%	
1.4.2004 – 31.3.2005	50%	(For small companies only)
1.4.2006 – 31.3.2007	50%	(For small companies only)
1.4.2007 – 31.3.2008	50%	(For small companies only)

   h) The qualifying conditions which a company must meet in order for it actually to qualify as small or medium sized in any financial year are expressed in terms of numerical criteria. A company satisfies the qualifying conditions in a financial year if it meets two or more of the criteria in that year (section 247 (3), Companies Act 1985). The criteria are as follows:

   Small company

a)	Turnover	$\leq$ £5.6m
b)	Balance sheet total	$\leq$ £2.8m
c)	Number of employees	$\leq$ 50

Medium sized company

a)	Turnover	≤£22.8
b)	Balance sheet total	□ £11.4m
c)	Number of employees	≤ 250

In the case of a company which is a member of a group of companies the requirements apply to the group as a whole, including overseas members.

These allowances are available for all sized companies

	%	
1.4.2001 –	100%	Energy saving plant and equipment
16.4.2002 –	100%	New low emission cars and equipment
1.4.2003 –	100%	Water saving plant

The new capital allowance system from 1st April 2008

3. Overview of the main changes:

a) Abolition of the Industrial Buildings Allowance and Agricultural Buildings Allowance phased over a period to 2011.

b) Abolition of First Year Allowances for small and medium enterprises at 40/50%.

c) Reduction of the Writing Down Allowance from 25% to 20%.

d) Introduction of a new 'Integral Features' allowance of 10% reducing balance. Integral features can broadly be defined as:

   i) electrical systems (including lighting systems);

   ii) cold water systems;

   ii) space or water heating systems, powered systems of ventilation, air cooling or air purification, and any floor or ceiling comprised in such systems;

   iv) lifts, escalators, and moving walkways;

   v) external solar shading; and

   vi) active facades

e) Introduction of a new Annual Investment Allowance (AIA) for corporations and groups of companies of up to a maximum of £50,000 per year.

f) These changes take effect from 1st April 2008 for incorporated entities.

Changes for FY 2009 effective from 1st April 2009

4. Overview of the main changes:

a) As outlined in Chapter 13, the basic capital allowance provisions relate to both incorporated and unincorporated entities. For the purposes of corporation tax, the changes are effective from 1st April 2009 as opposed to the start of the tax year, 6th April 2009, for unincorporated entities.

b) A temporary first year allowance of 40% available for one year is introduced for expenditure on general plant and machinery that would normally be allocated to the general pool when the AIA has already been utilised.

c) 100% First Year Allowance is available on low emissions cars producing 110 g/km or less CO_2.

d)   Capital allowances on other cars purchased from 1 April 2009 for companies will be:

i) a 20% Writing Down Allowance for cars with CO_2 emissions of 160 g/km or less;

ii) a 10% Writing Down Allowance for cars with CO_2 emissions of more than 160 g/km.

Example

K plc has the following data relating to its accounting period ended 31st March 2010.

	£
Trading profits for taxation purposes	1,865,550
Profit from land and property	173,200
Plant and machinery pool at 1.4.2009	88,000
Additions 1.8.2009 (non energy saving)	27,000

K's turnover is £40 million for the year ended 31st March 2010 and it employs 400 people with balance sheet total £20m.

Compute the capital allowances and the corporation tax liability for AP to 31st March 2010.

Solution

Capital allowances: plant and machinery

	Pool
	£
Written down value b/f	88,000
Writing down allowance @ 20%	(17,600)
Balance	70,400
Additions	27,000
AIA within £50,000 annual limit	(27,000)
	0
Written down value c/f	70,400

Corporation tax computation AP 31.3.2010

	£	£
Trading profits		1,865,550
Less capital allowances:		
Plant and machinery	44,600	
Trading profits		1,820,950
Profit from land and property		173,200
Profits chargeable to corporation tax		1,994,150
Corporation tax payable 1,994,150 @ 28%		558,362

Question without answer

1. Z Ltd has the following information relating to its accounting period for the 15 months to 30th April 2009. Prior to this date the company had always prepared accounts to the 31st January in each year.

		£
1.2.2008	Pool value of plant brought forward	5,800
11.3.2008	Machinery purchased	3,000
1.7.2008	Fixtures and fittings purchased	2,000
4.8.2008	Plant and machinery sold	2,800
10.2.2009	Plant and machinery sold	2,500
15.3.2009	Office equipment purchased	30,000
12.4.2009	Desktop computers purchased	20,000

Calculate the capital allowances available to Z Ltd for the two accounting periods to 30th April 2009. Assume Z Ltd meets the qualifying conditions for the FYA for small companies, where appropriate.

21 Charges on income/quarterly returns

Introduction

1. This chapter is concerned with the charges on income such as gift aid payments to a charity, and their treatment for corporation tax purposes. It begins with the definition of charges on income and the conditions which must be met if they are to be allowed as deductions where payments are made to both residents and non-residents.

The income tax aspects of charges and loan relationship interest and the manner in which such tax is collected form the remainder of the chapter.

2. Charges on income are allowed as a deduction in computing the profits chargeable to corporation tax for an accounting period. In equation form:

$$\text{Profits chargeable to corporation tax} = \text{Profits} - \text{Trading losses etc.} - \text{Charges on income} - \text{Group relief}$$

Charges are therefore deducted from total profits after trading losses etc. and before group relief.

Definition

3. Charges on income are defined to include:

a) qualifying donations to charities and gift aid payments (see below).

b) gifts of shares etc. to charity

Notes

i) Interest arising from loan relationships is not treated as a charge on income but as follows:
  trading interest – as an expense of trade
  non-trading interest – by way of loss relief. See Chapter 23, section 8.

A sum deductible in computing trading income cannot be a charge on income. See *Wilcock v Frigate Investments Ltd*, 1982 STC 198.

Gift aid payments

4. Payments made by a company to a charity are covered by the new Gift Aid Scheme. Under these rules:

i) The company does not deduct income tax at the basic rate when making the payment.

ii) The payment does not enter the quarterly CT61 scheme.

iii) The payment is treated as a charge on income.

iv) The charity recipient cannot recover any income tax in respect of the net amount it receives.

v) There is no limit on the amount payable by the company.

Qualifying donations

5. Companies (other than close companies) can treat as a charge on income gifts to a charity up to a maximum of $2^{1}/_{2}\%$ of dividends paid on ordinary share capital, during the companies' accounting period.

The above relief is in addition to any gifts made by way of gift aid payments.

Eligible deductions

6. To be eligible for deduction from profits the charges on income must comply with the following conditions.

a) They must be actually paid in the accounting period and not accrued except for a covenanted donation to a charity which is its parent.

b) The payments must be ultimately borne by the company making the payment.

c) They must be paid out of the company's profits brought into charge to corporation tax.

d) They must be made for valuable and sufficient considerations, except for covenanted donations to charity, and qualifying donations.

e) Income tax at the basic rate must be deducted at source from each payment, except for gift aid donations.

Adjustment to accounts

7. As the normal company accounts do not distinguish between charges on income and interest in arriving at profits before taxation it would be necessary to 'add back' some of the items for two reasons.

a) In the first place if they are charges on income then they are deducted from profits and not trading income.

b) Second, only charges actually paid in the accounting period are allowed, whereas for accounts purposes an element of accrual might have been made.

If the payments relate to an earlier accounting period, they are nevertheless allowed as a charge in the accounting period when the payments are made. Gift aid payments are classed as charges on income.

Collection of income tax on payments which are not distributions

8. The principles of the system for the collection of income tax are as follows.

Return periods

a) A company must make returns to the collector of taxes in respect of each of its accounting periods of *payments* (not accruals) subject to the deduction of income tax at source, and of income received not accrued which has been taxed at source.

b) The returns must be made for a quarter and the dates prescribed are 31st March, 30th June, 30th September, and 31st December. These are known as standard return periods, and if a company's accounting period does not coincide with any of the quarterly dates, then an additional return is required.

Income tax is deductible from the under mentioned payments at the rates shown.

	Basic rate 20%	Lower rate 20%
Yearly interest (to an individual)	–	✓
Interest paid by banks/building societies	–	✓
Income element of purchased life annuities	–	✓
Rents paid to non-UK residents	✓	–
Patent royalties (except to exempt bodies)	✓	–
Gift aid payments	–	–
Inter company interest payments	–	–

Note

Inter company payments of interest, royalties, annual payments and annuities are made gross where the recipient company is within charge to corporation tax.

Example

S Ltd has an accounting year ending on the 30th November 2009. The return periods relating to that accounting period are as follows:

2008	1st December to 31st December
2009	1st January to 31st March
	1st April to 30th June
	1st July to 30th September
	1st October to 30th November

The company here has five return periods and each return must be submitted within fourteen days of the end of the return period. If there are no transactions in the period a nil return is not required.

c) The return forms must show particulars of *payments made in the period*, and income tax deducted is due on the return date without the making of any formal assessment. Particulars of any unfranked investment income, including building society interest, must also be included on the returns, and any income tax suffered at source is set against that due on any annual payments paid.

The position at the end of a return period

9. a) If the income tax payable exceeds the income tax suffered, the balance may be set against any suffered from earlier return periods, within the company's accounting period.

b) In the absence of any excess as in (a) above, then the net amount is payable on the due date.

c) Where the income tax suffered at source is greater than the income tax payable on the charges on income, then the surplus may be carried back and set against any excess of income tax paid in return periods within the company's accounting period.

Example

F Ltd has an accounting period ended 31st March 2010 and during the year the following transactions took place.

2009	April 11th	Debenture interest paid – individuals	8,000
	June 30th	Interest received Net	4,000
	August 7th	Bank interest paid	12,000
	October 11th	Debenture interest paid – individuals	8,000
2010	January 1st	Interest received Net	4,000

All transactions are shown net as entered in the company's bank account.

Show the quarterly returns for the year to 31st March 2010.

Solution

Quarter	Income tax on annual payments and interest		Income tax deducted		Net amount
	Gross amount	Income tax	Gross amount	Income tax	Paid (received)
£	£	£	£	£	
30.6.09	10,000	2,000	5,000	1,000	1,000
30.9.09	–	–	–	–	–
31.12.09	10,000	2,000	–	–	2,000
31.3.10	–	–	5,000	1,000	(1,000)
20,000	(4,000)	10,000	2,000	2,000	

Notes

i) In the fourth quarter, the excess of income tax suffered can be set against the payment made in quarter 1 or 3.

ii) Bank interest paid is not subject to deduction of income tax and is, therefore, excluded from the return system.

iii) Interest paid and received is taxed at the 20% rate.

The position at the end of an accounting period

10. This may be summarised as follows.

Income tax deducted from income received net > income tax paid on annual payments and interest.

a) i) Excess can be set against corporation tax payable on the profits of the accounting period.

   ii) If the excess is greater than the corporation tax payable then a cash repayment can be obtained.

b) Income tax deducted from income received net < income tax paid on annual payments and interest.

   i) In this case since the excess has already been paid over within the quarterly return system, no further adjustment is necessary.

Example

B Ltd has an accounting period ended 31st March 2010 and during that year, the following transactions took place, all net.

2009	June 10	Interest on unsecured loan stock paid – individuals	1,600
	July 19	Interest received Net	2,000
	August 31	Building society interest received (gross)	2,500
	December 10	Interest on unsecured loan stock paid – individuals	1,600
2010	January 19	Interest received Net	2,000

The adjusted trading profits for the year ended 31st March 2010 amounted to £1,795,300 before any adjustment for loan interest paid. The unsecured loan interest is used for trade purposes. Property income in respect of the same period was £1,200.

Show the quarterly returns for the year to 31st March 2010 and the corporation tax computation for the same period.

Solution

Quarter	Income tax on annual payments and interest		Income tax deducted		Net amount	
	Gross	Income amount	Gross tax	Income amount	Paid tax	Excess (received)
	£	£	£	£	£	£
30.6.09	2,000	400	–	–	400	–
30.9.09	–	–	2,500	500	(500)	(100)
31.12.09	2,000	400	–	–	400	–
31.3.10	–	–	2,500	500	(500)	(100)
	4,000	800	5,000	1,000	–	(200)

Corporation tax computation AP to 31.3.2010

	£
Trading profits (1,795,300 – 4,000)	1,791,300
Property income	1,200
Income taxed at source	5,000
Building society interest	2,500
Profit chargeable to corporation tax	1,800,000
Corporation tax @ 28%	504,000
Less excess income tax as above	200
	503,800

Notes

i. Unsecured loan interest is a deduction for trading profit purposes, as it was used for trade purposes.

ii. As there was an excess of taxed income suffered, the income tax unrecovered is set against the corporation tax payable. From a cash flow point of view, the benefit will not be felt until the corporation tax becomes payable.

Excess charges

11. It should perhaps be noted here that as charges on income are deducted from total corporation tax profits situations can arise where the charges are greater than the total profits. The excess charges give rise to a claim for loss relief and this is examined in *Chapter 23, Relief for losses.*

Student self-testing question

K Ltd has the following data relating to its accounting period ended 31st March 2010.

	£
Trading profits	1,548,000
Building society interest (gross)	2,000
Bank interest received (gross)	10,000
Gift aid payment (net)	40,000
Debenture interest (gross) on trade loan	20,000

Compute the corporation tax payable for the AP to 31st March 2010.

Solution

Corporation tax computation AP to 31.3.2010

	£
Trading profits	1,528,000
Bank interest gross	10,000
Building society interest gross	2,000
	1,540,000

Charges on income paid

Gift aid payment (net)	40,000
Profits chargeable to corporation tax	1,500,000

Corporation tax payable	
1,500,000 @ 28%	420,000
Mainstream liability	420,000

Notes

i) Trading profits	1,548,000	
Less debenture interest trade (gross)	20,000	1,528,000

ii) The gift aid donation is not subject to deduction of basic rate income tax at source.

Questions without answers

1. P plc has the following entries in its cash book for the year ended 31st December 2009.

Cash book

	£			£
Jan 1 Dividend from UK company	800	Feb 1	Proposed final dividend for 2008	10,000
31 UK company interest (gross)	20,000	Mar 1	Debenture interest – individuals	16,000
Mar 1 Dividend from UK company	20,000	Sept 1	Debenture interest – individuals	16,000
31 Building society interest (gross)	2,250			
June 30 Bank deposit interest	12,000			
July 31 UK company interest (gross)	25,000			
Dec 31 Bank interest	5,180			

Adjusted trading profits for the year amounted to £1,600,000 (excluding the cash book entries) and property income £62,820.

Compute the profits charged to corporation tax for the year to 31st December 2009.

Assume bank interest is for trade purposes.

2. Stonyhurst Limited is a trading company, resident in the United Kingdom, which makes up its annual accounts to 31 March. It has no associated companies. The company's profit and loss account for the year ended 31 March 2010 was as follows:

	£	£
Gross trading profit		372,100
1. Add: surplus on sale of plant etc.	17,150	
Debenture interest (gross) UK company	3,250	
Dividends received from UK companies (net)	4,570	
Building society interest received (gross)	730	
2. Bank deposit interest	360	26,060
		398,160
Deduct:		
Lighting and heating	1,290	
Repairs and renewals	1,600	
3. Depreciation 34,650		
Wages and salaries	24,450	
Directors' remuneration	35,480	
4. Subscriptions and donations	1,350	
Postage, stationery and phone	525	
5. Loan interest payable	17,500	
6. Professional expenses	6,820	
7. Miscellaneous expenses	1,815	125,480
Net profit		272,680

Notes

1. Subscriptions and donations

	£
Golf club subscription for sales director (P11D)	150
National Trust	50
Political party	300
Local charities	75
Works social club	750
Trade association	25
	1,350

2. Loan interest

There was an accrued liability at 31 March 2010 for loan interest of £1,500. There was no opening accrual.

3. Professional expenses

	£
Audit and accountancy	3,000
Costs of successful tax appeal	500
Legal fees re collection of bad debts	180
Costs of defending action by a former director for wrongful dismissal	300
Legal costs on acquisition of a new seven-year lease on a warehouse	500
Architect's fees for designing a new warehouse which was not proceeded with	2,340
	6,820

4.   Miscellaneous expenses

Entertaining

–foreign suppliers	70
– UK suppliers	340
– UK customers	180
Round-sum expense allowances to company salesmen	1,225
	1,815

5. You are also given the following information.

a)   The company paid a dividend of £18,000 to its shareholders on 13 March 2010.

b)   The written down values of capital assets at 1 April 2009 were:

	£
Plant and machinery (main pool)	82,563
Car no. 1 CO2 150g/km(purchased 1.1.06)	8,598
Car no. 2 CO2 155g/km(purchased 1.1.06)	10,520

The following items were purchased and sold during the year ended 31 March 2010.

Purchases		£
11 August 2009	Car for salesman CO2 140g/km	6,500
23 October 2009		
Moveable office partitioning		3,518
7 March 2010	Plant and machinery	42,500
28 March 2010	Plant and machinery	17,192
Sales		£
19 April 2009	Plant and machinery	31,000
29 July 2009	Car no. 2	7,500
11 August 2009	Car (purchased on 13 August 2005 for £4,500)	2,150

Notes

i)   The private usage of the salesman's car is one-quarter.

ii)   The company's offices do not qualify for industrial buildings' allowances.

Compute the profits chargeable to corporation tax for the year ended 31st March 2010.

3. Unbeatable Undercarriages Limited (UUL) is a United Kingdom resident company which has been trading for many years and manufactures aircraft components. It has no associated companies. The company had always made up accounts to 31 December. The company's results for the year ended 31 December 2009 are as follows:

	£
Trading profits (as adjusted for taxation but before capital allowances and loan interest)	1,300,000
Payment under gift aid to a national charity (gross amount)	
Loan interest payable on trade loan (gross amount) (notes 3 and 5)	
Bank interest receivable - non trading relationship (note 4)	7,000
Dividends received from UK companies in June 2009	50,000

Notes:

1.   On 1 January 2009 the tax written-down values of plant and machinery were:

     £

     Pool   105,000

     On 1 August 2009 a car was sold for £7,000 and replaced by one costing £14,000 with CO_2 of 170g/km.

2.   The company had purchased a new industrial building on 1 July 2001 for immediate use for £200,000. On 31 May 2009 the building was sold for £400,000. The building was not situated in an Enterprise Zone. The chargeable gain on disposal of the building was £145,600.

3.   Included on the figure of £10,000 for loan interest payable is a closing accrual of £2,000. The £8,000 was paid on 1 July 2009. The loan was taken out in 2008.

4.   Included in the figure of £7,000 for bank interest receivable is a closing accrual of £2,440. The £4,560 was received on 30 September 2009. The bank account was opened in 2007.

5.   The gross amounts of loan interest payable are shown. Income tax has been deducted at source where appropriate.

Requirement: Calculate the corporation tax liability for the accounting period to 31 December 2009.   **17 marks**

NB. All apportionments should be made to the nearest month.

(ACCA Tax Framework June 97 amended)

22 Qualifying distributions

Introduction

This chapter is concerned with what are called qualifying distributions and these mainly relate to the payment of dividends by an incorporated entity.

Qualifying distributions – definition

1. Most of the tax laws do not in fact refer to dividends as such, but to qualifying distributions which is a general term covering a wide range of similar transactions. These include:

a)   Any dividends paid by a company including a capital dividend. Ordinary and preference dividends are thus included, together with any dividends which are described as capital dividends by the paying company, but not 'stock dividends', which are scrip shares issued in lieu of a dividend.

b)   Any other distributions out of the assets of a company whether in cash or otherwise. There are some exceptions to this rule, for example, repayments of share capital on a winding up are not qualifying distributions. However, where a company distributes in specie, assets or shares in another company, without additional consideration being received from its shareholders, then this is a qualifying distribution, as is interest in excess of a reasonable commercial return.

c)   Interest on bonus securities issued in respect of shares and securities.

d)   Interest on unquoted securities convertible into shares or with rights to shares or securities. Interest on quoted convertible loan stock is not a distribution, but a charge on income.

e)   Transfers of assets or liabilities to any member, where the value of any benefit received is greater than any consideration given. This does not apply to inter-company transfers between members of a 51% group.

f)   The repayment of capital that has been originally issued by way of a bonus issue of share capital.

g)   Benefits in kind to any participator or associate of a close company except, generally, where the recipient is charged to income tax. The latter would be the case for most participator directors.

h)   Excessive interest payments made to associated companies may be treated as a distribution in certain circumstances.

It should be noted that distributions made by an unquoted company on the purchase of its own shares are exempt.

Qualifying distributions

2. The following is a summary of the rules applicable to dividends or other qualifying distributions made by an incorporated entity:

a)   There is no tax payment due in respect of the distribution, by the company.

b)   Each dividend payment has attached to it a tax credit of one-ninth of the distribution which is equivalent to a rate of 10% of the sum of the distribution and the tax credit.

Example

K plc pays a dividend of £90,000 on the 30th June 2009.

Calculate the amount of the total gross dividend received by shareholders.

Solution	£
Dividend payment	90,000
Tax credit 1/9 × 9,000	10,000
Gross dividend	100,000

Student self-testing question

T plc has the following data relating to the year ended 31.3.2010.

	12 months to 31.3.2010
	£
Trading profits	1,550,000
Profits from land and property	125,000
Chargeable gains	125,000
Dividends paid 31.3.10	1,600,000
Dividend received	400,000

Compute the corporation tax liability for AP to 31.3.2010.

Solution: Corporation tax computation

	12 months to 31.3.2010
	£
Trading profits	1,550,000
Profits from land and property	125,000
Chargeable gains	125,000
	1,800,000

	12 months to 31.3.2010
Corporation tax payable	£
1,800,000 @ 28%	504,000

Notes

i)   The UK dividends paid are ignored in computing the CT liability.

ii) Dividends received are not subject to CT but are used in the calculation of marginal relief (see Chapter 24).

Questions without answers

1. Z Ltd has the following data relating to the year ended 31st March 2010.

	£
Trading profits	15,000
Other income	68,000
Debenture interest paid for non-trade purposes (gross)	3,000
Dividend paid	96,000

Compute the corporation tax liability for the AP to 31st March 2010.

2. Avril Showers Ltd makes up its accounts to 31 March each year. In the year to 31 March 2010 the following transactions took place:

1.	30 April 2009	Paid loan interest of £80,000 (gross) to T Ltd
2.	31 May 2009	Received interim dividend from Layne & Co. Ltd (a UK company) £8,000
3.	30 June 2009	Paid interim dividend of £160,000
4.	31 July 2009	Received half-yearly interest on £50,000 9½% debenture stock from Lesley & Co. Ltd
5.	31 October 2009	Paid final dividend of £300,000
6.	31 October 2009	Paid loan interest of £80,000 (gross) to T Ltd
7.	31 January 2010	Received final dividend from Layne & Co. Ltd (a UK company) £16,000
8.	31 January 2010	Received half-yearly interest on £50,000 9½% debenture stock from Lesley & Co. Ltd
9.	28 February 2010	Paid gift aid of covenant to charitable trade association of £1,000 (gross).

Notes

The company's adjusted trading profit for the year ended 31 March 2010 was £1,709,250.

There were chargeable gains of £135,000.

Required: Prepare the corporation tax computation for the year ended 31 March 2010 showing the corporation tax payable.

23 Relief for losses

Introduction

1. This chapter examines the various forms of loss relief available to a company which is not a member of a group of companies. The main emphasis is given to loss reliefs available in respect of trading losses. Non-trading loan relationship deficits are covered. Relief available in connection with charges on income and chargeable gains is also covered.

A company can claim to set a trading loss against other income in several ways. In summary form they may be depicted as follow:

Set against profits (income and gains) of the same period.

Sec 393A(1)(a)

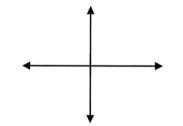

Carried back and set against profits (income and gains) of the previous year*.

Sec 393A(1)(b)

Carried forward and set against future *trading income* from the same source

Sec 393(1)

Surrendered as group relief.
Sec 402 (*current year*)

*Note: For the period from 24th November 2008 to 23rd November 2010, companies with accounting periods ending between these dates can carry back trading losses up to three years with a maximum of £50,000 in years two and three in total.

List of loss reliefs

2. i)   Trade losses   −   set against profits chargeable to corporation tax of the same accounting period. Sec 393 A(1)(a).

ii)   Trade losses   −   set against profits chargeable to corporation tax of the *previous* year. Sec 393 (A)(1)(b). (Also see Note above)

iii)   Trade losses   −   carried forward and set against future trade income. Sec 393(1).

iv)   Trade losses   −   and charges on Income. Sec 393(a).

v)   Trade losses   −   terminal loss relief. Sec 393A(2A)(2B).

vi)   Trade losses   −   surrendered to a 75% subsidiary (and consortium company) by way of group relief. *See Chapter 25.*

vii)   Trade losses   −   transfer to successor company. Sec 343.

viii)   Non-trading loan relationship deficit   −   set against taxable profits. Sec 83 FA1996

xi)   Pre-trading expenditure   −   treated as expenditure on 1st day of trading. Sec 401.

Trade losses

3. It is perhaps worth recalling that a trading loss is arrived at after deducting capital allowances and any interest arising from a trading loan relationship which may in fact turn a 'profit' into a 'loss' for tax purposes. Also, charges on income are deducted from total corporation tax profits and not income, but see (g) below.

Trade losses Section 393A(1)(a) and (b)

a) Under this section a company which has incurred a loss in its trade (excluding any loss brought forward) in any accounting period, which may claim to set off that loss against total profits (i.e. including chargeable gains) of the same accounting period.

b) Any balance of loss remaining after this set off in the current period can be set off against total profits of APs falling within the previous year.

c) A claim for the current year must be made before claiming relief for any preceding year.

d) A claim under this section must be made within two years of the end of the accounting period in which the loss is incurred, or within such longer period as the Inland Revenue may allow.

e) Relief for the loss under Section 393A(1)(a) appears in the computation before charges on income and group relief are deducted, but see (g) below.

f) Where the accounting period of the loss is less than 12 months' duration, the loss can nevertheless be carried back 12 months.

g) Where the loss is carried back under Section 393A(1)(b) then it is set off against profits *after* deducting trade charges on income but not non-trade charges such as gifts, aid, donations and covenants. In effect this does not disturb relief obtained for trade charges in earlier years.

h) For the period from 24th November 2008 to 23rd November 2010, companies with accounting periods ending between these dates can carry back trading losses up to three years with a maximum of £50,000 in years two and three in total. Losses must be allocated to recent years first. If the accounting period is less than 12 months the £50,000 cap is reduced on a pro-rata basis.

Example

Q Ltd has the following corporation tax profit/loss for its accounting years ended 31st March 2010 and 2009 and makes a claim for loss relief under Section 393A(1)(a) and (b).

Show the computations.

Q Ltd

	31.3.10	31.3.09
	£	£
Trading profit/(loss)	(30,000)	80,000
Income from property	11,000	10,000
Chargeable gains	2,100	9,000
Non-trading loan relationship deficit	(2,000)	–

Solution

Claim for relief under Section 393A(1)(a) and (b)

	£	£
Trading profit	–	80,000
Income from property	11,000	10,000
Chargeable gains	2,100	9,000
Non-trading loan relationship deficit	(2,000)	–
Total profits	11,100	99,000
Less Section 393A(1)(a) and (b) relief	11,100	18,900
Assessment	–	80,100

Loss memorandum	£
The trading loss of £30,000 has been utilised as follows:	
Set against other profits for the year to 31.3.2010-393A(1)(a)	11,100
Set against other profits for the year to 31.3.2009–393A(1)(b)	18,900
	30,000

Notes

i)   In making a claim under Section 393A(1)(a) for the year to 31st March 2010 it is not necessary to carry the losses back to the previous period.

ii) The carry back relief is only available when the total profits of the year of the loss have been absorbed.

iii) It is not possible to claim a partial relief for the year to 31st March 2010 and also claim relief for the period to 31st March 2009.

iv) The non-trading loan relationship deficit is deducted before the loss relief – see 8 below.

Trade losses carried forward Section 393(1)

4. Where a company incurs a trading loss in any accounting period, then apart from any claim for relief under Sections 393A(1)(a) and (b) the loss may be dealt with as follows:

a)   It may be carried forward to succeeding accounting periods so long as the company continues to trade.

b)   A loss carried forward is only deductible from future trading income not corporation tax profits, chargeable to corporation tax.

c)   The trading profit of a succeeding period is treated as being reduced by any such loss brought forward.

d)   A claim under this section must be made within six years of the end of the accounting period in which the loss was incurred.

e)   There may be a disallowance of trading losses carried forward arising from a change of ownership. Sec 768 TA 1988 – *see Chapter 25 section 24.*

Example

D Ltd has the following results for the two years ended 30th June 2009.

	30.6.08	30.6.09
	£	£
Trade profits/(loss)	(12,000)	7,000
Interest income	3,000	4,000
Chargeable gain	6,000	1,000

The company makes a claim under Sections 393A(1)(a) and 393(1).

Compute the assessments.

Solution

	30.6.08	30.6.09
	£	£
Trade profits	–	7,000
Less Section 393(1)	–	3,000
	–	4,000
Interest income	3,000	4,000
Chargeable gain	6,000	1,000
Profits chargeable to corporation tax	9,000	9,000
Less Section 393A(1)(a)	9,000	
Assessment	–	9,000

Notes

i) The trading loss of £12,000 incurred in the accounting period to 30th June 2008 has been utilised as indicated below.

			£
Accounting period to 30.6.08	Section393A(1)(a)		9,000
do. 30.6.09	Section 393(1)		3,000
			12,000

ii) The trading loss carried forward to 30.6.09 is deducted from trading profits and not total profits.

Trade losses and charges on income Section 393(9)

5. In any accounting period where the charges on income paid exceed total corporation tax profits, and include payments made wholly and exclusively for the purposes of a trade carried on by that company, then a measure of loss relief is available under Section 393(9).

This provides that the amount of the excess charges on income or of the trade payments, whichever is the less, may be carried forward as if they were a trading loss under Section 393(1).

Covenanted payments or gift aid donations would not be trade charges.

Example

P Ltd has the following results for the year ended 31st March 2010

		£	£
Trading loss			(88,000)
Interest income			4,000
Chargeable gain			10,000
Charges on income:	trade	27,000	
	non-trade	5,000	32,000

The company makes a claim for loss relief under Section 393A(1)(a) and 393(1).

Compute the assessment for the AP to 31.3.2010 and show the loss relief.

Solution: P Ltd AP to 31.3.2010

	£	£
Interest income		4,000
Chargeable gain		10,000
Total profits		14,000
Less loss relief. Section 393A(1)(a)		14,000
Assessment		–
Amount of losses carried forward:		
Trading loss for year to 31.3.10	88,000	
Less Section 393A(1)(a) relief	14,000	74,000
Charges on income the lower of:		
a) Excess charges 32,000 – 0 =	32,000	
or		
b) Trade charges only	27,000	27,000
Total trade losses carried forward		101,000

Note

Here the non-trade charges of £5,000 would not be relieved.

Example

Using the data in the previous example, if the company made no claim under Section 393A(1)(a) **recompute the losses carried forward.**

Solution

	£	£
Total profits as above		14,000
Less charges on income		32,000
Excess charges		18,000
Amount of losses carried forward:		
Trading loss for the year to 31.3.10		88,000
Charges on income the lower of:		
(a) Excess charges; or	18,000	
(b) Trade charges only	27,000	18,000
Total trade losses carried forward		106,000

Note

In this example by not claiming relief under Section 393A(1)(a), the non-trade charges are effectively relieved.

It should be noted that an excess of charges cannot be carried back like normal trade losses under Section 393A(1)(b).

Terminal loss relief Section 393A(2A)(2B)

6. Trading losses arising in the twelve months prior to the cessation of trading can be carried back against total profiting the previous three years on a LIFO basis.

Trade charges incurred in the final 12-month period can be used to augment a terminal loss.

Claims to relief must be made within two years of the end of the accounting period in which the loss is made or within such period as the Inspector of Taxes may allow.

Example

Z Ltd has the following data for the four years ended 31st March 2010 when it ceased trading.

	31.3.10	31.3.09	31.3.08	31.3.07
Trading profits	(180,000)	65,000	30,000	55,000
Income from property	9,000	9,000	8,000	7,000
Capital gains	1,000			

The company makes a claim for loss relief under sections 393A(1)(a) and 393A(2A)(2B).

Solution: Z Ltd APs ended 31st March

	2010	2009	2008	2007
Trading profits		65,000	30,000	55,000
Income from property	9,000	9,000	8,000	7,000
Capital gains	1,000	–	–	–
	10,000	74,000	38,000	62,000
Less section 393A(1)(a)	10,000			
section 393(A)(2a)(2b)	–	74,000	38,000	58,000
Revised assessments	–	–	–	4,000

Note

Loss Memo	£	£
Trade loss to 31.3.2010		180,000
Section 393(A)(1)(a) 31.3.10	10,000	
Section 393(A)(2a)(2b) 31.3.09	74,000	
Section 393(A)(2a)(2b) 31.3.08	38,000	
Section 393(A)(2a)(2b) 31.3.07	58,000	180,000

Transfer of losses Section 343

7. When a company ceases trading and another company takes over the same trade, then unrelieved losses can be carried forward to the successor company providing that certain conditions are met, which are:

a)   On or at any time within two years after the succession and within one year prior thereto, at least 75% of the interest in the trade is held by the same persons. This means that three quarters of the ordinary share capital in both companies must be held by the same persons throughout the three-year period. Throughout the same period the same trade must be carried on by a company in charge to corporation tax.

b)   It follows from this provision that the transfer of a trade from an individual to a company precludes the transfer of trading losses between the entities. However, in that case under Section 386 some relief for an individual is available whereby part of a business loss may be set against income which he or she receives from the company. *See Chapter 14.*

Where there is a transfer of trade then the following applies.

a)   The trade is not treated as if it had been discontinued and a new one started.

b)   Loss relief under Section 393(A) (1)(b) is not available to the company ceasing to trade. If the second company ceases to trade within four years of the succession, then loss relief can be carried back, where appropriate, to the first company.

c)   Relief under Section 393(1) for the carry forward of losses is available subject to any claim by the company ceasing to trade, under Section 393(A) (1)(a) i.e. set off against corporation tax profits chargeable to corporation tax.

        Where a trade or part thereof is transferred between two companies so that Section 343 applies, then relief to successor for losses brought forward is restricted where the amount of the 'relevant liability' immediately before the transfer exceeds the open market value of the 'relevant assets' at that time.

d)   No balancing adjustments are raised on the transfer.

e)   Unused capital allowances can also be carried forward under Section 77 CAA 1990.

f)   Losses can not be carried forward where at any time before the change in ownership the scale of activity becomes small or negligible and the change takes place before any considerable revival has occurred.

g)   Other losses or capital gains tax losses cannot be transferred.

The main provisions relating to the transfer of trades are contained in Sections 343 and 344 of the TA 1988.

Non-trading loan relationship / foreign exchange deficit

8. Interest incurred and receivable plus any other debits and credits relating to non-trade borrowing and lending must be pooled to produce either a non-trading credit or deficit for the period. This also includes any non-trading foreign exchange debt differences.

A net non-trading credit is included as interest income.

A net non-trading deficit is relieved by one or more of the following methods:

i)   By offset against the company's taxable profits (in whole or part) for the same period. A current year non-trading deficit is deducted against taxable profits *before*: any current year trading loss offset under S 393A, TA 1988; charges on income; and a non-trading deficit carried back from a subsequent period.

ii)   Against the taxable profits of fellow group members under the group relief provisions.

iii)   By carry-back (in whole or part) against the company's interest income loan relationships profits falling within the previous 12 months.

iv)   By carry-forward for offset against the company's non-trading profits for the next accounting period. (For this purpose, non-trading profits represent the company's total profits except those constituting trading income.)

The above reliefs must be claimed within two years of the end of the relevant accounting period or such further period as the Revenue may allow. Any surplus non-trading deficit remaining after the above claims is automatically carried forward as a non-trading debit for the next accounting period.

Example

Q Ltd has the following data relating to the year ended 31st December 2009.

	£
Adjusted trading profit	100,000
Income from property	5,000
Non-trade interest incurred	65,000
Non-trade interest received	15,000
Trade charges paid (gross)	7,000

Compute the profits chargeable to corporation tax for the AP to 31st December 2009.

Solution: Q Ltd corporation tax computation AP 31.12.09

Trading profits	100,000
Income from property	5,000
	105,000
Non-trading deficit	50,000
	55,000
Less charges on income	
Trade charges	7,000
Profits chargeable to CT	48,000

Notes

i) The non-trade deficit comprises:

interest paid	65,000
less interest received	15,000
	50,000

ii) Non-trade deficit is deducted from total profits and before charges on income paid, and group relief.

Pre-trading expenditure

9. Relief is available for expenditure by a company in the seven years before it commences to carry on a trade.

a) The expenditure must be allowable trading expenditure which would have been deducted in computing Case I or II trading income if incurred after commencement of trading.

b) Such expenditure is treated as a trading expenditure on the first day on which the trade commences.

c) The relief does not apply to pre-trading purchases of stock.

d) Charges on income paid by a company are also eligible for treatment as pre-trading expenditure. They will be deemed to be paid as a charge on the first day that trading commences.

Chargeable gains

10. The amount of any chargeable gain arising in an accounting period is reduced by any allowable capital losses of the same period and by those brought forward from a previous period.

Example

R Ltd has the following data relating to its AP to 31st March 2010.

	£
Capital losses brought forward 1.4.09	3,000
AP to 31.3.2010	
Trading profits	41,000
Chargeable gains 22,000	

Compute the corporation tax payable.

Solution: R Ltd AP to 31st March 2010

	£	£
Trading profits		41,000
Chargeable gains	22,000	
Less losses b/f	3,000	19,000
Profits chargeable to corporation tax		60,000
Corporation tax payable: 60,000 @ 21%		12,600

Non-trading losses and deficits

11. Non-trading loan relationship deficit

See section 8 above

Interest income

Since there are no permitted expenses allowed against income from this source there can be no loss or deficit for tax purposes, except the non-trading loan relationship deficit. See 8 above.

Income from overseas possessions

Losses would not normally arise under these cases but when a trade falls to be taxed under this section, then the loss relief under Section 393A(1)(a) and (b) is not available. A loss may only be carried forward and set against income from the same source.

Other annual profits

When a loss is incurred under this case, then it may be set against other income of the same type against the same or future accounting periods. Such a loss may not be carried back, or set against any other income.

Income from property

Relief for losses against current years total profits. *See Chapter 19.*

Capital losses

May be set against chargeable gains of same AP, or carried forward. They cannot be set against total profits.

Student self-testing questions

1. Trailer Limited has the following results for the two years to 31 August 2009

	y/e 31.8.08	y/e 31.8.09
	£	£
Trading profit/(loss)	(21,000)	17,000
Interest income - non trade relationship	6,000	9,000
Capital loss	(2,000)	
Chargeable gains		7,000

Requirement: Calculate PCTCT for the 2 periods, assuming that the loss is relieved under S393 (1) showing any losses carried forward at 1 September 2009.

Suggested solution

	31/8/08	31/8/09
	£	£
Trading profit	-	17,000
Less : S393 (1) relief		(17,000)
		NIL
Interest income	6,000	9,000
Chargeable gains (£7,000 - £2,000)		5,000
	6,000	14,000
PCTCT	6,000	14,000

Loss memorandum

	£
Loss for year ended 31/8/08	21,000
Relieved year ended 31/8/09 (S393(1))	(17,000)
Available for carry forward under S393 (1)	4,000

2. Caravan Limited has the following results for the accounting years ended 31 March 2009 and 31 March 2010.

	Year to 31/3/09	Year to 31/3/10
	£	£
Trading profit/(loss)	39,000	(49,700)
Income from property	2,000	1,500
Non trade charges (gross)	500	500

Requirement: Calculate PCTCT for both periods, assuming that relief under S393A is claimed for the loss in the period ended 31 March 2010. Show any losses available to carry forward at 1 April 2010.

Suggested solution

Caravan Limited: PCTCT computation for 2 years ending 31 March 2010

	Year ended 31/3/09	Year ended 31/3/10
	£	£
Trading profit	39,000	-
Income from property	2,000	1,500
	41,000	1,500
S393A 1 (b) relief	(41,000)	(1,500)
PCTCT	-	-
Unrelieved non trade charges	500	500

Loss memorandum	£
Loss for the year ended 31/3/10	49,700
Less S393A year ended 31/3/10	(1,500)
S393A year ended 31/3/09	(41,000)
Loss to carry forward	7,200

3. Buttercup Limited made up accounts to 30 September and ceased to trade on 31 March 2010.

Results have been as follows:

	30/9/07	30/9/08	30/9/09	Period ended 31/3/10
Trading profit/(loss)	5,200	4,700	3,200	(30,500)
Income from property	2,000	1,800	1,900	500
Interest income - non trading	750	900	840	400
Chargeable gains	3,000	-	2,000	-
Charges on income				
-Gift Aid payment	300	300	300	300

Requirement: Show the PCTCT for all years, assuming the loss is relieved under S393A terminal loss relief.

Suggested solution

	30/9/07	30/9/08	30/9/09	31/3/10
	£	£	£	£
Trading profit	5,200	4,700	3,200	-
Income from property	2,000	1,800	1,900	500
Interest income	750	900	840	400
Chargeable gains	3,000	-	2,000	-
Less S393 A relief	(10,950)	(7,400)	(7,940)	(900)
	0	0	0	0
Trade charges	-	-	-	-
Non trade charges - Gift Aid	-	-	-	-
PCTCT	Nil	Nil	Nil	Nil
Unrelieved Gift Aid Payment	300	300	300	300

	£
Loss incurred to 6 months 31/3/10	30,500

Less S393A	
6 months to 31/3/10	(900)
y/e 30/9/09	(7,940)
y/e 30/9/08	(7,400)
y/e 30/9/07	(10,950)
Loss remaining unrelieved	3,310

4. Z Ltd has the following results for the four years to 31st March 2010.

	2007	2008	2009	2010
	£	£	£	£
Trading profits/(loss)	100,000	40,000	(200,000)	60,000
Chargeable gains	10,000	20,000	5,000	8,000
Loan interest paid (non trade)	7,000	7,000	–	–

Show the assessments for all the years assuming that loss reliefs are claimed as soon as possible.

Suggested solution

	2007 £	2008 £	2009 £	2010 £
Trading profits	100,000	40,000		60,000
Less Section 393 (1)	–	–	–	60,000
	100,000	40,000	–	–
Chargeable gains	10,000	20,000	5,000	8,000
Corporation tax profits	110,000	60,000	5,000	8,000
Less loan deficit	7,000	7,000	–	–
	103,000	53,000	5,000	8,000
Less Section393A(1)(a)(b)	50,000	53,000	5,000	
Assessments	53,000	Nil	Nil	8,000

Loss memorandum

		2009 £	2010 £
Trade loss for year to 31.3.09			200,000
Section 393A(1)(a) 31.3.09		5,000	
Section 393A(1)(b) 31.3.08		53,000	
Section 393A(1)(b) 31.3.07		50,000	
Section 393(1)31.3.09	60,000	168,000	
Carried forward – section 393(1) 31.3.10			32,000

Notes

i) Loss relief for the current period is set against income and gains after any non trade loan relationship deficit.

ii) For the one year carry back the relief is set against income and gains after any non trade loan relationship deficit.

iii)   The loss for y/e 31.3.2009 falls between the 24th November 2008 and 23rd November 2009, therefore the extended carry back rules for 2009-2010 apply and the maximum cap of £50,000 has been utilised and applied to profits for the y/e 31.3.2007.

Questions without answers

1. O plc has the following results for the periods to 31st March 2010.

	12 months to 31.3.07	3 months to 31.3.08	12 months to 31.3.09	12 months to 31.3.10
	£	£	£	£
Trading profits	35,000	(17,000)	4,500	8,000
Income from property	1,000	2,000	3,000	2,000
Chargeable gain			5,000	(8,000)
Debenture interest paid (trade)	1,000	1,000	1,000	

Compute the assessment for each year assuming all available loss reliefs are claimed.

2. T Ltd has the following results to 30th June 2009.

	30.6.09	30.6.08	30.6.07	30.6.06
	£	£	£	£
Trading profits	(80,000)	(135,000)	7,500	30,000
Chargeable gains	120,000	7,500	–	–

Compute the assessments for all years, assuming all loss reliefs are claimed under Section 393A(1) (a), (b).

3. Uncut Undergrowth Limited (UUL) is a United Kingdom resident company which has been manufacturing garden machinery since 1997. It has no associated companies. The company results are summarised as follows:

	Year Ended 30/6/08	6 months to 31/12/08	Year Ended 31/12/09	Year Ended 31/12/10 (forecast)
	£	£	£	£
Trading Profit/(Loss)	25,000	(51,000)	(362,500)	87,000
Non-trade loan interest received (gross amount)	-	15,000	22,000	-
Bank interest received -non trade relationship	-	-	-	10,000
Income from property	25,000	-	-	-
Chargeable gains	-	-	30,000	-
Gift Aid payment to charity	1,000	1,000	1,000	1,000

On 1 July 2007 there were no trading losses brought forward but £40,000 of capital losses were available.

Requirements

(a) Calculate the corporation tax liabilities for all years in the question after giving maximum relief at the earliest time for the trading losses sustained and any other reliefs.
(11 marks)

(b) Show any balances carried forward.
(5 marks)

NB: All apportionments may be made to the nearest month.

Note Use FY 2009 tax rates for all years.
(ACCA December 1997 amended)

4. Loser Ltd's results for the year ended 30 June 2007, the nine month period ended 31 March 2008, the year ended 31 March 2009 and the year ended 31 March 2010 are as follows:

	Year ended 30 June 2007	Period ended 31 March 2008	Year ended 31 March 2009	Year ended 31 March 2010
	£	£	£	£
Trading profit/(loss)	90,200	(33,000)	34,600	(85,500)
Income from property	(3,600)	4,500	8,100	5,600
Non-trade charges paid (gross)	(1,400)	(800)	(1,200)	(1,100)

Required:

(a) State the factors that will influence a company's choice of loss relief claims. You are not expected to consider group relief. **(3 marks)**

(b) Assuming that Loser Ltd claims relief for its losses as early as possible, calculate the company's profits chargeable to corporation tax for;

the year ended 30 June 2007,

the nine month period ended 31 March 2008,

the year ended 31 March 2009 and

the year ended 31 March 2010.

Your answer should show any amount of unrelieved losses as at 31 March 2010.

(10 marks)

(c) Explain how your answer to (b) would have differed if Loser Ltd had ceased trading on 31 March 2010. **(2 marks)**

(15 marks)

ACCA past paper 2.3 December 2002 updated

Student note: Some of these questions contain brief elements of capital gains tax and this topic is covered in chapters 27-34.

24 Corporation tax rates and the small company

Introduction

1. This chapter is concerned with the taxation of 'small companies'. It begins with a summary of basic rates and the meaning of profits for small company purposes. There have been a number of changes in the rates of corporation tax for small companies over recent years. The 0% starting rate, marginal relief for small corporations and the non-corporate distribution rate were all abolished for FY 2006. The corporation tax rate for small corporations has increased from 19% to 20% for FY 2007 and again increased to 21% for the current year, FY 2008. The small companies' rate remains at 21% for FY 2009. This chapter will show the effect of the change in the rates for small companies.

Basic rates

2.

Rates	Financial years			
	2006	**2007**	**2008**	**2009**
	to 31.3.2007	**to 31.3.2008**	**to 31.3.2009**	**to 31.3.2010**
Small company profits	50,001–300,000	0-300,000	0-300,000	0-300,000
Small company rate	19%	20%	21%	21%
Marginal relief	300,001–1,500,000	300,001–1,500,000	300,001–1,500,000	300,001–1,500,000

Profits between £0 and £300,000 are taxed at the small company's rate of 21%. Profits in between £300,000 and £1,500,000 are taxed at the main rate of corporation tax, subject to marginal relief (see section 4 below).

Definition of profits

3. The definition of profits for both the starting rate and the small company rate is the sum of:

 a) profits chargeable to corporation tax i.e. total profits less charges on income, and group relief, *plus*

 b) franked investment income, excluding from group companies.

Example

Beta Ltd has the following data relating to the year ended 31st March 2010.

Trading profits	3,500
Chargeable gains	4,700

Calculate the corporation tax payable for the AP to 31st March 2010.

Solution: Corporation tax computation AP to 31.3.2010

	£
Trading profits	3,500
Chargeable gain	4,700
Profit chargeable to corporation tax	8,200
Corporation tax payable £8,200 @ 21%:	1,722

Example

AP Ltd has the following income and charges relating to the year ended 31st March 2010.

	£
Trading profits	127,000
Chargeable gain	3,500
Charges on income paid	1,500
Dividends received	14,400

Calculate the corporation tax payable for the AP to 31st March 2010.

Solution: Corporation tax computation AP to 31.3.10

	£
Trading profits	127,000
Chargeable gain	3,500
	130,500
Less charges on income	1,500
Profit chargeable to corporation tax	129,000
Add franked investment income 14,400 + (10/90 ×14,400)	16,000
Small company profits	145,000
Corporation tax payable:	
£129,000 @ 21%	27,090

Note The small company profit threshold for the year to 31.3.2010 is £300,000.

Marginal relief – small company rate

4. Where the small company profits exceed the lower maximum amount of £300,000, but fall below the upper maximum amount, then the position is as follows:

a) Corporation tax profits are chargeable at the full rate of 28%.

b) $\left[(M-P) \times \dfrac{I}{P} \times a\ fraction \right]$ is deducted from (a)

M = Upper maximum amount i.e. £1,500,000. FY to 31.3.10.

P = Profits chargeable to corporation tax + FII.

I = Basic profits i.e. profits chargeable to corporation tax.

P = B + FII.

c) The fraction is determined with respect to financial years, and the recent years to 31.3.2009 are as follows:

Financial years	Marginal relief fraction
2007 to 31.3.2008	1/40
2008 to 31.3.2009	7/400
2009 to 31.3.2010	7/400

d) Thus in respect of accounting periods for the financial year to the 31st March 2010 the formula is:

$$(1,500,000 - P) \times \frac{I}{P} \times \frac{7}{400}$$

Example

Z Ltd has the under mentioned data relating to its accounting year ended 31.3.2010.

	£
Trading profits	453,100
Chargeable gains	2,250
Charges on income	5,350
Dividend received	1,800
Dividend paid	24,000

Compute the corporation tax liability.

Solution: Calculation of small company profits

	£	
Trading profits	453,100	
Chargeable gain	2,250	
	455,350	
Less charges on income	5,350	
	450,000	i.e.I
Add franked investment income	2,000	
	452,000	i.e.P

Computation of marginal relief:

$$(1,500,000 - 452,000) \times \frac{450,000}{452,000} \times 7/400 \qquad 18,259$$

Z Ltd Corporation tax computation AP 31.3.2010

	£
Schedule D Case I	453,100
Chargeable gains	2,250
	455,350
Less charges on income	5,350
	450,000
Corporation tax @ 28% ×450,000	126,000
Less marginal relief	18,259
Corporation tax payable	107,741

Notes

i) From this example it will be noted that the marginal relief is in fact a calculated amount which is deducted from the profits charged at the full rate of 28%.

ii) As P > £300,000, marginal relief should be claimed.

Marginal rates of corporation tax

5. a) Small companies

The marginal rate of corporation tax refers to the rate of corporation tax borne on profits in between £300,000 and £1,500,000, and for the financial year to the 31st March 2008 this was 32.5%. For the financial year to 31st March 2009 this was 29.75%. For the financial year to 31st March 2010 the marginal rate is also 29.75%.

Example

B Ltd has profits chargeable to corporation tax of £400,000 for the year ended 31st March 2010. Calculate the corporation tax payable and show the marginal rate of tax.

Solution

	£
Profits chargeable to corporation tax	400,000
Corporation tax @ 28%	112,000
Less marginal relief	
(1,500,000 – 400,000 × 7/ 400	19,250
	92,750

Corporation tax liability

This can be shown to be equivalent to:

300,000 @ 21%	63,000
100,000 @ 29.75% (marginal rate)	29,750
400,000	92,750

The marginal rate of 29.75% compares with a marginal rate of income tax for 2009/10 of 40% (the higher rate).

Associated companies

6. A company is treated as an associate of another at a given time, if at that time, or at any time within one year previously, either one of the two has control over the other, or both are under the same control. Control is generally established with a shareholding of more than 50%. Control is also established if the parent company is entitled to acquire:

a) the greater part of the share capital or issued share capital, or voting power of the associate company.

b) such part of the issued share capital as would entitle the parent company to receive the greater part of the income of the associate company if it were distributed amongst the participators, ignoring the rights of loan creditors.

c) such rights as would on a winding up of the company, or in any other circumstance, entitle the parent company to the greater part of the assets of the company, available for distribution among the participators.

If a company has one or more associated companies in the accounting period, then the upper and lower relevant maximum and minimum amounts are divided equally between the company and the number of associates. Thus a company with two associates would have to allocate the relevant amounts threefold:

FY to 31.3.2010	Lower level £	Upper level £
The company	100,000	500,000
First associate	100,000	500,000
Second associate	100,000	500,000
	300,000	1,500,000

In determining the number of associated companies the following points should be noted.

a) An associated company which was not a trading company or has not carried on a trade at any time in the accounting period is to be disregarded.

b) A company which is only an associate for part of an accounting period is to be counted.

c) Two or more companies are to be counted even if they were associated for different parts of the accounting period.

2. Overseas subsidiaries are included in determining the number of associates.

Example

D Ltd, a company resident in the United Kingdom, owns 80% of the equity share capital of S Ltd., 52% of the ordinary share capital of J Ltd. and 25% of the ordinary share capital of N Ltd. The company prepares accounts to the year ended 31 December and provides the following information in respect of its accounting period of twelve months ended 31 December 2009:

INCOME	£
Trading profits	260,000
Bank interest	140,000
Capital gains	50,000
Rental income	200,000

Requirement: Compute the corporation tax liability for the above accounting period.

Solution

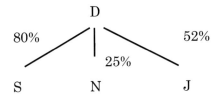

S & J are associates for the purposes of tax

Divide upper & lower limits by 3 :-

£300,000 / 3	Lower £100,000
£1,500,000 / 3	Upper £500,000

Calculation of PCTCT

Trading profits	260,000
Interest income	140,000
Income from property	200,000
Capital Gains	50,000
PCTCT	650,000

The company is taxed at full rate because 'profits' are £650,000 ('profits' = PCTCT as there are no dividends). If there was a change in the rates, the CT liability would need to be apportioned accordingly, this is shown below; however, the rate did not change between FY08 and FY09.

FY08

1.1.2009 to 31.3.2009 3/12 x £650,000 x 28%	45,500

FY09

1.4.2009 to 31.12.2009 9/12 x £650,000 x 28%	136,500
Total corporation tax liability	182,000

Accounting periods of less than 12 months

7. As already indicated, for corporation tax purposes a company's accounting period cannot exceed 12 months in duration. If the accounting period is less than 12 months in length then the relevant maximum amounts are reduced accordingly.

Thus with an accounting period of three months' duration ending in the financial year to 31.3.2009 the lower profit level would be £300,000/4 i.e. £75,000, and the upper profit level would be 1,500,000/4 i.e. £375,000. If the situation arises where a company has an accounting period of less than 12 months' length, and has an associated company, then the respective profit levels are first divided by the number of companies and then reduced in proportion to the length of the accounting period.

Student self-testing questions

1. Harold Limited has the following results for the year ended 31 March 2010.

PCTCT	150,000
Dividend received on 1 September 2009	15,000

Requirement: Calculate the corporation tax liability for the year ended 31 March 2010.

Solution

	£
PCTCT	150,000
FII (£15,000 x 100/90)	16,667
Profits	166,667

Less than £300,000 therefore tax at small company's rate

FY09	£
150,000 x 21%	31,500

2. Hannah Limited has the following results for the year ended 31 March 2010.

PCTCT	250,000
Dividend received on 1 September 2009	50,000

Requirement: Calculate the corporation tax liability for the year ended 31March 2010.

	£
PCTCT	250,000
FII (£50,000 x 100/90)	55,556
Profits	305,556

Therefore marginal relief band

FY09	£
250,000 x 28%	70,000
(1,500,000 - 305,556) x 250,000/305,556 x 7/400	(17,102)
	52,898

3. Freddie Limited makes up accounts to the year ended 31 December. For the year ended 31 December 2009 the profit and loss account was as follows:

PCTCT	200,000
Dividend received on 1 September 2009	50,000

Requirement: Calculate the corporation tax liability for the year ended 31 December 2009

	£
PCTCT	200,000
FII (£50,000 x 100/90)	55,556
Profits	255,556
Tax liability	£
FY08	
200,000 x 3/12 x 21%	10,500
FY09	
200,000 x 9/12 x 21%	31,500
	42,000

4. K plc has the undermentioned data relating to its accounting period ended 31st March 2010.

	£
Trading profits	327,000
Income from property	13,000
Chargeable gains	45,000
Charges on income paid	10,000
Dividend received 31.12.09	18,000
Dividend paid 31.12.09	24,000

Calculate the corporation tax liability for the AP to 31st March 2010.

Solution: Corporation tax computation AP to 31.3.2010

	£	
Trading profits	327,000	
Income from property	13,000	
Chargeable gains	45,000	
	385,000	
Less charges on income paid	10,000	
Profits chargeable to corporation tax	375,000	= I
Corporation tax payable	£	
375,000 @ 28%	105,000	
Less marginal relief	18,358	
Corporation tax payable	86,642	

Note

Marginal relief computation.

$I = 375,000$

$P = I + FII = 375,000 + 20,000 = 395,000$

$$(1,500,000 - 395,000) \times \frac{375,000}{395,000} \times 7/400$$

$$= 1,105,000 \times \frac{375}{395} \times 7/400 = 18,358.$$

Questions without answers

1. James Limited has 2 associated companies and a PCTCT for the year ended 31 March 2010 of £200,000.

Requirement Calculate the corporation tax liability in respect of the year ended 31 March 2010.

2. D Ltd has the following data relating to its accounting year ended 31st March 2010.

	£
Trading profits	440,000
Other income	10,000
Income from property	20,000
Chargeable gain	20,000
Debenture interest paid (gross) trading	10,000
Dividend received 31.12.09	4,500
Dividend paid 31.12.09	24,000

Compute the corporation tax liability for the AP to 31st March 2010.

3. The following information has been extracted from the records of Nerston Ltd, a UK resident company, for its trading year to 31st March 2010.

	£
Trading profits	18,000
Income from property	20,000
Debenture interest paid: trading purposes	3,200
Chargeable gain	2,400
Dividends paid in the year, to individuals.	30,000

Debenture interest was paid on 7th July 2009 and dividends were paid 1st December 2009.

Compute corporation tax payable for the accounting period to 31st March 2010.

4. N Ltd has owned 60% of the share capital of D Ltd for several years. Both companies are trading companies resident in the UK.

The following information relates to the ten month accounting period to 30 September 2009 of N Ltd:

INCOME	£
Adjusted trading profit (before capital allowances)	77,000
Bank interest - non trading	5,000
Capital gains	10,000
Rental income	5,000

The balances brought forward at 1 December 2008 for capital allowances purposes were as follows:

General pool	Car pool all 145g/km	Car CO_2 165g/km
£38,000	£16,000	£14,000

During the above period machinery was sold for £10,000 (original cost £11,000) and new desks were bought for £6,000 on 1st May 2009. The car CO_2 165g/km was traded in for £10,000 against the cost of a new car costing £12,000 on 1st June 2009.

Requirement

(a) **Compute the maximum capital allowances which N Ltd may claim for the ten month accounting period to 30 September 2009. Assume N Ltd qualifies for medium company first year allowances.**

(b) **Compute N Ltd's corporation tax liability for the ten month accounting period.**

5. DLT Ltd is a resident in the United Kingdom. It has one associated company. The board decided to alter the company's accounting date and prepared accounts for the fourteen months from 1 January 2009 to 28 February 2010. The following relates to this period.

INCOME	£	£
Trading profit (before capital allowances)		420,000
Rents receivable		
- February 2009	52,000	
- February 2010	25,000	
		77,000
Bank interest received - July 2009*		48,000
Capital gains		
- October 2009	120,000	
-February 2010	150,000	
		270,000

The written down balances for capital allowances purposes brought forward at 1 January 2009 were:

	£
General pool	160,000
Car CO2 180g/km	18,000

Capital transactions during the above period were as follows:

Purchases:

10/10/09	Lorry	24,000
05/01/10	Machinery	12,000

Disposals

02/01/10	Car CO2 180g/km sold for	11,000

*The bank interest wholly relates to the year ended 31/12/09 in a non-trading loan relationship.

Requirement: Compute the corporation tax liability payable in respect of the above accounting profits.

6. Upbeat Ukuleles Limited (UUL) is a United Kingdom resident company, which has been manufacturing musical instruments for many years. It has no associated companies. The company has previously made up accounts to 30 June but has now changed its accounting date to 30 September.

The company's results for the 15 month period to 30 September 2009 are as follows:

	£
Trading profits (as adjusted for taxation before capital allowances)	1,320,000
Debenture interest receivable (notes 3)	20,000
Bank interest receivable (note 4)	6,000
Chargeable gain (notes 5 and 6)	10,000
Gift aid payment (note 7)	5,000
Dividends received from UK companies (note 8)	30,000

Notes

1. Capital allowances

On 1 July 2008 the tax written-down value of the plant and machinery in the capital allowances pool was £100,000. There were no additions or sales in the period of account to 30 September 2009.

2. On 1 July 2008 the company had trading losses brought forward of £800,000.

3. Debenture interest receivable (non trading relationship)

	£
22.9.09 received	18,000
30.9.09 accrued	2,000
	20,000

The debenture had been acquired in July 2009.

4. Bank interest receivable (non trading relationship)

	£
30.11.08 received	3,000
30.5.09 received	1,000
30.9.09 accrued	2,000
	6,000

5. Chargeable gain

The chargeable gain of £10,000 is in respect of shares disposed of on 31 December 2008.

6. On 1 July 2008 the company had capital losses brought forward of £12,500.

7. Gift Aid Payment

£5,000 was paid to a charity on 31 December 2008.

8. Dividends received

	£
25.4.09	18,000
29.9.09	12,000
	30,000

Requirement: Calculate the corporation tax liabilities for the 15 month period ended 30 September 2009. Assume the company is small for capital allowance purposes

NB. All apportionments may be made to the nearest month.   **(22 marks)**

(ACCA Tax Framework updated December 1996)

7. Chandler Ltd has, for many years, prepared accounts to 30 September, but changes its accounting date to 31 December by preparing accounts for the 15 months ended 31 December 2009. The accounts show a profit, as adjusted for tax purposes (but before deducting capital allowances) of £200,000.

The tax written down value of the general pool was £18,000 at 1 October 2008. During the period ended 31 December 2009, the following transactions took place.

14 November 2008	Purchased machine at a cost of £17,500
3 February 2009	Sold a machine, purchased in 1992 for £2,500 realising proceeds of £3,000
11 November 2009	Purchased motor van, cost £10,000

The company also received income in the period as follows:

Bank Interest received:	31 December 2008	£50
Non Trading relationship	30 June 2009	£900
	31 December 2009	£800
Capital Gains: Disposal	15 December 2009	£25,000
UK Dividends received:	18 April 2009	£11,000
	3 November 2009	£14,865

Chandler Ltd has no associated companies.

Requirement: Calculate the mainstream corporation tax liabilities for this 15 month period of account.

Student note: Some of these questions contain brief elements of capital gains tax and this topic is covered in chapters 27-34.

25 Groups and consortia

Introduction

1. This chapter considers the main aspects of corporation tax where a company is a member of a group or consortium. It begins with a summary of the topics to be examined, each of which is considered in detail subsequently.

Topics to be considered

2. a) Group relief
(75% subsidiaries and consortia)

The set-off of trading losses against profits within a group is known as group relief.

b) Inter-company transfer of assets
(75% subsidiaries)

The transfer of assets between group companies without any chargeable gain or loss arising.

c) Company reconstructions

Without change of ownership.

d) Change in ownership

Disallowance of trading losses.

Group relief (groups and consortia) Section 402

3. This is the term used to describe the amount of trading losses, excess charges on income, or surplus management expenses which one company in a group of companies may surrender and another company in the same group may claim to be set against its corporation tax profits. The main provisions which deal with this form of relief are found in the TA 1988 Sections 402–413.

Meaning of group – world wide

4. Two companies are deemed to be members of a group of companies if the following four conditions all prevail.

a) One is the 75% subsidiary of the other, or both are 75% subsidiaries of a third company. A 75% subsidiary is defined under Section 838 TA 1988 in terms of the direct or indirect ownership of not less than 75% of the ordinary share capital, ordinary shares meaning all shares other than fixed rate preference shares. For the FY 2009 under the Finance Act 2009 an amendment to the 75% rule has been introduced to remove the reference to fixed rate preference shares. This is to ensure that corporations issuing new preference shares to external investors do not lose the right to group relief. The term 'fixed rate preference shares' is replaced with 'relevant preference shares'.

b) The parent company is beneficially entitled to not less than 75% of the profits available for distribution to equity holders of the subsidiary company. An equity holder is any person who holds ordinary shares or is a loan creditor in respect of a loan which is not a commercial loan. Loan creditor has the same meaning as that used in connection with close companies except that the proviso in favour of bank normal borrowings is not excluded and therefore is within the definition for the purposes of these conditions. A normal commercial loan is one which carries a reasonable rate of interest, with no rights to conversion.

c) The parent company would be entitled beneficially to not less than 75% of any assets of the subsidiary company available to its equity shareholders on a winding up.

d) The meaning of group includes non UK subsidiaries, and UK branches of overseas companies. Following the European Court of Justice Judgement in the Marks and Spencer case a small extension to the group relief rules was made in FY 2006. Relief for foreign tax losses from subsidiaries within the European Economic Area (EEA)or have a permanent establishment within the EEA(including indirectly held subsidiaries) that cannot be relieved elsewhere will be available if the loss is computed in line with UK regulations. The amount of the loss will be restricted to the level of foreign tax loss.

Example

B Ltd owns 75% of the ordinary share capital of W Ltd who in turn owns 75% of the ordinary share capital of Z Ltd.

Since B Ltd would only be entitled to 56.25% of the profits available for distribution by Z Ltd the three companies do not constitute a group for the purposes of group relief. B Ltd and W Ltd however would constitute a group, as would W Ltd and Z Ltd.

Example

T Ltd is the UK parent of two 100% subsidiaries, A Ltd and B Ltd, both being USA resident companies.

T Ltd and its USA subsidiaries would constitute a group for tax purposes.

Meaning of consortia – world wide

5. A company is owned by a consortium if 75% or more of its ordinary share capital is beneficially owned by companies, none of which:

    a)   beneficially owns less than 5% of the ordinary share capital,

    b)   would be entitled to less than 5% of any profits available for distribution to equity holders,

    c)   would be entitled to less than 5% of any assets available to equity holders on the wind up.

6. Group relief is also available to a consortium of companies in the following circumstances:

    a)   Where the company surrendering the loss is a trading or holding company owned by a consortium (not being a 75% subsidiary of any company) and the claimant company is a member of the consortium. A loss may also be surrendered from a member of the consortium to the trading or holding company.

    b)   Where a trading company is the 90% subsidiary of a holding company, which itself is owned by a consortium.

Example

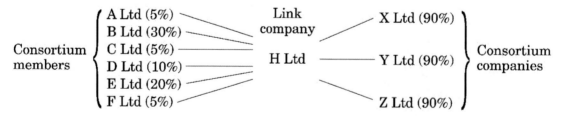

A loss in X, Y or Z could be transferred to the consortium members in proportion to their interests. In addition a loss by any of the consortium members could be claimed by X, Y or Z, and in this case the amount would be restricted to the profits of each claimant proportionately. However, *see Section 12 below.*

What may be surrendered

7. The following may be given by a surrendering company as group relief:

a) trading losses computed as for set off in accordance with Section 393A(1)(a) i.e. excluding any losses brought forward, but after claims for capital allowances.

b) any excess of capital allowances normally given against income of a special class, such as agricultural buildings allowances.

c) any excess of charges on income, whether trading or non-trading, over profits including chargeable gains.

d) any excess of management expenses of an investment company, other than a close investment holding company.

e) a net loss arising from a loan relationship.

In each of the above cases no amounts arising from earlier or succeeding accounting periods can be surrendered.

The surrendering company does not have to make any claim for loss relief, e.g. under Section 393A(1)(a), before surrendering any loss to claimants, although this is frequently done in practice.

The claimant

8. In the accounting period of the claimant company, the surrendered loss may be set against the claimant's total profits including chargeable gains determined as follows:

a) After taking into consideration any relief for losses from trading (or charges) brought forward from previous years under Section 393(1). These would be deducted in arriving at the normal trading profits.

b) After taking into consideration any loss relief under Section 393A(1)(a) for the current accounting period, whether claimed or not.

c) Before any loss relief under Section 393A(1)(b) in respect of a loss brought back from a subsequent accounting period.

d) After deducting charges on income, whether trade or non-trade.

e) Group relief is only available to companies resident in the UK or trading here through a branch.

Relief is to be set against the current profits of the claimant, and it cannot be either carried forward or backward to other accounting periods.

General points

9. a) Group relief is limited to the smaller of the surrendering company's losses relief, or the claimant company's profits available for group relief. Where the surrendering company's losses are greater than the claimant's available profits then the excess cannot be carried forward or backward as group relief. This does not prevent any other form of loss relief being obtained by the surrendering company, e.g. carry forward under Section 393(1).

b) More than one company in the group may make a claim relating to the same surrendering company.

c) If any payment takes place between the claimant and the surrendering company, and such a payment is not necessary to support a claim, then this transaction is:

   i) ignored for all corporation tax purposes as regards both payer and recipient

   ii) not treated as a distribution or as a charge on income.

Example

H Ltd has a wholly owned subsidiary company M Ltd and the results of both companies for their current accounting period of the same 12 months are given below:

	H Ltd £	M Ltd £
Trading profits	(75,000)	70,000
Less loss b/f under Section 393(1)	–	30,000
	(75,000)	40,000
Interest income	15,000	–
Chargeable gain	10,000	5,000
Charges on income	–	25,000

H Ltd decides to make a claim for loss relief under Section 393A(1)(a) and to surrender as much as possible of the balance of its loss to M Ltd.

Show the effects of the claims on H Ltd and M Ltd.

Solution	**H Ltd**
£	
Interest income	15,000
Chargeable gain	10,000
25,000	
Less Section 393A(1)(a) relief	25,000
Assessment	–
Utilization of losses	
Available trade loss	75,000
Less Section 393A(1)(a)	25,000
Available for group relief	50,000
Less surrendered to M Ltd under Section 402	20,000
Carried forward under Section 393(1)	30,000

Smaller amount taken for group relief

M Ltd	
Trading profits	40,000
Chargeable gain	5,000
45,000	
Less charges on income	25,000
Available for group relief	20,000
Group relief claimed under Section 402	20,000
Assessment	–

Notes

i)   In this example the group relief is limited to the claimant's profits of £20,000, as these are the lower amount.

ii) Group relief is deducted after charges on income by the claimant.

Overlapping periods

10. Where the accounting periods of the surrendering company and the claimant company do not coincide, but they have been members of the same group throughout their respective accounting periods, then the group relief is in effect restricted to the proportion of the loss/profit of the overlapping period. This may, in fact, cover two accounting periods of either company.

Example

X Ltd has a 75% subsidiary, Y Ltd, and the results of both companies for the last two accounting periods are as follows:

X Ltd

AP to 31.3.2009 Trading profit	10,000
AP to 31.3.2010 Trading profit/(loss)	(16,000)

Y Ltd

AP to 31.12.2009 taxable profits	6,000
AP to 31.12.2010 taxable profits	24,000

Compute the group relief available.

Solution

In this example the period of the loss by X Ltd covers two accounting periods of Y Ltd and it will be necessary to determine the lower of the profit or loss in each corresponding period.

Group relief available

	£	£
Overlapping period 1.4.2009 to 31.12.2009		
X Ltd 3/4 × (16,000)	(12,000)	
Y Ltd 3/4 × 6,000	4,500	
Restricted to the lower amount		4,500
Overlapping period 1.1.2010 to 31.3.2010	£	£
X Ltd ¼ × (16,000)	(4,000)	
Y Ltd ¼ × 24,000	6,000	
Restricted to the lower amount		4,000
Total		8,500

a) An overlapping period is the period throughout which both the claimant and the surrendering companies meet the qualifying conditions for group relief (as to membership of the group or consortium) and which is a common period within the corporation tax accounting periods of both companies.

b) The maximum loss to be surrendered is the smaller of the unused part of the total available or the unrelieved part of the total profit of the claimant company in the overlapping period.

c) The unused part of the loss is the part remaining after prior surrenders of loss. This assumes that the total loss available for the overlapping period is computed and successive surrenders of loss are deducted from that total until the whole of the loss for the overlapping period is exhausted.

d) The unrelieved part of the total profit assumes an apportionment of the total profit for the entire accounting period between the amount for the overlapping period and the balance. The profit for the overlapping period is then taken and successive group relief claims are deducted from it until, cumulatively, the profit is exhausted.

Companies joining or leaving a group

11. Group relief is generally only available if the claimant and surrendering companies are members of the same group (or fulfil the conditions relating to a consortium) throughout the accounting periods of both companies. However, when a company either joins or leaves a group or consortium, then some relief is available and a new accounting period is deemed to end or commence on the occurrence of that event.

Normally the profits/losses are apportioned on a time basis. However, if it appears that such an apportionment would produce an unreasonable result, then a more reasonable basis must be used.

Example

D Ltd, a trading company, acquires a 100% interest in W Ltd on the 30th June 2009. Both companies have the same year end and the results for the year to 31st December 2009 are as follows:

	D Ltd £	W Ltd £
Trading profit	17,000	(40,000)
Interest income	3,000	–
Chargeable gain	15,000	–
Chargeable loss	–	(10,000)
Charges on income – Trade charges	5,000	–

Compute the amount of group relief available.

Solution

On the acquisition of W Ltd who then with D Ltd forms a group, there is deemed to be a commencement of an accounting period for group relief purposes.

	£
Loss to be surrendered by W Ltd	
Loss for 12 months to 31.12.2009	40,000
Proportion for deemed accounting period from	
1.7.2009 to 31.12.2009 $^{6}/12 \times 40,000$	20,000
Loss to be claimed by D Ltd	
Trading profit	17,000
Interest income 3,000	
Chargeable gain	15,000
	35,000
Less charges on income	5,000
	30,000
Proportion from 1.7.2009 $^{6}/12 \times 30,000 =$	15,000

Since this is smaller than the amount of the loss of the surrendering company, this is the maximum available for group relief.

The computations for the year to 31st December 2009 are:

£

D Ltd

Taxable profits as above	30,000
Less group relief	15,000
Assessment	15,000

W Ltd

Trading loss	40,000
Less surrendered	15,000
Unused loss	25,000

Notes

i)   The balance of the loss of W Ltd is not available for future group relief, but it can be used by W Ltd under Section 393A(1)(b) or 393(1).

ii)   The capital loss of W Ltd may not be set against the chargeable gain of any other company.

Similar provisions apply when a company leaves a group, and the profits and losses up to the date of the demerger must be apportioned to determine the amount of any group relief available.

Consortium relief

12.   Where there is a consortium of companies as defined in section 6 above, the following relief may be available:

a)   surrender to consortium members

b)   surrender by the consortium members

c)   a mixture of group/consortium relief

d)   relief through a link company.

Relief is only available to a UK member of a consortium which can include overseas members.

Surrender to a consortium member

13.   K Ltd is owned by four companies A Ltd (20%), B Ltd (30%), C Ltd (10%) and D Ltd (40%).

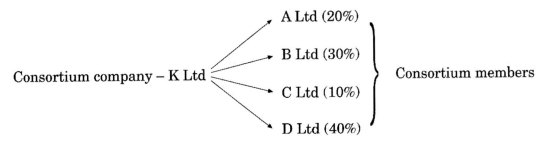

If K Ltd incurs a trading loss it may be surrendered to the consortium members A, B, C, D in proportion to their shareholding in K Ltd. Thus if K Ltd makes a loss of £20,000, the amount that can be surrendered to the consortium members is:

		£
A Ltd	20% × 20,000	4,000
B Ltd	30% × 20,000	6,000
C Ltd	10% × 20,000	2,000
D Ltd	40% × 20,000	8,000
		20,000

The amount of the loss that can be surrendered by K Ltd is reduced to the extent that it has profits of the same accounting period available to relieve the loss under Section 393A(1)(a). It should be noted that K Ltd does not have to make the claim under Section 393A(1)(a) but the consortium relief is restricted as though this had taken place whereas with group relief this restriction does not apply.

Surrender by the consortium members

14. Where a consortium member makes a loss then this can be surrendered to the consortium company. However, in this case the amount that can be surrendered is limited to the percentage of the *profits* of the consortium company.

Example

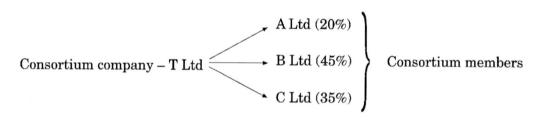

If C Ltd makes a loss then the amount that can be surrendered to T Ltd is restricted to 35% of the profit of T Ltd.

For example, if C Ltd makes a loss of £25,000 and T Ltd has profits of £50,000 then the amount of the loss that can be surrendered is limited to 35% □□□£50,000 i.e. £17,500.

In this case it is not necessary for C Ltd to consider any other profits available for set-off under Section 393A(1)(a).

A mixture of group/consortium relief

15. Under Sections 405 and 406 TA 1988 the position is as follows.

a) Where a consortium owned company is also a member of a group of companies then that company is known as a 'group/consortium company'.

b) If a group/consortium company incurs a loss then the amount that can be surrendered pro rata to the consortium members must first be reduced by:

i) any potential claim under Section 393(A)(1)(a) (set-off against other profits of the same period)

ii) any potential group relief claims that could be made under Section 402.

The potential loss claims do not have to be made, but their availability restricts the loss to be surrendered by the group/consortium company.

c) Where the group/consortium company has taxable profits and wishes to claim loss relief from any of its consortium members then the available profits must first be reduced by any potential group loss claims within the group/consortium company's own group.

d)   If the accounting periods of the members of the group/consortium are not co-terminus then an overlapping arises and the relief claimed cannot be more than the consortium members' proportionate share in the equity of the consortium subsidiary.

Example

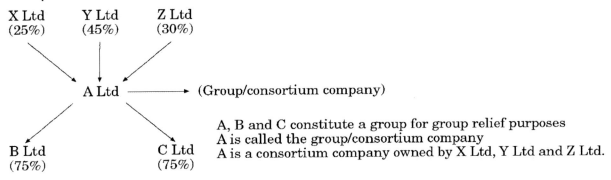

X Ltd (25%)   Y Ltd (45%)   Z Ltd (30%)

A Ltd ⟶ (Group/consortium company)

B Ltd (75%)   C Ltd (75%)

A, B and C constitute a group for group relief purposes
A is called the group/consortium company
A is a consortium company owned by X Ltd, Y Ltd and Z Ltd.

The following results relate to the year ended 31.12.2009.

		£
A Ltd	Trading loss	80,000
	Chargeable gain	12,000
B Ltd	Trading profits	25,000
C Ltd	Trading loss	10,000
	Chargeable gains	3,000

Compute the amounts that could be surrendered to X Ltd.

Solution

		£	£
a)	A Ltd trading loss		80,000
	Less potential reliefs:		
	Section 393A(1)(a) A Ltd	12,000	
	Section 402 B Ltd	25,000	
	Section 402 C Ltd	3,000	40,000
			40,000
	25% × 40,000 =		10,000
b)	A Ltd trading loss		80,000
	Less potential reliefs:		
	Section 393A(1)(a) A Ltd	12,000	
	Section 402 B Ltd	18,000	30,000
			50,000
	25% × 50,000 =		12,500

Notes

i)   In (a) the inter-group relief by B & C and the possible claim under Section 393A(1)(a) by C has not been exercised.

ii)   In (b) the amount of potential group relief is after taking:

C Ltd Section 393A(1)(a)	£10,000 – £3,000	=	£7,000 loss
B Ltd group relief with C Ltd	£25,000 – £7,000	=	£18,000 profit.

Relief through a link company

16. A link company is defined as a company which is a member both of a consortium and of a group.

Example

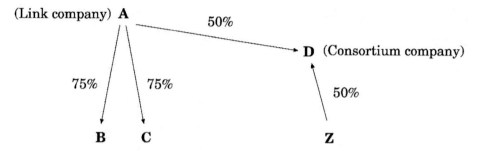

A, B and C constitute a group for group relief purposes.

A and Z jointly own the consortium company D.

A is a member of a group and a consortium.

Example

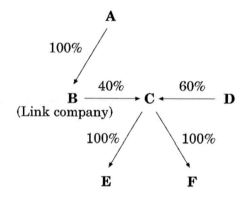

A and B constitute a group. C, E and F constitute a group. C is owned by a consortium of two members B and D. C is also a group consortium company.

In respect of the year ending 31st December 2009 the companies have the following results:

	£	
A Ltd	100,000	
B Ltd	(30,000)	loss
C Ltd	(20,000)	loss
D Ltd	Nil	
E Ltd	12,000	
F Ltd	(4,000)	loss

Calculate the possible claims for group relief and consortium relief.

Solution: AP to 31st December 2009

E Ltd	Profits before relief		12,000
	Less Group relief surrendered by F	4,000	
	do. C	8,000	12,000
	Assessment		–
A Ltd	Profits before relief		100,000
	Less Group relief surrendered by B	30,000	
	Consortium relief C:		
	40% × (20,000 – 8,000)	4,800	34,800
	Profits chargeable to corporation tax		65,200

Notes

The consortium relief available to A Ltd from C Ltd is the lower of:

A Ltd profits after group relief i.e.		100,000 – 30,000	=	70,000
B Ltd share of C Ltd loss i.e.	40%	(20,000 – 8,000)	=	4,800

Exemption from income tax – inter company transactions

17.   Payments of interest, royalty payments and annual payments and annuities, are made without the deduction of income tax where the companies concerned are within charge to UK corporation tax. For payments made on or after the 1st January 2004 the exemption is extended to interest and royalty payments where the recipient is an EU company.

Transfer of assets between group companies (groups only)

18. a) There is no method of group relief applicable to chargeable gains and losses which arise within different members of a group of companies. Accordingly, when a company disposes of a chargeable asset outside the group, then any capital gain arising will be chargeable to corporation tax. However, if the disposal is by a member of a group of companies to another group company then the provisions of Section 171 TCGA 1992 enable the transaction to be construed as if the disposal does not give rise to any chargeable gain or loss. This is achieved by deeming the consideration for the disposal of the asset to be such an amount that neither a gain nor a loss accrues to the company disposing of the asset. When the asset is ultimately disposed of outside the group, then a normal liability to corporation tax on any gain would arise.

b) The company actually disposing of the asset and another company in the group can elect that the disposal outside the group be treated as being made by the other company. The election must be made within two years after the end of the accounting period in which the actual disposal is made.

c) Companies and groups of companies may ask the Inland Revenue to agree the value of land and buildings held by them on 31st March 1982. The request must extend to the entire property portfolio of the company or group. The service is available only if the company or group have at least 30 properties held since 31st March 1982 or fewer such properties but with an aggregate current value greater than £30 million. Companies must provide values for checking, and these must be supported by professional valuations.

d) From 5th December 2005 anti-avoidance rules were introduced to deter corporations from deliberately creating capital losses, buying capital gains and losses and other creative capital gains/losses to off-set against income. The new rules adhere to the principal of a capital gain or loss arising as a result of a genuine commercial transaction.

Companies eligible

19. a) A group comprises of a principal company and all of its 75% subsidiaries.

b) A 75% subsidiary means a company whose ordinary share capital is owned by another company either directly or indirectly to the extent of at least 75%. Again ordinary share capital comprises all shares other than relevant preference shares.

c) Where the principal company is itself a 75% subsidiary of another company, then both its parent and its subsidiaries, together with the principal company, constitute a group.

d) From 1st April 2000, companies can transfer assets to one another on a no gain/no loss basis in a wider range of circumstances than at present. In particular, it is possible to make such transfers between:

   i)   two UK resident companies with a common non-resident parent company;

   ii) a UK resident company and a non-resident company within the same world wide group, where the latter company carries on a UK trade through a branch or agency.

e) A company is not a member of a group unless the principal member of the group has itself directly or indirectly a more than 50% interest in its profits and assets.

Members of a consortium are not eligible for treatment as a group for the purposes of this section, nor are close investment holding companies, unless the transfer is between close investment holding companies.

Assets available for group treatment

20.   The disposal of any form of property contained in Section 21 TCG ACT 1992 could give rise to the no gain or loss treatment, but there are some exceptions which are as follows.

a) Where the disposal is of redeemable preference shares in a company, on the occurrence of the disposal.

b) Where the disposal is of a debt due from a member of a group, effected by satisfying the debt or part of it.

c) Where the disposal arises from a capital distribution on the liquidation of a company.

d) Where the company is a dual resident member of a group of companies and any gain made by that company would be exempt.

If the transfer is of an asset which the recipient company appropriates to its trading stock, then that company is deemed to have received a capital asset and immediately transferred that asset to its trading stock. There would thus be no capital gain or loss arising on the inter-company transfer, as it would fall within the provisions noted above.

Where the asset transferred to a group company was trading stock of the transfer or company, then the latter is treated as having appropriated the asset as a capital asset immediately prior to the disposal. The value placed on the asset for trading purposes under Section 161 TCG ACT 1992 would be the transfer value giving rise to a 'no gain or loss' situation.

Other points

21. a) When an asset is disposed of by a group company to a company outside the group, then any capital allowances granted to any member of the group relating to the asset are taken into consideration in computing any gain or loss.

b) If a company to which an asset has been transferred ceases to be a member of a group within six years of the date of the transfer the position is as follows.

   i)   At the date of the acquisition of the asset by the company leaving the group or if later the beginning of the accounting period when the company left the group, it is deemed to have sold and reacquired the asset at its market value.

ii) There will therefore, be a chargeable gain or loss on the difference between the market value and the original cost to the group of the asset.

This provision does not apply if a company ceases membership of a group by being wound up.

c) The provisions of Section 152 TCG Act 1992 (rollover relief) is extended to groups and enables all trades carried on by the group to be treated as one.

For further details *see Chapter 34.*

Company reconstruction without change of ownership Section 393–4 TA 1988

22. When a company ceases trading and another company takes over the same trade, then unrelieved losses can be carried forward to the successor company providing that certain conditions are met, which are:

a) On or at any time within two years after the succession and within one year prior thereto, at least 75% of the interest in the trade is held by the same persons. This means that three quarters of the ordinary share capital in both companies must be held by the same persons throughout the three year period.

b) Throughout the same period the same trade must be carried on by a company in charge to corporation tax.

23. Where there is a transfer of trade then the following applies.

a) The trade is not treated as if it had been discontinued and a new one started.

b) Loss relief under Section 393A(1)(b) is not available to the company ceasing to trade. If the second company ceases to trade within four years of the succession, then terminal loss relief can be carried back, where appropriate, to the first company.

c) Relief under Section 393(1) for the carry forward of losses is available subject to any claim by the company ceasing to trade, under Section 393A(1)(a) i.e. set off against corporation tax profits.

Where a trade or part thereof is transferred between two companies after so that Section 343 applies, then relief to successor for losses brought forward is restricted where the amount of the 'relevant liability' immediately before the transfer exceeds the open market value of the 'relevant assets' at that time.

d) No balancing adjustments are raised on the transfer.

e) Unused capital allowances can also be carried forward.

f) Losses can not be carried forward where at any time before the change in ownership, the scale of activity becomes small or negligible and the change takes place before any considerable revival has occurred.

g) Other losses or capital gains tax losses cannot be transferred.

The main provisions relating to the transfer of trades are contained in Section 343 and 344 of the TA 1988.

Change in ownership – disallowance of trading losses Section 768 TA 1988

24. No relief for trading losses carried forward under Section 393(1) is available where:

a) within any period of three years there is both a change in the ownership of the company *and* (either earlier, later or simultaneously) a major change in the nature or conduct of a trade carried on by the company, *or*

b) there is a change in the ownership of the company at *any time* not just within a three year period – after the scale of the activities in a trade have become small or negligible and before any revival of the trade.

These provisions prevent the set-off of a loss incurred by a company in an accounting period beginning before the change of ownership against trading income of an accounting period ending after the change of ownership.

There is a change in the ownership of a company when:

a) a single person acquires more than 50% of the ordinary share capital of the company

b) two or more persons each acquire more than 5% or more of the ordinary share capital and together they own more than 50% of the ordinary share capital.

A major change in the nature of the trade is defined as

a) a major change in the type of property dealt in, or services or facilities in the trade, *or*

b) a major change in customers, outlets or markets of trade.

On a change in ownership, if the company fails to pay its corporation tax liability for an AP then it may in certain circumstances be assessed on the person who had control of the company before the change.

Miscellaneous

25. a) With effect from the 1st April 2004 the transfer pricing rules apply to transactions undertaken within the UK.

b) Parent companies which act as holding companies are treated as companies with investment business.

Student self-testing questions

1. The results of A Ltd and its wholly owned subsidiary B Ltd for the three years ended 31st March 2010 are as follows:

		31.3.2008 £	31.3.2009 £	31.3.2010 £
A Ltd	Trading profit/(loss)	1,200	(7,500)	4,800
	Income from property	500	500	500
B Ltd	Trading profit	2,500	3,500	5,000

A Ltd makes a claim for loss relief under Section 393A(1)(a) and (b) and then claims group relief under Section 402.

Show the computations.

Solution: Corporation tax computations

	31.3.2008 £	31.3.2009 £	31.3.2010 £
A Ltd			
Trading profit	1,200	–	4,800
Less Section 393(1)	–	–	1,800
	1,200	–	3,000
Income from property	500	500	500
	1,700	500	3,500
Less Section 393A(1)(a) and (b)	1,700	500	–
Assessments	–	–	3,500

B Ltd

Trading profit	2,500	3,500	5,000
Less group relief Section 402	–	3,500	–
Assessments	2,500	–	5,000

Loss memorandum		£	£
Loss year to 31st March 2009			7,500
Section 393A(1)(a)31.3.2009		500	
Section 393A(1)(b)31.3.2008		1,700	
Section 393(1)	31.3.2010	1,800	
Section 402	31.3.2009	3,500	7,500

(group relief surrendered to B Ltd)

Note. The maximum amount has been surrendered to B Ltd.

2. Arch Ltd owns 100% of the share capital of Bow Ltd and Can Ltd. The results of each company for the year ended 31 March 2010 are as follows:

	Arch Ltd	Bow Ltd	Can Ltd
	£	£	£
Tax adjusted trading profit/(loss)	(125,000)	650,000	130,000

Required

a) **Explain the group relationship that must exist in order that group relief can be claimed.** (3 marks)

b) **Explain how group relief should be allocated between the respective claimant companies in order to maximise the potential benefit obtained from the relief.** (4 marks)

c) **Assuming that reliefs are claimed in the most favourable manner, calculate the corporation tax liabilities of Arch Ltd, Bow Ltd and Can Ltd for the year ended 31 March 2010.** (8 marks)

ACCA Pilot paper modified

Solution

(a) (1) One company must be a 75% subsidiary of the other, or both companies must be 75% subsidiaries of a third company

(2) The holding company must have an effective interest of at least 75% of the subsidiary's share capital, excluding relevant preference shares.

(3) The holding company must have the right to receive at least 75% of the subsidiary's distributable profits and net assets on a winding up.

(b) (1) Group relief should be allocated to the company(s) with the highest marginal rate of tax first. The upper and lower limits for marginal relief for this group are £1,500,000 / 3 = £500,000 and £300,000 / 3 = £100,000. Profits of between £500,000 and £100,000 are taxed at the marginal rate of 29.75%. Next those companies that are taxed at the 28% rate should be given relief.

(c)

	£	£	£
	Arch Ltd	Bow Ltd	Can Ltd
Trading profit	-	650,000	130,000
Less group relief	-	(95,000)	(30,000)
PCTCT	-	555,000	100,000
Tax @ 21%			21,000
Tax @ 28%		155,400	

Questions without answers

1. Z Ltd, a UK trading company, acquired a 75% interest in Q Ltd on the 30th September 2009. Both companies have the same year end and their results for the AP 31.3.2010 are as follows:

	Z Ltd £	Q Ltd £
Trading profit/(loss)	75,000	(30,000)
Income from property	15,000	–
Chargeable gain	10,000	–
Debenture interest paid (gross)	5,000	5,000

Compute the amount of group relief available for the AP to 31st March 2010, and show the corporation tax computations.

2. Straight plc is the holding company for a group of companies. All of the companies in the group have an accounting date of 31 March. The group structure is as follows:

Straight plc
|
100%
|
Arc Ltd
|
80%
|
Bend Ltd
|
75%
|
Curve Ltd

For the year ended 31 March 2010 Straight plc has a trading profit of £185,000. As at 31 March 2009 the company had unused trading losses of £15,000 and unused capital losses of £10,000.

Straight plc sold a freehold office building on 20 June 2009 for £350,000, and this resulted in a capital gain of £80,000.

During the year ended 31 March 2010 Straight plc received dividends of £18,000 from Arc Ltd, and dividends of £9,000 from Triangle plc, an unconnected company. These figures are the actual amounts received.

Arc Ltd sold a freehold warehouse on 10 March 2010, and this resulted in a capital loss of £40,000.

   i)   **Explain why Straight plc, Arc Ltd, Bend Ltd and Curve Ltd form a group for capital gains purposes, and why Curve Ltd would be excluded from the group if Straight plc's holding in Arc Ltd were only 80% instead of 100%.**

ii) **Before taking into account any notional transfer of assets, calculate the corporation tax payable by Straight plc for the year ended 31 March 2010.**

(ACCA)

3. Animal Ltd is the holding company for a group of companies. The results of each group company for the year ended 31 March 2010 are as follows:

	Tax adjusted trading profit/(loss)	Income from property	Franked Investment Income
	£	£	£
Animal Ltd	450,000	5,000	20,000
Bat Ltd	65,000	15,000	–
Cat Ltd	85,000	–	–
Dog Ltd	100,000	–	–
Elk Ltd	–	–	–
Fox Ltd	60,000	–	5,000
Gnu Ltd	(200,000)	–	–

Animal Ltd owned 100% of each subsidiary company's ordinary share capital throughout the year ended 31 March 2010 with the following exceptions:

(1) Animal Ltd only owned 90% of Bat Ltd's ordinary share capital.

(2) Animal Ltd's shareholding in Cat Ltd was disposed of on 31 December 2009.

The trading profit of £85,000 is for the year ended 31 March 2010.

(3) Animal Ltd's shareholding in Dog Ltd was acquired on 1 January 2010. The trading profit of £100,000 is for the year ended 31 March 2010.

Elk Ltd was a dormant company throughout the year ended 31 March 2010.

Required:

(a) **Explain the group relationship that must exist in order that group relief can be claimed.** **(3 marks)**

(b) **Explain why there are six associated companies in the Animal Ltd group of companies. Your answer should identify the six associated companies.** **(3 marks)**

(c) **Assuming that relief is claimed for Gnu Ltd's trading loss of £200,000 in the most favourable manner, calculate the profits chargeable to corporation tax of Animal Ltd, Bat Ltd, Cat Ltd, Dog Ltd and Fox Ltd for the year ended 31 March 2010.** **(9 marks)**

(15 marks)

ACCA past paper 2.3 June 2003 (updated)

Student note: Some of these questions contain brief elements of capital gains tax and this topic is covered in chapters 27-34.

26 International aspects

Introduction

1. This chapter deals with some of the more common features of corporation tax arising from overseas operations under the following main headings:

> Interest income
>
> Income from overseas possessions
>
> Computation of underlying taxes
>
> Foreign tax credit and loss relief
>
> Non resident companies
>
> Controlled foreign companies.
>
> Transfer pricing.
>
> Foreign Branches – UK companies

Interest income

2. Interest receivable is brought within the loan debt relationship arrangements, and any profit taxed as interest income. Income arising from securities outside the UK is chargeable to corporation tax under interest income. 'Security income' means income from a mortgage or debenture, but not from stocks or shares.

Example

K Ltd has the following data relating to the 12 months AP to the 31st March 2010.

	£
Trading profits	1,280,000
Interest income:	
(foreign interest after 15% withholding tax)	85,000
Chargeable gains	250,000

Calculate the CT payable for the AP to 31st March 2010.

Solution

K Ltd corporation tax computation AP 31.3.2010

	£
Trading profits	1,280,000
Interest income (gross) $\frac{85,000}{85} \times \frac{100}{1}$	100,000
Chargeable gains	250,000
Profits chargeable to CT	1,630,000

Corporation tax payable	£
1,630,000 @ 28%	456,400
Less double tax relief	15,000
Corporation tax liability	441,400

Note

The double tax relief is the lower of the following:

Foreign income	100,000
UK tax @ 28%	28,000
Foreign tax	15,000

Income from overseas possessions

3. Income arising from possessions outside of the UK, not being income consisting of any remuneration of any office or employment, are chargeable to corporation tax under this case. Income from possessions embraces all income from trades, professions and vocations, income from stocks and shares, and foreign bank interest.

With Case V income the form of unilateral relief available under Section 790 TA 1988 is extended to 'underlying taxes' in special circumstances. Underlying taxes means taxes on profits out of which dividends have been declared attracting the withholding tax. The special circumstances are:

a)   The UK company must control not less than 10% of the voting power of the overseas company paying the dividend.

b)   The 10% holding can be established through the medium of sub-subsidiaries, providing that the direct and indirect linkage gives the minimum percentage.

c)   Unilateral relief can be extended to cover provincial, state and municipal taxes.

There are extensive anti-avoidance rules applicable to dividends paid where the relievable tax credit is enhanced through the use of a chain of overseas company investments and dividends.

Computation of underlying taxes

4. Underlying tax is the tax attributable to the relevant profits out of which the dividend has been paid, and following the rules outlined in the case of *Bowater Paper Corporation Ltd* v *Murgatroyd* 1969 the rate is calculated as follows:

$$\frac{\text{Actual tax paid}}{\text{Actual tax paid} + \text{Relevant profits}} \times 100 = \text{Rate \%}$$

Relevant profits = Profits after tax per accounts.

The actual amount of the underlying tax may be computed from the following formula:

$$\frac{\text{Overseas tax paid}}{\text{Relevant profits}} \times \text{Dividend (including withholding tax)}$$

Example

T Ltd received a dividend of £9,000 (after withholding tax of 10%) from its wholly owned subsidiary V Ltd. The profit and loss account of V Ltd for the AP to 31st March 2010 translated into sterling is as follows:

	£	£
Operating profit before taxation		30,000
Deduct:		
Taxation provision	12,000	
Deferred taxation	3,000	15,000
Profit after taxation		15,000
Proposed dividend (gross)		10,000
Retained profits		5,000

The actual tax paid on the profits of V Ltd was £10,000.

T Ltd had trading profits for the AP to 31st March 2010 of £30,000.

Compute the corporation tax payable.

Solution

i) **Calculation of overseas income income**

$$\text{Underlying tax rate} = \frac{10,000}{10,000 + 15,000} \times 100 = 40\%$$

	£		
Cash received	9,000		
Add withholding tax	1,000		
	10,000	=	60%
Add underlying tax	6,667	=	40%
Overseas income	16,667	=	100%

ii) **T Ltd corporation tax computation AP 31.3.2010**

	£
Trading profits	30,000
Overseas income (gross)	16,667
Profits chargeable to CT	46,667
CT payable: 46,667 @ 21%	9,800
DT relief	
Foreign income 16,667 @ 21%	3,500
CT payable	6,300

Notes

i) The excess foreign tax suffered, and unrelieved is:

	£
Overseas income	16,667
Less dividend received (net)	9,000
Total foreign tax	7,667
Less DTR	3,500
Unrelieved foreign tax	4,167

ii) The amount of the underlying tax is also computed as follows:

$$\frac{\text{Overseas tax paid}}{\text{Relevant profits}} \times \text{Dividend} = \frac{10,000}{15,000} \times 10,000 = £6,667$$

Example

T plc, a UK company, has corporation tax profits of £1,472,000 for the year ended 31st March 2010. During the same period T plc received a dividend from its foreign subsidiary Z Ltd of £17,850 after a deduction of 15% withholding tax, and underlying tax of 25% on its profits.

Calculate the gross amount of the foreign dividend and the CT computation for the AP to 31.3.2010.

Solution

	£	£
Foreign income grossed up		
Net dividend received	17,850	
Withholding tax: $15\% \times \dfrac{17,850}{100-15} \times \dfrac{100}{1}$	3,150	21,000
Underlying tax: $25\% \times \dfrac{21,000}{100-25} \times \dfrac{100}{1}$		7,000
		28,000

Corporation tax computation AP 31.3.2010

	£	£
Trading profits		1,472,000
Overseas income gross		28,000
		1,500,000
Corporation tax @ 28%		420,000
Less double tax relief: withholding tax	3,150	
underlying tax	7,000	
	10,150	
Restricted to lower UK tax:		
28,000 @ 28%	7,840	7,840
Unrelieved foreign tax	2,310	
Corporation tax liability		412,160

Foreign tax credit and loss relief

5. Where a UK company has foreign income then in order to preserve the maximum amount of DT relief the consideration of loss relief claims should be considered carefully.

Example

W Ltd and its wholly owned UK subsidiary□X Ltd have the following results for the year ended 31st March 2010.

	W Ltd £	X Ltd £
Trading profits	(30,000)	80,000
Overseas income gross	16,000	
(gross before withholding tax of 15%)		
Chargeable gains	2,000	1,000

Calculate the corporation tax payable in the following situations:

a) **W Ltd claims loss relief under Section 393A(1)(a) and surrenders the maximum loss to X Ltd.**

b) **W Ltd makes no claim under Section 393A(1)(a), and surrenders as much loss as possible to X Ltd.**

Solution

(a) **Corporation tax computations AP 31.3.2010**

	W Ltd £	X Ltd £
Trading profits	–	80,000
Overseas income	16,000	–
Chargeable gains	2,000	1,000
	18,000	81,000
Less Section 393A(1)(a)	(18,000)	
Section 402		12,000
Profits chargeable to CT	–	69,000
CT Payable @ 21%	–	14,490
Unrelieved foreign tax £2,400		
CT payable	–	14,490

	W Ltd £	X Ltd £
(b) **Trading profits**	–	80,000
Overseas income	16,000	–
Chargeable gain	2,000	1,000
	18,000	81,000
Less Section 402	–	30,000
Profits chargeable to CT	18,000	51,000
CT payable @ 21%	3,780	10,710
Less DTR	2,400	–
MCT	1,380	10,710

Notes

i) By not claiming loss relief under Section 393A(1)(a) the DT relief of £2,400 has been obtained.

Controlled foreign companies

6. Under Section 747 TA 1988 certain UK resident companies with interests in a controlled foreign company (CFC) may be charged to corporation tax on an apportionment of the profits of the CFC. Some of the main features of the existing legislation are noted below.

Controlled foreign company

The charge due to corporation tax, which only occurs on the direction of the Board of Inland Revenue, is applicable where the company is a controlled foreign company (CFC). The latter is defined to mean:

a) an overseas resident company which is under the control of persons resident in the UK, and,

b)   the overseas resident company is subject to a lower level of taxation in its country of residence than it would be in the UK. Lower in this case means that the tax paid in the country of residence < 75% of the tax payable had the company been resident in the UK.

c)   Control may exist where 40% is held by a UK company.

d)   On 22nd March 2006 additional anti-avoidance measures were introduced to extend the CFC regime to UK incorporated companies that are tax-resident outside of the UK.

e)   On the 12th March 2008 additional anti-avoidance measures were introduced to extend the CFC regime to those corporations that classified as Special Purpose Vehicles (SPV's) set up with the sole intention of avoiding UK corporation tax.

Tests of exclusion

7. No direction will be made to apportion the profits of the CFC if that company satisfies any one of the following tests of exclusion.

a)   *Pursues an acceptable distribution policy*
In general this means that a trading CFC must have paid to UK residents by way of dividends at least 90% of its available profits. For all other companies 90% of taxable profits less capital gains and foreign tax must be distributed.

b)   *Is engaged in exempt activities*
Under this heading a CFC is engaged in exempt activities if it has, throughout the accounting period, a business establishment in its territory of residence and its business affairs are effectively managed there. The latter is evidenced, amongst other things, if it has a sufficient number of employees in the territory to deal with its volume of business locally. Certain non- trading activities have to meet other criteria to benefit under this heading.

c)   *Fulfils the public quotation condition*
This is met where the CFC has at least 35% of its shares which have voting power, quoted on a recognised stock exchange in the country of residence. As for close companies in the UK, this requirement is not met where 85% of the company's voting power is in the hands of its principal members.

d)   *Satisfies the motive test*
Under this heading there are two conditions to be met if the CFC is to satisfy the motive test.

   i)   The existence of the CFC was not made mainly for the purposes of achieving a diversion of profits from the UK, and

   ii)   Any reduction of UK tax resulting from transactions is either minimal or is not the main reason for undertaking those transactions.

e)   *Has chargeable profits <£50,000*
Where the chargeable profits of the CFC are less than £50,000 for a 12 month accounting period then it automatically falls within the exclusion category.

Chargeable profits, including capital gains, if the company was resident in the UK, would be chargeable to corporation tax.

Assessable profits

8. a) Where a direction to apportion chargeable profits is made then corporation tax at the 'appropriate rate' is assessed on the following:

The apportioned amount of chargeable profits minus any creditable tax attributable to the apportioned profits such as DT relief.

The appropriate rate of corporation tax is the average rate applicable to the company's UK profits for the accounting period in which the accounting period of the CFC ends.

b)   Deductions at the appropriate rate can be made where the UK company has reliefs which have not been fully utilised against its UK taxable profits. The reliefs are:

    i)   relief for trading losses (Sec 393a(1)(2))

    ii)   relief for excess charges (Sec 393(9))

    iii)   group relief (Sec 402)

    iv)   relief for management expenses (Sec 75(1)).

c)   No self-assessment need be made unless the amount apportioned to a UK company and its associates of the CFC's chargeable profits amount to at least 10% of those chargeable profits.

Inland Revenue press releases have provided a list of what are known as 'excluded countries'. Where a company carries on a trade in one of these countries it is deemed to fall outside the charging provisions noted above.

CFC – self-assessment

9. a) The CTSA rules – i.e. corporation tax self-assessment rules – apply to CFCs. This means that UK companies have to include in their tax returns (Form 6T600B) their share of the CFCs profits in accordance with the CFC rules. A direction by the Board will no longer be needed. The charge to tax is triggered, however, if a UK company (including connected or associated persons) has a 25% or more interest in a non-exempt CFC.

b)   The de minimis level before CFC tax may be due is £50,000 of chargeable profits in the CFC for a year.

Transfer pricing

10. Under section 77A and Schedule 28AA TA 1988, a UK business is required to calculate its taxable income by reference to an arm's length result for transactions with connected businesses outside the scope of UK taxation, where this would increase the amount of UK taxable income. The following additional rules apply

i)   The transfer pricing rules include transactions within the UK.

ii)   Small and medium sized companies will be exempt except in relation to transactions with a related business in a territory which does not have a double tax treaty with the UK containing a suitable non discrimination article.

iii)   In exceptional circumstances a medium sized company may be required by the IR to apply transfer pricing rules.

Foreign branches of UK companies

11. Where a UK company carries on its trade through a foreign branch then the following rules apply:

    a)   The trade is subject to UK corporation tax and branch profits are taxed as Case I income.

    b)   Where the overseas branch is subject to foreign taxation then this is taken into consideration in determining the amount of double tax relief available.

    c)   Capital allowances are available in respect of plant and machinery purchased by the overseas branch and in respect of industrial buildings, providing the trade is taxed as Case I income.

Student self-testing question

A Ltd, a UK company, owns one third of the voting shares in B, a foreign company. The profit and loss account of B for the AP 31.3.2010 in sterling was:

	£	£
Profit before tax		1,000,000
Tax on profits	300,000	
Deferred tax	100,000	400,000
		600,000
Dividend (net)	240,000	
Withholding tax	60,000	300,000
Retained profit		300,000

Actual tax liability was agreed at £270,000. A Ltd has trading profits for the AP 31.3.2010 of £1,355,000. Compute the DTR and CT payable.

Solution: A Ltd corporation tax computation AP 31.3.2010

	£
Trading profits	1,355,000
Overseas income	145,000
Profits chargeable to CT	1,500,000
CT payable @ 28%	420,000
Less DT relief	40,600
Mainstream CT liability	379,400

Notes

i) Calculation of underlying tax

$$\frac{270,000}{270,000 + 600,000} = 31.034\%$$

	£	£
Net dividend received $\dfrac{240,000}{3} =$		80,000
Add withholding tax @ 25%		20,000
		100,000
Add underlying tax		
$\dfrac{100,000}{100 - 31.034} \times 100 =$	145,000	
Less	100,000	45,000
Overseas income		145,000

The amount of the underlying tax is also computed as:

$$\frac{270,000}{600,000} \ \square\square \ 100,000, \text{ i.e. } 45,000.$$

ii) Unrelieved foreign tax amounts to the following:

	£
Overseas income	145,000
Foreign taxes (20,000 + 45,000)	65,000
UK tax 145,000 × 28%	40,600
Unrelieved tax	24,400

Questions without answer

1. T Ltd, a UK company, owns 20% of A, a foreign resident company. T Ltd has the following results for the year ended 31st March 2010:

	£
Trading profits	2,000,000
Chargeable gains	66,000
Overseas income (gross)	280,000
Debenture interest paid (gross)	140,000
Dividend paid (net)	500,000

The foreign income is subject to overseas taxation of 45%.

Compute the CT payable for the AP to 31st March 2010.

2. Wash plc is a UK resident company that manufactures kitchen equipment. The company's trading profit for the year ended 31 March 2010 is £1,600,000. Wash plc has a 100% owned subsidiary, Dry Inc. that is resident overseas. Dry Inc. sells kitchen equipment that has been manufactured by Wash plc. The results for Dry Inc. for the year ended 31 March 2010 are as follows:

	£	£
Trading profit		580,000
Corporation tax		160,000
		420,000
Dividend paid – net	270,000	
– withholding tax	30,000	300,000
Retained profits		120,000

Dry Inc.'s dividend was paid during the year ended 31 March 2010. The company's corporation tax liability for the year ended 31 March 2010 was £8,000 more than that provided for in the accounts.

All of the above figures are in pounds sterling.

i) **Calculate Wash plc's corporation tax liability for the year ended 31 March 2010.**

ii) **Explain the tax implications if Wash plc were to invoice Dry Inc. for the exported kitchen equipment at a price that was less than the market price**

(ACCA)

End of section questions and answers

Corporation tax question NO. 1 Advance Ltd

Advance Ltd, a trading company, makes up its accounts annually to 31st January. The company had the following results for the year ended 31st January 2010.

	£	£
Sales		1,565,204
Less: Purchases	1,044,134	
Add: Stock at 1.2.09	264,216	
	1,308,350	
Less: Stock at 31.1.10	390,208	
		918,142
		647,062
Less: Salaries, NHI, pension contributions	244,778	
Rent, rates, light, heating	104,324	
Delivery expenses	43,211	
Sundry expenses (note 1)	14,409	
Professional charges (note 2)	12,602	
Repairs and maintenance (note 3)	8,040	
Interest payable (note 4)	7,491	
Depreciation plant and machinery	3,620	
		438,475
Trading profits		208,587
Investment income (note 5)		42,000
Profit before taxation		250,587
Taxation	120,000	
		130,587
Dividend (note 6)		70,000
		60,587
Add: Retained earnings brought forward		201,266
Retained earnings carried forward		261,853

1. Sundry expenses

Stationery, postage, telephone	4,866
Office teas, coffees etc.	1,982
Entertaining –	
UK customers	1,456
staff	2,514
Office cleaning	864
Removal expenses	1,256
Hire of vehicles	1,031
Donation (non-trade)	440
	14,409

2. Professional charges

	£
Audit and accountancy	7,420
Legal charges re new lease	2,650
Legal charges – re unfair dismissal claim	1,500
Debt collecting	1,032
	12,602

3. Repairs and maintenance

	£
Building alterations to new premises	3,200
Decoration of new premises	1,250
Annual maintenance contract	1,900
Sundry repairs	1,690
	8,040

4. Interest payable (to UK bank)

	£
Accrued at 1.2.2009	(2,444)
Paid during year	6,524
	4,080
Accrued at 31.1.2010	3,411
	7,491

5. Investment income

	£
Franked investment income	30,000
Debenture interest (received) gross – trading purposes	12,000
	42,000

6. Dividend. This was paid on 2nd January 2010. £70,000

7. The pool written down value at 1st February 2009 was £32,080. During the year items of plant and machinery were sold for £16,400 and the company acquired on the 28th April 2009 a second hand polishing machine for £26,000 and new items of plant costing £3,400.

8. Advance Ltd moved premises during the year acquiring a 99 year lease on 1st May 2009 of a showroom for a consideration of £180,000.

9. Advance Ltd is a qualifying small company for capital allowance purposes.

You are required to compute the profits subject to corporation tax for the year ended 31st January 2010 on the assumption that all available reliefs are claimed.

Solution: Advance Ltd AP to 31st January 2010

	£	£
Trading profits		
Adjustment of profits		
Profits before taxation		250,587
Add back:		
Entertaining	1,456	
Donation	440	
Legal charges re new lease	2,650	
Alterations to new premises	3,200	
Decoration of new premises	1,250	
Depreciation	3,620	12,616
		263,203
Less non-taxable investment income (42,000 – 12,000)		30,000
		233,203

Plant and Machinery

Capital allowances		£
Balance b/f		32,080
Less proceeds of sale		16,400
		15,680
WD allowance 20%		3,136
		12,544
Additions eligible for AIA – 28.4.2009	29,400	
100% on first £50,000	29,400	0
WDV c/f		12,544

Corporation tax computation. AP to 31st January 2010

	£	£
Trading adjusted profits	233,203	
Less : capital allowances (3,136 + 29,400)	32,536	200,667
Profits chargeable to corporation tax		200,667

Notes

i)   The amount invested in the new showroom was:

	£
99 year lease	180,000
Legal charges	2,650
	182,650
Non-revenue expenditure:	
Alterations	3,200
Decoration	1,250
	187,100

ii)   There would be no capital allowances available in respect of the new showroom nor any relief for the lease premium being greater than 50 years' duration.

iii) Small company profit rate of 21% would apply in this case.

iv)   Debenture interest received for trade purposes of £12,000 is treated as trading income.

v)   Capital expenditure on plant machinery of £29,400 is eligible for the 100% AIA (1.4.09 – 31.3.10)

Corporation tax question NO. 2 Threadbare Ltd

Threadbare Ltd is a manufacturer of quality clothing which makes its accounts up to the 31st March each year.

Its trading and profit and loss account for the year ended 31st March 2010, its centenary year, is as follows:

	£	£
Sales		787,315
Cost of sales		731,118
Gross profit		56,197
Add miscellaneous income		5,142
		61,339
Less expenses:		
Salaries	4,705	
Rent rates and insurance	1,650	
Lighting and heating	1,291	
Motor expenses	7,402	
Repairs and renewals	10,011	
General expenses	8,117	
Depreciation	5,483	
Debenture interest paid (gross)	7,500	
		46,159
Profit before taxation		15,180

You are given the following information:

1. Miscellaneous income comprises:

	£
Profit on sale of plant and machinery	1,542
Dividend from UK company (net) received 15.6.09	900
Building society interest received (gross) non trade	1,800
Bank interest received (gross) non trade	900
	5,142

2. Repairs and renewals comprise:

	£
Repairs to new premises, necessary to make them usable	2,502
Portable office partitioning	2,509
New microcomputers	5,000
	10,011

3. General expenses comprise:

	£
Bad debts written off	1,123
Increase in general bad debt provision	1,000
Legal costs of renewal of lease for 20 years	557
Entertaining	1,532
Promotional gifts of bottles of wine	2,055
Gift aid payment	100
Theatre outing for staff	1,750
	8,117

4. Capital allowances in respect of all qualifying expenditure have been agreed at £1,819.

5. The debenture interest is in respect of a trade loan.

a) Compute the profits chargeable to corporation tax.

b) Calculate the mainstream liability.

Solution: Threadbare Ltd AP to 31st March 2010

Adjustment of trading profits

	£	£
Profit before taxation		15,180
Add back:		
Repairs to make premises usable	2,502	
Office partitioning	2,509	
New microcomputers	5,000	
Increase in general bad debt provision	1,000	
Entertaining	1,532	
Promotional gifts	2,055	
Gift aid	100	
Depreciation	5,483	
Debenture interest	7,500	27,681
		42,861
Less non-trading income		5,142
		37,719

Corporation tax computation AP to 31st March 2010

	£	£	£
Adjusted trading profits	37,719		
Less: capital allowances	1,819		35,900
Non-trading loan deficit (7,500 − 2,700)			
			(4,800)
			31,100
Charges on income paid			
Gift aid			100
Profits chargeable to corporation tax			31,000
Corporation tax payable:			
31,000 @ 21 %			6,510

Notes

i) Non-trading loan deficit is:

Debenture interest paid	7,500	
Less interest received	2,700	4,800

ii)   F11 of £1,000 is included in P of £32,000.

Corporation tax question No. 3 XYZ Ltd

XYZ Ltd, a company with no associated companies, has been trading since 1990, making up its accounts to 31st March.

In arriving at a profit from all sources of £509,000 for the year ended 31st March 2010, the following items were included:

Income:	£	
Rent received	10,000	
Premium on a lease granted to a tenant	8,000	(note 1)
Interest on deposit account non trade	700	
Debenture interest non-trading		
Gross amount from UK company	1,000	
Dividend from UK company (received net 4,500 in August 2009)		

Gross amount	5,000	
Profit on sale of freehold property	126,850	(note 3)

Items charged in the accounts:

Depreciation	5,900	(note 5)
Legal charges:		
Negotiation of a new lease taken by the company	700	(note 2)
Blackmail payment made on 1.12.09	600	
Sale of premises	850	
General expenses	2,400	(note 4)

Notes

i)   The premium received was in respect of the granting of a lease for 21 years. (Ignore CGT in respect of this transaction.)

ii) The new lease took effect from 1st April, 2009 for a term of 21 years.

iii) The chargeable gain arising on the sale of the property has been agreed at £29,200.

iv) General expenses included:

	£
Gift aid	200
Staff Christmas party	400
Thefts by staff	1,000
Sundries (all allowable)	800
	2,400

v)   Capital allowances have been agreed at £61,200.

vi) Dividends paid:

a)   For year ended 31.3.09 £60,000 paid 20.7.09.

b)   Interim for year ended 31.3.10 £20,000 paid 1st January 2010.

Compute the corporation tax payable.

Solution: XYZ Ltd corporation tax computation. AP to 31st March 2010

	£	£
Trading income		
Profit from all sources		509,000
Add back:		
Depreciation	5,900	
Legal charges: New lease	700	
Blackmail payment	600	
Sale of premises	850	
General expenses: Gift aid	200	8,250
		517,250
Less non-trading income		
Rent received	10,000	
Premium on lease	8,000	
Non-trading interest	1,700	
Dividends	5,000	
Profit on sale of factory	126,850	151,550
		365,700
Less capital allowances		61,200
		304,500

Income from land and property	£

	£
Lease premium	8,000
Less $(21 - 1) \times 2\% \times 8,000$	3,200
	4,800
Rents received	10,000
	14,800

Corporation tax computation. AP to 31.3.2010

	£
Trading profits	304,500
Income from land and property	14,800
Interest received	1,700
	321,000
Chargeable gains	29,200
	350,200
Less charges on income paid:	
Gift aid	200
Profit chargeable to corporation tax	350,000
Corporation tax payable:	
£350,000 @ 28%	98,000
Less marginal relief:	

$$(1,500,000 - 355,000) \times \frac{350,000}{(350,000 + 5,000)} \times 7/400$$

$$= 1,145,000 \times \frac{350,000}{355,000} \times 7/400 \qquad 19,755$$

	78,245

Note: F11 is included in the calculation of the marginal relief.

Corporation tax question No. 4 Urban Usage Ltd

Urban Useage Ltd (UUL) is a waste re-cycling company and is resident in the United Kingdom. It has no associated companies. The company ceased to trade on 30 September 2009 and its summarised results to that date are:

	Year to 31.12.05 £	Year to 31.12.06 £	Year to 31.12.07 £	Year to 31.12.08 £	Period to 30.9.09 £
Trading profit/(loss)	500,000	250,000	100,000	(200,000)	(300,000)
Non-trade loan interest					
Received (gross amounts)	10,000	9,000	3,000	8,000	6,000
Chargeable gain/(loss)	–	(20,000)	–	30,000	(4,000)
Franked investment income (gross amounts)	2,500	3,000	3,500	–	–
Trade charges (gross amounts)	40,000	45,000	30,000	–	–
Payments to charity gift aid	7,000	7,000	7,000	7,000	7,000

Notes

i) Loan interest was received on 31 March each year.

ii) Bank interest was received on 30 June each year.

iii) Frank investment income was received on 31 October each year.

iv) Trade charges were made on 31 May each year.

v) Gift aid payments were made on 31 August each year.

vi) The trade charges were subject to deduction of tax at source.

You are required to calculate the corporation tax liabilities for all years for which information is provided after claiming maximum relief at the earliest possible time for the trading losses sustained.

(ACCA)

Solution: Urban Useage Ltd

	Year to 31.12.05 £	Year to 31.12.06 £	Year to 31.12.07 £	Year to 31.12.08 £	Period to 30.9.09 £
Trading profits	500,000	250,000	100,000	–	–
Non-trade loan interest	10,000	9,000	3,000	8,000	6,000
Chargeable gains	–	–	30,000	–	
Total profits	510,000	259,000	103,000	38,000	6,000
Loss reliefs	127,500	214,000	73,000	38,000	6,000
	382,500	45,000	30,000	– –	
Charges on income –					
Trade	(40,000)	(45,000)	(30,000)	– –	
Non-trade	(7,000)	—	–	–	
Profits chargeable	335,500	—	–	–	

1. Calculation of terminal loss

9 months to 30.9.09	300,000
3 months to 31.12.08	50,000
	350,000
Less period to 30.9.09	6,000
	344,000
Less year to 31.12.06	214,000
	130,000
Less 3 months to 31.12.05	127,500
Unrelieved loss	2,500

2. Loss memo

Loss AP 31.12.08		200,000
Less terminal loss	50,000	
Sec 393(A(1)(a)	38,000	
Sec 393(A)(1)(b)	73,000	161,000
Unrelieved loss		39,000

Corporation tax question No. 5 Andrell Ltd

Andrell Ltd was incorporated on 1st April 1990 and has always prepared accounts to the 31st March each year. The company have now decided to change their accounting date to the 30th June and the accounts for the 15 months to the 30th June 2009 are as follows:

		£	£
Gross trading profits			177,310
Add:	Bank deposit interest received (note 1)	3,450	
	Rents receivable (note 2)	1,000	
	Profit on sale of plant (note 3)	6,000	10,450
			187,760
Deduct:	Wages and salaries	43,000	
	Light and heat	23,000	
	Legal and professional charges (note 4)	1,860	
	Depreciation	3,000	
	Bad debts (note 5)	4,600	
	Debenture interest (gross) (note 6)	11,250	
	Rent and rates	10,000	96,710
			91,050

Andrell Ltd has no associates and the following information is given in relation to the above accounts.

1. The bank short-term interest was received on the following dates:

	£
30th June 2008	1,200
31st December 2008	1,850
30th June 2009	400

2. On the 1st June 2009 the company negotiated to rent out part of its storage facilities, the annual rent of £1,000 being payable in advance on the 10th June. Due to an industrial dispute however, the first payment was not received by Andrell Ltd until the 10th July 2009.

3. An extract from the asset disposal account relating to the sale of plant showed:

	£
Cost (purchased 1st March 2008)	12,000
Less accumulated depreciation	2,500
	9,500
Sale proceeds (sold 12th February 2009)	15,500
Profit on sale	6,000

The chargeable gain has been agreed in advance with the HMRC at £2,300

4. The legal and professional charges were made up of:

	£
Accountancy charge re annual audit	1,500
Accountancy charge for negotiating successful tax appeal	150
Legal charge for negotiating successful appeal against rates	210
	1,860

5. Bad debts comprise:

	£
Increase in specific reserve	1,800
Increase in general reserve	2,000
Bad debts written off	1,200
	5,000
Less bad debts recovered	400
	4,600

6. The debenture interest paid related to an issue of debentures for trade purposes, the interest on which is payable half yearly on 30th June and 31 December and includes an accrual of £2,500 as at the 30 June 2009.

The company had a pool balance brought forward for plant and machinery of £276,000 and the only capital additions during the period of account were:

	£
1st December 2008 purchased new plant	3,000
1st May 2008 purchased 16 saloon motor cars for use by the company salesmen, each car costing £12,000 (average CO2<160)	192,000

Compute the mainstream corporation tax payable. Assume that all allowances and reliefs are claimed as soon as possible. The company qualifies as a medium company for capital allowance purposes.
(ACCA)

Solution: Andrell Ltd AP 15 months to 30.6.2009

Adjustment of profits

	£	£
Net profit per accounts		91,050
Add back: Legal and professional fees	150	
Depreciation	3,000	
Bad debts	2,000	
		5,150
		96,200
Less non-trading income		
Bank deposit interest	3,450	
Rents receivable	1,000	
Profit on sale of plant	6,000	10,450
		85,750

Corporation tax computation AP

	12 months to 31.3.2009 £	3 months to 30.6.2009 £
Adjusted profits 12/15 × 85,750	68,600	
3/15 × 85,750		17,150
Less capital allowances	55,800	20,160
Trading profits	12,800	(3,010)
Interest income	3,050	400

Income from land and property	–	1,000
	18,850	1,400
Chargeable gain	2,300	
	18,150	1,400
Less Section 393A(1)(a)(b) (total 2,410)	(1,610)	(1,400)
Profits chargeable to CT	16,540	NIL
Corporation tax @ 21%	3,473	

	AP to 31.3.09 £	AP to 30.6.09 £
Capital allowances		
Pool balance b/f	276,000	211,200
Proceeds of sale (restricted to cost)/additions	(12,000)	192,000
	264,000	403,200
WD allowance 20%	52,800 $20\% \times \frac{1}{4}$	20,160
	211,200	

AIA addition	3,000		
AIA 100%	3,000	nil	
Balance c/f		211,200	383,040

Summary of allowances		AP to 31.3.09	AP to 30.6.09
Plant and machinery WD allowance		52,800	20,160
	FYA	3,000	–
Motor cars	WD allowance	–	–
		55,800	20,160

Notes

i)   The loss of £3,010 is carried back to the accounting period to 31.3.2009 under Section 393A(1)(b).

ii) As the motor vehicles do not cost more than £12,000 and have an average CO_2 of <160 g/km each they are pooled collectively with the plant.

iii) Debenture interest for trade purposes is allowed in computing trading income.

iv) Only the adjusted profit **before** capital allowances is time apportioned.

Corporation tax question No. 6 XYZ Ltd

XYZ Ltd has a 100% subsidiary, PQR Ltd, and each company prepares its accounts annually for the year ended 31st March.

The following are summarised results of each company for the year ended 31st March 2010:

	XYZ Ltd £	PQR Ltd £
Adjusted trading profit/(loss) before capital allowances	279,600	(112,000)
Deposit interest received	4,000	2,000
Chargeable gains/(losses)	7,900	(4,000)
Capital allowances	2,400	1,800

XYZ Ltd has a capital loss brought forward of £2,700.

a) Show how the losses of PQR Ltd may be most effectively utilised, assuming that it is not expected to make a profit for several years.

b) Calculate the mainstream corporation tax payable by XYZ Ltd.

c) State with reasons the advice that should have been given in respect of the capital transactions of PQR Ltd. (CIMA)

Solution

a) **Corporation tax computation AP. 31.3.2010**

	£	XYZ Ltd £	PQR Ltd £
Adjusted Trading profit	279,600		–
Less capital allowances	2,400	277,200	
Interest income		4,000	2,000
		281,200	2,000
Chargeable gain	7,900		
Less losses b/f	2,700	5,200	–
		286,400	2,000
		286,400	–
Less S393A 1 (a)			2,000
Less group relief Section 402		111,800	
Profits chargeable to corporation tax		174,600	–

b) **Corporation tax payable:**

£174,600 @ 28% =		49,392

Marginal relief:

$$(750,000 - 174,600)\ \frac{174,600}{174,600} \times 7/400$$

= 575,400 × 7/400		10,070
Mainstream liability		39,322

Loss memorandum:

Trading loss	112,000
Add capital allowances	1,800
S393A 1 (a)	2,000
Group relief	111,800

Notes

1) Small company rate for two companies in 1,500,000/2 = 750,000 and 300,000/2 = 150,000

2) The capital loss incurred by PQR Ltd cannot be surrendered to XYZ Ltd by way of group relief. It can be carried forward and set against future gains incurred by PQR Ltd. In view of the group relationship it would be advantageous to elect for the matching of the gain in XYZ Ltd against the loss in PQR Ltd. The position would have been:

	£
Net gain per computation	5,200
Less transferred from PQR Ltd	4,000
	1,200

Corporation tax question No. 7 Fell Ltd

Fell Ltd, a UK resident company, commenced trading in 1995 and makes up accounts to 31 December each year.

The accounts for the year ended 31 December 2009 show a net profit of £649,885. A detailed examination of the accounts reveals that the following items of income and expenditure have been included in arriving at that figure.

Income	£
Bank interest received December 2009	683
Building society interest received November 2009	420
Dividends from UK companies received November 2009	1,125
Expenditure	
Depreciation	22,000
Gift aid	1,000
Staff Christmas party (20 staff @ £32.50 each)	650
Provision for bad debts @ 5% of debtors	2,500
Debenture interest payable (gross) – trade purposes	3,250

Capital allowances are due in the sum of £10,395.

Fell Ltd has two UK resident trading subsidiaries, in which it has the following shareholdings:

Moor Ltd	100%
Hill Ltd	80%

The results of the subsidiary companies for the year ended 31 December 2009 were as follows:

	Trading profit/(loss) £	Charges £	Rental income £
Moor Ltd	(25,000)	(5,000)	–
Hill Ltd	(50,000)	–	3,000

All charges are trade charges.

Compute the tax payable by each company for the year ended 31 December 2009, assuming that all reliefs are claimed as soon as possible and show the losses to be carried forward, if any. *(CIOT)*

Solution: Fell Ltd corporation tax computation AP 31.12.2009

	£	£
Adjusted trading profits	673,157	
Capital allowances	10,395	662,762
Interest income 683 + 420		1,103
		663,865
Less charges paid: gift aid		1,000
		662,865
Less Group relief Moor Ltd	30,000	
Hill Ltd	47,000	77,000
Profits chargeable to CT		585,865
Corporation tax payable:		
FY 08 £146,466 @ 28%		41,010
FY 09 £439,399 @ 28%		123,032
Total corporation tax		164,042

Notes

i)

Net profit per accounts			649,885
Add back:Depreciation	22,000		
gift aid	1,000		
Bad debt provision	2,500	25,500	
		675,385	
Less:Bank interest	683		
BSI	420		
Dividends	1,125	2,228	673,157

ii) **Group relief. Moor Ltd**

Trading loss	25,000	
Charges on income	5,000	30,000

Both trade and none trade charges may be group relieved.

iii) **Group relief. Hill Ltd**

Trading loss	50,000
Rental income	3,000
Less Section 393A(1)(a)	3,000
	–
Loss available for group relief	47,000

iv) With three companies in the group the upper levels of profits are:

FY to 31.3.2009 $\dfrac{1,500,000}{3} \times 3/12 =$ 125,000

Profits chargeable to CT 585,865 x 3/12 = 146,466

FY to 31.3.2010 $\dfrac{1,500,000}{3} \times 9/12 =$ 375,000

Profits chargeable to CT 585,865 × 9/12 = 439,399

Therefore, the full rates of corporation tax apply.

Questions without answers

1.   Zoom plc

Zoom plc is a manufacturer of photographic equipment. The company had profits chargeable to corporation tax of £860,000 for the year ended 31 March 2010. The summarised profit and loss account of Zoom plc for the year ended 31 March 2010 is as follows:

	£
Operating profit (note 1)	812,500
Other operating income (note 4)	16,400
Income from investments	
Bank interest (note 5)	10,420
Loan interest (note 6)	22,500
Income from property (note 7)	44,680
Dividends (note 8)	49,500
Total other income	127,100
	956,000
Interest payable (note 9)	46,000
Profit before taxation	910,000

Note 1 – Operating profit

Depreciation of £48,100 has been deducted in arriving at the operating profit of £812,500.

Note 2 – Plant and machinery

On 1 April 2009 the tax written down values of plant and machinery were as follows:

	£
General pool	19,600
Motor car CO2 180g/km	20,200
Short-life asset	3,600

The following transactions took place during the year ended 31 March 2010:

		Cost/(Proceeds)
		£
15 April 2009	Purchased equipment	4,600
19 June 2009	Purchased a computer	2,280
29 July 2009	Sold the motor car	(24,200)
31 July 2009	Purchased motor car CO2 150g/km (1)	16,600
3 August 2009	Sold a lorry	(9,800)
22 December 2009	Purchased motor car CO2 140g/km (2)	10,800
1 February 2010	Purchased motor car (3)	14,200
28 February 2010	Sold the short-life asset	(800)

The expensive motor car sold on 29 July 2009 for £24,200 originally cost £23,400. The lorry sold on 3 August 2009 for £9,800 originally cost £17,200. Motor car (3) purchased on 1 February 2010 is a low emission motor car (CO2 emission rate of less than 110 grams per kilometre).

Zoom plc is a large company as defined by the Companies Acts.

Note 3 – Industrial building

On 1 April 2009 Zoom plc purchased a second-hand factory for £360,000 (including £120,000 for the land and £55,000 for general offices). The factory was originally constructed at a cost of £285,000 (including £100,000 for the land and £40,000 for general offices). The factory was first brought into use on 1 October 2002. It has always been used for industrial purposes.

Note 4 – Other operating income

The other operating income consists of patent royalties that were received during the year ended 31 March 2009.

Note 5 – Bank interest received

The bank interest was received on 31 March 2010. The bank deposits are held for non-trading purposes.

Note 6 – Loan interest receivable

The loan was made for non-trading purposes on 1 July 2009. Loan interest of £15,000 was received on 31 December 2009, and interest of £7,500 was accrued at 31 March 2010.

Note 7 – Income from property

Zoom plc lets out two unfurnished office buildings that are surplus to requirements.

The first office building was let from 1 April 2009 until 31 January 2010 at a rent of £3,200 per month. On 31 January 2010 the tenant left owing two months rent which Zoom plc was unable to recover. This office building was not re-let until May 2010.

The second office building was not let from 1 April 2009 to 31 July 2009. During this period Zoom plc spent £4,800 on advertising for new tenants, and £5,200 on decorating the office building. On 1 August 2009 the office building was let at an annual rent of £26,400, payable in advance.

Zoom plc insured its two office buildings at a total cost of £3,360 for the year ended 31 December 2009, and £3,720 for the year ended 31 December 2010. The insurance is payable annually in advance.

Note 8 – Dividends received

The dividends were all received from unconnected UK companies. The figure of £49,500 is the actual cash amount received.

Note 9 – Interest payable

The interest is in respect of a debenture loan that has been used for trading purposes. Interest of £23,000 was paid on 30 September 2009 and again on 31 March 2010.

Note 10 – Other information

Zoom plc made quarterly instalment payments in respect of its corporation tax liability for the year ended 31 March 2010.

Zoom plc has three associated companies.

For the year ended 31 March 2009 Zoom plc had profits chargeable to corporation tax of £780,000.

Required:

(a) (i) Calculate the amount of capital allowances and industrial buildings allowance that Zoom plc can claim for the year ended 31 March 2010. (12 marks)

(ii) Prepare a computation for the year ended 31 March 2010 reconciling Zoom plc's profit before taxation with its profits chargeable to corporation tax. Your reconciliation should commence with the profit before taxation figure of £910,000, clearly identify the tax adjusted trading profit and the amount of profit from land and property, and end with the figure of £860,000 for profits chargeable to corporation tax. (8 marks)

(b) Explain why Zoom plc was required to make quarterly instalment payments in respect of its corporation tax liability for the year ended 31 March 2010.

(3 marks)

(c) Calculate Zoom plc's corporation tax liability for the year ended 31 March 2010, and explain how and when this will have been paid. You should assume that the company's profits chargeable to corporation tax of £860,000 accrued evenly throughout the year. (3 marks)

(d) Explain how your answer to part (c) above would differ if Zoom plc had no associated companies. Your answer should include a calculation of the revised corporation tax liability for the year ended 31 March 2010. (4 marks)

(30 marks)

Past ACCA question December 2004

2. Scuba Ltd

Scuba Ltd is a manufacturer of diving equipment. The following information is relevant for the year ended 31 December 2009:

Operating profit

The operating profit is £162,400. The expenses that have been deducted in calculating this figure include the following:

	£
Depreciation and amortisation	45,200
Entertaining customers	7,410
Entertaining employees	2,470
Gifts to customers (diaries costing £25 each displaying Scuba Ltd's name)	1,350
Gifts to customers (food hampers costing £80 each)	1,600

Leasehold property

On 1 April 2009 Scuba Ltd acquired a leasehold office building that is used for business purposes. The company paid a premium of £80,000 for the grant of a twenty-year lease.

Disposal of industrial building

On 30 June 2009 Scuba Ltd sold a factory for £195,000 (including £65,000 for land). The factory was purchased new from a builder on 1 January 2005 for £215,000 (including land of £65,000), and was immediately brought into use. It has always been used for industrial purposes.

Purchase of industrial building

Scuba Ltd purchased a new factory from a builder on 1 July 2009 for £240,000, and this was immediately brought into use for industrial purposes. The cost was made up as follows:

	£
Drawing office serving the factory	34,000
General offices	40,000
Factory	98,000
Ventilation system	8,000
Land	60,000
	240,000

Plant and machinery

On 1 January 2009 the tax written down values of plant and machinery were as follows:

	£
General pool	47,200
Expensive motor car	22,400
Long-life asset	105,000

The following transactions took place during the year ended 31 December 2009:

		(Cost/Proceeds) £
3 January 2009	Purchased machinery	7,300
10 January 2009	Purchased a computer	1,400
4 May 2009	Purchased a motor car CO2 180g/km	10,400
18 August 2009	Purchased machinery	14,800
29 September 2009	Purchased computer software	1,100
15 November 2009	Sold a lorry	(12,400)

The motor car purchased on 4 May 2009 for £10,400 is used by the factory manager, and 40% of the mileage is for private journeys. The lorry sold on 15 November 2009 for £12,400 originally cost £19,800.

Scuba Ltd is a small company as defined by the Companies Acts.

Income from property

Scuba Ltd lets a retail shop that is surplus to requirements. The shop was let until 31 December 2008 but was then empty from 1 January 2009 to 30 April 2009. During this period Scuba Ltd spent £6,200 on decorating the shop, and £1,700 on advertising for new tenants. The shop was let from 1 May 2009 to 31 December 2009 at a quarterly rent of £7,200, payable in advance.

Interest received

Interest of £435 was received from the Inland Revenue on 31 October 2009 in respect of the overpayment of corporation tax for the year ended 31 December 2008.

Profit on disposal of shares

On 8 November 2009 Scuba Ltd sold 5,000 £1 ordinary shares in Deep Blue Sea plc for £42,400. The shareholding had been purchased on 19 March 2007 for £26,900. The retail prices index (RPI) for March 2007 was 204.4, and for November 2009 it was 211.3 (estimated).

Other information

Scuba Ltd has no associated companies, and the company has always had an accounting date of 31 December.

Required:

(a) Calculate Scuba Ltd's tax adjusted trading profit for the year ended 31 December 2009. You should assume that no other adjustments are required to the operating profit except in respect of the expenses that have been deducted. (21 marks)

(b) Calculate Scuba Ltd's corporation tax liability for the year ended 31 December 2009. You should ignore any capital gains implications arising in respect of the disposal of the industrial building on 30 June 2009. (6 marks)

(c) State the date by which Scuba Ltd must pay its corporation tax liability for the year ended 31 December 2009, and explain the implications for the company if this liability is paid three months late. (3 marks)

(30 marks)

Past ACCA question December 2005

3. Tock Tick

Tock-Tick Ltd is a clock manufacturer. The company's summarised profit and loss account for the year ended 31 March 2010 is as follows:

	£
Gross profit	822,280
Operating expenses	
Bad debts (note 1)	9,390
Depreciation	99,890
Gifts and donations (note 2)	3,090
Professional fees (note 3)	12,400
Repairs and renewals (note 4)	128,200
Other expenses (note 5)	426,920
Total expenses	679,890
Operating profit	142,390

Profit from sale of fixed assets

Disposal of office building (note 6)	78,100

Income from investments

Loan interest (note 7)	12,330
	232,820
Interest payable (note 8)	48,600
Profit before taxation	184,220

Note 1 – Bad debts

Bad debts are as follows:	£
Trade debts recovered from previous years	(1,680)
Trade debts written off	7,970
Decrease in specific bad debt provision	(3,100)
Increase in general provision for doubtful debts	6,200
	9,390

Note 2 – Gifts and donations

Gifts and donations are as follows:	£
Gifts to customers (pens costing £45 each displaying Tock-Tick Ltd's name)	1,080
Gifts to customers (food hampers costing £30 each)	720
Long service award to an employee	360
Donation to a national charity (made under the gift aid scheme)	600
Donation to a national charity (not made under the gift aid scheme)	250
Donation to a local charity (Tock-Tick Ltd received free advertising in the charity's magazine)	80
	3,090

Note 3 – Professional fees

Professional fees are as follows:	£
Accountancy and audit fee	5,400
Legal fees in connection with the issue of share capital	2,900
The cost of registering the company's trademark	800
Legal fees in connection with the renewal of a 35-year property lease	1,300
Debt collection	1,100
Legal fees in connection with a court action for not complying with health and safety legislation	900
	12,400

Note 4 – Repairs and renewals

The figure of £128,200 for repairs and renewals includes £41,800 for replacing the roof of an office building, which was in a bad state of repair, and £53,300 for extending the office building.

Note 5 – Other expenses

Other expenses include £2,160 for entertaining suppliers; £880 for counselling services provided to two employees who were made redundant; and the cost of seconding an employee to a charity of £6,400. The remaining expenses are all fully allowable.

Note 6 – Disposal of office building

The profit of £78,100 is in respect of a freehold office building that was sold on 20 February 2010 for £276,000.

The office building was purchased on 18 November 2001 for £197,900. Assume the indexation allowance from November 2001 to February 2010 is £51,100.

The building has always been used by Tock-Tick Ltd for trading purposes.

Note 7 – Loan interest received

The loan interest is in respect of a loan that was made on 1 July 2009. Interest of £8,280 was received on 31 December 2009, and interest of £4,050 was accrued at 31 March 2010. The loan was made for non-trading purposes.

Note 8 – Interest payable

The interest payable is in respect of a debenture loan that is used for trading purposes. Interest of £24,300 was paid on 30 September 2009 and again on 31 March 2010.

Note 9 - Plant and machinery

On 1 April 2009 the tax written down values of plant and machinery were as follows:

	£
General pool	12,200
Motor car CO2 170g/km	20,800
Short-life asset	3,100

The following transactions took place during the year ended 31 March 2010:

	Cost/(Proceeds) £
28 May 2009 Sold the motor car CO2 170g/km	(34,800)
7 June 2009 Purchased a motor car	14,400
1 August 2009 Sold the short-life asset	(460)
15 August 2009 Purchased equipment	6,700

The motor car sold on 28 May 2009 for £34,800 originally cost £33,600. The motor car purchased on 7 June 2009 is a low emission motor car (CO2 emission rate of less than 110 grams per kilometre).

Tock-Tick Ltd is a small company as defined by the Companies Acts.

Required:

(a) Calculate Tock-Tick Ltd's tax adjusted Trading profit for the year ended 31 March 2010. Your computation should commence with the profit before taxation figure of £184,220. **(19 marks)**

(b) Calculate Tock-Tick Ltd's profits chargeable to corporation tax for the year ended 31 March 2010. **(5 marks)**

(c) State the effect on Tock-Tick Ltd's profits chargeable to corporation tax for the year ended 31 March 2010 if Tock-Tick Ltd had:

> **(i) For capital allowances purposes been a large-sized company as defined by the Companies Acts rather than a small company;** **(2 marks)**

> **(ii) Claimed the maximum possible group relief from a 100% owned subsidiary company that had made a trading loss of £62,400 for the year ended 31 December 2009;** **(4 marks)**

(30 marks)

Past ACCA question June 2005 (modified)

Part IV

Taxation of chargeable gains

27 General principles

Introduction

1. A comprehensive form of capital gains tax was introduced by the Capital Gains Tax Act 1965, and applied to all 'chargeable gains' arising after the 5th April 1965. The basic principle of capital gains tax is that when an asset is sold, any gain over the original cost is considered to be a taxable gain. In 1982 a system of indexation was introduced to take account of rising prices. In 1998 indexation was abolished for individuals (with any indexation being frozen at 1998 rates) but still remains for incorporated entities. A simplified system of taper relief with different percentages being applied depending on the length of ownership and whether the asset was a business or non business asset replaced the indexation allowance. In 2008 both frozen indexation allowances and taper relief was abolished and replaced with a simplified system of a flat rate of capital gains tax, again depending on the type of asset.

For the tax year, 2008-2009, some significant changes were implemented in relation to capital gains tax and these changes will be considered in detail in this and subsequent chapters. It is important to recognise that for individuals a separate regime exists in the computation of chargeable gains to that of incorporated entities. The main difference is that individuals do not get any relief for effects of increases in the general retail prices index (indexation allowance and taper relief) for the length of time they have owned an asset. This could be valuable depending on the length of time an asset is owned. Incorporated entities do continue to get indexation allowance up to the date of disposal; however, they are not subject to the rates of capital gains tax in the same way as individuals. Instead corporations are charged tax on capital gains at their corporation tax rate.

FA 2008 – fundamental changes

2. The following is an outline of the main changes to the taxation of chargeable gains introduced by the FA 2008 details of which are incorporated in various chapters of this section of the book. The main change to have an impact on individuals is the abolition of indexation and taper relief on the disposal of assets on or after 6th April 2008. Prior to this date the calculation of the chargeable gain was reduced by indexation and/or taper relief depending on the amount of time the asset had been held.

For individuals, including sole traders and partnerships:

a) For gains realised on or after 6th April 2008 the basic basis of computation of the chargeable gain is made by reference to the disposal proceeds less any allowable costs.

b) Chargeable gains are charged at a flat rate of 18% for non business assets or an effective rate of 10% (5/9ths of the gain is chargeable) on the first £1 million of gains for business assets that qualify for Entrepreneurs Relief. Any excess over £1 million is then charged at the full rate. The £1 million is a lifetime allowance, so that over an individual's lifetime, total gains are cumulative in arriving at the £1 million. The lifetime allowance commences for any disposals made on or after 6th April 2008.

For incorporated entities the position is as follows:

a) Chargeable gains are calculated by reference to the disposal proceeds, less any allowable costs and indexation allowance. The resulting gain is added to the profits chargeable to corporation tax figure and tax is calculated by reference to the corporation's effective tax rate. For a large corporation the rate will be 28%, for a small corporation the rate will be 21%. For those corporations in the marginal rate band, the effective tax rate will be between 21% and 28 for the current tax year.

b)   Share and securities are 'pooled' together and a weighted average cost is used to determine the allowable cost on disposal.

Disposal of assets by individuals on or before 5th April 2008;

3.   a)   For gains realised on or after 6th April 1998 up to 5th April 2008 indexation is only given for periods up to 5th April 1998 on assets acquired before that date. This includes the April 1998 RPI.

b)   For assets acquired on or after 1st April 1998 indexation allowance is not available in computing any chargeable gain for individuals.

c)   Indexation was replaced by a system of tapering relief which reduces the amount of the chargeable gains by reference to the period of time the asset has been held after 5th April 1998.

d)   Taper relief percentages were far more generous for business assets than non business assets.

Persons chargeable

4. The following classes of persons are chargeable to capital gains tax:

Individuals and personal representatives

Companies, who pay corporation tax at the appropriate company rate

Trusts and trustees.

Rates of tax 2009/10

5.	Person	Exemption	Rate of tax
	Individuals	£10,100	Chargeable gains after exemption are taxed at a flat rate of 18% or an effective rate of 10% on the first £1 million for those assets that qualify under the Entrepreneurs Relief scheme. Husband and wife are taxed separately.
	Companies	Nil	Chargeable gains taxed at company corporation tax rate, i.e. small company rate, marginal rate or full rate.

Chargeable assets

6. In accordance with Sections 21 and 22 of the TCGA 1992 all forms of property are assets for the purposes of capital gains tax, whether situated in the UK or not, including:

a)   options, debts, and incorporeal property in general

b)   currency other than sterling

c)   any form of property created by the person disposing of it, or coming to be owned without being acquired

d)   capital sums derived from assets.

Property

7. This includes anything capable of being owned such as freehold and leasehold land, shares and securities, and other tangible assets and intangible assets such as purchased goodwill.

Options

8. An option is a right of choice and where a person grants an option to another person then this is a disposal of a chargeable asset. If an option is exercised, any consideration received is added to any made with the initial grant, to form a single transaction.

Where an option is abandoned then this is not a disposal by the grantee so that he or she cannot establish a capital loss, except where the option is to subscribe for shares in a company or to acquire a business asset. The abandonment of a traded option in gilt edged securities, bonds, or loan stocks can also produce an allowable CGT loss.

Debts

9. An ordinary debt is not a chargeable asset in the hands of the original creditor, his or her personal representative or legatee. However, a person acquiring a debt say by an assignment, obtains a chargeable asset.

A debt on security is a chargeable asset and this includes any holding of loan stock of a government, local authority or company.

A loan to a trader, or payment by way of guarantee, where it is not a debt on a security, if irrecoverable, can be used to establish a capital loss.

Incorporeal property

10. This is other intangible property such as a tithe or easement, or a right to exploit a copyright.

Currency

11. Any currency other than sterling is a chargeable asset, but foreign currency acquired by an individual for personal use is exempted.

Created property – intangible fixed assets

12. This would include such assets as goodwill, copyright, patents and trade marks or know how. Goodwill, trade marks and copyright are chargeable assets.

Patents are not chargeable assets since any excess over cost is taxed as patent income.

Know how is treated as a chargeable asset where its disposal includes any part of a trade, with some exceptions. For the corporation tax treatment of intangible assets *see Chapter 19:* 8.

Capital sums

13. These are defined to include:

a)   Any capital sums received by way of compensation for any kind of damage or injury, to assets or for the loss, destruction or dissipation of assets or for any depreciation of an asset

b)   Capital sums received under a policy of insurance of the risks of any kind of damage or injury to, or the loss or depreciation of assets.

c)   Capital sums received in return for forfeiture or surrender of rights, or for refraining from exercising rights.

d)   Capital sums received as consideration for use or exploitation of assets.

When a person derives any capital sum from an asset, then the disposal of a chargeable asset occurs. If any part of the amount received is used to restore or replace the original asset then special reliefs apply. *See Chapter 32.*

Non-chargeable assets and exemptions

14. The following assets are either exempt assets or chargeable assets, on whose disposal there may not be a chargeable gain or loss.

a) Private motor vehicles.

   This includes private cars and vintage cars purchased for investment.

b) Savings certificates.

   All non-marketable securities are included under this heading such as National Savings Certificates, and Defence Bonds.

c) Gambling winnings.

   This covers winnings from pools, lotteries, premium bonds and bingo prizes.

d) Decorations for valour.

   These are exempt assets if disposed of by the individual to whom they were awarded, or their legatee. If purchased they become chargeable assets.

e) Currency.

   Foreign currency acquired for personal use is exempt.

f) Compensation.

   Any compensation or damages obtained for any wrong or injury suffered by a person, or in connection with his or her profession or vocation.

g) Life assurance and deferred annuities.

   No chargeable gain arises on the disposal of any rights under a life assurance policy or deferred annuity, providing the disposal is made by the original owner. The acquisition of such rights from an original owner is a chargeable asset.

h) British government securities and qualifying corporate bonds. QCBs held by corporate investors are chargeable to CT under the loan relationship rules.

i) Private residence. *See Chapter 29.*

j) Chattels. *See Chapter 29.*

k) Gifts to a recognised charity.

l) Certain disposals conditionally exempt from IHT e.g. works of art.

m) Tangible moveable property with useful life of less than 50 years, not used for trade purposes.

Exempt persons

15. The under-mentioned persons are exempted from capital gains tax:

a) Pension funds approved by the Inland Revenue.

b) Registered charities providing the gains are used for charitable purposes.

c) Registered friendly societies.

d) Local authorities.

e) Scientific research associations.

f) Community amateur sports clubs.

Administration

16. The capital gains tax pages of a tax return do not have to be completed for any year in which the total chargeable gains do not exceed the annual exemption (£10,100 – 2009/10) unless either

a)   the proceeds exceed four times the annual exemption (£40,400 – 2009/10) or

b)   there are allowable losses to be set against gains.

In general appeals can be made to either the General or Special Commissioners except:

a)   appeals in respect of the valuation of any land, which will be heard by a Lands Tribunal.

b)   appeals in respect of the valuation of unquoted shares which will be heard by the Special Commissioners.

c)   Where an election to appeal to the Special Commissioners is disregarded by the General Commissioners.

Payment of tax

17.   Capital gains tax is due when the final balancing payment is made under the income tax rules for self assessment, as described in Chapter 2. The due date is as follows:

2007/08	-	31st January 2009
2008/09	-	31st January 2010
2009/10	-	31st January 2011

It is possible to pay capital gains tax by instalments where the consideration is payable over a period exceeding 18 months, and payment of capital gains tax in one sum would cause undue hardship. Payment of tax by ten equal instalments is also available in respect of tax due on gifts not eligible for holdover relief (*see Chapter 33*).

Rebasing

18. Rebasing is only relevant to corporations that have held an asset prior to 31st March 1982, which was when the indexation system was introduced. The base date was changed from the 6th April 1965 to the 31st March 1982 and for disposals after the 5th April 1988 only gains or losses accruing from 31st March 1982 need be brought into charge to tax.

For assets held on 31st March 1982 re-basing means that the asset is assumed to be sold and immediately re-acquired on 31st March 1982 at that date.

In general, if the gain under the re-basing method is greater than it would be under the 'old rules' then the latter may be used. The taxpayer can make a once and for all election that all gains and losses acquired before 31st March 1982 are to be computed by reference to the 31st March 1982 re-basing method. In practice most assets that are re-valued with reference to the rebased amount will produce a lower gain, therefore the rebased amount will normally be used.

Indexation – Incorporated entities

19.   Assets acquired before 31st March 1982 can be re-valued at 31st March 1982 and that value substituted for the initial cost plus incidental expenses, under the re-basing principle.

The indexation allowance is calculated by reference to changes in the Retail Prices Index which was re-based to 100 in January 1987.

Where an asset was held on the 31st March 1982 then indexation allowance is automatically based on the higher of the original cost or market value at 31st March 1982.

Indexation cannot be used to create or increase a capital loss.

Outline computations

20. I.   Chargeable assets held by incorporated entities   **2009/10**

	£	£
Gross consideration or market value		–
Allowable deductions		
Initial cost of asset plus incidental expenses	–	
Enhancement expenditure (not repairs)	–	
Incidental costs of disposal	–	–
Unindexed gain		–
Indexation		–
Taxable gain added to PCTCT		–

		2009/10
	£	£
II. *Chargeable assets held by individuals*		
Gross consideration or market value		–
Allowable deductions		
Initial cost of asset plus incidental expenses	–	
Enhancement expenditure (not repairs)	–	
Incidental costs of disposal	–	–
Chargeable gain subject to capital gains tax		

Rates of interest

21. Rate of interest charged on outstanding tax 2.5% for individual and 1.75% for corporations at 24th March 2009.

Interest on tax repaid 0% at 24th March 2009

Retail prices index

22.

	Jan	Feb	Mar	April	May	June	July	Aug	Sept	Oct	Nov	Dec
1982	–	–	79.44	81.04	81.62	81.85	81.88	81.90	81.85	82.26	82.66	82.51
1983	82.61	82.97	83.12	84.28	84.64	84.84	85.30	85.68	86.06	86.36	86.67	86.89
1984	86.84	87.20	87.48	88.64	88.97	89.20	89.10	89.94	90.11	90.67	90.95	90.87
1985	91.20	91.94	92.80	94.78	95.21	95.41	95.23	95.49	95.44	95.59	95.92	96.05
1986	96.25	96.60	96.73	97.67	97.85	97.79	97.52	97.82	98.30	98.45	99.29	99.62
1987	100.00	100.40	100.60	101.80	101.90	101.90	101.80	102.10	102.40	102.90	103.40	103.30
1988	103.30	103.70	104.10	105.80	106.20	106.60	106.70	107.90	108.40	109.50	110.00	110.30
1989	111.00	111.80	112.30	114.30	115.00	115.40	115.50	115.80	116.60	117.50	118.50	118.80
1990	119.50	120.20	121.40	125.10	126.20	126.70	126.80	128.10	129.30	130.30	130.00	129.90
1991	130.20	130.90	131.40	133.10	133.50	134.10	133.80	134.10	134.60	135.10	135.60	135.70
1992	135.60	136.30	136.70	138.80	139.30	139.30	138.80	138.90	139.40	139.90	139.70	139.20
1993	137.90	138.80	139.30	140.60	141.10	141.00	140.70	141.30	141.90	141.80	141.60	141.90
1994	141.30	142.10	142.50	144.20	144.70	144.70	144.00	144.70	145.00	145.20	145.30	146.00
1995	146.00	146.90	147.50	149.00	149.60	149.80	149.10	149.90	150.60	149.80	149.80	150.70
1996	150.20	150.90	151.50	152.60	152.90	153.00	152.40	153.10	153.80	153.80	153.90	154.40
1997	154.40	155.00	155.40	156.30	156.90	157.50	157.50	158.50	159.30	159.50	159.60	160.00
1998	159.50	160.30	160.80	162.60	163.50	163.40	163.00	163.70	164.40	164.50	164.40	164.40
1999	163.40	163.70	164.10	165.20	165.60	165.60	165.10	165.50	166.20	166.50	166.70	167.30
2000	166.60	167.50	168.40	170.10	170.70	171.10	170.50	170.50	171.70	171.60	172.10	172.20
2001	171.10	172.00	172.20	173.10	174.20	174.40	173.30	174.00	174.60	174.30	173.60	173.40
2002	173.30	173.80	174.50	175.70	176.20	176.20	175.90	176.40	171.60	177.90	178.20	178.50
2003	178.40	179.30	179.90	181.20	181.50	181.30	181.30	182.60	182.50	182.60	182.70	183.50
2004	183.10	183.80	184.60	185.70	186.50	186.80	186.80	187.40	188.10	188.60	189.00	189.90
2005	188.90	189.60	190.50	191.60	192.00	192.20	192.20	192.60	193.10	193.30	193.60	194.10
2006	193.40	194.20	195.00	196.50	197.70	198.50	198.50	199.20	200.10	200.40	201.10	202.70
2007	201.60	203.10	204.40	205.40	206.20	207.30	206.10	207.30	208.00	208.90	209.70	210.90
2008	209.80	211.40	212.10	214.00	215.10	216.80	216.50	217.20	218.40	217.7	216.00	212.90
2009	210.10	211.40	211.30	211.50	212.20							

28 The basic rules of computation

Introduction

1. This chapter is concerned with the basic rules of computation used in the taxation of chargeable gains. It begins with an examination of the meaning of consideration and market price, and the allowable deductions, this applies to both individuals and incorporated entities. The chapter goes on to consider the disposal of an asset by an individual. The chapter concludes with the rules of the disposal of an asset by an incorporated entity.

Consideration and market price

2. As a general principle a chargeable gain is computed by deducting from the total consideration obtained the initial cost of acquisition, any allowable expenditure, and what is known as the 'indexation allowance'. Consideration is taken to be the gross sales price without any deduction for expenses of sale. However, in the under-mentioned cases the disposal is deemed to be at market price:

a) where the disposal is by way of a gift

b) where the transaction is not at arms length, e.g. between connected persons such as husband and wife or group companies

c) where an asset cannot be readily valued, or is acquired in connection with a loss of employment

d) on a transfer into a settlement by a settlor.

3. Where the market value for a disposal is used, then the person who acquires the asset is also treated as acquiring at the market value.

Market value means the price which assets might reasonably be expected to fetch in a sale on the open market. There are a number of special rules which relate to particular assets, and these are noted below.

Deferred consideration

4. The general rules of computation are not affected where the consideration is payable by instalments as the whole of the consideration is brought into account with no discount for the future receipt of monies. Where all or part of the consideration is deferred because it cannot be quantified at the date of the original disposal, the value of the right to receive that additional amount is included with any ascertainable consideration at the date of the original disposal. The value of this right (known as a 'chose in action') is deducted from the deferred consideration when that is received at a later date. See *Marren v Ingles* 1980 STC 500. *Marson v Marriage* 1980 STC 177.

Allowable deductions

5. The following may be deducted from the consideration:

a) The cost of acquisition, including incidental expenditure.

b) Any enhancement expenditure, but not repairs or maintenance.

c) Expenditure incurred in establishing or protecting the right to any asset.

d) Incidental costs of disposal (*see below*).

e) The indexation allowance for incorporated entities (*see below*).

6. Incidental costs include: fees, commission, or professional charges such as legal accountancy or valuation advice: costs of transfer and conveyance including stamp duty: advertising to find a buyer or seller. The following items of expenditure are specifically disallowed:

a)   Costs of repair and maintenance.

b)   Costs of insurance against any damage injury or loss of an asset.

c)   Any expenditure allowed as a deduction in computing trading income.

d)   Any expenditure which is recouped from the Crown or public or local authority.

Entrepreneurs' relief

7. For chargeable assets disposed of after 5th April 2008 a system of entrepreneurs' relief has been introduced. Entrepreneurs' relief is available in respect of gains made by individuals on the disposal of:

a)   all or part of a trading business the individual carries on alone or in partnership;

b)   assets of the individual's or partnership's trading business following the cessation of the business;

c)   shares in (and securities of) the individual's "personal" trading company (or holding company of a trading group). The relief will have effect for gains on disposals of shares in (and securities of) a trading company (or the holding company of a trading group) provided that throughout a one-year qualifying period the individual making the disposal:

   i)   is an officer or employee of the company, or of a company in the same group of companies; and

   ii)   owns at least 5 per cent of the ordinary share capital of the company and that holding enables the individual to exercise at least 5 per cent of the voting rights in that company.

d)   assets owned by the individual and used by his / her "personal" trading company (or group) or trading partnership.

e)   The rules for entrepreneurs' relief are extended to assets held by trustees and personal representatives.

f)   Entrepreneurs' relief results in a charge to capital gains tax at an effective rate of 10% (5/9ths of the gain being chargeable x 18%).

The basic computation for individuals

8. This section illustrates the basic computation for an individual

a)   The basic computation for an individual who disposes of an asset that does not qualify for entrepreneurs' relief is illustrated as follows:

Example 1:

Peter purchased a house that was not his main residence, in January 1986 for £50,000. He incurred legal fees and survey fees of £500 on the acquisition of this property. In September 1990 Peter added an extension to the property at a cost of £15,000. He sold the house on 1st May 2009 for £350,000, incurring legal fees and selling costs amounting to £2,000. Peter has no other disposals for the tax year 2009-2010. Compute the chargeable gain and capital gains tax payable on the disposal.

Suggested solution	£	£
Proceeds from sale		350,000
Allowable deductions:		
Initial cost	50,000	
Costs of acquisition	500	
Enhancement expenditure, September 1990	15,000	
Incidental costs of disposal	2,000	67,500
Chargeable gain		282,500
Less annual exemption		(10,100)
Gain subject to capital gains tax		272,400
Capital gains tax @ 18% of £272,400		**49,032**

b) The basic computation for an individual who disposes of a business asset that qualifies for entrepreneurs' relief is shown in the following example:

Example 2:

Simon purchased a retail shop selling electrical goods in October 1984 for £85,000. He incurred acquisition costs of £1,500. In September 1999 the shop was extended and structurally improved at a cost of £30,000. Simon has been running this business as a trade since buying the shop. On 1st June 2009 Simon sold the shop for £750,000, incurring legal costs and other selling expenses of £3,500. Simon has no other capital gains during the tax year. Compute the chargeable gain and the capital gains tax payable.

Suggested solution:	£	£
Proceeds from sale		750,000
Allowable deductions:		
Initial cost	85,000	
Costs of acquisition	1,500	
Enhancement expenditure, September 1999	30,000	
Incidental costs of disposal	3,500	120,000
Chargeable gain		630,000
Gain chargeable Entrepreneurs relief 5/9ths x 630,000		350,000
Less annual exemption		(10,100)
Gain subject to capital gains tax		339,900
Capital gains tax @ 18% of £339,900		**61,182**

Notes:

i) This is an asset used for the purposes of a trade and therefore qualifies

ii) If the chargeable gain had exceeded £1 million, the excess over this amount would be taxed at 18%.

iii) Simon has used up £630,000 of his lifetime allowance for capital gains tax entrepreneurs' relief purposes. He therefore has a lifetime balance left of £370,000.

Part disposals

9. Where the part disposal of an asset takes place then the attributable cost of acquisition is determined by the following general formula:

$$\text{Attributable cost} = \text{Cost of acquisition} \times \frac{A}{A+B}$$

A is the consideration for the disposal, excluding any expenses of sale.

B is the market value of the un-disposed portion.

Indexation allowance – Incorporated entities

10. For incorporated entities an indexation allowance applies to disposals. The main general provisions relating to disposals are as follows.

a) The indexation allowance is calculated by reference to the change in the Retail Price Index between the date of the disposal and:

   i)   the date of acquisition, or

   ii) the 31st March 1982 if that is later than the date of acquisition.

b) The indexation applies to the initial cost of acquisition and any enhancement expenditure but not to the incidental costs of disposal.

c) Where an asset was held on the 31st March 1982 indexation will automatically be based on the market value at that date or the actual allowable expenditure whichever is the greater.

d) On a part disposal the indexation allowance is calculated referencing the apportioned cost, before getting the actual gain. The allowable cost carried forward is not indexed at that stage.

e) The indexation allowance cannot be used to create or increase a capital loss.

Calculation of indexation allowance

11. The calculation of the indexation allowance commonly called the 'indexation factor' is made according to the following formula rounded to three decimal places, using the formula table provided at the end of chapter 27:

$$\frac{\text{RPI in month of disposal} - \text{RPI in month of acquisition (or if later 31st March 1982)}}{\text{RPI in month of acquisition (or if later 31st March 1982)}}$$

Example

Q Ltd purchased an office for use in its trading business for £10,000 in January 1983. Legal charges and other allowable costs of acquisition amounted to £500. In January 1984 an extension to the property was built for £3,000, and major repairs undertaken amounting to £1,000. The whole property was sold for £100,000 on 28th February 2009 with incidental costs of disposal of £1,500. RPI January 1983 82.61, January 1984 86.84, February 2009 211.40. Q Ltd is a large company for corporation tax purposes.

Compute the chargeable gain arising on the disposal of the office.

Suggested solution: Calculation of indexation allowance

		£	£
Cost of acquisition January 1983	10,000		
Acquisition expenses January 1983	500	10,500	
Enhancement expenditure January 1984		3,000	13,500
Indexation allowance:			
Cost 1983 10,500			

$$\frac{211.40 - 82.61}{82.61} = 1.559 \times 10,500 = \qquad\qquad 16,370$$

Cost 1984   3,000

$$\frac{211.40 - 86.84}{86.84} = 1.434 \times 3,000 = \qquad\qquad 4,302$$

| Indexation | | | 20,672 |

CGT computation		£	£
Proceeds of sale			100,000
Less: Cost of acquisition		10,000	
Expenses of acquisition		500	
Enhancement expenditure		3,000	
Expenses of disposal		1,500	15,000
Un-indexed gain			85,000
Indexation allowance to February 2009			20,672
Chargeable gain added to PCTCT			64,328

Notes:

i) As the disposal took place in February 2009 the gain will be taxable at Q Ltd corporation tax rate, which for FY 2008 was 28% for a large corporation.

Assets held on 31st March 1982

12. For assets held on 31st March 1982, from the 6th April 2008 the following rules apply.

a) The asset is assumed to be sold on 31st March 1982 and immediately re-acquired at its market value at that date. This is the general re-basing rule and applies to all taxpayers.

b) In the case of incorporated entities, any indexation allowance cannot be used to increase a loss on disposal, therefore the indexation allowance will be restricted to the point at which the gain is zero.

Example

X purchased a painting in 1979 for £10,000 which he sells for £85,000 in August 2009 after incurring expenses of disposal amounting to £5,000. The market value at 31st March 1982 was £36,000.

Calculate the chargeable gain for 2009/10, assuming that X has no other gains.

Solution: Capital gains tax computation 2009/10

	£	Re-basing 31.3.82 £	£	Original cost £
Proceeds of sale		90,000		90,000
Less cost of acquisition	–	10,000		
MV at 31.3.82	36,000		–	
Cost of disposal	5,000	41,000	5,000	15,000
Gain		49,000		75,000
Annual exemption		(10,100)		(10,100)
Chargeable gain subject to CGT		38,900		64,900
Subject to capital gains tax @ 18%		7,002		11,682

Note

i) The smaller gain of £38,900 obtained from re-basing will be taken as the chargeable gain. Where the March 1982 value is greater then the original cost computation will not normally be required.

Indexation – losses

13. The Indexation allowance claimed by corporations cannot be used to turn a gain into a loss or to increase a loss.

Example

B Ltd owns freehold property which has a market value of £20,000 on 3rd March 1982. The property was sold on 28th February 2009 for:

  a) £300,000 b) £50,000

Compute the chargeable gain/loss.

Solution: B Ltd chargeable gains tax computation

a) Proceeds of sale — 300,000
   March 1982 value — 20,000

   Unindexed gain — 280,000
   $$\text{IA } \frac{211.40 - 79.44}{79.44} = 1.661 \times 20,000 = \qquad 33,220$$
   Chargeable gain — 246,780

b) Proceeds of sale — 50,000
   March 1982 value — 20,000

   Unindexed gain — 30,000
   IA of £33,220 restricted to — 30,000

   No gain/loss — nil

Disposals still treated as no gain / no loss

14. The following transactions are to be treated as no gain/no loss disposals:

i) Acquisitions of quoted securities before 6th April 1965 where the substitution of the market value at 6th April 1965 converts a gain into a loss or vice versa.

ii) Disposals between spouses.

iii) Transfers within a group of companies.

iv) Deemed disposals on the death of a life tenant.

v) Company reconstruction and amalgamations.

vi) Gifts etc. involving heritage property.

Student self-testing questions

1. Z purchased a painting for £100,000 in August 1984 which he sold for £200,000 on the 3rd March 2010. Selling expenses amounted to £10,550.

Compute the capital gains tax assuming no other gains during the year.

Suggested solution: Z CGT computation 2009/10

	£	£
Proceeds of sale		200,000
Less cost of acquisition	100,000	
Selling expenses	10,550	110,550
Gain		89,450
Annual exemption		(10,100)
Gain subject to CGT		79,350
Capital gains tax @ 18%		14,283

Question without answer

1. An asset qualifying for entrepreneurs' relief was acquired in February 1988 at a cost of £70,000. The asset was sold in January 2010 for sale proceeds of:

i) £1,300,000

ii) £850,000

Requirement

Compute the capital gains tax payable in each case.

29 Land and chattels

Introduction

1. This chapter deals with the CGT rules applicable to land and chattels under the following headings:

Freehold/leasehold land and buildings

Part disposals of land

Small part disposals of land

Disposals of short leases

Granting a lease from a freehold interest

Private residence

Chattels

Freehold/long leasehold land and buildings

2. There are no special rules for the computation of capital gains arising on the disposal of assets under this heading.

A long lease is a lease with more than 50 years to run.

Land includes houses, hereditaments and buildings.

Where the property is also the main residence of the owner then exemption is normally available. *See below.*

Part disposals of land

3. Where there is a part disposal of freehold or long leasehold land then unless the disposal is 'small', *(see below)* the normal part disposal formula applies.

$$\text{Attributable cost} = \text{Cost of acquisition} \times \frac{A}{A + B}$$

$$\text{Attributable cost} = \text{Market value at } 31.3.1982 \times \frac{A}{A + B} \quad \text{(Assets held on 31.3.82)}$$

Example

G purchased a plot of land of 10 acres for £10,000 in May 1977, and an adjacent further 2 acres for £5,000 in June 1980. In December 2009 a sale of 5 acres was made for £60,000, from the original 10 acres, the remaining 5 acres being worth £75,000 at that time. The market value of the 10 acres of land at 31st March 1982 was £22,000. The land was not used for business purposes. Compute the capital gains tax payable, assuming no other disposals during the year.

Solution: CGT computation 2009/10

	£
Proceeds of sale	60,000
Market value 31.3.82: $22,000 \times \dfrac{60,000}{60,000 + 75,000}$	9,778
Gain	50,222
Annual exemption	(10,100)
Chargeable gain subject capital gains tax	40,122
Capital gains tax @ 18%	7,222

In this case, since the disposal was out of the first identifiable plot, there is no need to combine the acquisition costs of the two plots.

If the sale had been 5 acres out of the total of 12 acres (valued at £25,000 at 31.3.82) with the remaining 7 acres being valued at £85,000 at the date of disposal then the computation would be:

	£
Proceeds of sale	60,000
Market value 31.3.82: $25,000 \times \dfrac{60,000}{60,000 + 85,000}$ =	10,345
Gain	49,655
Annual exemption	(10,100)
Chargeable gain subject to capital gains tax	39,555
Capital gains tax @ 18%	7,120

Small part disposals of land

4. There are some special rules which relate to land where:

a)   the value of the part disposal does not exceed £20,000;

b)   the part disposal is small relative to the market value of the entire property, before the disposal. Small in this context means 20% of the value immediately prior to the disposal.

Given these conditions, then the taxpayer can claim to have any consideration received for the part disposal deducted from the allowable expenditure of the whole property. In this case there would be no chargeable gain on the part disposal.

The £20,000 exemption does not apply to a compulsory purchase by a public authority.

The taxpayer's total consideration for disposals of land in an income tax year must not exceed £20,000, for him or her to be eligible to claim relief under this section.

Example

Z owns land which he acquired in April 1982 for £20,000 comprising some 10 acres. The costs of the acquisition amounted to £500. In August 2009 Z sells 1.5 acres for £13,500 incurring disposal costs of £750. At the date of sale the remainder of the land had a market value of £135,500.

Compute the chargeable gain arising in 2009/10. If Z makes a claim under Section 242 show the computations.

Solution: CGT computation 2009/10

	£	£
August 2009 proceeds of sale		13,500
Deduct – allowable cost $\dfrac{13,500}{13,500 + 135,500} \times 20,500$	1,857	
Cost of disposal	750	2,607
Gain		10,893
Claim under Section 242 TCGA 1992		
Cost of acquisition		20,500
Less proceeds of sale August 2009 (13,500 – 750)		12,750
Revised allowed cost		7,750

Notes

i)   In this example, rather than claim relief under Section 242 it might be more advantageous to accept the chargeable gain since most of it falls within the exemption level of £10,100 for 2009/10 which might otherwise go unused.

ii)   The election under Section 242 TCGA 1992 can be made where the proceeds of sale are less than 20% of the value of the entire property before the disposal.

$$\frac{\text{Disposable value}}{\text{Total value before sale}} = \frac{13,500}{13,500 + 135,500} \times \frac{100}{1} = 9\%$$

Private residence

5. Any gain accruing to an individual on the disposal of his or her only or main residence can be exempt from capital gains tax. The exemption also extends to one other residence provided for a dependent relative, if the property is rent free and without other consideration, and has been occupied continuously since 6th April 1988.

Residence includes a dwelling house (or part) together with land up to half a hectare in area, or more if justified, and a mobile home. See *Makins v Elson* 1981 STI 326.

Full exemption is available where there has been a continuous period of ownership, and the following are to be taken into consideration in determining the total periods of exemption.

a)   Actual periods of occupation.

b)   Any period of absence during the last three years of ownership providing that at some time the residence has been occupied as the principal private residence of the taxpayer. This period of absence applies even where the occupancy was only before 31st March 1982.

c)   Absences for whatever reasons, for periods which in total do not exceed three years.

d)   Absence for any period of time during which the owner was in employment, carrying out duties abroad.

e)   Absences amounting in total to not more than four years during which the owner:

   i)   was prevented from living at home because of the distance to the place of employment.

   ii)   lived away from home at the employer's request, in order to perform his or her employment more effectively.

In general, absence under items (c) to (e) above only qualify if the owner actually occupies the home *both before and after the period of absence*, and there is no other house to which the absence could be related. However, if the owner is unable to resume residence because employment forces him or her to work elsewhere, periods of exemption under (d) and (e) still qualify.

Where the period of absence under (c) and (d) is exceeded then only the excess is treated as giving rise to a chargeable gain.

Where the main residence qualifies for occupancy for part of period since 31st March 1982, the exempt gain is:

$$\frac{\text{Period of exemption as main residence}}{\text{Total period of ownership}} \times \text{Gain}$$

6. The following additional points should be noted.

a)   If part of any house is used *exclusively* for business purposes, then that part of any gain attributable to the business portion is not eligible for any exemptions.

b)   If a house, or part of it, is let for residential purposes then the part of the gain attributable to that letting is exempt up to the smaller of:

i)   the gain otherwise exempt by reason of owner occupation

ii) £40,000

iii) the gain attributable to the letting period.

Example

A purchased a house on 1st July 1986 for £25,806 in which he lived until the 31st March 1987. The property was then let for five years, followed by occupancy by A until he sold the house for £600,000 on the 31st March 2010.

Compute the chargeable gain.

Solution: Computation 2009/10

		£
Proceeds of sale		600,000
Cost of acquisition	25,806	
Total gain before exemption		574,194
Less exemption:		
Proportion of total gain $\frac{261}{285} \Box\Box 574,194$		525,841
		48,353
Less let property exemption: Lower of:		
maximum amount	40,000	
gain otherwise exempt	525,841	40,000
letting gain		48,353
chargeable gain subject to capital gains tax (before annual exemption)		8,353

Notes

		Years	Months	Total months
Period of ownership	1.7.86 – 31.3.10	23	9	285
Period of absence	1.4.87 – 31.3.92	5	–	60
Periods of occupancy	1.7.86 – 31.3.87	–	9	9
	1.4.92 – 31.3.10	18	–	216

	Months	
Last three years	36	
Period of absence preceded and followed by occupancy	36	
Occupancy additional to last three years		
1.7.86 – 31.3.87	9	
1.4.92 – 31.3.07	180	189
		261

c)   A husband and wife can only have one residence for the purposes of any exemptions. If they are permanently separated or divorced, then each qualifies individually for the residence exemption.

d)   Exemption is extended to the trustees of a settlement where a person is entitled to occupy the house under the terms of the settlement.

e)   The exemption also applies to an individual who lives in job-related accommodation and who intends in due course to occupy a house owned by that individual, as his or her main residence. It also applies to self-employed people living in job-related accommodation.

Chattels

7. The chattels discussed here are personal chattels or tangible movable property which for capital gains tax purposes are put into three categories.

a) Chattels which are specifically exempt from capital gains tax, e.g. private cars, or decorations for valour.

b) Chattels which are wasting assets.

c) Chattels, not being wasting assets, disposed of for £6,000 or less.

Chattels which are wasting assets

8. A wasting asset is one with an estimated useful life of less than 50 years at the time of the disposal. A chattel which is a wasting asset is exempt from capital gains tax unless:

a) the asset has been used since first owned, for the purposes of a trade, profession or vocation, and capital allowances were available in respect of the expenditure, whether claimed or not, or

b) it consists of commodities dealt with on a terminal market.

Where capital allowances have been claimed, then no chargeable gain will arise unless the disposal value is greater than the original cost. If the proceeds are less than £6,000 then the exemption noted below can be claimed.

Chattels disposed of for £6,000 or less – marginal relief

9. Any gain arising on the disposal of a chattel, not being a wasting asset, is not a chargeable gain where the gross disposal value is £6,000 or less.

Marginal relief applies where the disposal value is greater than £6,000 and the cost less than £6,000. The marginal relief limits the gain to:

$$\frac{5}{3} \times (\text{gross proceeds} - £6,000)$$

Thus the maximum assessable gain is the lower of:

i) $\frac{5}{3} \times$ (gross proceeds − £6,000) or

ii) The actual gain i.e. gross proceeds less.

Example

H buys a piece of pottery for £800 in June 1982 which he sells in October 2009 for (a) £4,800, (b) £6,800.

Compute the chargeable gains.

Solution: H CGT computation 2009/10

a) As the proceeds of sale are less than £6,000 no chargeable gain arises.

b)

	£	£
Proceeds of sale		6,800
Less: cost of acquisition		800
Chargeable gain		6,000
Limited to $\frac{5}{3}$ (6,800 − 6,000)		1,333
Net chargeable gain subject to capital gains tax (before annual exemption)		1,333

Restriction of loss

10. If the chattel which cost more than £6,000 is sold for less than £6,000 then the allowable loss is calculated by reference to £6,000 and not the actual disposal value. If both the disposal price and the cost price are less than £6,000 then the loss is not allowed at all.

   Where two or more chattels form part of a set, then any disposal of part of the set is to be aggregated with any disposal of the other parts, and treated as a single transaction.

Student self-testing question

1. In March 2010, Neil sells an oil painting, which he had acquired in June 1992 for £10,000. He sells the painting for:

   a)   £7,200   b)   £5,700

Requirement

Compute the allowable loss in each of the above cases

Solution

a)   The disposal is not exempt from CGT as the proceeds exceed £6,000. The allowable loss is therefore calculated in the normal way at £2,800 (£10,000 - £7,200).

b)   The asset was acquired for more than £6,000 and therefore a loss is allowed. This is calculated by substituting £6,000 for the disposal proceeds. The allowable loss is therefore £4,000 (£6,000 - £10,000).

Questions without answers

1. K purchased a painting for £500 on the 1st June 1975. The painting was sold for £7,500, after sales commission of 10% in May 2009 at auction. The market value at 31st March 1982 was £4,000.

   Compute the chargeable gain for 2009/10.

2. James purchased a house in Oxford, 'Millhouse', on 1st July 1984 and took up immediate residence. The house cost £50,000. On 1st January 1987 he went to work and live in the United States where he stayed until 30th June 1989. On 1st July 1989 James returned to the UK to work for his United States employers in Scotland where it was necessary for him to occupy rented accommodation. On 1st July 1990 his mother became seriously ill and James resigned from his job to go and live with her. His mother died on 30th September 1991 leaving her house to James. James decided to continue to live in his mother's house and finally sold 'Millhouse' on 30th June 2009 for £300,000.

   Calculate the chargeable gain assessable on James for 2009/10.

   (ACCA)

3. Mr and Mrs Scott had the following transactions in assets in the year to 5 April 2010.

   Mr Scott

   Sold an antique for £7,250, incurring expenses of £250, on 1 December 2009, which he had bought on 19 April 1982 for £2,950, including expenses of purchase.

   A holiday cottage, which had been bought for £31,000 on 3 April 1983, was sold on 1 November 2009. On 14 May 1984 an integral garage costing £3,000 was added. The net proceeds of sale were £80,000.

   Sold a vintage Rolls Royce for £38,000 on 9 May 2009, which had cost £15,000 on 6 April 1982.

Mrs Scott

On 4 June 2009 sold an antique silver brooch for £4,800, incurring expenses of £54. It had cost £6,200, including expenses, on 5 April 1983.

Sold 5 acres of land on 14 October 2009 for £11,000, incurring expenses of £480. It was part of a 25 acre plot, which had been purchased on 14 March 1984 for £17,000, including expenses. The remaining 20 acres have been valued at £33,000.

Requirement

Compute the capital gain accruing to Mr and Mrs Scott in each of the cases above. **15 marks**

4. Lord Scarlet carried out the following capital transactions in January 2010.

Sold a cricket bat, signed by the 1978 England test team, which he had bought at an auction in May 1982 for £1,400. The net proceeds, after paying auctioneer's fees of £520, were £11,520.

Sold £20,000 13.75% Treasury stock for £27,400. He had acquired the stock in September 1987 at par.

Sold an antique book for £3,000. He had bought it in May 1987 for £8,000.

Sold a third interest in a plot of land for £11,500. Lord Scarlet had acquired the land in June 1984 for £15,000. The value of the remaining two thirds interest in January 2010 was £28,000.

Requirement

Compute the total capital gains tax payable by Lord Scarlet for 2009/10. 8 marks

30 Stocks and securities

Introduction

1. This chapter is concerned with the CGT rules applicable to stocks and securities and begins with the general method of computation following the changes introduced by the FA 2008; In line with other areas of capital gains tax, major changes have taken place in respect of the treatment of gains and losses in respect of stocks and securities transactions involving individuals. From 6th April 2008 the frozen indexation allowance and taper relief is abolished for individuals and a simplification of the cost apportionment of shares of the same class has been introduced. For corporations, gains and losses on transactions in stocks and securities remain broadly the same as the previous year, with indexation using the weighted average cost being available for the current year. This chapter commences with an overview of the rules for the current year for shares or securities of the same class and then examines bonus and rights issues and takeover bids.

FA 2008 – main changes for individuals

2. The following are the main provisions concerning stocks and securities introduced by the FA 2008:

a)   The system of cost allocation on disposal of a shareholding by an individual were simplified for the FA 2008 year. The cost is calculated on a weighted average basis so that all shares of the same class purchased over a period of time are 'pooled' together. Anti avoidance rules are in place to prevent unlawful gains, such as insider trading, whereby same day acquisitions and buy backs within the next 30 days are treated as being the deemed cost for capital gains tax purposes. This is referred to as 'bed and breakfasting' of share and is considered in section c below.

b)   If a shareholding qualifies as a business asset under the entrepreneurs' relief scheme, any gain arising on the first £1 million will be chargeable to capital gains tax at the reduced rate (5/9ths of the gain chargeable at 18%, up to £1 million limit). The following conditions apply, provided that throughout a one-year qualifying period the individual making the disposal:

   i)   is an officer or employee of the company, or of a company in the same group of companies; and

   ii)   owns at least 5 per cent of the ordinary share capital of the company and that holding enables the individual to exercise at least 5 per cent of the voting rights in that company.

c)   Stocks and securities held at or prior to 31st March 1982 are deemed to be valued at their 31st March 1982 market value for the computation of any disposal.

d)   When part of the share holding is disposed of, the cost of acquisition relating to the disposal is the proportionate part of the cost of all the shares in the holding. A weighted average cost is computed.

e)   Shares that meet the criteria as investments in the Enterprise Investment Scheme, Venture Capital Trust and the Corporate Venturing Scheme are exempt from capital gains tax.

Weighted average cost - individual

3. Example 1

Denis has the following transactions in the 25p ordinary shares of Z plc, a quoted trading company.

				£
6th April 1982	purchased	3,500	shares at cost	2,500
31st March 1984	purchased	1,000	shares at cost	1,500
3 rd April 1998	purchased	2,000	shares at cost	7,500

Calculate the value of the general pool at 6th April 2009.

Suggested solution

General pool   Denis ordinary shares in Z plc

		Number of shares	Qualifying expenditure
		£	£
6.4.82	Purchased	3,500	2,500
31.3.84	Purchased	1,000	1,500
3.4.98	Purchased	2,000	7,500
Pool values at 6.4 2009		6,500	11,500

$$\text{Average cost per share: } \frac{£11,500}{6,500} = £1.77$$

Notes:

i)   If all the shares were sold the qualifying expenditure would be £11,500.

ii)   If part of the holding is disposed of the allowable cost would be allocated on a pro-rata basis

Example 2

Colin has the following transactions in the 25p ordinary shares of K plc, a quoted trading company.

				£
1.6.1990	purchased	1,000	shares at cost	525
1.9.2000	purchased	500	shares at cost	575
2.1.2003	purchased	2,500	shares at cost	3,500
10.10.2009	sold	3,000	shares, proceeds	36,000

The shares do not qualify for entrepreneurs' relief.

Calculate the chargeable gain for 2009/10 before annual exemption.

Suggested solution

General pool K plc		Number of shares	Qualifying expenditure £
1.6.1990	Purchase 1,000	525	
1.9.2000	Purchase 500	575	
2.1.2003	Purchase	2,500	3,500
	Total	4,000	4,600
10.10.2009	Disposal	3,000	3,450
11.10.2009	Balance remaining in pool	1,000	1,150

Colin CGT computation 2009/10

		£
10.10.2009	Proceeds of sale of 3,000 shares	36,000
	Allowable cost	3,450
	Chargeable gain before annual exemption	32,550

Incorporated entities pooling rules

4. The following are the main provisions which apply to shares or securities of the same class, where they are held by an incorporated entity.

a)   Separate pools must be established as follows.

    i)   Shares or securities acquired on or after the 1st April 1982 'the section 104 Pool'. The s.104 pool indexation factor at each step is specifically <u>not</u> rounded to 3 decimal places like all other CGT indexation factors, but is left unrounded (due to the possibility for multiple small-step calculations in a fast changing shareholding)

    ii)   Shares or securities acquired prior to 1st April 1982 are called the 1982 Holding.

b)   The re-basing rules apply to shares and securities held at the 31st March 1982 and the market value at that date forms the basis of valuation of the 1982 Holding.

c)   Disposals are first deducted from the Section 104 Holding and then from the 1982 Holding.

c)   The weighted average cost plus indexation allowance is used to calculate the allowable cost against the sale proceeds.

d)   Indexation cannot increase or create a loss.

e)   The chargeable gain is added to the corporations PCTCT.

Example

Incorporated entity 1982 Holding, Section 104 pool.

V Ltd had the following transactions in the quoted shares of Z plc, a quoted trading company.

23.11.1980	Bought	6,000	shares costing	£14,000
31.1.1983	Bought	8,000	shares costing	£15,600
31.5.1998	Bought	12,000	shares costing	£36,000
28.2.2009	Sold	22,000	shares for	£176,000

The market value of the shares at the 31st March 1982 was £2.75.

Compute the chargeable gain.

Suggested solution

The first step is to construct the section 104 pool and then the 1982 Holding.

Section 104 pool		Number of shares	Qualifying expenditure £	Indexed pool £
31.1.1983		8,000	15,600	15,600
IA to 28.2.2009	1.559			24,320
$\dfrac{211.40-82.61}{82.61}$				
31.5.1998		12,000	36,000	36,000
IA to 28.2.2009	0.292			10,512
$\dfrac{211.40-163.50}{163.50}$				
Total		20,000	51,600	86,432
28.2.2009 Disposal		20,000	51,600	86,432
		–	–	–

1982 Holding	Nominal value	Qualifying expenditure £	Re-basing 31.3.1982 £
23.11.1980	6,000	14,000	16,500
IA to 28.2.2009			27,406
$\dfrac{211.40-79.44}{79.44}=1.661$			
Total			43,906
28.2.2009 Disposal	2,000	5,500	14,635
Balance remaining	4,000		29,271

V Ltd CGT computation

		£
Sales proceeds		176,000
Allowable deductions:		
Cost Section 104 pool	51,600	
Cost 1982 Holding	5,500	57,100
Un-indexed gain		118,900
Indexation Section 104 pool	34,832	
Indexation 1982 Holding	9,135	43,967
Chargeable gain added to PCTCT		74,933

Notes:

i)   All the Section 104 holding has been disposed of and a proportion of the 1982 Holding, the remaining balance will be held until such time that another disposal is made.

ii)   Indexation should be shown separately in case a loss on disposal is incurred. In the case of a loss the indexation allowance is restricted so as not to create or increase a loss on disposal. Thus if the shares in this example were disposed of for, say, £80,000, this would result in a gain of nil and no loss being allowed, with indexation restricted to £22,900 (sales proceeds less cost less restricted indexation). A capital loss can only be allowed when the shareholding is sold for less than cost.

iii)   The sale proceeds could also be allocated to each pool holding allowable cost.

Bonus issues of similar shares

5. When a company makes a bonus or scrip issue of shares of the same class, then the average cost (or market value at 31.3.1982) of all the shares held is not affected, but their number is increased, and hence the average cost per share is reduced. The indexation allowance principle is not affected by a bonus issue, so that the normal rules for identification noted above apply in the case of incorporated entities. The number of shares in each pool is increased by the bonus issue.

Example

T Ltd makes a bonus issue of 1 for 5 in respect of its ordinary shares on 1st August 1984. Alex had acquired 500 ordinary shares in T Ltd on 1st May 1972 at a cost of £1,000. In June 2009 Alex sells 250 of the shares for £6,500. The market value of the shares before the bonus issue at 31.3.1982 was £2.50 per share. The shares do not qualify for entrepreneurs' relief.

Compute the chargeable gain.

Suggested solution

Cost of shares, 1982 holding

		Cost £	Market value at 31.3.82 £
1.5.1972 cost of	500 ordinary shares	1,000	1,250
1.8.1984 cost of	100 bonus shares	–	–
	600	1,000	1,250

The deemed date of acquisition of the bonus shares is the date of the original purchases.

	Cost £	Market value at 31.3.82 £
CGT computation 2008/09		
Proceeds of sale June 2009		6,500
MV of 250 shares sold as at 31.3.1982:		
$\dfrac{250}{600} \times 1,250$	521	
		521
Chargeable gain subject to CGT (before annual exemption)		5,979

Notes

i) The value of the 250 shares sold, as at 31.3.1982, is 250 × £2.083 = £521 (£1,250 ÷ 600 = £2.083).

ii) The value of the 350 shares carried forward is £1,250 – 521 i.e. £729.

Example

AB Ltd makes a bonus issue of 1 for 10 on the 30th June 1987. John had acquired 10,000 ordinary shares in AB Ltd in April 1980 at a cost of £14,000. John sells 2,000 shares in May 2009 for £8,000. The market value of the shares in issue at 31st March 1982 was £1.50 per share, i.e. before the bonus issue. The shares do not qualify for entrepreneurs' relief.

Compute the chargeable gain.

Solution: CGT computation 2009/10

		£
Proceeds of sale – 2,000 shares		8,000
MV at 31.3.1982:		
10,000 @ £1.50 =	15,000	
$\frac{2000}{11000}$ × 15,000 (i.e. 2,000 × £1.364)	2,727	2,727
Chargeable gain subject to capital gains tax (before annual exemption)		**5,273**

Notes

i) **1982 holding:**

	Number	Cost	MV 31.3.82
April 1980 cost	10,000	14,000	15,000
June 1987 bonus	1,000	Nil	Nil
	11,000	14,000	15,000

Market value of shares plus the bonus issue is $\frac{£15,000}{11,000}$ = £1.364 per share i.e. the price as adjusted for the bonus issue. 2,000 shares @ £1.364 = £2,727.

ii) The MV carried forward is £15,000 – £2,727 = £12,273.

Bonus issues of shares or debentures of a different class

6. A bonus issue of shares of a different class, or debentures, gives rise to two distinct classes of holdings, and the original cost of the shares must be apportioned. The method of apportionment is as follows:

a) Quoted investments. Apportionment by reference to the market value of the new holding on the first day a price is quoted on the stock exchange.

b) Unquoted investments. The part disposal formula is applied as and when a disposal occurs.

Example

T plc, a quoted company, made a bonus issue on the 31st August 2009 of 1 new ordinary share for every 5 held, and £1.00 of 8% debenture stock for every 2 shares held. First day dealing prices on 1st September were 160p for the ordinary, and par for the debentures. Andrew acquired the shares from his father's estate on 1st July 1984: 1,000 ordinary shares in T plc value £1,500.

Compute the apportioned cost.

Solution

Calculation of apportioned cost

	Market value 1.9.2009	Apportioned cost	
After bonus issue of 1 for 5. 1,200 shares held at a cost of	£1,500		
	£	£	
1,200 ordinary shares @ 160p	1,920	1,190	see below
£500 8% debenture @ £100	500	310	
	2,420	1,500	

Ordinary shares:	$\dfrac{1,920}{2,420} \times 1,500$ i.e.		1,190
Debentures:	$\dfrac{500}{2,420} \times 1,500$ i.e.		310

Rights issues of the same class

7. Where a company makes a rights issue of the same class of shares as existing ones, and they are taken up, then for CGT purposes the following rules apply.

a) The consideration paid for the shares by way of the rights issue is deemed to take place at the time when the cost of the rights becomes due.

b) Each pool cost is increased accordingly.

c) For incorporated entities indexation from the date of the rights issue.

Example

T plc makes a rights issue on the 7th February 1984 of 1 new ordinary share for every 2 held, at a price of 125p per share. Jack acquired 1,000 ordinary shares in T plc for £1,300 on the 1st October 1982. He sells 750 shares for £10,000 on the 25th October 2009. The shares do not qualify for entrepreneurs' relief.

Compute the chargeable gain.

Solution: CGT computation 2009/10

Pool at October 2009		Number of shares	Qualifying expenditure
1.10.1982	Acquisition	1,000	1,300
7.2.1984	Rights issue	500	625
Pool value @ 25th October 2009		1,500	1,925
25.10.2009 Disposal 750 shares		750	
$\dfrac{750}{1,500} \times 1,925$			963
Value of pool c/f		750	962

CGT computation 2009/10	£
Proceeds of sale	10,000
Less pool cost at 25th October 2009	963
Chargeable gain subject to capital gains tax before annual exemption	9,037

Note

The rights issue of 1 for every 2 is 500 new shares at a cost of 125p per share i.e. £625.00.

Rights issues of a different class

8. Where the shareholder is offered shares of a different class, or securities, by way of a rights issue, then the same rules apply as for a bonus issue of shares of a different class, noted above. The different treatment for quoted and unquoted shares also applies to this type of rights issue.

For indexation purposes the additional consideration becomes a separate asset as for rights issues in general.

Takeover bids

9. Where a company makes a bid for the shares of another company the following situations could arise.

a) The consideration is satisfied entirely by cash. In this case a shareholder who accepts the offer has made a chargeable disposal.

b) The consideration is a share for share exchange. In this case an accepting shareholder is deemed to have acquired the new shares at the *date and cost of the original holding*, or the 1982 value.

c) The consideration is either a partial cash settlement, or it consists of two or more shares or securities by way of exchange. In both cases it will be necessary to use the market value of the separate components of the bid, in order to apportion the original cost.

Example

Arthur owns 1,000 ordinary shares in P Ltd which he acquired for £1,500 on 27th June 1983. On the 30th May 2009 Z plc makes a bid for P Ltd on the following terms:

For every 200 shares: £30.00 in cash, 100 ordinary shares in Z plc, and £50.00 of 7% unsecured loan stock. MV when first quoted: ordinary 375p, 7% loan stock at par.

Compute the apportioned cost and CGT computation for 2009/10.

Solution

	Market value £	Apportioned cost £
Cash 5 × 30	150	99
7% loan stock 5 × 50	250	165
500 ordinary share 500 × 375p	1,875	1,236
	2,275	1,500

CGT computation 2009/10

Disposal cash receipt		150
Less apportioned cost	99	
Chargeable gain subject to capital gains tax before annual exemption		51

Notes

i) The cost apportionments are as follows:

$$\text{Cash} \quad \frac{150}{2,275} \times 1,500 = 99$$

$$\text{7\% loan stock} \quad \frac{250}{2,275} \times 1,500 = 165$$

$$\text{Ordinary shares} \quad \frac{1,875}{2,275} \times 1,500 = 1,236$$

ii) See 11 below for treatment of 'small' disposals. In this case $\frac{150}{2,275} = 6.5\%$.

Example

Using the data in the previous example Arthur sells all his 500 ordinary shares in Z plc for £10,000 on the 1st December 2009.

Compute the chargeable gains.

Solution: CGT computation 2009/10

	£	£
Proceeds of sale 500 shares in Z plc		10,000
Less cost of acquisition (as above)	1,236	
Chargeable gain subject to capital gains tax before annual exemption		8,764

Small capital distributions Section 122

10. Where a person receives cash by way of a capital distribution, e.g. on a takeover bid, in the course of a liquidation, or by the sale of any rights, then there is a part disposal for capital gains tax purposes. However, if the cash received is small relative to the value of the shares, then it may be deducted from the cost of acquisition. Small here is taken to be the highest of 5% or £3,000 of the value of the shares, before the sale of rights and in other cases after the distribution is made.

Example

Terry acquired 5,000 ordinary shares in A Ltd at a cost of £1,500 on 8.2.1978. On the 12th June 2009 the company made a rights issue of 1 for 10 at a price of 25p, Terry sold his rights for 60p each on the 1st August 2009 when the market value of the 5,000 ordinary shares was £7,000.

Compute the allowed cost carried forward, and any CGT liability for 2009/10. MV at 31.3.82 was 75p per share.

Solution Terry CGT computation 2009/10

	£
Proceeds of sale of rights 500 × 60p	300
As this is less than 5% of the market value of the shares of £7,000, the cost of acquisition can be reduced for any future disposal:	
1982 holding	
5,000 × 75p of 5,000 ordinary shares	3,750
Less sale of rights	300
Allowed value carried forward	3,450

Note

i)   As there is no part disposal there is no CGT liability for 2009/10.

ii) 5% of MV of £7,000 = £350.

Example

Alex holds 100,000 ordinary shares in Beta plc which he bought in September 1988 for £50,000. In May 2009 there was a rights offer of 1 for 10 which Alex did not take up. The rights were sold for £20,000, paid when the ex rights price of the shares was £120,000.

Compute the chargeable gain for 2009/10.

Solution: Alex CGT computation 2009/10

Proceeds of sale of rights	20,000
Allowable cost	
$50,000 \times \dfrac{20,000}{20,000 + 120,000}$	7,143
Chargeable gain subject to capital gains tax before annual exemption	12,857

Note

5% × ex rights price £120,000 = £6,000 which is less than the proceeds of sale from the rights, therefore this gain cannot be deducted from the cost of the original acquisition.

Stock dividends

11. For capital gains tax purposes, if an individual shareholder elects to receive shares instead of cash, then on a subsequent disposal of shares the amount of the Cash Equivalent will be treated as the consideration given for the new shares.

The number of new shares to be allotted to electing shareholders is calculated by multiplying the number of shares on which an election has been made by the cash dividend per share and dividing by the cash equivalent share price, being the price determined using the average middle market quotation of an ordinary share in the company, as derived from the London Stock Exchange Daily Official List. New shares may be allotted up to the maximum whole number possible. Fractions of new shares cannot be allotted and any fractional entitlement will be dealt with in accordance with the notes below. The number of new shares to be allotted is calculated as follows:

$$\frac{(N \times D) + F}{P}$$

N is the number of shares on which the shareholder has elected to receive a scrip dividend

D is the cash dividend per share

F is the fractional entitlement carried forward from previous scrip dividends (where a standing election mandate has been given and not revoked); and

P is the cash equivalent share price of one new share

The issue of a stock dividend does not constitute a reorganisation of capital and accordingly the receipt is treated as a separate acquisition for CGT purposes, from the date they are issued. Any taper relief starts from the date of the stock dividend and not from the date of the purchase of the original shares.

Student self-testing questions

1. Peter acquired the following shares in Hirst plc.

Date of acquisition	No. of shares	Cost
9/11/90	17,000	£25,000
4/8/05	7,000	£19,400
15/7/09	6,000	£19,000

He sold 24000 shares on the 20th July 2009 for £80,000. The shares are not business assets for the purposes of entrepreneurs' relief. Calculate the chargeable gain arising.

Suggested solution

General pool	Number of shares	Cost £
9/11/90 Acquisition	17,000	25,000
4/8/05 Acquisition	7,000	19,400
15/7/09 Acquisition	6,000	19,000
Total	30,000	63,400
20/7/09 sales (x24/30)	(24,000)	(50,720)
Balance to carry forward	6,000	12,680

Peter CGT computation 2009/2010 £

Sale proceeds	80,000
Cost	50,720
Chargeable gain subject to capital gains tax before annual exemption	**29,280**

2. Paul had the following transactions in Super Ltd, in which he holds the position of Finance Director.

1.10.95	Bought 20,000 shares (10%) holding for £30,000
11.9.03	Bought 4,000 shares for £10,000
1.2.04	Took up rights issue 1 for 2 at £2.75 per share
14.10.09	Sold 10,000 shares for £40,000

Compute the gain arising in October 2009 and the capital gains tax payable assuming Paul has no other gains during the year.

a) General pool	Number	Cost £
1.10.95 purchase	20,000	30,000
11.9.03 purchase	4,000	10,000
Pool at 1.2.04	24,000	40,000
Rights issues 1.2.04	12,000	33,000
	36,000	73,000
14.10.09 sale	(10,000)	(20,278)
C/F	26,000	52,722

Paul CGT computation 2009/2010 £

Sale proceeds	40,000
Cost	(20,278)
Chargeable gain	19,722
Entrepreneur's relief 5/9ths chargeable	10,956
Annual exemption	(10,100)
Chargeable gain subject to CGT	856
CGT payable @ 18%	154

Note: The shares meet the qualifying conditions for entrepreneurs' relief.

3. Hull Limited had the following transactions in the shares of City plc.

October 1976	purchased 1,000 shares for £1,500
November 1980	purchased 1,200 shares for £1,900
April 1984	purchased 600 shares for £1,100
January 1989	purchased 700 shares for £1,350
February 1991	bonus issue of one for five
1st March 2009	sold 2,000 shares for £8,000

The price of City plc shares on 31 March 1982 (as adjusted for the bonus issue) was £1.50.

Required: Calculate the chargeable gain or allowable loss arising on the sale in March 2009.

Suggested solution

(a) Shares matched against the Section 104 pool

	£
Proceeds 1,560/2,000 x £8,000 (W1)	6,240
Less: Cost (W1)	2,450
Un-indexed gain	3,790
Less: Indexation allowance (5,193 – 2,450)	2,743
Chargeable gain	1,047

(b) Shares matched against the 1982 holding

	Cost	31.3.82 Value £
Proceeds (2,000 - 1,560 = 440)		
440/2,000 x £8,000	1,760	1,760
Less: Cost/March 1982 value		
£567 (W2) / £1.50 x 440	567	660
Unindexed gain	1,193	1,100
Less: Indexation allowance (to February 2009) £660 x 1.661	1,096	1,096
$\dfrac{211.40 - 79.44}{79.44} = 1.661$	97	4

The chargeable gain is the smaller gain, i.e. £4.

Total gain on disposal is thus £1,051 (1,047 + 4)

Workings - construction of pool costs

(W1) Shares held in the S104 pool

	Shares	Unindexed Cost £	Indexed Cost £
April 1984 purchase	600	1,100	1,100
Indexation 1,100 x $\dfrac{211.40 - 88.64}{88.64} = 1.385$			1,523
January 1989 purchase	700	1,350	1,350
Indexation 1,350 x $\dfrac{211.40 - 111.00}{111.00} = 0.904$			1,220
Total	1,300	2,450	5,193
Feb. 1991 bonus issue (1 for 5)	260		
	1,560	2,450	5,193
sale	1,560	2,450	5,193

(W2) Shares in 1982 holding

	Shares	Cost £
October 1976 purchase	1,000	1,500
November 1980 purchase	1,200	1,900
Feb. 1991 bonus issue	440	-
	2,640	3,400
Mar 2008 sale (2,000 - 1,560 (W1))	440	*567
	2,200	2,833

*cost of shares is   440 / 2,640 x £3,400 = 567

4. Tony has the following transactions in the 10p ordinary shares of W plc, a quoted trading company.

				£
11.10.1977	purchased	500	shares cost	600
10.11.1980	purchased	1,000	shares cost	800
20.5.1983	purchased	500	shares cost	750
25.10.1999	purchased	500	shares cost	1,000
30.3.2010	sold	1,200	shares proceeds	10,000

The market value at 31st March 1982 was 165p per share.

The shares are not eligible for entrepreneurs' relief.

Compute the chargeable gain for 2009/10.

Solution: Tony CGT computation 2009/10

	General Pool	**Number of shares**	**Qualifying expenditure**
			£
i)	20.5.1983 Purchase	500	750
	25.10.1999 Purchase	500	1,000
		1,000	1,750
	30.3.2010 Sale	1,000	1,750
	31.3.1982 Market value of share acquired		
	(500+1,000) x 1.65p.	1,500	2,475
	30.3.2010 Sale	200	330
	Pool carried forward	1,300	2,145
	Sale proceeds		10,000
	Allowable cost		
	General pool	1,750	
	March 1982 market value	330	2,080
	Chargeable gain subject to capital gains tax		**7,920**

Questions without answers

1. Frank acquired 10,000 ordinary shares in Trent plc on 12th May 1980 for £1,500. On 15th December 1983, T plc made a rights issue of 1 for 5 at a price of 130p. Frank took up the rights and then sold half of his total holding on 10th May 2009 for £16,000.

    The market value of the shares at 31st March 1982 was £1,300. Compute the CGT liability of Frank for 2008/09. The shares do not qualify as a business asset.

2. Trevor has the following transactions in the 10p ordinary shares of Baker plc, a quoted company.

					£
4.5.80	purchased	5,000	@	80p	4,000
4.12.81	purchased	300	@	75p	225
16.5.82	purchased	1,000	@	104p	1,040
30.4.83	purchased	3,000	@	125p	3,750
5.9.00	purchased	2,000	@	150p	3,000
31.3.10	sold	9,000	@	180p	27,000

    The market value as at 31st March 1982 was £1.00.

    Compute CGT liability for 2009/10. The shares do not qualify as a business asset.

3. Patrick Limited bought 1,000 shares in Target plc in September 1991 for £20,000. On 3 June 2009 the entire share capital of Target plc was acquired by Bidder plc. Target plc shareholders received 2 Bidder plc shares and £5.00 cash for each share held. Bidder plc shares were quoted at £12.50.

    Requirement: Calculate the chargeable gain or allowable loss, if any, accruing to Patrick Limited as a result of the takeover in June 2009.

    You may assume the following indexation factor:

    September 1991 - June 2009   0.490 (estimated)

31 Taxable persons

Introduction

1. This chapter is concerned with the persons who are responsible for chargeable gains tax liabilities. It states the CGT position of individuals, husband and wife and personal representatives, with examples showing the effects of the unification of the income tax rates and capital gains tax rates. The CGT aspect of other persons is outlined.

Individuals

2. An individual is liable to capital gains tax if he or she is resident, or ordinarily resident in the UK in an income tax year, wherever he or she may be domiciled. If domiciled outside the UK, then any capital gains tax arising from the disposal of foreign assets is only chargeable to the extent that the sums are remitted to the UK. For this purpose the terms residence, ordinary residence and domicile, have the same meaning as for income tax.

> Rates   2009/10   –   First £10,100 (£9,600 – 2008/09) of net gains in the income tax year is exempt.

The following points should be noted.

a)   Net gains are added together and the annual exemption deducted from the total net gains.

b)   Where a taxpayer has no taxable income any unused allowances and reliefs cannot be deducted from the chargeable gains.

c)   Capital gains tax rate is a flat 18% after the annual exemption. Where a business asset qualifies for the entrepreneurs' relief the first £1 million of any gain is charged at 5/9ths of the gain and then charged at the rate of 18%, after the annual exemption, giving an effective rate of 10%.

d)   Husband and wife are treated separately.

Losses

3. i)   A capital loss can only be offset against a capital gain. Losses of the current year must be set against gains of the current year before being carried forward. The annual exemption amount of £10,100 is deducted from the net gains.

ii)   Losses brought forward can be set off against gains of the current year.

iii)   Losses brought forward are only utilised to the extent that they are used to reduce any gains to the £10,100 level.

Example

Barry makes a chargeable gain of £20,000 in 2009/10 arising from shares held at 17th March 1998. He also incurred a capital loss in the same period of £2,500.

The shares are not eligible for entrepreneurs' relief.

Compute Barry's CGT liability for 2009/10

Solution: Barry CGT computation 2009/10

	£
Chargeable gain	20,000
Less capital loss	2,500
Gain	17,500
Less exempt amount	10,100
Taxable gain	7,400
CGT payable 7,400 @ 18% =	1,332

Husband and wife

4.   The following points should be noted.

a)   Husband and wife are treated as separate individuals, each with an exemption allowance of £10,100 for 2009/10.

b)   Chargeable gains are recorded by husband and wife in their respective Self Assessment Tax Returns (SATR).

c)   The transfer of chargeable assets between husband and wife in any year of assessment does not give rise to any CGT charge where they are living together in the year of assessment; however the next owner takes on the previous one's exact CGT base cost at the date of transfer.

d)   Losses of one spouse cannot be set against the gains of the other.

e)   Where assets are jointly owned then in the absence of a declaration of beneficial interest, the 50–50 rule applies and each is treated as owning 50% of the assets.

f)   Where a married couple live together they can have only one residence which can qualify as their principal private residence.

Example

Mr and Mrs Johnson have the following data relating to the year ended 5th April 2010:

	Mr J £	Mrs J £
Capital gains (non-business) assets acquired June 2009	15,200	14,000
Capital losses	–	1,000

Compute the CGT liabilities for 2009/10.

Solution: CGT computation 2009/10

	Mr J £	Mrs J £
Capital gains	15,200	14,000
Less losses	–	1,000
Gains	15,200	13,000
Less exempt amount	10,100	10,100
Chargeable gain	5,100	2,900
CGT payable@ 18%	918	522

Notes

i)   Tax is payable by Mr & Mrs Johnson individually.

Trading losses set against chargeable gains

5. Where a trading loss is incurred in the year then to the extent that it has not been fully relieved under a claim for relief against any chargeable gain can be made. The amount to be claimed cannot exceed the chargeable gain for the year, before deducting the exemption amount of £10,100.

Example

Nick, who is single, has the following data relating to the year 2009/10:

	£
Trade profits 2009/10 (year to 31.3.2010)	15,000
Chargeable gain (asset acquired 1.4.2006)	12,500

In the year to 31st March 2011 Nick has a trading loss of £16,000, and no other income.

Compute the income tax liability and CGT liability for 2009/10.

Solution

N Income tax computation 2009/10

	£
Trade profits	15,000
Less loss relief	15,000
Assessment	–

CGT computation 2009/10

		£
Chargeable gain	12,500	
Less trading loss		1,000
Chargeable gain		11,500
Less annual exemption		10,100
		1,400
CGT payable @ 18%		252

Notes

i)   Nick's personal allowance of £6,475 would be wasted.

ii) The trading loss of £16,000 has been dealt with as follows:

	£
Carry back 2009/10	**15,000**
Capital gain 2009/10	1,000

The trading loss for the year ended 31st March 2011 can be used in either 2009/10 or 2010/11. However, since there is no other income in the period to 31st March 2011 the carry back has been used. Nick could also have decided to carry the loss forward against future trading income.

iii) CGT is payable at the 18%.

Personal representatives

6. The executor or administrator of a deceased person's estate is deemed to have acquired all the chargeable assets at the market value at the date of death, but there is no disposal. Legatees are also deemed to have acquired assets passing to them, at their market value at the date of death, so that any transfer to a legatee is not a chargeable disposal.

Rates   The first £10,100 of net gains is exempt in the year of assessment in which the death occurs and the subsequent two years of assessment.

Balance within the time scale noted above, at 18%.

Losses   Losses of the personal representative cannot be set against previous gains of the deceased.

Losses of the deceased in the year of his or her death can be carried back against the previous three years of assessment.

Within the time scale of the year of death and the next two years, losses need only be utilised to the extent that they reduce the net gains to the exempt amount.

Overseas aspects

7. Non-domiciled

An individual who is resident or ordinarily resident in the UK, but who is not domiciled in the UK, is only charged on gains in foreign assets to the extent that the proceeds from those gains are remitted to the UK. As there is no equivalent concept of remitting loss, there is no relief for losses realised by a non-domiciled individual on foreign assets.

Gains are computed at the date of disposal in accordance with normal computational rules. It is the individual's domicile status at the date of the disposal, not the date of the remittance, which determines the treatment of the gain.

Temporary non-resident

The following rules apply to individuals who become non-UK resident and non-UK ordinarily resident after 16th March 1998 but who are abroad for less than five complete tax years. Such individuals are still liable to UK CGT on certain gains made during that period of temporary non-residence.

A gain or loss of the tax years between the years of departure and return ('the intervening years') in the UK will be taxed as a gain or allowed as a loss of the year of return provided that:

a)   the individual was resident or ordinarily resident for at least four out of seven tax years before the tax year of departure; and

b)   the intervening years do not exceed five tax years; and

c)   the gain or loss arose on an asset acquired by the individual before actual departure from UK.

Splitting the tax year

Normally, an individual's residence status is determined for a complete tax year. However, where a person comes to or leaves the UK, the tax year can in certain circumstances be split into resident and non-resident periods under Extra Statutory Concession D2 (ESC).

This concession applies when the individual:

1)   comes to the UK to take up permanent residence or to stay for at least two years; or

2)   ceases to reside in the UK if he has left for permanent residence abroad.

It is also extended to the situation where an individual goes abroad to work under a full-time employment contract and:

1)   the absence and the employment both extend over a period covering a complete tax year; and

2)   interim visits to UK during period do not exceed 183 days in any year or 91 days on average,so that the individual is regarded as not resident and not ordinarily resident for

the whole of the contract. However, the concession is restricted where any individual ceases to be resident or ordinarily resident in the UK on or after 17th March 1998 or becomes resident or ordinarily resident in the UK on or after 6th April 1998.

Where an individual arrives in the UK, the year of arrival can be split into resident and non-resident periods, but only if the individual has been non-resident and non-ordinarily resident in the UK throughout the whole of the preceding five tax years. Gains made between the previous 6th April and the day before arrival are not charged to tax in this case.

Where an individual is leaving the UK, the year of departure can be split into resident and non-resident periods, but *only* if the individual was not resident and not ordinarily resident in the UK for at least four out of the seven preceding tax years. Gains made between the day of departure and the following 5th April are not charged to tax in this case.

An important case is *R v HMIT ex parte Fulford Dobson 1987 STC 344* which was on ESC D2 and established that a taxpayer could not use an ESC for tax avoidance.

Companies

8. Companies are not liable to capital gains tax as such, but they are liable to corporation tax on the disposal of any chargeable assets. The following should also be noted:

i)   Indexation continues to apply to disposal of assets by incorporated companies.

Partners

9. A partner is assessed as an individual in respect of his or her share of any chargeable gains accruing from the disposal of partnership assets. Accordingly any personal chargeable gains can be set against his or her share of any partnership capital losses, and vice versa.

Student self-testing question

Roger bought a painting for £2,500 in June 1973 which he sold for £65,000 on the 8th May 2009. Incidental costs of acquisition amounted to £200, costs of disposal £2,200.

Roger's wife Vanessa has capital losses of £3,500 for 2009/10. The painting had a market value of £15,000 on 31st March 1982. Roger's taxable income for 2009/10 is £40,000, i.e. after all allowances and reliefs.

Compute the 2009/10 CGT liability.

Solution: CGT computation 2009/10

	£	£
Proceeds of sale 8.5.2009		65,000
Less MV 31.3.82	15,000	
Cost of disposal	2,200	17,200
Gain	47,800	
Less exempt amount		10,100
CGT assessment		37,700
CGT payable @ 37,700 @ 18%		6,786

Notes

i)   The losses of Vanessa can only be used against her own future gains.

Questions without answers

1. Frank has chargeable gains of £11,500 for the year 2009/10, and capital losses of £500. His wife sells a piece of land for £10,000 on 10th May 2009 being part of a larger plot purchased in 1975 for £3,000. The remaining part had a value of £30,000 on 10th May 2009. Frank's taxable income for 2009/10 is £21,300 and his wife's Florence is £1,000.

    The market value of the land at 31st March 1982 was £2,500.

    Compute the CGT liability for 2009/10 of Frank and Florence.

2. Arnold purchased a painting in 1970 for £2,000 which he sells for £50,000 in January 2010. The painting was valued at £20,000 in 1982.

    Arnold's wife Patricia owned a small business which she acquired for £15,000 on the 1st January 1982. On the 1st January 2010 she sells the business for £165,000, incurring disposal costs of £344.

    The market value as at 31st March 1982 was £16,000.

    Compute the CGT liability of Arnold and Patricia for 2009/2010

32 Chargeable occasions

Introduction

1. A chargeable gain or loss arises on the occasion of a disposal of a chargeable asset. For this purpose a disposal takes place in the following circumstances, each of which is examined in this chapter:

> on a sale by contract
>
> on the compulsory acquisition of assets
>
> where capital sums are derived from assets destroyed or damaged, e.g. from insurance claims
>
> where assets have negligible value
>
> on the part disposal of an asset
>
> by value shifting
>
> on a death
>
> where a gift is made

Disposal by contract

2. Where an asset is disposed of by way of a contract then the date of the disposal is the time the contract is made and not, if different, the time when the asset is conveyed or transferred. For shares and securities the date of the contract note is the disposal date, and for land and buildings and house property the date of the contract to sell is the relevant date, and not the date of completion.

Compulsory acquisition

3. Where there is a compulsory acquisition of an interest in land, then the date of the disposal is the date when the amount of compensation is formally agreed.

Capital sums derived from assets

4. Compensation or insurance monies received in respect of an asset, amounts to a disposal by the owner. Thus if A has property which is damaged or destroyed by fire, then any insurance money received constitutes a disposal for CGT purposes. However, this is varied to some extent where the capital sum is used for the following purposes:

a)   to restore a non-wasting asset or

b)   to replace a non-wasting asset lost or destroyed.

Restoration of a non-wasting asset

5. If a capital sum is received in respect of a non-wasting asset, which is not lost or destroyed, the taxpayer can claim to have the sum deducted from the cost of acquisition, rather than treated as a part disposal. Such a claim can only be made if:

a)   the capital sum is used wholly for restoration, or the amount not restored is small relative to the capital sum or

b)   the capital sum is small relative to the value of the asset.

Small is normally taken to be 5% or less.

Example

Terry purchased a picture for £10,000 in June 1972, which was damaged by fire in May 2009 Insurance proceeds of £1,000 were received in December 2008, the whole amount being spent on restoring the picture. T claims to have the sum of £1,000 not treated as a disposal. The value of the painting after the fire was estimated at £8,000. Market value at 31.3.1982 was £35,000.

Show the computation of the allowable expenditure carried forward.

Solution: Computation 2009/10

	£
Market value 31.3.82	35,000
Less insurance sum	1,000
	34,000
Add expenditure on restoration	1,000
Allowable expenditure c/f	35,000

Note

From a capital gains tax point of view, Terry is in exactly the same position as he was before the picture was damaged.

Example

Sam purchased a piece of antique furniture for £10,000 in May 1978. The item was damaged by water in January 2009 for which £1,500 was received by way of insurance in July 2009. The amount spent on restoration was (a) £1,500 (b) £1,430. The market value at 31.3.1982 was £12,000. Compute the allowable costs in each case.

Solution

a) As the whole sum was spent on restoration there is no disposal if Sam claims, and no overall adjustment to the cost of the antique.

b) In this case the whole sum was not spent, but the unused amount of £70 is less than 5% of the capital sum, i.e. £75. The £70 not spent on restoration need not be treated as a disposal, but may be deducted from the allowed cost.

Computation 2009/10

	£	£
MV of antique 31.3.1982		12,000
Less insurance claim:		
Spent on restoration	1,430	
Not spent	70	1,500
	10,500	
Add expenditure on restoration		1,430
Allowable expenditure		11,930

Note

This is equivalent to the MV at 31.3.1982 less the amount not spent i.e. £12,000 – £70 = £11,930.

Example

Valerie has a collection of rare books purchased in February 1991 for £70,000 which were damaged by fire in May 2009 when they were estimated to be worth £100,000. The value of the collection as damaged by the fire was £70,000. In July 2009 Valerie received £30,000 insurance compensation and the collection was restored.

Compute the CGT effects of a) restoring and b) not restoring the book collection.

Solution

a) **Restoring**

CGT computation 2009/10

	£
Original cost of collection	70,000
Less insurance claim	30,000
	40,000
Add expenditure on restoration	30,000
Allowed expenditure c/f	70,000

As the whole sum has been spent on restoration there is no disposal if Valerie so claims and no adjustment to the cost of acquisition.

b) **Not restoring**

CGT computation 2009/10

	£
Insurance proceeds	30,000
Apportioned cost $\dfrac{30,000}{30,000+70,000} \times 70,000$	21,000
Gain subject to CGT before annual exemption	9,000

Replacement of non-wasting assets

6. Where an asset is lost or destroyed and a capital sum is received by way of compensation, or under a policy of insurance, then if it is spent on a replacement asset within 12 months of the receipt of the sum (or such longer period as the Inspector of Taxes may allow), and the owner so claims, then:

a) the consideration for the disposal of the lost or damaged asset is taken to be such that neither a gain or loss arises.

b) the cost of the replacement asset is reduced by the excess of the capital sum over the total of the consideration used in (a) above, plus any residual or scrap value of the old asset.

Example

Quentin purchased a picture for £3,000 in 1969 which was destroyed by fire in July 2009. Insurance of £20,000 was received in December 2009 and Quentin decided to purchase another picture using the full amount of the insurance money. The scrap value of the picture was £100.

Show the computations, with and without a claim under Section 23. Market value of £8,000 at 31st March 1982.

Solution: CGT Computation 2009/10

a) **If no claim is made**

	£	£
Capital sum received December 2009	20,000	
Add residual value	100	20,100
Less MV at 31.3.82	8,000	8,000
Chargeable gain subject to CGT		12,100

b)   If a claim is made

Deemed proceeds of sale December 2009		8,000
MV at 31.3.1982		8,000
No gain or loss		–
Replacement picture at cost		20,000
Less capital sum	20,000	
Less deemed proceeds	8,000	
	12,000	
Add scrap value	100	12,100
Allowable cost carried forward		7,900

Note

Where the whole sum is not spent on a replacement asset, then some relief is available providing that the amount not spent is less than the amount of the gain.

Assets whose value becomes negligible

7. The occasion of the entire loss, destruction, or extinction of an asset (wasting or non-wasting) amounts to a disposal of that asset, whether or not any capital sum is received. Where the value of an asset has become negligible, and the inspector is satisfied that such is the case, then the owner may make a claim to the effect that the asset has been sold and immediately required for a consideration equal to the negligible value. Thus if P owns a building which is destroyed by fire, and it was not insured, then he may claim to have made a disposal and reacquisition at the scrap value. An allowable loss for capital gains tax purposes would arise, assuming that the building was not an industrial building eligible for capital allowances.

The replacement of business assets

8. Where a qualifying 'business asset' is disposed of, including the occasion of the receipt of a capital sum, then special provisions apply if the assets are either wholly or partially replaced. This aspect which relates to assets used for the purposes of a trade is covered in Chapter 33 and 34.

Value shifting

9. Under these sections a disposal is deemed to occur where for example the value of a controlling interest in a company is 'watered down' in such a way that the value is passed into other shares or rights, without the occurrence of a disposal.

Hire purchase

10. Where a person enters into a hire purchase or other transactions, whereby he or she enjoys the use of an asset for a period of time, at the end of which he or she may become the owner of the asset, then the acquisition and disposal is deemed to take place at the beginning of the period of use. If the transaction is ended before the property is transferred then 'suitable adjustments' are to be made in agreement with the Inspector of Taxes. See *Lyon* v *Pettigrew* March 1985 STI 107.

Part disposals

11. In general any reference to a disposal also includes a part disposal, and where this occurs it is necessary to make some apportionment of the cost of acquisition. This is explained in Chapter 28.

Death

12. On the death of a person there is no disposal of any chargeable assets for capital gains tax purposes. The personal representative is deemed to have acquired any assets at their market value at the date of death, and any legatee also acquires the assets at the same market value, the date of acquisition being the date of death.

If a personal representative disposes of any assets other than to a legatee, e.g. in order to raise funds to pay any inheritance tax, then a chargeable occasion arises. However, in the year of death and in the two following years of assessment, the personal representative is entitled to the same annual exemptions as an individual.

Losses incurred by a personal representative cannot be set against any previous gains of the deceased. However, if the deceased had incurred any losses in the year of his or her death, then if they cannot be relieved in that year, then they can be carried back and set against gains in the previous three years.

Gifts

13. A gift of a chargeable asset does amount to a disposal, and this aspect together with the special reliefs available is examined in Chapter 33.

Student self-testing question

Jane has a collection of rare prints which cost £3,000 in May 1983. They were damaged by water in November 2008 and Jane received £17,000 by way of insurance compensation in May 2009. She spent £15,000 on restoration. The value of the prints in a damaged state was £6,000.

Compute any CGT liability arising and the amount of allowable expenditure carried forward.

Solution: CGT computation 2009/10

Capital sum received May 2009	17,000
Less spent on restoration	15,000
Part disposal	2,000
Proportion of cost: $3,000 \times \dfrac{2,000}{2,000 + 6,000} =$	750
Gain subject to CGT	1,250
Allowable expenditure carried forward	
Cost of acquisition	3,000
Less part disposal cost	750

Question without answer

Zachariah had a painting which was badly damaged by fire in January 2009. The picture was originally purchased for £1,000 in July 1973. In May 2009 Zachariah received insurance compensation of £20,000 which he decides to spend on a new painting. The scrap value of the damaged painting was £50.

Show the CGT position for 2009/10 on the basis that

a) **Zachariah makes a claim under Section 23 TCGA 1992**

b) **Zachariah makes no such claim.**

Market value of the painting at 31st March 1982 was £10,000.

33 Gifts – holdover relief

Introduction

1. This chapter is concerned with capital gains tax arising from gifts of chargeable assets. It begins with a list of exempt gifts and then examines the general holdover relief available. Holdover relief can be considered here as any gain that normally arises on the gift of a business asset being deducted from the deemed acquisition cost of the person receiving the gift. Thus the person making the gift has potentially avoided a charge to capital gains tax. In the case of gifts of business assets then the relief can be valuable and provide succession for a family business or when a business asset is disposed of in a 'not at arm's length' transaction.

2. A gift or a bargain not made at arm's length of a chargeable asset amounts to a disposal for capital gains tax purposes and is deemed to be made for a consideration equal to its market value. Thus in the case of *Turner* v *Follett* 1973, 48 TC 614, a gift of shares to the taxpayer's children was held to be a disposal at their market value.

Exemptions

3. The following gifts do not give rise to any chargeable gain or loss.

a) A gift to a charity or other approved institution such as the National Gallery, or the British Museum. Such a transfer is deemed to take place on a no gain or loss basis.

b) Gifts of works of art, manuscripts, historic buildings, scenic land etc., if the conditions required for inheritance tax exemption are satisfied.

c) A gift of a chattel with a market value of less than £6,000. See Chapter 29.

d) A gift of an exempt asset such as a private motor car, or the principal private residence of the taxpayer, unless otherwise taxable.

e) Gifts between husband and wife, these are treated as a no gain/no loss situation.

f) Transfers between members of a group of companies (see chapter 25 para 19-21).

Gifts of business assets – Section 165

4. The following are the main provisions relating to gifts of business assets.

a) Holdover relief is available to an individual who makes a transfer at less than market price to a person of:

   i) business assets used for the purposes of a trade, profession or vocation carried on by:

      1. the transferor, or

      2. his or her personal company

      3. a member of a trading group of which the holding company is his or her personal company.

   ii) Shares or securities of a trading company, or of the holding company of a trading company where:

      1. the shares are neither quoted nor dealt in on the AIM/USM or,

      2. the trading company or the holding company is the transferor's personal company.

   iii) agricultural property qualifying for the 100% IHT relief.

b) A personal company is one in which the individual is entitled to exercise 5% or more of the voting rights.

c) The relief must be claimed jointly by the transferee and the transferor, within six years of the date of transfer.

d) The relief is only available in respect of a business asset.

e) Holdover relief is not available:

    i) if the donee is non-resident or is exempt from CGT by reason of a double tax treaty.

    ii) if the recipient is a company controlled by non-residents who are connected with the donor.

f) the held over gain (in isolation) also becomes chargeable on the donee, as a CGT disposal in the year of emigration, if he/she emigrates permanently from the UK within 6 years of the transfer

Example

Beryl purchased the goodwill and freehold property of a retail business for £12,000 in 1970, which she gave to her son in May 2009 when it was worth £200,000.

The market value of the business at 31st March 1982 was £90,000.

Compute the chargeable gain that can be held over.

Solution: Computation 2009/10

	£	£
Disposal at market price		200,000
Less MV at 31.3.82	90,000	90,000
Chargeable gain held over		110,000
Acquisition by Beryl's son		
Market value of assets transferred		200,000
Less held over gain		110,000
Deemed cost		90,000

Example

William purchased his business premises in September 1988 for £40,000, which he gave to his son in May 1999 when it was worth £120,000. The election for hold over relief was given. In June 2009 William's son sold the premises for £200,000.

Compute the chargeable gain for 2009/10.

Solution: CGT 1999/00

	£	£
Value of premises		120,000
Cost of acquisition	40,000	40,000
Held over gain		80,000
Chargeable gain		NIL
CGT 2009/10		
Proceeds of sale		200,000
Base cost (120,000 – 40,000)		80,000
Chargeable gain subject to CGT		120,000

Note

i)   5/9ths of the gain is chargeable as the asset qualifies for entrepreneur's relief.

ii)   The annual exemption of £10,100 will also be available.

Gift of shares in personal company

5. If the transfer by an individual is of shares in his or her personal company then the held over gain is restricted. Where there are any non-business assets the gain is restricted where either

a)   at any time within 12 months of disposal not less than 25% of the company's voting rights were exercisable by the transferor, or

b)   the company is his or her personal company at any time within that period.

$$\text{Chargeable gain} \times \frac{\text{Chargeable business assets of the company at date of disposal}}{\text{Chargeable assets of the company at date of disposal}} = \frac{\text{CBA}}{\text{CA}}$$

Example

Terry acquired all the shares of X Ltd, a trading company, for £9,000 in March 1984, and transferred them by way of a gift to Phil in May 2009 when they were worth £140,000. At the date of the gift the company's assets were valued as follows:

	£
Freehold land and buildings	30,000
Goodwill	30,000
Plant and machinery – all items > £6,000	25,000
Investment in quoted company	60,000
Stocks, debtors and cash	18,750

Solution: Computation 2009/10

	£	£
Proceeds of sale of shares		140,000
Less cost of acquisition	9,000	9,000
Chargeable gain		131,000
Held over gain: $\frac{\text{CBA}}{\text{CA}}$ x 131,000		76,793
Chargeable gain		54,207
Entrepreneur's relief 5/9ths x £54,207		30,115
Gain subject to CGT before annual exemption		**30,115**

Notes

i)   The deemed cost to Phil is £140,000 – 76,793 i.e. £63,207

ii)   Plant and machinery is treated as a business asset. Items valued at less than £6,000 per item are exempt and not chargeable business assets.

iii) Stock, debtors and cash are exempt from capital gains tax.

iv)   A business asset is an asset used for the purpose of trade.

v)   The investment is not a chargeable business asset.

vi) Chargeable business assets are any assets on the disposal of which any gain would be a chargeable gain, and excludes, therefore, motor cars and items of moveable plant purchased and sold for £6,000 or less.

	Chargeable business assets (open market value at date of disposal)	Chargeable assets
	£	£
Freehold land	30,000	30,000
Goodwill	30,000	30,000
Investment	–	60,000
Plant and machinery	25,000	25,000
	85,000	145,000

Gifts of non-business assets, works of art etc.

6. Holdover relief is also available on gifts, where both the transferor and the transferee are individuals or trusts for:

i) gifts which are immediately chargeable transfers for IHT purposes i.e. gifts to discretionary trusts.

ii) gifts which are either exempt or conditionally exempt for IHT purposes e.g. gifts to political parties or gifts of heritage property, but not PETs.

Payment of tax by instalments

7. a) Capital gains tax on gifts not eligible for full holdover relief may be paid by ten equal annual instalments where an election is made. This only applies to the following assets:

i) Land or any interest in land.

ii) Shares or securities in a company which immediately before the disposal gave control to the person making the disposal.

iii) Shares or securities of a company (not falling in (ii)) and not quoted on a recognised stock exchange nor dealt in on the USM/AIM.

b) Where the gift is to a connected person, tax and accrued interest become payable where the donee subsequently disposes of the gift for a valuable consideration.

c) The first instalment is due on the normal due date. Instalments are not interest free unless the gifted property is agricultural land qualifying for IHT agricultural property relief.

Student self-testing questions

1. Karen purchased a business in 1980 which she gave to Mark in May 1998 when the market value was £125,000. Both Karen and Mark elected to hold over the computed gain. Mark sold the business in May 2009 for £180,000. The market value @ March 1982 was £40,000. The business qualifies for entrepreneur's relief.

Show the CGT computations.

Solution

Karen CGT Computation 1998/99

	£	£
Deemed proceeds of sale (May 1998)		125,000
Market value (March 1982)	40,000	40,000
Gain held over		85,000

Mark CGT Computation 2009/10

	£	£
Proceeds of sale (May 2009)		180,000
Deemed base cost (125,000 – 40,000)		85,000
Chargeable gain		95,000
Entrepreneur's relief 5/9ths x £95,000		52,778
Chargeable gain before annual exemption		52,778

Notes:

i)   5/9ths of the gain is chargeable as the asset qualifies for entrepreneur's relief.

ii)   No CGT is payable by Karen upon the gift of the asset to Mark.

2. On 5th December 2009 Michael sold to his son Simon a freehold shop valued at £250,000 for £75,000, and claimed gift relief. Michael had originally purchased the shop from which he has run his business in July 2001 for £45,000. Simon continued to run a business from the shop premises but decided to sell the shop in May 2011 for £230,000.

Compute any chargeable gains arising. Assume the rules of CGT in 2009/10 continue to apply in May 2011.

Suggested solution

Michaels CGT position 2009/10	£
Proceeds	250,000
Less cost	(45,000)
Gain	205,000
Less gain deferred	
£205,000 – (£75,000-£45,000)	(175,000)
Gain left in charge subject to CGT	30,000

Simons CGT position 2011/12	£
Proceeds	230,000
Less cost £250,000 – £175,000	(75,000)
Gain subject to CGT	155,000

Notes:

i)   In this case for Michael the excess of consideration over the original cost (£30,000) becomes chargeable to CGT.

ii)   Simon is deemed to have purchased the shop for £75,000.

iii)   5/9ths of the gain is chargeable as the asset qualifies for entrepreneur's relief.

Question without answer

1. Frank purchased a controlling interest in Nominal Ltd, a trading company, for £20,000 in 1991 which he gave to his son on 1st April 2004 when he was 48 years of age. The market value of the interest at the date of the gift was £500,000. A joint claim under Section 165 TCGA 1992 was made. Franks's son sells the business for £650,000 in June 2009.

The estimated market value of the controlling interest at 31st March 1982 was £100,000. There were no non-business, chargeable assets.

Compute the chargeable gains arising in 2009/10.

2. Jack Chan, aged 45, has been in business as a sole trader since 1 May 2001. On 28 February 2010 he transferred the business to his daughter Jill, at which time the following assets were sold to her:

(1)   Goodwill with a market value of £60,000. The goodwill has been built up since 1 May 2001, and has a nil cost. Jill paid Jack £50,000 for the goodwill.

(2)   A freehold office building with a market value of £130,000. The office building was purchased on 1 July 2003 for £110,000, and has always been used by Jack for business purposes. Jill paid Jack £105,000 for the office building.

(3)   A freehold warehouse with a market value of £140,000. The warehouse was purchased on 1 September 2003 for £95,000, and has never been used by Jack for business purposes. Jill paid Jack £135,000 for the warehouse.

(4)   A motor car with a market value of £25,000. The motor car was purchased on 1 November 2005 for £23,500, and has always been used by Jack for business purposes. Jill paid Jack £20,000 for the motor car.

Where possible, Jack and Jill have elected to hold over any gains arising.

Jack has unused capital losses of £6,400 brought forward from 2008-09.

Required:

Calculate Jack's Capital gains tax liability for 2009–10, and advise him by when this should be paid.

(15 marks)

ACCA past examination question December 2002 (updated)

34 Business assets and businesses

Introduction

1. The disposal of a business or of any business, assets requires special consideration for chargeable gains tax purposes as there are valuable relief's available to the owners. In this chapter the following topics will be examined:

a) Replacement of business assets Sections 152 to 158.

b) Reinvestment relief for individuals.

c) Transfer of a business to a company Section 162.

d) Transfer of assets between group companies.

e) Trading stock.

f) Loans to traders.

The holdover relief in respect of a gift of business assets is outlined in the chapter on gifts, see Chapter 33.

Replacement of business assets Sections 152–158

2. Relief under these provisions enables a taxpayer to 'roll over' any gain arising on the disposal of a 'business asset', by deducting it from the cost of a replacement. The main rules are:

a) A business asset is one used for the purposes of a trade and falling within the under mentioned classes:

> land and buildings occupied by the taxpayer; fixed plant and machinery; satellites, space stations, space craft; ships, aircraft and hovercraft; goodwill; milk and potato quotas; EC agricultural quotas. Since 2002, goodwill and quotas are not chargeable assets for corporate taxpayers, and so are now excluded from this list in the case of companies only, but remain qualifying assets for individuals

b) The assets disposed of must be used throughout the period of ownership, and the latter includes assets held by a 'personal company'.

c) The new asset must be acquired within 12 months before the disposal, or within three years after, although the Inspector of Taxes has power to extend these limits.

d) Where a trader re-invests in business assets to be used in a new trade then relief is available providing the interval between the two trades is not greater than three years.

e) Partial relief is available where the whole of the proceeds of sale are not used in the replacement. In these circumstances the gain attracting an immediate charge to tax is the lower of:

   i)   the chargeable gain, and

   ii) the uninvested proceeds.

   By concession HMRC regard proceeds net of disposal costs for this purpose.

f) There are special provisions where the replacement asset is a depreciating asset. *See below.*

g) The relief is also available to non-profit making organisations such as trade and professional associations.

h) Where a person carrying on a trade uses the proceeds from the disposal of an 'old asset' on capital expenditure to enhance the value of other assets, such expenditure is treated for the purposes of these provisions as incurred in acquiring other assets provided:

i)   the other assets are used only for the purposes of the trade, or

ii)   on completion of the work on which the expenditure was incurred the assets are immediately taken into use and used only for the purposes of the trade.

i)   Where a 'new asset' is not, on acquisition, immediately taken into use for the purposes of a trade, it will nevertheless qualify for relief provided:

     i)   the owner proposes to incur capital expenditure for the purpose of enhancing its value;

     ii)   any work arising from such capital expenditure begins as soon as possible after acquisition, and is completed within a reasonable time;

     iii)   on completion of the work the asset is taken into use for the purpose of the trade and for no other purpose; and

     iv)   the asset is not let or used for any non-trading purpose in the period between acquisition and the time it is taken into use for the purposes of the trade.

j)   As a general rule rollover relief should not be claimed by an individual where the gain would be covered by the annual exemption.

k)   Incorporated entities use the indexation allowance in the computation of any gains to be rolled over, unincorporated entities and individuals do not use indexation.

Example

Peter purchased the goodwill of a retail business in 1979 for £5,000 and sold it on 1st December 2009 for £40,000. On 31st December 2009 Peter purchased the goodwill of a new business for £50,000. The market value of the business at 31st March 1982 was £15,000.

Compute the chargeable gain.

Solution: Computation 2009/10

	£	£
Proceeds of sale		40,000
Less market value 31.3.82	15,000	15,000
Chargeable gain		25,000
Cost of new business		50,000
Less rolled over gain on old business		25,000
Deemed cost		25,000

Notes:

i)   The deemed cost on any subsequent disposal of the new business asset is £25,000.

i)   There is no charge to CGT on the first disposal as all of the proceeds have been re-invested.

Example

Karen purchased a freehold factory for her business use in 1979 for £22,000. This was sold for £250,000 on 31st May 2009, and a new factory acquired for £230,000.

The market value of the factory at 31st March 1982 was £75,000.

Compute the chargeable gain.

Solution: Computation 2009/10

	£	£
Proceeds of sale		250,000
Less market value at 31.3.82	75,000	75,000
Chargeable gain		175,000
Less rollover relief:		
Gain	175,000	
Less amount of consideration not invested	20,000	155,000
Chargeable gain		20,000

Notes

i) The base cost for subsequent disposals would be £230,000 – £155,000 i.e. £75,000.

ii) The rolled over gain is restricted by any part of the consideration not reinvested, i.e. (250,000 – 230,000) = 20,000.

iii) 5/9ths of the gain is chargeable as the asset qualifies for entrepreneur's relief.

Replacement with a depreciating asset

3. Where the asset is replaced with a depreciating asset then the gain is not deducted from the cost of the asset, i.e. the replacement asset, but is frozen until the earliest of the following occurs:

a) the depreciating asset is itself sold, or

b) the depreciating asset ceases to be used by the person in his or her trade, or

c) the expiry of 10 years from the date of the replacement.

A depreciating asset is one with an estimated life of 50 years or less, or one which will have such a life expectancy within 10 years from the date of acquisition, i.e. a total of 60 years at the date of acquisition.

Where a gain on a disposal is held over against a depreciating asset then provided that a non-depreciating asset is bought before the held over gain on the deprecating asset crystallises, it is possible to transfer the held over gain to a non-depreciating replacement.

Example

John sold his freehold shop property used for trade purposes for £120,000 on 1st August 2007. The property was bought for £50,000 on 1st May 1982. In December 2007 John acquired fixed plant for £130,000 which he used immediately for trade purposes until he ceased trading altogether on 31st March 2010 when the plant was scrapped. He had no other gains in the year 2009/2010.

Compute the chargeable gains when the plant was scrapped.

Solution

John's CGT computation 2007/08

	£	£
1.8.2007 Proceeds of sale of property		120,000
1.5.1982 Cost of acquisition	50,000	50,000
Chargeable gain		70,000
Less amount held over		70,000
Assessable gain		Nil

John's CGT computation 2009/10

	£
Held over gain	70,000
Entrepreneurs relief 5/9ths chargeable	38,889
Less annual exemption	10,100
Gain subject to CGT	28,789
CGT at 18%	5,182

Notes

i) As the business ceased to trade the held over gain has crystallised.

ii) No gain arises on the scrapping of the plant, as any proceeds of sale would be < cost.

iii) The business asset qualifies for entrepreneurs' relief at 5/9ths of the gain.

iv) The gain is held until the earlier of 10 years or the business ceasing to trade.

v) The held over gain is not deducted from the cost of the replacement depreciating asset.

Transfer of a business to a company Section 162

4. The transfer of a business to a company is a disposal of the assets of the business and can therefore give rise to a chargeable gain or loss.

A form of rollover relief exists where an individual transfers the whole of his or her business to a company in exchange for shares, wholly or partly. In effect the held over gain is deducted from the costs of the shares acquired. The gain to which this section relates is that arising on the transfer of chargeable business assets, and the amount deferred is equal to:

$$\text{The net gain} \times \frac{\text{Value of shares received}}{\text{Total value of consideration ie shares and loans}}$$

All assets of the business must be transferred although cash balances and other non-business assets may be retained as a general rule.

The taxpayer can elect for the rollover relief *not* to apply, which may be advantageous in terms of his entrepreneurs relief entitlement

Example

Andrea transfers her business to Trent Ltd on 6th April 2009 in exchange for 100,000 ordinary shares of £1 each fully paid, having a value of par, and £25,000 by way of loans. Chargeable gains on the transfer of business assets to Trent Ltd amounted to £75,000. Andrea had been in business since 1990.

Compute the chargeable gain.

Solution

Calculation of rolled over gain 2009/10

	£
$75,000 \times \dfrac{100,000}{100,000 + 25,000} =$	60,000
Chargeable gain	75,000
Less amount rolled over	60,000
Gain subject to CGT	15,000

Deemed cost of shares carried forward	£
Value of shares	100,000
Less rolled over gain	60,000
Net cost	40,000

Transfer of assets between group companies

5. There is no method of group relief applicable to chargeable gains and losses which arise within different members of a group of companies. Accordingly, when a company disposes of a chargeable asset outside the group, then any capital gain arising will be chargeable to corporation tax. However, if the disposal is by a member of a group of companies to another group company then the provisions enable the transaction to be construed as if the disposal does not give rise to any chargeable gain or loss. This is achieved by deeming the consideration for the disposal of the asset to be such an amount that neither a gain nor a loss accrues to the company disposing of the asset. When the asset is ultimately disposed of outside the group, then a normal liability to corporation tax on any gain would arise.

The company actually disposing of the asset and another company in the group can to elect that the disposal outside the group be treated as being made by the other company. The election must be made within two years after the end of the accounting period in which the actual disposal is made.

Companies eligible

6. a) A group comprises a principal company and all of its 75% subsidiaries.

b) A 75% subsidiary means a company whose ordinary share capital is owned by another company either directly or indirectly to the extent of at least 75%. Again ordinary share capital comprises all shares other than fixed preference shares.

c) Where the principal company is itself a 75% subsidiary of another company, then both its parent and its subsidiaries, together with the principal company, constitute a group.

d) From 1st April 2000, companies are able to transfer assets to one another on a no gain/no loss basis in a wider range of circumstances than at present. In particular, it is possible to make such transfers between:

i) two UK residents companies with a common non-resident parent company;

ii) a UK resident company and a non-resident company within the same world-wide group, where the latter company carries on a UK trade through a branch or agency.

e) A company is not a member of a group unless the principal member of the group has itself directly or indirectly more than 50% interest in its profits and assets.

Members of a consortium are not eligible for treatment as a group for the purposes of this section, nor are close investment holding companies, unless the transfer is between close investment holding companies.

Example

Zodiac Ltd and its 75% subsidiary company Burnham Ltd had the following results for the year ended 31st March 2009.

	Z Ltd	B Ltd
Trading profits	125,000	80,000
Chargeable gains (loss)	(75,000)	100,000

Zodiac Ltd and Burnham Ltd elect that the capital loss arising from the disposal of an asset by Zodiac Ltd be treated as a disposal by Burnham Ltd.

Show the effects of the election.

Solution: Corporation tax computations AP 31.3.2009

	Z Ltd	B Ltd
Schedule D Case I	125,000	80,000
Chargeable gains		
(100,000 – 75,000)		25,000
	125,000	105,000
Corporation tax @ 21%	26,250	22,050

Notes

i) It is not necessary for Z Ltd to transfer the asset, giving rise to the loss of £75,000, to B Ltd under section 171.

ii) The election has to be made within two years of the end of the AP in which the assets disposed of outside the group i.e. by 31.3.11.

iii) The election can be made in respect of part of an asset.

iv) Without the transfer B Ltd would be taxed on the full £180,000 of its profits chargeable to corporation tax at the marginal rate. (2 companies $300,000 \div 2 = 150,000$)

v) Group cash savings $(305,000 – 230,000)$ @ 21% = £15,750.

Assets available for group treatment

7. The disposal of any form of property could give rise to the no gain or loss treatment, but there are some exceptions which are as follows:

a) where the disposal is of redeemable preference shares in a company, on the occurrence of the disposal

b) where the disposal is of a debt due from a member of a group, effected, by satisfying the debt or part of it

c) where the disposal arises from a capital distribution on the liquidation of a company.

If the transfer is of an asset which the recipient company appropriates to its trading stock, then that company is deemed to have received a capital asset and immediately transferred that asset to its trading stock. There would thus be no capital gain or loss arising on the inter-company transfer, as it would fall within the provisions noted above.

Where the asset transferred to a group company was trading stock of the transferor company, then the latter is treated as having appropriated the asset as a capital asset immediately prior to the disposal. The value placed on the asset for trading purposes under would be the transfer value giving rise to a 'no gain or loss' situation.

Miscellaneous points

8. a) When an asset is disposed of by a group company to a company outside the group, then any capital allowances granted to any member of the group relating to the asset are taken into consideration in computing any gain or loss.

b) If a company to which an asset has been transferred, ceases to be a member of a group within six years of the date of the transfer the position is as follows.

    i) At the date of the acquisition of the asset by the company leaving the group, it is deemed to have sold and reacquired the asset at its market value.

    ii) There will therefore be a chargeable gain or loss on the difference between the market value and the original cost to the group of the asset.

This provision does not apply if a company ceases to be a member of a group by being wound up.

    iii) The gain is chargeable in the A.P. the company leaves the group but it is the gain arising on inter-group transfer known as 'degrouping charge'.

c) The provisions of rollover relief are extended to groups and enable all trades carried on by the group to be treated as one.

d) Where a company is a dual resident member of a group of companies detailed provisions exist which are designed to prevent:

    i) the transfer of assets at a no gain/no loss value where the dual resident company would be exempt from CGT

    ii) the granting of rollover relief for the replacement of business assets where the replacement assets are required by a dual resident company.

e) Capital losses brought into a group as a result of a company joining the group will be 'ring fenced' for disposals. In effect such capital losses will only be available for unrestricted set-off against gains on:

    i) assets held by the company at the date that it joined the group or

    ii) assets acquired by that company from outside the new group and used in a trade carried on by that company before joining the group.

Substantial disposals of shares – exempt from CGT

9. Sales by United Kingdom companies of 'substantial shareholdings' in other companies are to be tax free. Although dividends from foreign subsidiaries remain fully taxable, disposals of shares in foreign and United Kingdom subsidiaries are exempt from corporation tax on gains, provided that certain conditions are met.

i) The relief is available for disposals by trading companies or members of a trading group (the 'investing' company).

ii) It applies to gains on the disposal of a substantial shareholding in a trading company or holding company of a trading group (the 'investee' company).

iii) A substantial shareholding means, broadly, at least a 10% interest.

iv) The substantial shareholding must have been held for a continuous period of at least 12 months in the two years immediately before the disposal.

In order to hold a substantial interest, the investing company needs to be beneficially entitled to at least 10% of the investee company's:

i) ordinary share capital; and

ii) profits available for distribution to equity holders; and

iii) assets available for distribution to equity holders in the event of a winding-up.

In determining whether a holding amounts to a substantial shareholding, shares held by other group members are aggregated over the world-wide group.

Trading stock

10. Trading stock is not a business asset for capital gains tax purposes as it is normally taken into consideration in computing taxable trading income.

Where an asset is appropriated to stock in trade then there is a deemed disposal at the date of the appropriation if a gain or loss would have arisen from a sale of the asset at its market value. An election can be made to have the gain (or loss) deducted (or added) from the value of the asset so that the ultimate profit is taxed as trading income.

If an asset is appropriated from trading stock for any purpose then it is deemed to be acquired for CGT purposes at the value taken into account in computing the taxable profit.

Example

Keith purchased an asset in October 1986 for £20,000 which he held as an investment until 31st July 2009 when it was transferred to trading stocks. Market value at 31st July was £45,000. It was sold as trading stock in December 2009 for £60,000.

Show the effects of the above both with and without an election

Solution

Without election. CGT computation 2009/10

	£	£
July 2009 market value		45,000
Less cost of acquisition	20,000	20,000
Chargeable gain subject to CGT		25,000
Trade profits		
Sale of trading stock		60,000
Less cost		45,000
Taxable profit		15,000

With election. CGT computation 2009/10

	£	£
Trade profits		
Sale of trading stock		60,000
Market value on appropriation	45,000	
Less gain (as above)	25,000	20,000
Taxable trade profits		40,000

Notes

i) The asset must be of a kind sold in the ordinary course of trade.

ii) The appropriation must be made with a view to resale at a profit.

iii) An election is only available by a person taxable with trade profits.

Loans to traders

11. Loans made to traders may be claimed as a CGT loss in the following circumstances:

i) where a loss is incurred on a qualifying loan.

ii) where the taxpayer has to meet a guarantee made on a qualifying loan, or

iii) where a loss is incurred on a qualifying corporate bond.

The borrower must be resident in the UK and the money advanced must be used wholly for the purposes of the trade or profession carried on, or for letting qualifying holiday accommodation.

The loss arises at the time the claim is made, and not the date of the loan transaction so that indexation does not arise.

Tax efficient schemes

12. Shares that qualify for exemption from capital gains tax will not need to make use of any rollover conditions. Such shares, in addition to the ones identified in this are chapter, are included in schemes such as:

i) Enterprise Investment Scheme (EIS)

ii) Venture Capital Trusts

iii) Corporate Venturing Scheme

Student self-testing questions

1. A sole trader bought a freehold factory in October 1998 and sold it for £140,000 on 18 May 2009 giving a gain of £35,900. He bought a replacement factory on 6 June 2009 for £120,000.

Requirement: Assuming a claim for rollover relief was made what is the base cost of the new factory.

Suggested solution

Total gain		35,900
Amount not reinvested	(140,000 - 120,000)	20,000
Gain eligible for roll-over		15,900
Cost of new factory		120,000
Rolled over gain		15,900
Base cost of new factory		104,100
Gain chargeable immediately		20,000

2. Linda is a sole trader who bought a qualifying business asset for £341,250 on 5/11/1991 and sold it for £982,800 on 31/12/2009. A replacement business asset was acquired on 1/11/2009 at a cost of £1,092,000. This asset was sold on 3/9/2013 for £1,829,100. A rollover claim was made on the first sale only. Assume existing rules apply in 2013.

Requirement: Calculate the capital gain on the sale of the second asset.

Suggested solution

31/12/09 disposal

Sale proceeds	982,800
Cost	(341,250)
Gain rolled over	641,550

3/9/13 disposal

Sale proceeds		1,829,100
Cost (1/11/09)	1,092,000	
Rollover relief	641,550	450,450
Gain subject to CGT		1,378,650
Gain chargeable		555,556
On first 1,000,000 x 5/9ths		
Gain chargeable		378,650
Excess 378,650		
Total gain subject to CGT		934,206
Annual exemption		(10,100)
Total		924,106
CGT @ 18%		166,339

3. Hadley Limited purchased a factory in November 1988 for £250,000. Not needing all the space, the company let out 15% of it. In April 2009 the company sold the factory for £600,000 and bought another in the same month for £700,000. Assume an indexation factor of 0.786 from November 1988 to April 2009.

Requirement:

Calculate:

(a) **The chargeable gain or allowable loss, if any, arising on the disposal in April 2009**

(b) **The allowable expenditure (base cost) of the new factory.**

Suggested solution

(a) Split the old factory & the new factory into qualifying and non qualifying parts and compute the gains on them separately:

	Qualifying £	Non qualifying £
Disposal proceeds (85%/15%)	510,000	90,000
Less cost	(212,500)	(37,500)
Unindexed gain	297,500	52,500
Indexation allowance	(167,025)	(29,475)
212,500 and 37,500 x 0.786		
Indexed gain	130,475	23,025

The gain of £23,025 will be taxed immediately as it does not qualify for rollover relief.

b) The base cost of the new factory is reduced by the amount of the gain rolled over. It is therefore:

	£
Purchase cost	700,000
Less gain rolled over	(130,475)
	569,525

4. Harold bought a freehold shop for use in his business in June 2008 for £150,000. He sold it for £175,000 on 1st August 2009. On 8th July 2009 Harold bought some fixed plant and machinery to use in his business costing £178,000. He then sells the plant and machinery for £192,000 on 20th November 2011.

Show Harolds CGT position.

Suggested solution

	£
Gain deferred	
Proceeds of shop	175,000
Less cost	(150,000)
Gain	25,000

The gain is deferred in relation to the plant and machinery.

	£
Sale of plant and machinery	
Proceeds	192,000
Less cost	(178,000)
Gain	14,000
Total gain chargeable on sale	
(gain on plant and machinery plus deferred gain)	
£25,000 + £14,000 subject to CGT	39,000

5. Barbera, a full-time working director of Zenith Ltd, sells her controlling interest of 100% of the ordinary share capital for £950,000 on 10th May 2009 in Zenith Ltd. Net assets consisted of the following as at 10th May 2009.

	£
Goodwill	360,000
Plant and machinery (all items > £6,000)	150,000
Freehold factory premises (cost £50,000)	140,000
Investments (short term)	90,000
Net current assets	60,600
	800,600

Barbera purchased the shares in Zenith Ltd for £50,000 in May 1979. The market value of the shares at 31st March 1982 was £130,000. **Compute the chargeable gain arising on the sale of her shares.**

Solution: CGT computation 2009/10

	£	£
Proceeds of sale of shares		950,000
Less market value at 31.3.82	130,000	130,000
Chargeable gain		820,000
Entrepreneur's relief 5/9ths x £820,000		455,556
Chargeable gain subject to CGT before annual exemption		**455,556**

Questions without answers

1. Z sold his business on 10th May 2009. The proceeds of sale amounted to £1,500,000 for the chargeable business assets. Z had purchased the business for £200,000 on 9th May 1980. The market value of the business at 31st March 1982 was £250,000.

Compute the chargeable gain arising.

2. Tony purchased a grocery business on 1st June 1978 which he is considering selling in December 2009 for an estimated price of £400,000. The sale price is allocated between the business assets on the following basis.

	Consideration £
Freehold premises	275,000
Flat above premises occupied by Tony since acquisition as only residence	40,000
Goodwill	50,000
Trading stock	20,000
Shop fixtures	15,000
	400,000

The value of the business at 31st March 1982 was estimated to be £150,000 comprising the following:

	£
Freehold premises	60,000
Flat above premises	30,000
Goodwill	40,000
Trading stock	15,000
Shop fixtures	5,000

Calculate the CGT liability which would arise should Terry sell the business and retire. He has no other chargeable gains arising in 2009-2010.

3. Chandra Khan disposed of the following assets during 2009/10:

a) On 15 June 2009 Chandra sold 10,000 £1 ordinary shares (a 30% shareholding) in Universal Ltd, an unquoted trading company, to her daughter for £75,000. The market value of the shares on this date was £110,000. The shareholding was purchased on 10 July 1997 for £38,000. Chandra and her daughter have elected to hold over the gain as a gift of a business asset.

b) On 8 November 2009 Chandra sold a freehold factory for £146,000. The factory was purchased on 3 January 1997 for £72,000. 75% of the factory has been used in a manufacturing business run by Chandra as a sole trader. However, the remaining 25% of the factory has never been used for business purposes. Chandra has claimed to rollover the gain on the factory against the replacement cost of a new freehold factory that was purchased on 10 November 2009 for £156,000. The new factory is used 100% for business purposes by Chandra.

c) On 8 March 2010 Chandra incorporated a wholesale business that she has run as a sole trader since 1 May 2003. The market value of the business on 8 March 2010 was £250,000. All of the business assets were transferred to a new limited company, with the consideration consisting of 200,000 £1 ordinary shares valued at £200,000 and £50,000 in cash. The only chargeable asset of the business was goodwill, and this was valued at £100,000 on 8 March 2010. The goodwill has a nil cost.

Calculate the capital gains arising from Chandra's disposals during 2009/10. You should ignore the annual exemption. *(ACCA)*

4. Astute Ltd sold a factory on 15 February 2010 for £320,000. The factory was purchased on 24 October 1997 for £164,000, and was extended at a cost of £37,000 during March 1999. During May 2000 the roof of the factory was replaced at a cost of £24,000 following a fire. Astute Ltd incurred legal fees of £3,600 in connection with the purchase of the factory, and legal fees of £6,200 in connection with the disposal.

Indexation factors are as follows:

October 1997 to February 2010	0·337 (estimated)
March 1999 to February 2010	0·282 (estimated)
May 2000 to February 2010	0·238 (estimated)

Astute Ltd is considering the following alternative ways of reinvesting the proceeds from the sale of its factory:

(1) A freehold warehouse can be purchased for £340,000.

(2) A freehold office building can be purchased for £275,000.

(3) A leasehold factory on a 40-year lease can be acquired for a premium of £350,000.

The reinvestment will take place during May 2010. All of the above buildings have been, or will be, used for business purposes.

Required:

(a) State the conditions that must be met in order that rollover relief can be claimed. You are not expected to list the categories of asset that qualify for rollover relief. *(3 marks)*

(b) Before taking account of any available rollover relief, calculate Astute Ltd's chargeable gain in respect of the disposal of the factory. *(5 marks)*

(c) Advise Astute Ltd of the rollover relief that will be available in respect of EACH of the three alternative re-investments. Your answer should include details of the base cost of the replacement asset for each alternative. *(7 marks)*

(15 marks)

ACCA past examination question December 2001 (updated)

End of section questions and answers

Chargeable gains tax question No. 1 T

An examination of the books and records of Trevor, a retired Army officer aged 68, and his wife Amelia for the year ended 5th April 2010 showed the following.

i) December 16th. Sale of 4,000 ordinary £1.00 shares in Beta plc (non-business asset) at a price of 835p per share. Trevor's records showed that his total holding prior to the sale consisted of the following:

		£
1.6.1969	purchased 300 ordinary shares, cost	300
30.9.1975	purchased 1,500 ordinary shares, cost	1,750
1.10.1980	rights issue of 1,800 shares at cost	2,000
30.10.1984	purchased 1,400 ordinary shares cost	1,800

The market value of the ordinary shares at 31st March 1982 was 150p.

ii) December 30th. Sold painting for £9,900 which he had purchased in 1970 for £2,100. The painting had an estimated value of £4,800 at 31st March 1982.

iii) December 30th. Sale of entire holding of ordinary shares in Kornet Ltd an ice cream business, for £42,000 representing a 50% share of the business. Amelia had purchased the shares in Kornet Ltd, an unquoted company, for £8,000 on 6th April 1970. Their market value at 31st March 1982 was £18,000.

Calculate the CGT liabilities for 2009/10 arising

Solution: Trevor capital gains tax computation 2009/10

i) Sale of 4,000 shares in Beta plc

Section 104 pool	Nominal value £	Qualifying expenditure £
30.10.1984 purchase	1,400	1,800
	1,400	1,800
16.12.2009 sale	1,400	1,800

1982 pool		Nominal value £	Cost £	Re-basing market value 31.3.82 £
1. 6.1969	purchase	300	300	450
30.9.1975	– do –	1,500	1,750	2,250
1.10.1980	– do –	1,800	2,000	2,700
		3,600	4,050	5,400

16.12.2009 sale   2,600

Proportionate cost: $\dfrac{2,600}{3,600} \times 5,400$ — 3,900

Chargeable gain subject to CGT

	Nominal value	Cost	Re-basing: market value 31.3.82
	£	£	£
Section 104 pool Proceeds of sale $\frac{1,400}{4,000} \times 33,400$		11,690	
Less pool cost		1,800	9,890
1982 Holding Proceeds of sale $\frac{2,600}{4,000} \times 33,400$		21,710	
Less pool cost		3,900	17,810
			27,700

Note

Proceeds of sale are 4,000 × £8.35 = £33,400.

ii) 30.12.2009 Sale of painting	£	£
Proceeds of sale		9,900
Market value at 31.3.82	4,800	
		5,100

Marginal relief, gain restriction

$\left(\frac{5}{3} \times 9,900 - 6,000\right)$ = 6,500, lower of £5,100 and £6,500

Chargeable gain subject to CGT		5,100

iii) **Amelia sale of shares in Kornet Ltd**		Cost	Market value 31.3.82
		£	£
30.12.2009	Proceeds of sale	42,000	42,000
6.4.1970	Cost	8,000	
31.3.1982	Market value		18,000
Chargeable gain subject to CGT		34,000	24,000

The gain based on the market value at 31st March 1982 is taken. .

Trevor and Amelia capital gains tax computations 2009/10

	Trevor	Amelia
	£	£
Shares in Beta plc	27,700	–
Painting	5,100	–
Shares in Kornet Ltd	–	24,000
Chargeable gain	32,800	24,000
Entrepreneurs relief 5/9ths	-	13,333
Less exemption	10,100	10,100
Capital gain	22,700	3,233
CGT payable 18%	4,086	582

Amelia's shares qualify for entrepreneurs' relief.

Chargeable gains tax question No. 2 David Plaine

David Plaine resigned as a full-time working director of Plaine Sailing Ltd, an unquoted personal company, on 1st July 2009, to become non-executive chairman and president of the company. He had joined the company on 1st July 1977, acquiring 30% of the ordinary shares at a cost of £95,000.

On 1st July 2009 he sold his entire interest for £800,000.

The following is a summary of the balance sheet of Plaine Sailing Ltd as at 30th June 2009 at market values:

	£
Freehold land and buildings	800,000
Goodwill	500,000
Plant and machinery (all items > £6,000)	300,000
Stocks and work in progress	300,183
Trade debtors	210,146
Cash in hand	32,000
Trade creditors	100,184
Bank overdraft	164,239

Plaine's 30% interest has been valued at £180,000 at 31st March 1982.

Compute the chargeable gain for 2009/10 after any claim for relief Plaine could make.

Plant and machinery was sold at a loss.

Solution: David Plaine CGT computation 2009/10

	£	£
1st July 2009 Sale proceeds		800,000
Less market value at 31.3.82	180,000	
Gain subject to CGT	620,000	
Gain chargeable entrepreneur's relief 5/9ths		344,444
Annual exemption	(10,100)	
Chargeable gain	334,344	
CGT @ 18%		60,182

Chargeable gains tax question No. 3 Robert Jones

Robert Jones held 140,000 shares in MNO plc. He sold 125,000 shares on 5 October 2009 for £3.20 per share. He had acquired the shares as follows:

Date	Number acquired	Price per share
21 June 1980	30,000	£1.30
9 December 1983	70,000	£1.35

In June 1988 there was a rights issue of 2 ordinary shares for every 5 held at £1.10 per share. Robert took up his full rights issue. The shares were quoted at £1.25 on March 1982.

The shares do not qualify for entrepreneurs' relief.

Calculate the amount of chargeable gain on the disposal. **(ATT)**

Solution

Section 104 pool.

	No. of shares	Indexed pool
9/12/83 Bought	70,000	94,500
	70,000	94,500
6/88 RI 2 for 5	28,000	30,800
	98,000	125,300
Sale 5.10.09	98,000	125,300
Carried forward	Nil	Nil

1982 Pool

	No. of shares	MV 31.3.82
21/6/80 Cost	30,000	37,500
6/88 RI	12,000	13,200
	42,000	50,700
5/10/09 Sale	27,000	32,593
C/forward	15,000	18,107

Chargeable gains computation 2009/10
Section 104 Pool.

Proceeds of sale 98,000 @ 3.20	313,600	
pool cost	125,300	
Gain		188,300
1982 Holding proceeds of sale 27,000 @ 3.20	86,400	
Less MV at 31.3.82	32,593	
Gain		52,843
Total gain subject to CGT before annual exemption		241,143

Questions without answers – Capital Gains Tax

1. Earth Ltd sold the following shareholdings during the year ended 31 March 2010:

(a) On 20 November 2009 Earth Ltd sold 25,000 £1 ordinary shares in Venus plc for £115,000. Earth Ltd had originally purchased 40,000 shares in Venus plc on 19 June 1987 for £34,000. On 11 October 2002 Venus plc made a 1 for 4 bonus issue. Retail price indices (RPIs) are as follows:

June 1987	101.90
October 2002	177.90
November 2009	215.50 (estimated)

(b) On 22 January 2010 Earth Ltd sold 30,000 £1 ordinary shares in Saturn plc for £52,500. Earth Ltd purchased 30,000 shares in Saturn plc on 9 February 2001 for £97,500. The indexed value of the 1985 pool on 3 January 2004 was £103,200. On 3 January 2004 Saturn plc made a 1 for 2 rights issue. Earth Ltd took up its allocation under the rights issue in full, paying £1·50 for each new share issued.

(c)   On 28 March 2010 Earth Ltd sold its entire holding of £1 ordinary shares in Jupiter plc for £55,000. Earth Ltd had originally purchased 10,000 shares in Mercury plc on 5 May 1995 for £14,000. The indexed value of the 1985 pool on 7 March 2010 was £19,000. On 7 March 2010 Mercury plc was taken over by Jupiter plc. Earth Ltd received two £1 ordinary shares and one £1 preference share in Jupiter plc for each £1 ordinary share held in Mercury plc. Immediately after the takeover each £1 ordinary share in Jupiter plc was quoted at £2·50 and each £1 preference share was quoted at £1·25.

Required: Calculate the chargeable gain or capital loss arising from each of Earth Ltd's disposals during the year ended 31 March 2010.

Each of the three sections of this question carries 5 marks each

ACCA past examination question June 2003

2. Malcolm Collasal is planning to restructure his business interests, with the sale of some assets and the partial gifting of other assets to his daughter, Marillion. Together they intend to claim all relevant reliefs available from capital gains tax in order to minimise or delay payment of capital gains tax wherever possible. Malcolm's present business interests consist of a wholesale clothing company and more recently he acquired a holiday home park in 2001. He intends to sell the wholesale clothing company and focus more on generating rental income for the future. Additionally he wishes to partially gift the holiday park to his daughter.

Malcolm has built up his wholesale clothing company over many years, and purchased the present premises in October 1992 for £115,000. The business was sold as a going concern on the 10th January 2009 for £750,000. Malcolm wishes to re-invest all or some of the proceeds in a replacement asset, but is unsure which asset to purchase. He is considering 2 choices:

> Purchasing a warehouse for £800,000, which he would then rent out to the present occupier who uses it for storage or

> Purchasing a 2nd holiday home park as a going concern for £700,000.

Malcolm wishes to gift his existing holiday home park to his daughter, Marillion. He originally purchased this in September 2001 at a cost of £200,000. The value of the holiday home park is now £600,000. On 25th March 2009 Marillion paid her father £250,000 for the holiday home park.

Required:

a)   **Calculate the capital gains arising for Malcolm on the sale of his wholesale clothing company, showing clearly any claim for relief available, assuming he:**
> **purchases the warehouse**
> **purchases a 2nd holiday home park**   **10 marks**

b)   **Calculate any capital gains arising on the gift of the holiday home park from Malcolm to Marillion, showing clearly any claim for relief.**   **6 marks**

c)   **What advice can you offer Malcolm and Marillion in terms of their capital gains tax position?**   **4 marks**

Total 20 marks

3. Individual. 85 Pools, bonus & rights issues. Calculation of capital gains tax.

Claudius had the following transactions.

(1)   Sold 2,250 quoted ordinary shares of Nero plc for £23,150 in March 2010. Before making the sale he owned 6,750 shares, of which 4,500 were purchased in December 1988 for £4,599 and 2,250 were acquired in August 1992 on the occasion of the company's rights issue of 1 for 2 at 160p per share.

(2)   Sold 2,550 quoted shares of Livia plc for £12,375 in June 2009. His previous transactions in those shares had been as follows.

April 1988	Purchased	1,500	cost	£3,093
August 1990	Purchased	900	cost	£2,700
May 1992	Bonus issue	1 for 2		

(3)   Sold 13,500 units of the Tiberius Unit Trust for £11,480 in June 2009, which had cost £3,450 upon their original offer to the public in June 1987.

(4)   Gave his brother 12,000 quoted shares in Augustus plc out of his holding of 30,000 shares in March 2010. He had originally purchased 22,500 shares in January 1989 at a cost of £49,500 and received a scrip issue of 1 for 3 June 1991. At the date of the gift the shares were quoted at 150p each.

Requirement:

Calculate Claudius' liability to capital gains tax in respect of the year ended 5 April 2010. None of the transactions qualify for entrepreneur's relief.

(14 marks)

Part V

Inheritance tax

35 General principles

Introduction

1. In this chapter the basic features of inheritance tax are outlined. Chapter 36 goes on to consider some basic inheritance tax computations and other points such as relief for the inheritance of business assets. It should be noted that inheritance tax is a complex area and these chapters aim to provide a basic introduction to the key concepts and principles of inheritance tax. There are many more detailed aspects to this area of taxation which are not covered in chapters 35 and 36. The main consolidating legislation is to be found in the Inheritance Tax Act 1984 (IHTA 1984).

Basic rates

2. There is one table of scale rates of IHT which apply to transfers of value. The rates applicable to transfers made on or after 6th April 2006 together with 'grossing up' tables are reproduced at the end of this chapter.

Where tax is chargeable in respect of any gift inter vivos, e.g. a gift by an individual to a trust, then usually the rate of tax used is 50% of the death scale rates.

For the current tax year to 5th April 2010, the first £325,000 (£312,000 to 5th April 2009) of an estate at death is chargeable at a nil rate (0%); any excess over this limit is chargeable at 40%. This is a basic explanation and many other detailed factors may influence the assessment of what elements of an estate are subject to inheritance tax.

The exempt bands up to 5th April 2012 are also reproduced at the end of this chapter.

Transfers of value

3. A transfer of value occurs where an individual's estate is reduced in value as a result of a gift or disposition and the amount of that decrease in value is the value transferred.

In the case of transfers on a death the value transferred is the value of the estate immediately prior to the death.

Chargeable transfers

4. A chargeable transfer is a transfer which is not an exempt transfer or a potentially exempt transfer (PET).

Potentially exempt transfers (PETs)

5. A potentially exempt transfer is a transfer of value made by an individual:

i)   to another individual, or

ii)   to a trust for the disabled

Although a PET is a transfer of value no inheritance tax is due at the time the transfer is made. IHT falls due for payment only if the transferor dies within seven years of the date of the transfer.

A PET made more than seven years before death is an exempt transfer. Tax payable on a PET, which may be subject to taper relief, is the responsibility of the recipient first, and secondly the personal representative (to a lesser extent) of the donor.

A PET is assumed to be an exempt transfer during the seven years following the transfer or, if earlier, until immediately before the transferor's death.

Other chargeable transfers

6. Other chargeable transfers made by an individual are not PETs and these would include:

i)   transfers by an individual to a discretionary trust

ii)   transfers by an individual to a company.

IHT is chargeable on these transfers at the time the transfer is made, at 50% of the death scale rates. Chargeable transfers also include:

i)   transfers by an individual to an accumulation and maintenance trust

ii)   transfers by an individual to an interest in possession trust

Taper relief

7. Any inheritance tax payable in respect of any chargeable transfer made within seven years of the death of the donor is reduced by reference to the following table

Years between date of transfer and date of death	% of normal tax charged	% of normal tax deducted
0 − 3	100	−
3 − 4	80	20
4 − 5	60	40
5 − 6	40	60
6 − 7	20	80

Gifts with reservation

8. Where an individual makes a transfer of value, and still retains some interest in the property, then in general on his or her death the property is treated as part of the estate. He or she is deemed to be beneficially entitled to the property and it is taxed together with the rest of the possessions.

Examples of gifts with a reservation are:

i)   a gift of a house where the donor remains in residence.

ii)   a gift to a discretionary trust where the donor retains an interest as a beneficiary.

9. Property is subject to a reservation if:

i)   possession and enjoyment of the property is not bona fide assumed by the donee at or before the beginning of the 'relevant period', or

ii)   at any time in the 'relevant period' the property is not enjoyed to the entire exclusion, or virtually so, of the donor and of any benefits to him or her by contract or otherwise.

The relevant period is the period ending on the date of the donor's death and beginning seven years before then, or, if later, the date of the gift.

General scope of the tax

10. If the individual making the transfer of value is domiciled in the UK, tax applies to his or her property wherever it is situated.

Where the transferor is domiciled outside the UK then in general only property situated in the UK is chargeable. For IHT purposes there are special rules by which an individual is deemed to be domiciled in the UK.

Excluded property

11. The following items of property are not liable to IHT on a lifetime transfer and do not form part of an individual's estate on death:

a)   property situated outside the UK where the owner is also domiciled outside the UK.

b)   reversionary interests in a settlement except those acquired for money or money's worth or those where either the settlor or his or her spouse is beneficially entitled to the reversion.

Thus if property is settled on X for life with remainder to Y, then Y has a reversionary interest in the property which is ignored for IHT purposes.

X's interest is deemed to be an absolute interest in the property and is not excluded property.

c)   property of individuals killed on active service.

Location of assets

12. To qualify as excluded property owned by a non-UK domicile, the individual assets must be situated outside the UK. The location of assets is determined in accordance with the general principles of law as follows:

Land	–	Land including leasehold property is situated where the land is physically located.
Tangible moveable property	–	Assets such as furniture and paintings are situated where they are located.
		Coins and bank notes are situated where they are at the time of the transfer.
Shares/securities	–	These are situated where the register is kept.
Bearer shares	–	These are situated where the certificate of title is kept.
Debts	–	These are located where the debtor resides.
Business assets	–	Assets of a business are located where the place of business is situated.
		An interest in a partnership is located where the head office is found.
Goodwill	–	This is located where the business is carried on.
Trademark	–	This is situated where it is registered.

General exemptions and reliefs

13. The following are the main exemptions and reliefs available in respect of lifetime and death transfers.

	PET/other lifetime transfers	Death
a) Transfers between husband and wife (no limit).	3	3
b) Transfers each year up to £3,000.	3	
c) Small gifts to any one person not exceeding £250.	3	
d) Transfers by way of normal expenditure out of taxed income.	3	
e) Gifts in consideration of marriage	3	

   £5,000 max: donor is parent to one of the parties to the marriage
   £2,500 max: donor is grandparent/great grandparent
   £1,000 max: donor is in any other relationship.

f) Gifts to charities £ no limit: whenever made.	3	3
g) Gifts to political parties £ no limit: whenever made.	3	3
h) Gifts for national purposes or for public benefit.	3	3
i) Gifts made during lifetime for family maintenance including the education of children.	3	

From 9th October 2007 a surviving spouse or civil partner may claim the unused proportion of a deceased spouse's or civil partner's nil rate band, if arrangements have not already been made for this. Effectively this results in a doubling of the nil rate band for a couple.

Business and agricultural property reliefs

14. These important reliefs are available in respect of both transfers inter vivos (PETs and other transfers) and on death. They are given effect to by a reduction in the value transferred.

a) Relief for business property.

Percentage reductions available are as follows: %

i) Transfers of a business or partnership interest 100

ii) Transfers of business assets 50

iii) Transfers of shares in unquoted companies including USM, AIM 100

iv) Transfers of a controlling interest in a quoted company 50

b) Relief for agricultural property

Percentage reductions available are as follows: %

i) Where the transferor has the right to vacant possession or could obtain it within 12 months after a transfer 100

ii) Where the transferor does not have the right to vacant possession or cannot obtain it within 12 months of the transfer. 100

Growing timber

15. Where land in the UK, not subject to agricultural or business relief, includes growing timber then the value of the timber may be excluded from a person's estate at death. IHT becomes payable on the later sale or lifetime transfer of the timber on the value at the date of the disposal.

Quick succession relief

16. This is available in respect of property transferred on the death of a person which has borne inheritance tax within the preceding five years. The relief is given by way of a percentage reduction of the original tax paid as follows:

		% Reduction
Death within	1 year	100
Death within	2 years	80
Death within	3 years	60
Death within	4 years	40
Death within	5 years	20

Sale within 1 or 4 years of death

17. Where shares are sold within one year of death, or land sold within four years of death and the proceeds of sale are less than their market value at the date of death, then a reduction of IHT payable may be claimed.

Liabilities and expenses

18. In general, liabilities are taken into account in computing the value of an estate for IHT purposes insofar as they have been incurred for a consideration in money's worth or imposed by law. Liabilities forming a charge on any property, such as a mortgage on a house, are deducted from the value of that property.

Post-death events

19. The beneficiaries under a will or intestacy can vary the terms of the disposition where it is not in the interests of all concerned. The 'Deed of Variation' must satisfy the following conditions.

a)   The instrument in writing must be made by the persons or any of the persons who benefit or would benefit under the dispositions of the property comprised in the deceased's estate immediately before his or her death.

b)   The instrument must be made within two years after the death.

c)   The instrument must clearly indicate the dispositions that are the subject of it, and vary their destination as laid down by the deceased's will, or under the law relating to intestate estates, or otherwise.

d)   A notice of election to vary the will must be given within six months of the date of the instrument, unless the Board sees fit to accept a late election.

e)   The notice of election must refer to the appropriate statutory provisions.

f)   Variation will automatically apply without election if the instrument states that it is to have that effect.

Any liability to IHT on death will be calculated on the basis of the revised estate distribution resulting from the Deed of Variation.

Intestacy

20. Where a person dies without making a will then there are rules of intestacy which prescribe the manner in which an estate must be distributed.

Administration and payment

21. a) The HM Revenue and Customs Offices which deal with IHT are known as the Capital Taxes Offices.

b)   Reporting lifetime transfers to the Capital Taxes Office is carried out as follows.

   i)   In the case of a chargeable transfer, the transferor must report unless some other person such as the donee liable for the tax has already done so. The account must be delivered within 12 months or, if later three months from the date on which he or she first becomes liable for the tax.

   ii)   In the case of a PET it is the transferee's duty to report the transfer within 12 months after the end of the month in which death occurs.

c) Appeals against an assessment are to the Special Commissioners or to the appropriate Land Tribunal.

d) For transfers on death, probate or letters of administration are not given until the appropriate account (provisional, if necessary) has been rendered and any IHT due paid.

e) Where the estate is 'excepted', then there is no duty to make a return on death. This applies where:

    i) the gross value of the property + certain life time-transfers ≤ Nil rate band and the deceased died domiciled in the UK;

    ii) The aggregate gross value of the estate + certain lift time transfers ≤ £1.0m and the aggregate value − (liabilities + spouse and charity transfer) ≤ nil rate band. Deceased domiciled in UK.

    iii) The deceased was never domiciled in UK and value of UK estate (cash quoted share) ≤ £100,000.

f) Payments of IHT may be made by instalments for the following transfers on death:

    i) land and buildings (freehold and leaschold wherever situated);

    ii) a controlling interest in a company, quoted or unquoted;

    iii) unquoted shares and securities where the value transferred exceeds £20,000 and the shares represent at least 10% of the nominal share capital;

    iv) the net value of a business, profession or vocation;

    v) timber where the proceeds of sale basis of valuation is not used.

g) Instalments are payable by 10 equal yearly amounts. Interest on IHT due on land other than land used for business or agricultural purposes is calculated on the whole amount outstanding and added to each instalment.

IHT due on other property payable by instalments only incurs interest when an instalment is in arrears.

The payment of tax by instalments is available on lifetime transfers of the appropriate property where the IHT is paid by the donee.

h) IHT is due for payment as follows:

    i) On a transfer on death – six months after the end of the month in which the death takes place.

    ii) On a lifetime transfer:

        made from 6th April to 30th September – the following April 30th

        made from 1st October to 5th April – six months after end of month of transfer.

i) Interest accrues on overdue tax at the rate of 4% from 6th January 2008. This applies to both lifetime and death transfers. The same rate applies to repayments.

j) IHT is paid on income that has accrued at the date of death but paid after that date and therefore subject to income tax on the recipient. Relief for this element of double taxation is given to the beneficiaries by an adjustment to their personal income tax liability where they are higher rate taxpayers.

Inheritance tax rates

Death rates

	Chargeable transfers (gross)	IHT %	Tax on band	Cumulative tax	IHT on transfer (net)
	£	%	£	£	
6.4.09 – 5.4.10	0 – 325,000	Nil	Nil	Nil	Nil
	325,001	40			2/3
6.4.08 – 5.4.09	0 – 312,000	nil	nil	nil	nil
	312,001	40	-	-	2/3
6.4.07 – 5.4.08	0 – 300,000	nil	nil	nil	nil
	300,001	40	-	-	2/3
6.4.06 – 5.4.07	0– 285,000	nil	nil	nil	nil
	285,001	40	-	-	2/3

Lifetime transfers

	Chargeable transfers (gross)	IHT %	Tax on band	Cumulative tax	IHT on transfer (net)
6.4.09 – 5.4.10	0 – 325,000	nil	nil	nil	nil
6.4.09 – 5.4.10	325,001	20	-	-	1/4
6.4.08 – 5.4.09	0 – 312,000	nil	nil	nil	nil
6.4.08 – 5.4.09	312,001	20	-	-	1/4
6.4.07 – 5.4.08	0 – 300,000	nil	nil	nil	nil
6.4.07 – 5.4.08	300,001	20	-	-	1/4
6.4.06 – 5.4.07	0– 285,000	nil	nil	nil	nil
6.4.06 – 5.4.07	285,001	20			1/4

Exempt bands to 5.4.12

6.4.07 – 5.4.08	£300,000
6.4.08 – 5.4.09	£312,000
6.4.09 – 5.4.10	£325,000
6.4.10 – 5.4.11	£350,000
6.4.11 – 5.4.12	£360,000

36 Basic rules of computation

Introduction

1. In this chapter the basic rules of IHT computations ignoring exemptions are examined under the following headings:

Grossing up procedures

Taper relief and gifts inter vivos

Chargeable lifetime transfers

Chargeable lifetime transfers – death within seven years

Potentially exempt transfers within seven years of death

Death with no chargeable transfers within seven years of death

Transfers of value made within seven years of death and earlier transfers.

Transfers of business assets

Grossing up procedures

2. Where a lifetime transfer is made and any IHT is paid by the donor, e.g. on a transfer to an eligible trust, then it is necessary to 'gross up the net transfer' as IHT is payable on the gross amount.

Example

Amy makes a net lifetime gift of £340,000 on 15th May 2009.

Compute the amount of the gross transfer.

Solution

	£
15.5.2009 Net gift	340,000
IHT is $\dfrac{20}{80} \times (340,000 - 325,000) =$	3,750
Gross transfer	343,750
Check Gross transfer	343,750
IHT $(343,750 - 325,000) \times 20\%$	3,750
Net transfer	340,000

Taper relief and gifts inter vivos

3. The inheritance tax payable in respect of transfers of value made within seven years of the death of an individual is reduced by reference to the following table.

Years between date of transfer and date of death	% of normal tax charged	% of normal tax deducted
0 – 3	100	–
3 – 4	80	20
4 – 5	60	40
5 – 6	40	60
6 – 7	20	80

4. For potentially exempt transfers no tax is payable unless death occurs within seven years of the date of the transfer. When this arises IHT calculated at the death rates subject to any taper relief is payable by the donee.

Other chargeable transfers (non-PETs) are taxed at 50% of the death rate at the time of making the transfer. If death occurs more than seven years after the date of the transfer then the position is as follows.

i)   The chargeable transfer is ignored in computing the IHT payable on the value of the estate.

ii)   There is no additional tax payable by the donee.

iii) IHT already paid when the transfer was made is not recoverable.

Taper relief does not affect the amount of inheritance tax payable on an estate by the executors.

The computational principles of taper relief are illustrated in the examples given below.

Chargeable lifetime transfers (non-PETs)

5. These transfers are chargeable at half the death rate at the time of the transfer, and where necessary must be grossed up.

Example

Mike makes a transfer of £400,000 to a discretionary trust on 1st December 2009 agreeing to pay any IHT. All exemptions had been used and Mike had made no previous transfers.

Compute any IHT payable.

Solution

	£
1.12.09 Gift to discretionary trust	400,000
IHT on net gift of £400,000	
$(400,000 - 325,000) \times \frac{1}{4}$	18,750
Gross transfer	418,750
IHT payable by Mike at lifetime scale rate	18,750
Check $(418,750 - 325,000)$ at 20% =	18,750

Chargeable lifetime transfers (non-PETs) – death within seven years

6. When the transferor dies within seven years of making a chargeable transfer then the gift is retaxed at the death rates, together with any taper relief. Any IHT payable when the gift was first made is then deducted in arriving at any additional tax due by the donee.

The value of the transfer is taken at the date of the gift but any additional tax arising on the death of the donor can be calculated by reference to the *lower* of:

i)   the market value at date of donor's death, or

ii)   the proceeds of an earlier sale.

Example

Noel dies leaving an estate valued at £100,000 on 11th June 2009. On 1st June 2006 he made a gift of £350,000 gross to a discretionary trust, inheritance tax of £13,000, being paid by the trustees.

Calculate the IHT due in respect of Noel's estate and any additional tax payable on the chargeable lifetime transfer.

Solution

		£
11.6.2009 Value Noel's estate		100,000
Chargeable transfers within previous 7 years		350,000
		450,000
IHT payable FA 2009 death scale rate		
325,000 – Nil		–
125,000 @ 40%		50,000
450,000		50,000
Less notional tax on transfers of £350,000 within last 7 years.		
325,000 per table		–
25,000 @ 40%	10,000	10,000
350,000		
Payable by executors		40,000
Additional tax payable on gift:		
1.6.06 Gross transfer		350,000
11.6.09 IHT (as above)		10,000
Less taper relief:		
(3-4 years) 20% × 10,000		2,000
80% payable after taper relief		8,000
Less paid by trustees on gift by X		13,000
Additional tax due (irrecoverable) by trustees		(5,000)

Notes

i)   As the additional tax payable is a 'negative amount', none is payable, or recoverable

ii)   There can be no refund of the IHT payable on the original gift.

iii) Tax on the estate is borne at the highest slice, i.e. after taking into consideration gifts within seven years of death.

iv)   Where the cumulative lifetime transfers exceed the exempt band then the estate will simply be the value of the estate ☐ ☐the death rate. In this example £100,000 @ 40% = £40,000.

v)   The IHT paid by the trustees on the gift by Mike is (350,000 – 285,000)☐ ☐ ☐20% = 13,000. (£285,000 being the nil rate band for 2006-2007)

v)   The exempt band for 2009/10 is £325,000, using FA 2009 rates.

Potential exempt transfer within seven years of death

7. There is no inheritance tax payable when the transfer is made. At the date of death where this is within seven years of the transfer, the PET is taxable at the death rate subject to any tapering relief. In addition the PET is added to the value of the estate to determine the rates of tax payable.

As with all lifetime transfers brought into charge, the estate is treated as the highest slice and the cumulative transfers in the previous seven years, as the lowest slice.

8. For the purposes of calculating the tax payable by the donee, (but not the estate) then the market value at the date of death or the proceeds of an earlier sale may be used if lower than the value of the PET at the date of the transfer.

Example

Arthur dies on 10th October 2009 leaving a net estate valued at £250,000. On 1st of December 2007 Arthur made a gift to his son with a value of £400,000 after having used all his exemptions. Arthur had made no previous transfers of value.

Calculate the IHT payable.

Solution

			£
10.10.2009 Value of Arthur's estate			250,000
Add cumulative transfers in previous 7 years			400,000
			650,000
IHT thereon (650,000 – 325,000) × 40%			
(FA 2009 Death Rates)			130,000
Less notional tax on transfers within previous 7 years		400,000	
325,000 per table (2009/10)	—		
75,000 @ 40%	30,000		
400,000	30,000		30,000
IHT payable on estate			100,000
Tax payable by Arthur's son			
1.12.2007 Value of gift			400,000
IHT thereon as above			30,000
Less taper relief: (0–3 years) 0% × 30,000			—
IHT payable			30,000

Example

Using the data in the previous example compute the IHT payable if the value of the gift to Arthur's son was only worth £350,000 at the date of Arthur's death.

Solution

	£
10.10.2009 Value of Arthur's estate	250,000
Add cumulative transfers in previous 7 years	400,000
	650,000
IHT payable on estate	130,000 (as above)

IHT payable by A's son	£
1.12.07 Value of gift	400,000
Less fall in value	50,000
10.10.2009 Value	350,000
IHT on £350,000	
(350,000 – 325,000) × 40%	10,000
Less taper relief 10,000 × 0%	—
IHT payable	10,000

Notes

i) The value of the *original gift* is included in calculations for the IHT payable on the estate.

ii) The reduced value of £350,000 is used to determine the amount of additional tax borne by the donee, which in this case is £10,000.

Death with no chargeable transfers or PETs within previous seven years

9. On the death of a person who has not made any chargeable transfers within the previous seven years, the death scale rates are applied to the value of the estate, subject to any permitted exemptions and reliefs.

Example

Tony died on 14 June 2009, leaving a chargeable estate of £485,000. He had made no lifetime transfers. Compute the IHT payable.

Solution: Tony deceased IHT computation 14.6.2009

Total value of estate:	485,000
Tax payable:	
325,000 per table	–
160,000 @ 40%	64,000
485,000	64,000

Notes

Estate rate of IHT = $\dfrac{64,000}{485,000} \times 100 = 13.19\%$

This is required where there is any IHT payable by instalments e.g. UK land, or by different persons.

Transfers of value made within seven years of death and earlier

10. Transfers of value made more than seven years before the date of death are not accumulated to arrive at the IHT rate at the date of death. However, where a transfer of value is made within the seven years before the date of death, then in determining any additional IHT payable on death by the recipient, any transfers made in the seven years before the date of that transfer must be considered.

Example

Kate makes a gross chargeable transfer to Pete of £350,000 on 1st February 2001. On 1st November 2005 Kate gives her son £75,000. Kate dies on 30th August 2009, leaving an estate of £500,000. **Calculate the IHT payable on the estate of K and on the PET of £75,000.**

Solution

	£
30.8.2009 **Value of Kate's estate**	500,000
Add transfers of value made within previous 7 years	
1.11.05 Gift to son	75,000
	575,000
IHT payable: (FA 2009 Rates)	
325,000 Nil	–
250,000 @ 40%	100,000
575,000	100,000

		£	£
Less notional tax on transfers within previous 7 years		£75,000	
IHT paid within the nil rate band		Nil	–
Payable by executors			100,000

Tax payable by Kate's son

		Gross (FA 2009 death rates)	IHT
1.2.01	Gross transfer to Pete (350,000 – 325,000 @ 40%)	350,000	10,000
1.11.05	Gift to son	75,000	30,000
		425,000	40,000

IHT	325,000		–
	100,000 @ 40%	40,000	
	425,000	40,000	

Deduct transfers made more than 7 years prior to date of death	350,000	10,000
	75,000	30,000

less taper relief 3–4 years 20% × 30,000	6,000
IHT payable	24,000

Notes

i)   The IHT payable at the death rate is calculated by reference to the value of **all** chargeable transfers in the seven years before the date of the gift.

ii) The tax due on the PET of £24,000 is not the amount deducted in computing the IHT payable on the estate by the executors.

iii) The taper relief for a transfer made in between three and four years is 20%.

Business Property Relief

11. Relief is available for transfers of value inter vivos or on a death of an individual, of relevant business property.

The relief is given by way of a percentage reduction from the valuation of the property.

This section begins with a summary of the relief available, followed by a definition of relevant business property and the associated rules. Worked examples then show the computations to be made.

12. Summary of relief

a) Property consisting of a business or interest in a business such as a partnership or sole trader. A business includes total assets including goodwill, less liabilities.   100%

b) Shares or securities in unquoted companies including USM/AIM.   100%

c) Shares or securities of a quoted company which gave the transferor control of   50%
the company immediately before the transfer.

d) Business assets such as land and buildings, plant and machinery owned by   50%
the transferor as a sole trader, partner, or as a controlling director, and used
in that business.

e) Business assets such as land and buildings, plant and machinery used by the   50%
transferor in a business which was settled property in which he or she had an
interest in possession.

13. Relevant business property

In addition to the details shown in the summary above, the following points should be noted.

a)   To qualify for relief, the property must have been owned by the transferor for at least two
years immediately prior to the transfer. Where property replaces other property and the
two years criteria cannot be met then relief is still available, provided aggregate
ownership is greater than two years out of the previous five.

b)   Assets not used wholly or mainly for the purposes of the business within the two year
period noted in (a) above are excepted assets e.g. investments or surplus cash and relief is
not available for those items.

c)   Relief is not available for a transfer of business property which is used wholly or mainly
for the following purposes:

   i)   Dealing in stocks, shares or securities. (Stock market makers and discount houses
are, however, eligible for relief.)

   ii)   Dealing in land or buildings.

   iii)   Making or holding investments.

d)   The expression business includes a profession or vocation but does not include a business
carried on otherwise than for gain.

e)   Shares in a holding company qualify if the subsidiaries themselves qualify for relief.

f)   The original property (or if sold, its replacement) must be owned by the transferee
throughout the period beginning with the chargeable transfer and ending on the
transferor's death to retain the full benefit of the relief.

g)   Where the original property is disposed of before the transferor's death and the proceeds
are used to purchase replacement property full relief is available if:

   i) the whole of the proceeds are used to purchase a replacement

   ii) both sale and purchase take place within three years of each other.

h)   If only part of the original property (or its replacement) is in the transferee's possession
on the death of the transferor, then only that part will be eligible for relief.

i)   Relief reduces the value of the transfer before any available exemptions are given.

Where any of the relief is clawed back the additional tax payable by the transferee is calculated
on the transfer before BPR. However, the net transfer i.e. after BPR included in the transferor's
cumulative total remains unchanged.

Excepted assets

14. The BPR will be restricted on a transfer of shares if the company holds 'excepted assets' on its balance sheet. An 'excepted asset' is an asset that is not used for business purposes throughout the two years immediately preceding a transfer, or is not required for future use in the business. The amount of the transfer qualifying for BPR, is the value of the shares gifted multiplied by the fraction below:

$$\text{Qualifying transfer} = \text{Gift} \times \left(\frac{\text{Total assets - excepted assets}}{\text{Total assets}} \right)$$

If the company has no excepted assets, all of the value of the shares will qualify for BPR. If non-trading assets make up more than 50% of total assets, the IR may seek to deny BPR completely on the grounds that the company is not trading.

PET and business property relief

15. If the property eligible for business property relief is transferred by a PET then tax will only become payable on the death of the transferor within seven years of the date of the transfer. For other chargeable transfers, tax is due at the date of the transfer and at the date of death if within the seven year period.

Example

A who had made no previous transfers gave his controlling interest in Z Ltd, a private company, to his son on April 12th 2006. The interest was valued at £440,000. A's controlling interest was acquired for £50,000 in 1992. A died on the 10th August 2009 leaving an estate of £380,000. A's son has retained the controlling interest in Z Ltd.

Compute the IHT arising on A's death.

Solution

	£	£
10.8.2009. Value of A's estate		380,000
Add transfers made within previous 7 years		
12.4.06 gift to son	440,000	
Less business property relief 100% × 440,000	440,000	–
		380,000
IHT payable thereof FA 2009 rates:		
325,000 @ Nil	–	
55,000 @ 40%	22,000	22,000
380,000		22,000
Less notional IHT on gift to son of	440,000	Nil
IHT payable by executors		22,000
IHT payable on PET		Nil

Notes

i)   IHT is not payable in respect of the transfer on 12th April 2006 as the transfer of value is a PET.

ii) As the business property relief of 100% applied there would be no IHT payable by A's son on the death of his father, as he has retained the business.

iii) BP relief is given at the rate appropriate to the property at the time the gift was made.

Student self-testing questions

1. Z dies on 22nd October 2009 leaving a net estate of £250,000. During his lifetime he had made the following transfers of value, after using all available exemptions.

1st December 2003	Gift to his daughter of £130,000.
20th June 2006	Gift to an accumulation and maintenance trust of £240,000.

Compute the IHT payable on the death of Z.

Solution

	£	£
22.10.2009 Z's estate		250,000
Add transfers of value made in previous 7 years		
1.12.03 Gift to daughter	130,000	
20.6.06 Gift to trust	240,000	370,000
		620,000

IHT payable (FA 2009 rates):

325,000		–	
295,000 @ 40%		118,000	
620,000		118,000	118,000

		£
Less notional tax on lifetime transfers of £370,000		
(370,000 – 325,000) × 40% =		18,000
IHT payable by executors		100,000
IHT payable by donees:		
1.12.03 gift to daughter within nil rate band	130,000	nil

		£
20.6.06 **Gift to accumulation and maintenance trust**		240,000
Add gifts in previous 7 years		
Gift to Z's daughter (1.12.03)		130,000
		370,000

IHT payable:		
(370,000 – 325,000) × 40%		18,000
Less notional IHT on gift to Z's daughter of £130,000		–
		18,000
Less taper relief: (3-4 years) 20% × 18,000		3,600
Tax payable by trustees		14,400

Cumulative transfers	Gross £	Tax £
1.12.2003 Gift to daughter	130,000	
IHT payable @ FA 2009 death rates	–	–
	130,000	–
20.6.06 Gift to accumulation trust	240,000	18,000
	370,000	18,000
Taper relief		3,600
Less transfers made more than 7 years prior to 22.10.2009		Nil
	370,000	14,400

Notes

i) Both of the transfers during Z's lifetime are PETs.

ii) The tax due in respect of each gift is computed separately beginning first with the one furthest from the date of death, within the seven years period.

iii) IHT payable on the second gift is calculated after deducting any notional tax on the previous gift to Z's daughter which in this case is nil.

iv) Taper relief 20.6.06 –22.10.09 is three-four years.

2. B dies on 7th April 2009 leaving the following estate:

	£
20% interest in Q Ltd, an unquoted private company	125,000
Freehold land used by Q Ltd	35,000
Shares in Z plc, a quoted company (< 1% holding)	15,000
Other property (net)	312,500

Three years before his death B had transferred a 15% interest in the shares in Q Ltd to his son. B has made no other transfers but has used all his annual exemptions. B's son has retained his interest in Q Ltd which at the date of the gift was valued at £40,000, and on B's death was worth £280,000.

Calculate the IHT arising on B's death.

Solution

	£	£
7.4.2009 value of B's estate:		
20% interest in Q Ltd	125,000	
Less business property relief 100% × 125,000	125,000	–
Freehold land used by Q Ltd		35,000
Shares in Z plc		15,000
Other property		312,500
		362,500
Add transfer within previous 7 years		
Gift of shares in Q Ltd	40,000	
Business property relief 100% × 40,000	40,000	–
		362,500
IHT thereon FA 2009 rates:		
325,000 per table 2009/10	Nil	
37,500 @ 40%	15,000	
362,500	15,000	15,000
Less notional IT on gift within last 7 years	–	–
IT payable executors		15,000

Notes

i) There is no inheritance tax payable in respect of the gift as it was below the threshold level of £325,000 for 2009/10.

ii) The BP rate of 100% applies to the shares in Q Ltd and the gift to B's son.

iii) No relief is available for the freehold land used by Q Ltd as B did not have a controlling interest.

iv) The PET is valued at the date of the transfer and not the date of B's death for estate purposes. Where the death value is lower than the transfer value, that value is used to compute any IHT on the transfer at death borne by the donor.

Part VI

Value added tax

37   General principles

Introduction

1. Value added tax is a tax on the supply of goods and services made by a registered taxable person within the UK. The Chancellor announced a temporary reduction in VAT in November 2008, cutting the standard rate by 2.5% from 17.5% to 15% for a period of 13 months. From 1st January 2010 the standard VAT rate will revert back to 17.5%. The questions and answers in this book therefore apply the standard rate of 17.5% throughout given the temporary nature of the 15% standard rate.

This chapter begins with a summary of the headings under which the tax will be examined.

Summary of topic headings

2.

Legislative background	Voluntary registration
VAT rates	Voluntary de-registration
Classification of goods and services	Group registration
Zero rated goods and services	Companies organised into divisions
Exempted goods and services	Accounts and records
Land and buildings	Accounting for VAT
Taxable persons	Administration
Business splitting	Late registration
Registration limits	Offences and penalties
Default surcharge	Errors on VAT returns

Legislative background

3. Value added tax was first introduced in the UK with effect from 1st April 1973, superseding purchase tax and selective employment tax. The main provisions of the VAT legislation are now contained in the Value Added Tax Act 1994. In addition to that Act there are a large number of Statutory Instruments which have introduced changes and provided information about the detailed machinery of the Act.

VAT rates

4. VAT has to be paid on the supply of goods and services within the UK by a taxable person unless they are exempt supplies, at the following rates:

	%
Standard rate to 31st December 2009	15.0
Standard rate from 1st January 2010	17.5
Lower rate	5.0
Zero	0.0

The Chancellor announced in November 2008 that the standard rate of VAT would be cut by 2.5% to 15% on 1st December 2008 for a period of 13 months as a temporary measure in an attempt to stimulate the economy. The 5% rate applies to: Fuel for domestic use, installation of energy saving materials, installation of home securing goods, children's car seats, renovations and conversions of residential property.

The tax element of an SR 17.5% VAT-inclusive price is $7/47$.

The tax element of an SR 15.0% VAT-inclusive price is $3/23$.

Classification of goods and services

5. For VAT purposes goods and services are classified into three broad groups:

Standard rate supplies – These are goods and services not zero rated or exempt, chargeable at the standard rate of 15% or 17.5% after 1ˢᵗ January 2010.

Zero rated supplies – These are goods and services which are subject to a positive rate of tax of nil% e.g. publications and most food.

Exempt supplies – These are goods and services which are not subject to VAT, such as postal services and insurance.

Details of the zero rated and exempted supplies are contained below.

A taxable supply is a supply of goods or services made in the UK, other than exempt supplies.

Zero rated goods and services

6. Particulars of the goods and services which are zero rated are contained in Schedule 8 to the VAT Act 1994 and there are sixteen broad groups classified as follows.

Group 1   Food. Most food for human consumption is zero rated unless supplied as a meal when it is taxable. However, hot food for consumption off the premises is taxable. In addition, some food products such as ice cream, sweets and chocolate, fruit juice and minerals are taxable. Pet foods are taxable but not general animal feeding stuffs.

Group 2   Sewerage services and water. The supply of water is zero rated but not distilled and mineral water. The supply of water and sewerage services to industry is standard rated.

Group 3   Books etc. The supply of books and magazines, newspapers, music, maps and charts is zero rated. Diaries and stationery are taxable.

Group 4   Talking books for the blind and handicapped, and wireless sets for the blind. Zero rated items include magnetic tapes, tape recorders and accessories, if supplied to approved agencies such as the Royal National Institute for the Blind and similar charities.

The supply of information other than photographs to newspapers or to the public by news agencies is zero rated.

Group 5   Construction of buildings. The position under this heading may be summarised as follows.

Zero rated
i)   Construction of new domestic buildings.
ii)   Approved alterations to domestic listed buildings.

Standard rated
i)   Construction of new non-domestic buildings (previously zero rated).
ii)   Repair, maintenance or alteration of existing buildings.
iii)   Civil engineering services or new work.
iv)   Civil engineering services or repair, maintenance or alteration of existing buildings.
v)   Demolition of domestic and non domestic buildings.
vi)   The construction of a building for own use in business.

Group 6   Protected buildings.

Group 7   International services. The supply of certain services such as professional advice or entertainment outside the UK with exceptions for EEC residents, is zero rated.

Group 8   Transport. Zero rating applies to a wide range of activities such as the supply of passenger transport both inland and international, international freight transport, and the supply, repair and maintenance of certain ships and aircraft. Standard rating applies to taxis and hire cars, car parking and luggage storage.

Group 9   Caravans and house-boats. Caravans are zero rated if they exceed 7 metres in length or 2.3 metres in width, the size permitted for use on public roads. The smaller towable caravans are taxable as is the supply of caravan accommodation. House-boats if suitable for permanent habitation are also zero rated.

Group 10   Gold. The supply of gold coins which are legal tender is taxable at the standard rate. The supply of gold held in the UK, by a central bank to another central bank or a member of the London Gold Market, and reciprocal transactions are zero rated.

Group 11   Bank notes. The issue of bank notes payable to bearer is zero rated.

Group 12   Drugs, medicines, aids for the handicapped etc. The following supplies are zero rated: goods dispensed by a registered pharmacist on prescription, medical and surgical appliances, electrical and mechanical appliances for a handicapped person. Other drugs and medicines dispensed without prescription are taxable.

Group 13   Imports, exports etc. The supply of imported goods before the 'delivery of an entry' within the meaning of Section 37 Customs and Excise Management Act 1979, is zero rated. The transfer of goods or services from the UK, by a person carrying on a business both inside and outside the UK, to the overseas business is also zero rated. This would cover, for example, the transfer of parts to be assembled from a UK company to its overseas branch.

Group 14   Tax-free shops.

Group 15   Charities etc. Zero rating applies to the supply by a charity established primarily for the relief of distress or the benefit or protection of animals, of goods donated for sale, any exports, medical or scientific equipment used solely in medical research, and appliances for the handicapped. The supply of goods and services purchased for resale are taxable in the ordinary way as there is no general exemption for charities.

Group 16   Clothing and footwear. Children's clothing and footwear are zero rated. Protective boots and helmets are standard rated when supplied to a person for use by his or her employees. Supplies of protective boots and helmets to any other person for industrial use remain zero rated. Also zero rated are motor cycle helmets.

Exempted goods and services

7. Particulars of the goods and services which are exempt supplies are contained in the 9th Schedule to the VAT Act 1994 and there are 15 groups classified as follows.

Group 1   Land. See separate heading below.

Group 2   Insurance. All forms of insurance are exempted and this includes insurance broking and agency services.

Group 3   Postal services. The conveyance of postal packets other than telegrams, by the post office is exempted. Services rendered by persons other than the post office are taxable.

Group 4   Betting gaming and lotteries. Examples of exempt services under this group are bookmakers, charges for bingo and profits from casino games. Admission charges to any premises where betting or the playing of games of chance takes place are however taxable as are takings from gaming or entertainment machines.

Group 5   Finance. In general, banking services such as those relating to the receipt and transfer of money are exempt. Specific services offered such as executorship and trustee work, portfolio management etc. are taxable as are the commissions from stockbroking, and management fees of unit trusts.

Group 6   Education. Educational services provided by schools, colleges, universities and youth clubs are exempted as are the supply of goods and services to those establishments. Services provided by organisations with a view to profit such as correspondence courses are taxable.

Group 7   Health and welfare. The supply of goods and services by registered persons such as doctors, dentists, opticians, occupational therapists etc. is exempted. Goods supplied under a prescription by a pharmacist are zero rated.

Group 8   Burial and cremation. The services of undertakers in connection with a funeral or cremation are exempt, and within limits this includes charges for the supply of a coffin, shroud etc. but not flowers.

Group 9   Trade unions and professional bodies. Exemption is covered for membership, services and related goods supplied by a trade union and most non-profit making professional, learned or representational bodies.

Group 10   Sports competitions. The grant of a right to enter a competition in sport or physical recreation, where the consideration for the grant consists in money which is to be used wholly for the provision of prizes, is exempt.

Group 11   Works of art etc. The disposal of works of art in circumstances where there is no liability to capital transfer tax or capital gains tax is exempt.

Group 12   Fund raising activities by charities.

Group 13   Cultural services etc.

Group 14   Supplies of goods where input tax cannot be recovered.

Group 15   Investment gold.

Land and buildings

8. *Exempt*

i)   The sale of used domestic and non-domestic buildings

ii)   Leases of used domestic and non-domestic buildings

iii) Leases of new domestic buildings

iv)   The sale of building land for domestic building

Zero rated

i)   Sales of new domestic buildings provided that the seller is the person constructing the building

ii)   Leases of new domestic buildings where the lease is capable of exceeding 21 years.

Standard rated

i)   Sales of new non-domestic buildings.

ii) Sales of building land for non-domestic building.

iii) The grant of any interest, right or licence consisting of a right to take game or fish.

iv) The provision in an hotel, inn, boarding house or similar establishment of sleeping accommodation or of accommodation in rooms which are provided in conjunction with sleeping accommodation or for the purpose of a supply of catering.

v) The provision of holiday accommodation in a house, flat, caravan, house-boat or tent.

vi) The provision of seasonal pitches for caravans, and the grant of facilities at caravan parks to persons for whom such pitches are provided.

vii) The provision of pitches for tents or of camping facilities.

viii) The grant of facilities for parking a vehicle.

ix) The grant of any right to fell and remove standing timber.

x) The grant of facilities for housing, or storage of, an aircraft or for mooring or storage of, a ship, boat or other vessel.

xi) The grant of any right to occupy a box, seat or other accommodation at a sports ground, theatre, concert hall or other place of entertainment.

xii) The grant of facilities for playing any sport or participating in any physical recreation.

Taxable persons

9. A taxable person is any person registered for VAT purposes. Person includes an individual, partnership, company, club, society or trust.

Business splitting

10. Customs & Excise have indicated that the following factors will be taken into consideration in deciding whether or not an independent business exists for VAT registration purposes.

i) Appropriate premises and equipment for the business should be provided by the person carrying on the business.

ii) Day-to-day records identifying the business should be kept and where appropriate separate annual accounts.

iii) Purchase and sales invoices should be in the name of the person carrying on the trade who should be legally responsible for all trading activities.

iv) A separate bank account should be opened for the business.

v) All payroll payments should be paid by the person carrying on the business.

vi) The business should be treated as an independent business for income tax purposes.

vii) The person carrying on the business should be legally responsible for all trading activities.

At present, Customs cannot require separate businesses to register as a single trader for VAT purposes unless it can show that the main reason (or one of the main reasons) for keeping those businesses separate was to avoid a liability to be registered.

This limitation has been removed, and 'connected businesses which have avoided liability for VAT by artificially separating will be liable to be treated as one, whatever the purported reason for the separation'. For example, a series of limited companies running a pub, launderette or other retail outlet for only one month a year in order to keep the turnover of each company below the registration threshold will be treated as one business.

Artificial separation of business activities

11. According to Customs & Excise it is impracticable to give a complete list of all the circumstances in which a separation will be artificial, as each case will depend on its own facts. However, Customs 'would at least make further enquiries' where:

a) Separate entities supply registered and unregistered customers.

b) The same equipment and/or premises is used by different entities on a regular basis – this may be particularly relevant where an ice cream van (for example) is used by traders in rotation.

c) A supply, which is usually a single supply, is split into separate parts – for example, a bed-and breakfast establishment where the bed is said to be supplied by the husband and the breakfast by the wife.

d) Where the separated parts retain the appearance of a single business: the example given being that of pub catering where 'in most cases the customer will consider the food and the drinks as bought from the pub and not from two independent businesses'. However, franchised 'shops within shops' will usually be accepted as truly independent businesses.

e) One person has a controlling influence in two or more businesses which make the same type of supply at separate locations.

Registration limits

12.

UK taxable supplies	Past turnover		Future turnover
	1 year	Unless turnover for next year will not exceed:	30 days
	£	£	£
1.4.2006	61,000	59,000	61,000
1.4.2007	64,000	62,000	64,000
1.4.2008	67,000	65,000	67,000
1.5.2009	68,000	66,000	68,000

Notes

i) Turnover of taxable supplies includes all zero and positive rates.

ii) Registration is mandatory in the following circumstances:

   a) At the end of any month if the value of the taxable supplies in the past year has exceeded the table limits.

   b) At any time if there are reasonable grounds for believing that the value of the taxable supplies in the next 30 days will exceed the future turnover figure.

iii) For ii) a) notification to Customs & Excise must be made within 30 days of the end of the relevant month. Registration is effective from the end of the month following the relevant month or such earlier date as may be mutually agreed.

iv) For ii) b) notification must be made before the end of the 30 day period. Registration is effective from the beginning of the 30 day period.

v) The relevant month is the month at the end of which liability to registration arises.

vi) For the current tax year 2009-2010 the effective date of the new turnover limits apply from 1st May 2009 and not 1st April 2009.

Voluntary registration

13. Where a person who is not liable to be registered satisfies the Customs & Excise that he or she:

i)   makes taxable supplies; or

ii)   is carrying on a business and intends to make such supplies in the course or furtherance of that business;

then, if the person so requests, he or she will be registered, with effect from the day on which the request is made or such earlier date as may be mutually agreed.

Voluntary de-registration

14. A registered person may apply for de-registration if his or her taxable turnover excluding VAT is not expected to exceed £66,000 (£65,000 previously) in the next year.

Group registration

15. Under Section 43 VATA 1994 two or more UK resident companies are eligible to be treated as members of a group if either:

  i)   one controls each of the others or,

  ii)   one person (being either a company, an individual or partnership) controls all of them.

Control exists where a person controls the composition of the board of directors of a company or holds more than 50% of the company's voting rights.

Applications for the VAT group registration must satisfy the definition contained in the Companies Act 1985.

A company is a subsidiary if another company:

  i)   holds a majority of the voting rights in it, or

  ii)   is a member of it and has the right to appoint or remove a majority of its board of directors, or

  iii)   is a member of it and under an agreement with other shareholders or members controls alone a majority of the voting rights in it, or

  iv)   is a subsidiary of a company which is itself a subsidiary of that other company.

Two further tests apply where a jointly owned entity is able to join a VAT group.

  i)   grouping will not be allowed where the majority of the economic benefits from the entity in question go to a third party.

  ii)   under GAAP the entity's accounts are consolidated in the group accounts of the VAT group or would be so if group accounts were prepared.

In general, the effects of a group registration are as follows.

  i)   The VAT affairs are vested in one group company known as the representative member and only one VAT return is required.

  ii)   Inter-group supplies are not subject to VAT.

  iii)   All members of the group are jointly and severally liable for the VAT due from the representative member.

  iv)   Rules exist for VAT groups with a turnover > £10m to prevent suppliers and customers being in the same VAT Group.

Companies organised into divisions

16. A UK resident company carrying on business in several divisions may be registered in the name of its divisions as follows.

i) All divisions of the company must be registered separately. It is not possible to exclude certain divisions e.g. where they fall below the registration limits.

ii) Separate returns are made by each division.

iii) The separate divisions are not separately taxed persons and the company remains liable for the whole VAT.

iv) Inter-divisional transfers are not subject to VAT.

v) Each division should be an independent unit with its own accounting and administration, carrying on business activities in separate locations.

vi) Input tax attributable to exempt supplies (exempt input tax) by the corporate body as a whole must be less than the limits referred to in *Chapter 38* (Section 20).

Divisional registration is subject to the approval of Customs & Excise.

Accounts and records

17. There are a number of detailed regulations concerning the 'book-keeping' arrangements required for VAT purposes, and some of these are noted briefly below.

a) Any standard or zero rated supply of goods or services must be supported by a 'tax invoice', which is described in the next chapter.

b) At regular intervals, usually quarterly, a return must be completed showing the amounts of output and input tax for the period and the net amount payable or receivable from the Customs & Excise. The period covered by a return is known as a tax period and each return must be submitted not later than one month after the end of that tax period. A separate VAT account must be sent for each quarter.

c) Adequate records and accounts of all transactions involving VAT must be maintained to support both the amount of output tax chargeable, and the claim, for deductible input tax. These will be checked from time to time by Customs & Excise officers.

d) Books and records must be kept for a period of six years. Business records include the following:

Orders and delivery notes

Relevant business correspondence

Purchase and sales books

Cash books and other account books

Purchase invoices and copy sales invoices

Records of daily takings e.g. till rolls

Annual accounts – balance sheet and profit and loss accounts

Import and export documents

Bank statements and paying-in-slips

Any credit/debit notes issued or received.

e) There are some special schemes for retailers for VAT purposes and these are outlined in *Chapter 39.*

Accounting for VAT

18. The following is an extract from the Statement of Standard Accounting Practice No. 5 concerning the treatment of VAT for persons exempt or partially exempt.

a) General

VAT is a tax on the supply of goods and services which is eventually borne by the final consumer but collected at each stage of the production and distribution chain. As a general principle, therefore, the treatment of VAT in the accounts of a trader should reflect his or her role as a collector of the tax and VAT should not be included in income or in expenditure whether of a capital or of a revenue nature. There will however be circumstances, as noted below, in which a trader will bear VAT and in such circumstances the accounting treatment should reflect that fact.

b) Persons not accountable for VAT

Persons not accountable for VAT will suffer VAT on inputs. For them VAT will increase the cost of all goods and services to which it applies and should be included in such costs. In particular, the VAT on fixed assets should be added to the cost of the fixed assets concerned and capital allowances claimed accordingly.

c) Accountable persons who also carry on exempted activities

In the case of persons who also carry on exempted activities there will be a residue of VAT, which will fall directly on the trader and which will normally be arrived at by division of his or her activities as between taxable outputs (including zero rated) and those which are exempt. In such cases, the principle that such VAT will increase the costs to which it applies and should be included in such costs will be equally applicable. Hence the appropriate portion of the VAT allocable to fixed assets should, if irrecoverable, be added to the cost of the fixed assets concerned and the proportion allocable to other items should, if practicable and material, be included in such other items. In some cases, for example where financial and VAT accounting periods do not coincide, an estimate may be necessary.

d) Non-deductible inputs

All traders will bear tax in-so-far as it relates to non-deductible inputs (for example, motor-cars, other than for resale, and certain business entertaining expenses). Such tax should therefore be included as part of the cost of those items.

e) Amounts due to or from the revenue authorities

The net amount due to or from the revenue authorities in respect of VAT should be included as part of debtors or creditors and will not normally require separate disclosure.

Administration

19. The department of Customs & Excise is the government department responsible for the administration and collection of VAT. In the event of a dispute between a taxable person and the VAT office it is possible to appeal to a VAT tribunal, providing that it is concerned with one of a number of prescribed matters. The main areas which can be dealt with are as follows.

a) Registration or cancellation of registration.

b) Assessment of tax.

c) Amount of tax chargeable.

d) Amount of input tax deductible.

e) Bad debt claims.

f) Group registration matters.

g) Matters concerned with the value of supplies.

On questions of law an appeal can be made to the High Court from the tribunal.

Late registration

20. a) Failure to notify the Customs & Excise at the proper time that a business should be registered for VAT purposes may incur a penalty, subject to a minimum of £50.00 based on the following rates.

Number of months late for registration	% of VAT due
0 – 9	5%
10 – 18	10%
19 –	15%

The amount of VAT due is the sum due from the date the registration should have been made.

The penalty is not due if the trader can satisfy the Customs & Excise that there was a reasonable excuse for the failure.

The following does not amount to reasonable excuses:

i) insufficiency of funds to pay the tax

ii) reliance on a third party to pay the tax

iii) ignorance of the law relating to registration.

b) Customs & Excise have indicated that the following *guidelines* show circumstances where there might be a reasonable excuse for *late registration*.

i) **Compassionate circumstances** where an individual is totally responsible for running a small business and he or she, or a member of the immediate family, was seriously ill or recovering from such illness at the time notification was required.

ii) **Transfer of a business as a going concern** where such a business is taken over with little or no break in the trading activities and returns have been submitted and tax paid on time under the registration number of the previous owner.

iii) **Doubt about liabilities of supplies** where there is written evidence of an enquiry to Customs & Excise about the liability of supplies and liability has remained in doubt. *See G Davies, LON/ 84/174 (2126).*

iv) **Uncertainty about employment status** where there are genuine doubts as to whether a person is employed or self-employed or where correspondence with the Inland Revenue can be produced about these doubts.

v) **Effective date of registration earlier than required** where a person has requested registration from an earlier date than was legally required in the mistaken belief that he or she had to do so to recover input tax on stocks and assets for the business. This excuse could only apply if there was no reason to believe that taxable turnover would exceed the registration threshold from the required date.

The default surcharge – Section 59 VATA 1994

21. The following points should be noted under this heading.

a) A person will be in default if by the last day on which a return is required, the Customs & Excise have not received that return, or the tax.

b) Taxpayers can be in default for two return periods (i.e. quarters or months) in any 12 month period without incurring a monetary penalty.

c) Where the taxpayer is in default for the first time then a surcharge liability notice will be issued. The surcharge liability notice once issued remains in force for a period of 12 months during which time there must be no default.

d)   While the notice is in force a default charge will arise in any quarter in which a default occurs, at the following rates, if greater than £30.00:

	% of VAT
1st default	2%
2nd default	5%
3rd and subsequent defaults	10%
4th and subsequent	15%

e)   A person is not liable to a surcharge if he or she satisfies the Commissioners that in the case of a default which is 'material to the surcharge' :

    i)   the return, or as the case may be the tax shown on it, was despatched at such time and in such manner that it was reasonable to expect that it would be received within the appropriate time limit, or

    ii)   there is a reasonable excuse for the return or tax not having been despatched.

The following are not reasonable excuses (FA 1985 Sec 33(2)):

    i)   Insufficiency of funds to pay any tax

    ii)   Where reliance is placed on any other person to perform any task, the fact of that reliance or any other dilatoriousness or inaccuracy on the part of the person relied upon.

f)   Automatic penalties for late payment of VAT do not apply to businesses with a turnover of less than £150,000.

Errors on VAT returns

22. a) The procedures for the *voluntary disclosure of errors* are as noted below:

Errors amounting to £2,000 or less	Separate disclosure not required.
	No interest charged on underpayments whether notified or not.
Errors amounting to more than £2,000	Customs & Excise must be notified in writing by letter or using VAT Form 652.
	Interest is chargeable from date when VAT was outstanding.
Default interest	This will be charged on net payments to the Customs & Excise at the prescribed rate of interest.
	The interest charge is not an expense of trade for income tax purposes.

b)   A Serious Misdeclaration Penalty can arise if the Customs & Excise find as a result of their enquiries that VAT has been misdeclared.

A penalty of 15% of the VAT due can be imposed but this will only apply where:

Amount misdeclared for a VAT accounting period $\geq$ which is the lesser of:

    (i)   30% of the true amount of tax payable, or

    (ii)   the greater of £1.0 million and 5% of the true amount of tax for the period

c)   A Serious Misdeclaration Penalty will not normally be imposed:

    i)   during the period from the end of an accounting period to the due date for furnishing the VAT return for the following accounting period

ii) when a VAT return is misdeclared but this has been corrected by a compensating misdeclaration in respect of the same transaction for the following accounting period, with no overall loss of VAT.

Default interest

23. The rate of default interest charged on under-declared VAT is 7.5%. Interest on overpaid VAT is 4% from the same date.

Tax avoidance schemes

24. Businesses with supplies ≥ £600,000 must disclose their use of specific avoidance schemes which C&E will publish in a statutory list. This must be done within 30 days of the date when the first return affected by the scheme becomes due. Failure to disclose incurs a penalty of 15% of tax avoided. Businesses with taxable supplies > £10m. must disclose the use of schemes that have the hallmarks of avoidance.

Student self testing question with answer

A Ltd owns a quarry. It extracts stone from this quarry and sells the stone to B Ltd for £10,000 plus VAT. B Ltd converts all the stone into paving slabs and sells these slabs to C Ltd for £18,000 plus VAT. C Ltd owns and runs a garden centre, where the slabs are sold to the general public for a total of £32,000 plus VAT.

Requirement:

Show how VAT is charged and collected at each stage of the process. (Assume that VAT is to be accounted for at 17.5% throughout).

Suggested answer

	Cost price before VAT	Input tax	Selling price before VAT	Output tax	Paid to C&E
	£	£	£	£	£
A Ltd	-	-	10,000	1,750	1,750
B Ltd	10,000	1,750	18,000	3,150	1,400
C Ltd	18,000	3,150	32,000	5,600	2,450
					5,600

Question without answer

Elaine makes patchwork quilts. She can make a maximum of 40 quilts in a year which she can sell to members of the general public for £500 each. She does not think that her customers would be willing to pay more. Alternatively, she could sell her total production for the year to an exclusive retail outlet, again for £500, excluding VAT, a quilt. The materials to make a quilt cost £100 before VAT. Under what circumstances should Elaine apply for voluntary registration?

38 The VAT system

Introduction

1. This chapter contains the main features of the VAT system covered under the following main topic headings:

The VAT return	Imports – removal from warehouse
Zero rated and exempt supplies	Exports
Taxable supply of goods and services	Goods for personal use
Taxable persons	Partial exemption
The supply of goods and services	Bad debts
Place of supply	Transfer of business
Tax point	Sale of business assets
Tax invoice/credit notes	Business assets – capital allowances
Value of goods and services	VAT on capital goods – partly exempt businesses
Mixed supplies/composite supplies	Self supplies
Input tax – deductions	Cash/annual accounting
Input tax – no deduction	Flat rate scheme – small firms
Private motoring	Rents
Miscellaneous	Changes in tax rates
Flat rate scheme – small firms	

The VAT return

2. A taxable person is required to charge VAT on taxable supplies to customers, called output tax, but he or she is also able to claim credit for the tax paid on business purchases and expenses, and assets known as the input tax.

At the end of an accounting period, usually a month or three months, a business has to submit a return of Value Added Tax to the Customs & Excise. This must show the total taxable supplies made and the VAT charged, together with the total purchases and expenses and any VAT paid. If the tax charged exceeds the amount paid then the balance is payable to the Customs & Excise. Where the output tax is less than the input tax then a repayment can normally be obtained.

Example

	£	£
Total taxable turnover for the period	100,000	
Output tax @ 17.5%		17,500
Total taxable inputs for the period	80,000	
Input tax @ 17.5%		14,000
Balance payable to Customs & Excise		3,500

Zero rated and exempt supplies

3. Goods or services which fall within the zero rated or exempt supplies categories are not subject to VAT at the standard rate. However, there are some important differences between the two supplies.

a)   Zero rated goods or services are taxable at a nil rate of output tax. It follows that any input tax incurred in providing those outputs can be reclaimed since there is no output tax to give a normal means of set-off.

b)   Supplies of exempt goods and services are really outside the VAT system and therefore any input tax incurred cannot be reclaimed, and there is no available set-off. However, such input tax would in effect be an allowable expense for business taxation purposes in most circumstances.

c)   A business which makes only exempt supplies cannot normally register for VAT.

d)   Details of the implications of being partially exempt are noted below.

Taxable supply of goods and services

4. Tax is chargeable on any supply of goods and services which are made in the UK or imported where the supply counts as being taxable. The supply must be made by a taxable person in the course of a trade, profession or vocation.

Taxable persons

5. A taxable person is any person who has registered for VAT, and this is required if the total value of his or her taxable supplies for any one year are greater than £68,000. All business activities must be aggregated in order to determine whether or not a person should register. Registration can be for an individual, partnership or limited company. The total of taxable business supplies is called taxable turnover.

The supply of goods and services

6. The supply of goods can include any of the following:

a)   sale by ordinary commercial transaction

b)   sale by auction or through agents

c)   sale under a credit sale agreement or by hire purchase.

d)   goods supplied for further processing

e)   goods supplied for personal use.

The supply of services covers any which are provided for money or money's worth, and includes the hire, lease or rental of any goods. Services which are ancillary to the supply of goods such as postage and packing and delivery are normally treated as services and not as part of the goods sold, if they are shown separately on the sales invoice.

Place of supply

7. In general only goods and services supplied in the UK are chargeable to VAT so that the determination of the place of supply is important. If the goods to be supplied are physically located in the UK then they are liable to VAT even where they may be subsequently exported. However, if the goods are located overseas and remain there, then the supply is outside the UK and hence not subject to VAT. This could arise, for example, where a shipping company arranges for a consignment of goods to be sold and transferred from one country to another.

With regard to the supply of a service then this is treated as occurring where the supplier 'belongs', which is usually the place of business. If this is the UK then any service provided from that place could be liable to VAT, and using the example noted above, the provision of the shipping facility would be a taxable supply.

For VAT purposes the UK includes the Isle of Man but not the Channel Isles.

Time of supply – tax point

8. The tax point determines the period in which a supply falls, and is therefore taxable. For goods the basic taxpoint is generally the date when the goods are removed or made available, and for services the basic tax point is the date of the performance. However, there are two key exceptions.

a)   If an invoice is issued within 14 days after the time when the goods are removed or made available, then the date of the invoice normally becomes the actual tax point. This practice is widely followed and enables the VAT return to be completed from copy invoices.

b)   If payments are made in advance of the date when the goods are removed or made available, then it is the date of the invoice or payment which determines the actual tax point.

The same rules apply for deciding the period in which the inputs arise, and in general relief for input tax is available before the invoice is paid. Although in principle tax on imports is due at the date of importation, a business is allowed to pay tax with the next return providing the imports are included in the VAT return for the period in which the importation occurs.

Under the standard method of accounting for VAT by retailers the actual tax point is the date on which the retailer receives payment for goods sold.

A system of cash accounting available. *See below.*

Tax invoice

9.   A tax invoice is a sales invoice issued by a registered person in respect of any goods or services supplied by him or her to another taxable person. The invoice must contain:

a)   supplier's name, address and VAT registration number

b)   customer's name and address

c)   type of supply i.e. whether a sale, sale by HP, hire or rental

d)   description of goods or services supplied together with the amount payable excluding VAT

e)   total amount payable without VAT

f)   particulars of any cash discounts offered

g)   total amount of tax chargeable.

A less detailed invoice may be used where individual supplies by a retailer amount to less than £250 including VAT.

Credit notes

10. Regulations have been issued requiring all businesses to issue credit or debit notes whenever a price adjustment alters the amount of VAT due on an invoice.

Value of goods and services

11. The general rule is that the value on which VAT is chargeable is the amount of money (excluding VAT) which a customer has to pay for the goods or services supplied. The following should be noted.

a)   Cash discounts must be deducted from the invoiced amount to determine the VAT value.

b)   If the supply is not made for money then the open market value less any VAT should be taken.

c)   The cost of the goods to the supplier may be used to determine the value of a taxable supply. This would apply to goods appropriated from trading stock for personal use, and to the trader's own built plant and machinery.

Mixed supplies

12. A mixed supply occurs where a single inclusive price is charged for a number of separate supplies of goods and services. Where all the supplies are taxable at the same rate then the normal rules of computation apply. However, where different rates apply then an apportionment must be made which is 'fair and justifiable'. *(See Card Protection Plan VCIR. 2001 STC)*

Example

B makes a mixed supply of goods at a VAT-inclusive price of £160.00. The product costs show zero rated goods costing £30.00 and standard rated goods costing £50 (exclusive of VAT).

Solution

Computation of VAT

Proportion of total cost at SR $\dfrac{50 + VAT}{(50 + VAT) + 30} = \dfrac{58.75}{58.75 + 30} = \dfrac{58.75}{88.75}$

VAT inclusive price of standard rated goods $\dfrac{58.75}{88.75} \times £160 = £105.90$

VAT included $= 106 \times \dfrac{7}{47} = 16$

Value of zero rated supply $= 160 - 106 = 54$.

Analysis of total price as apportioned

	£
Value of standard rated supply (106 – 16)	90
VAT on standard rated supply 17.5% × 90	16
Zero rated supply	54
Mixed supply	160

Other methods of apportionment eg based on market values can be used. Apportionment must not be made where the supply is a composite supply. *See below.*

Examples of mixed supply are:

   Annual subscription to the AA *(C & E v AA QB 1974 STC 192)*

   Fees for correspondence courses *(Rapid Results College Ltd 1973 VAT TR 197)*

   (Books are zero rated. Tuition is standard rated).

Composite supply

13. This occurs where goods and services supplied together make up a single indivisible supply, and apportionment must not be made.

Composite supplies include:

Services of a launderette (supplies of water, heat, use of machinery)	*Mander Laundries Ltd 1973 VAT TR 136*
A course in dress design (material and guidance notes)	*Betty Foster (Fashion Sewing) 1976 VAT TR 229*

Input tax – *Deduction*

14. Input tax is the VAT charged on business purchases and expenses including imported goods, goods removed from a warehouse, and capital expenditure.

To be deductible, the input tax must be in respect of goods and services for the purposes of the business and not of a class where the tax is specifically non-deductible.

Input tax can be reclaimed providing that it is attributable to:

i) standard or zero rated supplies

ii) supplies made in the course of business which are outside the scope of UK VAT but would have been subject to standard or zero rate if made in the UK

iii) supplies or warehoused goods.

Input tax incurred in relation to exempt supplies may be wholly recoverable where it falls within the de minimis rules. (See partial exemption section below.)

Input tax incurred in respect of any other activity not covered by (i) to (iii) above is not reclaimable.

Input tax on business overheads or research and development expenditure can be claimed as input tax provided that it is attributable to the three activities noted above. If the expenditure is partially attributable to exempt supplies or to activities outside the three categories then only part of the input tax attributable to the three activities is reclaimable.

Input tax – *No deduction*

15. Input tax charged in respect of the following is non-deductible.

a) The purchase of private motor cars except:

i) Cars used exclusively for business.

ii) Cars used primarily for business es such as taxis, self drive hire cars and cars used for driving construction.

iii) Cars purchased for resale.

VAT on the purchase of commercial vehicles is allowed as a deduction.

b) Normally only 50% of the input tax applicable to the leasing of all cars is deductable for VAT purposes. The net rental plus 50% of VAT incurred is charged in the accounts as an allowable expense for tax purposes.

c) Motor accessories. When a motor is purchased, VAT on the accessories is not reclaimable even if invoiced separately. VAT on accessories purchased and fitted later is deductible provided that the car remains in business ownership.

d) Business entertainment expenses. Input tax on this kind of expenditure is only allowable where it is incurred for staff entertainment for the purposes of the business eg provision of meals and seasonal entertainment.

Private motoring

16. Input tax on all road fuel purchased for business or private use is reclaimable providing that it is attributable to the specified supplies. For example, where exempt supplies are made, part of the input tax may not be recoverable.

A fuel scale charge was introduced for fuel for private use in a similar manner to that used for employment income purposes. Output tax is charged on the deemed taxable supply, by reference to the following scales.

A new method linked to the CO_2 emissions has been introduced for the current tax year. This replaces the previous method that was linked to the engine size and aligns the VAT treatment of fuel for private motoring to the other income tax benefit in kind charges. Both are now charged depending on the CO_2 emissions of the car.

VAT fuel rates 2009/10 (from 1st May 2009)

Vat Fuel Scale Charges for 3 Month Periods

CO_2 band	VAT fuel scale charge, 3 month period	VAT on 3 month charge 15%	VAT on 3 month charge 17.5%
	£	£	£
120 or below	126.00	16.43	18.76
121-139	189.00	24.65	28.14
140	201.00	26.21	29.93
145	214.00	27.91	31.87
150	226.00	29.49	33.65
155	239.00	31.17	35.59
160	251.00	32.73	37.38
165	264.00	34.43	39.31
170	276.00	36.00	41.10
175	289.00	37.69	43.04
180	302.00	39.39	44.97
185	314.00	40.95	46.76
190	327.00	42.65	48.70
195	339.00	44.21	50.48
200	352.00	45.91	52.42
205	365.00	47.60	54.36
210	378.00	49.30	56.29
215	390.00	50.86	58.08
220	403.00	52.56	60.02
225	416.00	54.26	61.95
230	428.00	55.82	63.74
235 or above	441.00	57.52	65.68

For monthly or annual VAT return periods, pro-rate the above charges accordingly.

Imports – removals from the warehouse

17. Imports of goods

VAT is charged on most goods imported into the UK (including acquisitions from the EC) whether or not the importer is registered for VAT. The tax is in addition to any customs duty or other charges which might be incurred and is calculated on a value which includes all such charges.

Payment of VAT on imported goods is due at the time of importation or removal from a warehouse unless deferment arrangements have been made.

A registered trader approved by Customs & Excise may defer payment of tax on goods imported in the course of business during a calendar month until the 15th of the following month (or the next working day after the 15th if that day is a holiday). The VAT is normally collected by a direct debit mandate which forms part of the procedure an application for deferment must comply with.

VAT on imported goods can be claimed as input tax subject to the normal rules. The claim for the VAT as input tax must be made in the return for the accounting period during which the importation or removal from the relevant warehouse occurs.

Certain goods imported into the UK from the EC are eligible for VAT import relief.

Warehoused goods

When goods are warehoused for customs and excise purposes then payment of any VAT is usually suspended. VAT becomes payable when the goods are removed from the warehouse for use in the UK.

Imports of services

Where services such as banking, insurance, and business consultancy are received from outside the UK then the taxable person may have to account for the output tax on those transactions as if he or she had made the supply personally. In this case there would be a set-off of input tax of an equivalent amount.

Exports

18. The export of goods and services to an overseas customer including a EC member country are mainly zero rated under group 15. Where goods are sent to a final exporter in the UK then in general they will not be zero rated, but this does not include delivery to a port or central clearance depot for shipment.

Goods for personal use

19. Where goods which belong to a business are put to private use outside the business then a taxable supply is made and output tax is chargeable. Thus if trading stock is withdrawn from the business for private use or an employee uses a business asset for private purposes, a taxable supply occurs.

VAT is chargeable on the cost (for income tax purposes it is the market value) of the supply or service to the business and the tax point is the time when the goods or services are made available for non-business use.

There are special rules for the private use of motor cars (*see above*).

Partial exemption

20.   The rules for the determination of partial exempt are outlined below.

i)   Where a business makes exempt supplies of financial or land related services, and these are not incurred in the course of carrying on a business in the financial sector, then all exempt input tax can be recovered provided it has been incurred in relation to any of the following supplies:

* the granting of any lease or tenancy of land, or any licence to occupy land (provided that the exempt input tax related to all such supplies made by the business is less than £1,000 per tax year, and that the business does not incur any exempt input tax other than that related to those supplies listed in this paragraph)
* any deposit of money

- any services of arranging insurance
- any services of arranging mortgages
- any services of arranging hire-purchase, credit sale or conditional sale transactions
- the assignment of any debt in respect of a supply of goods or services by the assignor.

If the exempt input tax is incurred in relation to supplies other than those listed above, then the tax must be taken into consideration in determining the 'de minimis limit'.

ii) A business can be treated as fully taxable providing its exempt input tax is not more than £625 per month on average.

In addition businesses must also satisfy the additional condition that exempt input tax is no more than 50% of the VAT on all purchases.

iii) Exempt input tax must be considered where financial businesses are carried on, such as a bank, building society, money lender, credit card company etc.

iv) The standard method of calculation to be used where the business cannot be treated as fully taxable is as follows.

a) Identify the non-attributable input tax.

b) Calculate percentage rounded up to the next whole number of such input tax which is equal to:

$$\frac{\text{Value of taxable supplies (excl. VAT)}}{\text{Value of taxable supplies (excl. VAT)} + \text{Value of exempt supplies}}$$

vi) The use of the standard method is not mandatory and a business can use a special method more suited to its business provided advance agreement obtained from C&E. Commonly used special methods include those based on staff numbers, floorspace, purchases (the standard method uses sales) or transaction counts. The scheme has to be 'fair and reasonable'.

Example

A Ltd had the following transactions in the quarter to 31st March 2010:

	£
Standard-rated supplies (excluding VAT)	150,000
Zero-rated supplies	50,000
Exempt supplies	100,000

Input tax has been paid as follows:

	£
Standard-rated supplies	12,000
Zero-rated supplies	–
Exempt supplies	17,000
General overheads	4,000

The general overhead input tax cannot be directly attributed to any of the listed supplies.

Compute the VAT payable for the quarter to 31st March 2010.

Solution: A Ltd VAT return: quarter to 31st March 2010

			£
Output tax 150,000 @ 17.5%			26,250
Input tax:	Standard-rated	12,000	
	Zero-rated	–	
	Overheads	2,680	14,680
VAT due			11,570

Notes

i) VAT attributable to overheads:

$$\frac{150,000(SR) + 50,000(ZR)}{150,000(SR) + 50,000(ZR) + 100,000(EX)} \quad \square \; 4,000 = 67\% \; \square \; 4,000 = 2,680$$

ii) As the de minimis levels for exempt input tax have been exceeded, the business is partially exempt.

iii) An annual computation is required to adjust any quarterly fluctuations.

iv) Where the amount of residual input tax is greater than £50,000 per year, then an annual override calculation is required to compare with the standard method.

Bad debts

21. Relief is available for bad debts incurred by a taxable person, and a claim for a refund of the appropriate output tax can be made where:

a) the goods or services were supplied for a monetary consideration, and VAT on the supply was paid.

b) the customer has become insolvent. This means an official determination of inability to pay debts such as bankruptcy, or the winding up of a company.

c) a trader can obtain a certificate from the 'administrator' or 'administrative receiver' of a company stating that in his or her opinion if the company went into liquidation its assets would be insufficient to pay secured and preference debts.

d) any debt which is more than six months old which has been written off in the trader's accounts can be claimed as a bad debt for VAT purposes. The six-month period is from the date the payment was due (previously the time of supply).

e) Any business that has made a claim for input tax on a supply but has not paid the supplier of the goods within six months, must repay the VAT.

Bad debts – *Claim*

22. The amount of the claim will usually be readily ascertainable by reference to the actual debt outstanding. However, where there are payments on account (not allocated by the debtor to any particular supply) then these are allocated to the earliest supplies in the account after adjusting for any mutual supplies ie contra items.

Example

R Ltd is registered for VAT. One of its customers, X Ltd, went into liquidation on 31st July 2009.

The sales ledger account for the last two months to 31st July 2009 was as follows:

R Ltd sales ledger account with X Ltd

£

1.5.09	Balance b/f	12,000	30.6.09	Cheque May a/c paid	12,000
25.5.09	1. Goods (including VAT)	36,000	23.7.09	Cheque payment on a/c	10,000
15.6.09	2. Goods (zero rated)	9,000	31.7.09	Balance c/f	50,000
20.7.09	3. Goods (including VAT)	15,000			
		72,000			72,000

31.7.09 Balance b/d   50,000

Compute the bad debt relief available to R Ltd.

Solution

Amount due from X Ltd at 31st July 2009 £50,000

		Gross	VAT
		£	£
Invoice	No. 3	15,000	2,234.04
	No. 2	9,000	–
	No. 1 (part)	26,000	3,872.34
		50,000	6,106.38

Notes

i)   VAT on Invoice No.1 $36,000 \times {}^{7}/_{47} = 5,361.70$

Proportion $\dfrac{26,000}{36,000} \times 5,361.70 = 3,872.34$

ii)   VAT recoverable is £6,106.38.

iii)   Assuming VAT at 17.5% standard rate.

Transfer of a business as a going concern

23.a) The sale of the assets of a business as a going concern is not a supply of goods or services and not therefore chargeable to VAT provided that:

i)   the assets are to be used by the purchaser in carrying on the same kind of business whether as part of an existing business or not.

ii)   in a case where the seller is a taxable person, the purchaser if not already registered must register immediately.

b)   A sale of part of a business is also not subject to VAT provided that the part sold is capable of separate operation.

c)   The purchaser cannot claim any input tax in respect of the purchase of the business even where this has been incorrectly charged to him or her.

d)   The provisions do not apply where the business is a different one after the transfer to that carried on by the seller.

e)   The transfer of a sole trader's business to a limited company or into partnership with one or more other persons falls within the transfer provisions and is therefore not chargeable to VAT.

f)   Where the business is transferred as a going concern then it is possible for the VAT Registration number of the vendor to be transferred to the purchaser subject to certain conditions, and the approval of the Custom & Excise.

g) Where a business carried on by a taxable person is transferred to another person who is not registered at the time of the transfer then the new owner is liable to register for VAT immediately.

Sale of business assets

24. The sale of assets used by a person in the course of business, e.g. plant and machinery, is subject to VAT as a taxable supply. This also applies where a person ceases to trade and the business assets are sold.

VAT is not chargeable on the disposal of a motor car unless it is sold for more than the price paid when purchased. Where the latter occurs VAT is chargeable to the disposer on the difference between the purchase and sale price.

Business assets – *Capital allowances*

25. In general there is no difference between the treatment of capital goods and other inputs for VAT purposes and in most cases the input tax can be set against the output tax in the normal way. However, where a trader's supplies are exempt, or partially exempt or the taxable turnover is below the threshold limits, he or she will not be able to recover all or part of the input tax on the capital goods. In such cases the VAT not reclaimable can be added to the cost of the asset for capital allowance purposes.

For motor cars the VAT is not recoverable input tax and is therefore added to the cost of the asset for capital allowance purposes.

VAT on capital goods – *Partly exempt businesses*

26. Input tax recovered by a trader on certain assets when first acquired can be repaid where there is a change in the use to which they are applied eg from taxable to exempt use.

The assets to which these rules apply are:

a) computers and computer equipment worth over £50,000, if their use changes within five years of acquisition.

b) land and buildings worth over £250,000, if their use is changed within ten years of acquisition.

Self supplies

27. The main circumstance where self supply of goods or services gives rise to a taxable supply is the self supply of motor cars by vehicle manufacturers or car dealers. Where this takes place there is a self supply at cost to the trader (excluding any input tax recovered)..

Cash accounting

28. The cash accounting scheme is optional for all businesses with a turnover of less than £1,350,000 (£1,350,000). The main features of the scheme are;

a) VAT on inputs and outputs can be accounted for by reference to cash paid and received rather than on the basis of invoice dates as under other systems.

b) Applications for the scheme, once approved, remain in force for two years.

c) The problem of VAT on bad debts does not arise in the first place.

Annual accounting

29. This scheme is available to all businesses which have been registered for at least one year and whose turnover is < £1,350,000. The main features of the scheme are;

a) Businesses choosing the scheme will make only one VAT return a year instead of the usual four.

b) There will be nine equal payments on account by direct debit and a tenth balancing payment with the annual return.

c) Businesses already using the scheme will be able to continue until their turnover reaches £1,600,000.

Rents

30. Landlords can elect to charge VAT on rents from non-domestic buildings. The election must be made on a building by building basis, and once made will apply to all future transactions in the property, i.e. lettings or sales by the landlord. Businesses which are fully taxable will not be greatly affected by this change but those which are exempt or partially exempt may be affected, such as Group 2 Insurance and Group 5 Finance.

Changes in the tax rates

31. When a change in the standard rate of VAT occurs or a new rate is introduced, the following rules apply.

a) Output tax is calculated under the normal rules i.e. by reference to the tax point unless the special change of rate provisions are applied

b) Under these provisions where the rate goes up, the tax at the old rate can be charged on goods removed or services performed before the date of change even though a tax invoice would normally have been issued after the date of change.

c) Where a supply of services takes place which crosses the threshold date of change in rate then the supply can be apportioned by reference to normal costing or pricing procedures. Tax at the old rate would be charged on the services performed before the date of the change.

d) Input tax following a change in rate is obtained from the supplier's invoice and only the amount charged can be reclaimed. For less detailed tax invoices which do not show the VAT separately, the amount of input tax can be computed at the rate appropriate at the tax point.

Miscellaneous

32. i) Annual Returns and Payments. Traders whose turnover is below the registration threshold but who have registered voluntarily will be required to adopt the Annual Returns and Payments system (ARP). This involves a single annual return and one lump sum payment of VAT.

ARP will be extended by way of option to other traders whose turnover is less than £100,000.

ii) Pre-registration expenditure. Input tax on pre-registration business expenditure can be included in the first VAT return. In the case of input tax on goods (as distinct from services) the goods must either be retained or converted into other goods still retained. For services the expenditure must have been incurred six months prior to registration.

iii) Business gifts. In general traders are not required to account for VAT as a taxable supply on the value of small business gifts such as diaries and calendars. The limit on such goods is £50.00 per item. The treatment of a series of business gifts in any 12 month period to the same person is aligned with that of a single gift. Where the limit is exceeded output tax is due on all the gifts made up to that point.

Flat rate scheme – small firms

33. A flat rate scheme of VAT has been introduced the main features of which are:

i) Under the flat-rate scheme, traders avoid having to account internally for VAT on all their purchases and supplies, and instead they calculate the net VAT liability as a percentage of their total turnover, including all their reduced, zero rated and exempt supplies.

ii) Once operating a flat rate scheme the distinction between standard, reduced and zero rated supplies, in addition to input tax attributable to exempt supplies becomes irrelevant. The trader merely applies the standard quoted percentage to all business income including exempt supplies and supplies to other member states to arrive at the 'net amount of VAT' for the period. This amount reflects a notional 'credit' for recoverable input tax (the amount actually incurred will not be relevant) and is the only calculation needed to operate the scheme.

iii) The scheme is available to businesses where the annual taxable turnover, including reduced and zero rated supplies, does not exceed £150,000 in the year of entry to the scheme, and with total VAT exclusive turnover, including the value of exempt supplies and/or other non-VATable income, of no more than £125,000 a year. The turnover threshold differs from that for the annual and cash accounting schemes, which is based on VATable income only.

iv) The flat rate percentage applied to turnover depends on the business trade classification used by Customs & Excise. These vary between 2% for food, tobacco, newsagents retailers to 13% for computer and IT service providers.

v) The calculation of the rates for the flat rate scheme allows for low value capital expenditure purchases. However, VAT on VAT-inclusive expenditure over £2,000 can be recoverable outside the flat rate scheme. Such separate treatment does not cover items such as cars where the VAT on purchases is excluded. However, where capital purchases are dealt with outside the flat rate scheme, output tax on their disposal (or deemed disposal in the case of an asset held as at the time of de-registration)is also dealt with outside the scheme.

vi) Traders using the flat rate scheme continue to charge VAT at the standard zero rates and show the relevant details on their sales invoices. The flat rate percentage is applied to the VAT inclusive sales.

vii) For businesses who use the VAT flat rate scheme in general the accounts will be prepared using gross receipts less flat rate VAT percentage for turnover and expenses will include the irrecoverable input VAT. Limited companies are required by law to show their turnover net of VAT.

Student self testing question with answer

You are provided with the following information relating to Octavius Limited for the quarter ended 31 March 2010:

The VAT-exclusive management accounts:

	£	£
Sales		16,500
Sales returns		(1,100)
		15,400
Purchases	9,600	
Purchases returns	(300)	
	9,300	
Bad debts written off	1,500	
Other expenses	2,400	
		13,200
Profit		2,200

The sales and other expenses are all standard-rated for VAT.

The purchases are all deductible for VAT.

The sales and purchases returns are all evidenced by credit notes issued and received.

The bad debts were written off in March 2010. Payment for the original sales was due by November 2009.

A sales invoice for £3,000 excluding VAT had been omitted in error from the VAT return for the quarter to 28 December 2008.

Included in the expense figure is the cost of both business and private petrol for Managing Directors car, which had an engine capacity of 1800cc and CO2 emissions of 210.

Requirement

Complete the VAT account for the three month period ended 31 March 2009, showing how much VAT is payable to Customs and Excise. The 'cash accounting' scheme is not being used. **7 marks**

When is the tax shown by (a) above payable? **1 mark**

State the course of action is open to a taxpayer who disagrees with a decision by Customs and Excise on the application of VAT before lodging a formal appeal to a VAT tribunal? **1 mark**

What are the consequences of any action taken by the taxpayer in (c) above?

(ACCA Tax Framework updated June 95)

415

Suggested solution

(a)

VAT account

	£		£
Input tax on purchases 9,600 at 17.5%	1,680	Output tax on sales 16,500 at 17.5%	2,888
Input tax on expenses 2,400 at 17.5%	420	Understatement of Output tax on previous return	
	2,100	3,000 at 17.5%	525
		Car fuel charge	56
Input tax on returns to suppliers 300 at 17.5%	(53)		3,469
	2,047	Output tax on returns from customers	
VAT payable	1,229	1,100 at 17.5%	(193)
	3,276		3,276

(b)   The VAT is payable within one month of the end of the quarter, i.e., by 30 April 2010.

(c)   A taxpayer who disagrees with a decision by Customs & Excise on the application of VAT may apply within 30 days to the local VAT office asking them to re-consider their decision.

(d)   After re-considering their decision the Customs & Excise will either:

Confirm their original decision. The taxpayer then has 21 days to submit an appeal to a VAT tribunal; or

Revise their original decision. The taxpayer then has 30 days to submit an appeal to a VAT tribunal, if appropriate.

Questions without answers

1. You are provided with the following information relating to Portia Limited, a consultancy company, for the quarter ended 30 November 2009:

	£
Fees (standard-rated and exclusive of tax)	60,000
Rent received from sub-letting part of her offices	6,000
Car purchase (exclusive of VAT)	18,000
Overheads (standard-rated and exclusive of VAT)	9,000
Input VAT attributable to taxable supplies	2,000

Notes

The car was purchased on 1 September 2009 and had an engine capacity of 1900cc. Petrol for both private and business motoring was charged through the business and not refunded. The CO_2 emissions of the car are 190.

Bad debts of £550 (exclusive of VAT) were written off during November 2009; the date payment was due for the services was January 2009.

Requirement:

Calculate the VAT payable for the quarter ended 30 November 2009 and to state when this will be payable to HM Customs and Excise.   **9 marks**

Advise Portia Limited on the VAT consequences of (1) purchasing a computer on hire purchase and (2) renting a computer. **2 marks**

Total: 11 marks

(ACCA Tax Framework updated Dec 96)

2. Antrobus Limited had the following transactions in the quarter to 30 June 2009:

	£
Standard-rated supplies (excluding VAT)	150,000
Zero-rated supplies	50,000
Exempt supplies	100,000

Input tax had been paid as follows:

	£
Standard-related supplies	12,000
Zero-related supplies	5,000
Exempt supplies	9,000
General overheads	4,000

The general overhead input tax cannot be directly attributed to any of the listed supplies.

Requirement

Calculate the VAT payable by Antrobus Limited for the quarter **5 marks**

State the records and accounts which must be kept for VAT purposes and to state for how long they must be retained by the trader. **6 marks**

Total: 11 marks

(ACCA Tax Framework updated Dec 95)

39 Special retail schemes

Introduction

1. In between the 1st August 1997 and the 1st April 1998 the following changes were made to the VAT Retail Schemes:

a)   There are five standard retail schemes:

       Point of sale scheme

       Apportionment scheme (2 schemes)

       Direct calculation scheme (2 schemes)

b)   No trader will be allowed to use any retail scheme if it is reasonably practicable for them to account for VAT in the usual way.

c)   Retail schemes can only be used for retail sales. If a trader makes some retail sales and others to VAT registered traders than the usual VAT procedures must be applied to the latter date.

d)   A trader whose tax exclusive retail turnover exceeds £10 millions is not allowed to use a standard retail scheme. Instead he must agree a bespoke scheme with the Revenue and Customs.

e)   Existing traders have the following choices:

   i)   adopt a successor scheme;

   ii)   migrate to one of the other five new standard schemes;

   iii)   agree a bespoke scheme with Customs & Excise.

f)   All retail schemes require a record of the value of retail supplies called daily gross takings (DGT).

g)   DGT includes:

   i)   all payments as they are received from cash customers;

   ii)   the full VAT inclusive value of credit and other non-cash sales;

   iii)   details of any adjustments made to (i) and (ii).

In general the record of DGT will normally be till rolls and/or copy sales invoices and not just cash in hand.

Daily gross takings (DGT) checklist

2. The following is a copy of the DGT checklist:

a)   Inclusions in DGT

   i)   You must include and record the following in your DGT as they are received from your customers:

       cash

       cheques

       debit or credit card vouchers

       Switch, Delta or similar electronic transactions

       electronic cash.

ii)   Additionally you must add the following to and record in your DGT on the day you make the supply:

> the taxable value of credit sales (excluding any disclosed exempt charge for credit)
>
> the value of any goods taken out of the business for your own use
>
> the cash value of any payment in kind for retail sales
>
> the face value of gift, book and record vouchers etc. redeemed
>
> any other payments for retail sales.

iii)   If you are involved in part-exchange, sale or return, credit sales, deposits, vouchers, coupons or other special transactions, you will have to make other adjustments to your DGT.

b)   Adjustments to the DGT

Your till roll or other record of sales together with the additions explained in paragraph 1 above constitutes your DGT and it is this figure (not simply the cash in the till) which you must use when calculating output tax due under your retail scheme. However, you may reduce your DGT for the following:

- void transactions (where an incorrect transaction has been voided at the time of the error);
- illegible credit card transactions (where a customer's account details are not legible on the credit card voucher and therefore cannot be presented and redeemed at the bank);
- unsigned cheques or dishonoured cheques from cash coupons (but not from credit customers);
- counterfeit notes;
- where a cheque guarantee card is incorrectly accepted as a credit card;
- acceptance of out of date coupons which have previously been included in the DGT but which are not honoured by promoters;
- supervisor's float discrepancies;
- till breakdown (where incorrect till readings are recorded due to mechanical faults, for example, till programming error, false reading and till reset by an engineer);
- use of training tills (where a till used by staff for training has been returned to the sales floor without the zeroing of figures);
- customer overspends using Shopacheck;
- inadvertent acceptance of foreign currency (where discovered at a later time, for example when cashing up):
- receipts recorded for exempt supplies;
- receipts for goods or services which are to be accounted for outside the scheme;
- refunds given to customers in respect of taxable supplies to cover accidental overcharges or where goods are unsuitable or faulty; and
- instalments in respect of credit sales.

Remember you must be able to provide evidence to support any adjustments to your DGT figure.

If you make an adjustment but subsequently receive a payment the amount received must be included in your DGT.

The five schemes

3. Point of sale scheme

This scheme works by identifying the VAT liability at the time the sale is made. The scheme requires a till system or other mechanism by which goods at different rates of VAT can be distinguished at the time of sale.

Output tax is computed by:

$$\text{Daily Gross Takings for standard rated supplies} \times 7/47$$

Apportionment scheme 1

4. This scheme is available to retailers with a tax exclusive turnover not exceeding £1 million.

Output tax is computed as follows:

a)   The daily gross takings, zero and standard, are recorded in the normal way.

b)   The cost of goods received including VAT at each positive rate is recorded, and the proportion at each rate is applied to the total takings.

c)   Once a year a total calculation is made and any necessary adjustments made.

Example

	Tax period ending 31.3.2010
	£
Daily gross takings, standard and zero rated	480,000
Cost of goods received with VAT standard rate	250,000
Cost of goods received with VAT zero rate	90,000
Total cost	340,000
	52,566

$$\text{Output tax is } \frac{250,000}{340,000} \times 480,000 \times 7/47 =$$

This scheme is acceptable where the mark-up for zero rated and standard rated supplies is on average very similar. If the mark-up on zero rated supplies is higher than that on standard rated supplies, this scheme can produce an excessive tax liability.

Apportionment scheme 2

5. This scheme is available to businesses with a tax exclusive turnover not exceeding £100 million.

Output tax is calculated over ESP (Expected Selling Prices) and DGT (Daily Gross Takings) as follows:

$$\frac{\text{ESP (including VAT) of SR goods}}{\text{ESP (including VAT) of all goods}} \times \text{DGT} \times \frac{7}{47}$$

a)   A full record of daily gross takings must be kept.

b)   For each positive rate, the opening stock and purchases for resale must be valued at their VAT inclusive selling prices.

c)   For the first three quarters the opening stock must be included in the computation.

d)   Expected selling prices should take into consideration the following:

- price changes – increases and decreases, for example, sell by date reductions;
- special offers and promotion schemes;
- wastage;
- freezer breakdowns;
- breakages.

Example

	Quarter to 31.3.2010	
	Std rate	Zero rate
	£	£
Opening stock 1.1.10 at SP and VAT	30,000	10,000
Purchases from 1.1.10 at SP and VAT	120,000	40,000
	150,000	50,000
Gross takings for the quarter to 31.3.2010	£50,000	

Output tax is $\dfrac{150,000}{200,000} \times 50,000 \times 7/47$

ie 37,500 $\square$ 7/47 = £5,585

Direct calculation scheme 1

6. This scheme may only be used if the traders' tax exclusive retail turnover does not exceed £1.0 million.

Output tax is calculated as follows:

a)   The expected SP of 'minority goods' must be calculated. These are the goods at the rate of tax which forms the smallest proportion of all retail supplies.

b)   Where the zero rated supplies are the minority goods

$$\text{output tax} \quad = \quad \text{Total sales} - \text{zero proportion} \times \frac{7}{47}$$

c)   Where the standard rated supplies are the minority goods

$$\text{output tax} \quad = \quad \text{SR supplies} \times \frac{7}{47}$$

Example

	Quarter ending 31.3.2010
Daily gross takings for the period	65,000
Less ESP of zero rated goods	15,000
Output tax	$50,000 \times \dfrac{7}{47} = \underline{7,447}$

In the above example if the zero rated goods are £65,000 and the S Rated are £15,000, the output tax would be $\dfrac{7}{47} \times 15,000 = £2,234$

Direct calculation scheme 2

7. This scheme is successor to the old scheme B1 and E1 and must be used where the tax exclusive retail turnover is greater than £100 million.

It is similar in computation to the direct calculation scheme 1 but requires an annual stock adjustment to correct any under or overpayment of VAT during the year.

Miscellaneous

8. Cash accounting

The system of cash accounting for businesses with a taxable turnover of not more than £1,350,000 p.a. is not likely to be advantageous for most retailers who already account for VAT on the basis of cash receipts. They would lose the advantage of reclaiming VAT on purchases as soon as they are invoiced and could only claim set-off at the end of the accounting period in which the payment was made.

Flat rate scheme – small firms

9. The flat rate scheme outlined in *Chapter 38* is available for retail traders.

VAT worked examples

Introduction

1. This chapter provides some worked examples of VAT under the following headings:

    Registration
    VAT return – non-retailing
    Bad debt recovery
    Partial exemption
    Retail apportionment sheme

Registration

2. **Example**

A has been the owner of a retail store for a number of years. He has not previously registered for VAT as his turnover has consistently been below the minimum criteria. However he now feels that he should register and seeks your advice. Turnover since January 2007 has been as indicated below:

	2007 £	2008 £	2009 £
January	1,125	2,775	8,000
February	950	1,450	16,000
March	1,000	2,400	15,000
April	950	2,550	18,000
May	1,450	3,700	17,000
June	1,150	4,200	19,000
July	1,400	3,900	22,000
August	1,425	4,500	25,000
September	1,500	4,000	
October	1,550	2,000	
November	1,675	1,500	
December	2,500	1,500	

Solution

Moving annual total sales

	£
12 months to 30.9.08 =	35,200
12 months to 31.10.08 =	35,650
12 months to 30.11.08 =	35,475
12 months to 31.12.08 =	34,475
12 months to 31.1.09 =	39,700
12 months to 28.2.09 =	54,250
12 months to 31.3.09 =	66,850
12 months to 30.4.09 =	82,300

As the annual total to 30.4.09 has exceeded £68,000 (the registration limit at 1.5.2009) A must notify the Customs & Excise by 31st May 2009. Registration will be effected from 31st March 2009.

3.   Example

D commenced trading on 1st January 2009 with the following taxable turnover.

	£
Quarter to 31st March 2009	8,000
Quarter to 30th June 2009	10,000

As a result of an unexpected UK order, obtained on 1st May 2009, budgeted sales evenly spread for the remainder of the financial year to 31st December 2009 are as follows:

	£	
Quarter to 30th September 2009	150,000	(budget)
Quarter to 31st December 2009	200,000	(budget)

D wants to know when he should register for VAT.

Solution

When the order was obtained in May 2009 it was clear that the annual turnover would exceed £68,000 the level for registration from 1st May 2009.

With the sales evenly spread the cumulative sales up to the month of July would be:

	£
Quarter to 31.3.09	8,000
Quarter to 30.6.09	10,000
July 2009 $\dfrac{150,000}{3}$	50,000
	68,000

Registration would be required either:

a)   by 30th August 2009, or

b)   at an earlier mutually agreed date.

VAT return – *non-retailing*

4.   Example

Z Ltd is registered for VAT, and is in the process of completing its VAT return for the quarter ended 31 March 2010. The following information is available.

i)   Sales invoices totalling £128,000 were issued in respect of standard rated sales. Z Ltd offers its customers a 2.5% discount for prompt payment.

ii)   On 15 March 2010 Z Ltd received an advance deposit of £4,500 in respect of a contract that is due to be completed during April 2010. The total value of the contract is £10,000.

iii)   Standard rated expenses amounted to £74,800. This includes £4,200 for entertaining customers.

iv)   On 31 March 2010 Z Ltd wrote off £12,000 due from a customer as a bad debt. The debt was in respect of three invoices; each of £4,000, that were due for payment on 15 August, 15 September and 15 October 2009 respectively.

v)   On 1 January 2010 the company purchased a motor car costing £10,900 for the use of its sales manager. The sales manager is provided with free petrol for private mileage. The car has a CO_2 emission of 195. The relevant quarterly scale charge is £339. Both figures are inclusive of VAT.

Unless otherwise stated all of the above figures are exclusive of VAT

Calculate the amount of VAT repayable by Z Ltd for the quarter ended 31 March 2010.

Solution: Z Ltd VAT Return quarter to 31.3. 2010

		£
Output tax:		
Sales invoices	124,800 × 17.5%	21,840
Advance payment	4,500 × 17.5%	787
Car fuel charge	339 × 7/47	50
		22,677
Input tax:		
Expenses	(74,800 – 4,200) × 17.5%	12,355
Bad debts	8,000 × 17.5%	1,400
		13,755
Net Tax payable		8,922

Notes:

i)   Tax on sales after discount of 2.5% i.e. 128,000 – 3,200 = 124,800.

ii) Input tax on business entertainment is not claimable.

iii) Bad debt relief is restricted to invoices due 6 months from the date of payment.

Bad debt recovery

5. T, a trader registered for VAT, has made the following supplies to P Ltd.

Date	Rate	Value of goods	VAT	Gross value
25.1.09	Zero	3,000	–	3,000
3.2. 09	SR	1,200	210	1,410
5.3. 09	Exempt	450	–	450
22.3. 09	SR	1,600	280	1,880
2.4. 09	SR	2,500	438	2,938
10.4. 09	SR	2,000	350	2,350
		10,750	1,278	12,028

T has received the following payments on account:

	£
15.3.09	1,646
11.5.09	1,000
20.5.09	1,000

P Ltd was the subject of a creditors' voluntary winding up order on the 30th May 2009.

Calculate the amount of bad debt relief for VAT. Assume a standard rate of 17.5% throughout.

Solution

Amount of debt outstanding 12,028 – 3,646 = 8,382
This would be represented by the following:

	Gross value	VAT
10.4.09	2,350	350
2.4.09	2,938	438
22.3.09	1,880	280
5.3.09	450	–
3.2.09	764	114
	8,382	1,182

Proportion of invoice dated 3.2.09

$$\frac{764}{1,410} \times 210 = 114$$

VAT recoverable £1,182

Partial exemption

6. S Ltd has the following data relating to the quarter ended 31st March 2010

	£
Sales standard rated (excluding VAT)	95,000
Zero rated	15,000
Exempt	28,000
Input tax	
Attributable to taxable supplies	9,500
Attributable to exempt supplies	1,100
Attributable to overheads	2,500
	13,100

Apportionment of overhead expenditure	%
Standard rate supplies	50
Zero rate supplies	35
Exempt supplies	15
	100%

Calculate the VAT payable for the quarter ending 31st March 2010.

Solution: VAT payable quarter to 31 March 2010

	£	£	£
Output tax £95,000 @ 17.5%			16,625
Input tax			
Attributable to taxable supplies		9,500	
Attributable to overheads 85% × 2,500		2,125	
Attributable to exempt supplies	1,100		
Add % of overheads 15% × 2,500	375		
		1,475	13,100
VAT Payable			3,525

Note

As the input tax attributable to the exempt supplies of £1,475 (1,475 ÷ 3 = 492) is less than £625 on average per month and the exempt input tax of £1,475 is less than 50% of the total input tax of £13,100, the total input tax is recoverable.

VAT apportionment scheme

7. Example

P is registered for VAT as a retailer and uses the apportionment scheme 1. His data for the four quarters to 31st March 2009 are as follows:

	Gross takings £	Cost of goods Std rate (inc. VAT) £	Total cost of goods (inc. VAT) £
Quarter to 30.6.08	19,500	9,500	14,200
Quarter to 30.9.08	25,500	12,300	19,150
Quarter to 31.12.08	14,700	4,200	9,100
Quarter to 31.3.09	20,500	8,500	15,100
	80,200	34,500	57,550

Compute the output tax for each quarter together with the annual adjustment, assuming a standard rate of 17.5% throughout.

Solution

Quarter to 30.6.08

Output tax $= \dfrac{9,500}{14,200} \times 19,500 = $ £13,046.00

Output tax $= 13,046 \times \dfrac{7}{47} = $ £1,942.98

Quarter to 30.9.08

Output tax $= \dfrac{12,300}{19,150} \times 25,500 = $ £16,378.00

Output tax $= 16,378 \times \dfrac{7}{47} = $ £2,439.27

Quarter to 31.12.08

Output tax $= \dfrac{4,200}{9,100} \times 14,700 = $ £6,785.00

Output tax $= 6,785 \times \dfrac{7}{47} = $ £1,010.53

Quarter to 31.3.09

Standard output $= \dfrac{8,500}{15,100} \times 20,500 = $ £11,540.00

Output tax $= 11,540 \times \dfrac{7}{47} = $ £1,718.68

Annual adjustment

Standard output $= \dfrac{34,500}{57,550} \times 80,200 = $ £48,078.00

Output tax $= 48,078 \times \dfrac{7}{47} = $ £7,160.58

Less: recorded	Quarter 1	1,942.98	
	Quarter 2	2,439.27	
	Quarter 3	1,010.53	
	Quarter 4	1,718.68	7,111.46
Under declaration			49.12

Questions without answers

1. P operates a café in a busy holiday resort which is open from March to October each year on a full-time basis and the remainder of the year on special occasions. Turnover since the business started on 1st January 2008 is as follows:

	2008 £	2009 £
January	100	300
February	–	150
March	500	1,100
April	3,200	4,400
May	2,900	3,800
June	4,500	5,500
July	2,500	10,200
August	2,700	9,500
September	4,900	16,200
October	200	20,000
November	–	24,000
December	400	29,000

Advise P as to when, if at all, he should register for VAT.

2. T is a small manufacturer registered for VAT. The following information relates to transactions for the quarter to 30th June 2009.

Sales invoices		**Value excluding VAT £**
No. 1	Standard rate goods	75,000
No. 2	Standard rate goods	42,000
No. 3	Zero rate goods	19,000
No. 4	Exempt goods	56,000

Purchase invoices		**Value excluding VAT £**
No. 1	Raw materials	39,500
No. 2	Raw materials	65,300
	(15% attributable to exempt supplies)	
No. 3	Printing and stationery	1,250
No. 4	Canteen food	3,500
No. 5	Repairs to factory roof	9,500
No. 6	Gas and electricity	12,000
No. 7	Rates	1,500
No. 8	Transport and delivery costs	7,500

Overhead expenditure is to be apportioned on the following basis:

SR goods (70%) zero rated goods (10%); exempt goods (20%)

Calculate the VAT payable for the quarter to 30th June 2009. Assume a standard rate of 17.5% throughout.

Part VII

Tax Planning

40 Elements of tax planning

Introduction

1. This chapter is concerned with some of the basic principles of tax planning which can be applied where a taxpayer has a choice of alternative courses of action. The chapter starts by defining tax planning and outlining some of the objectives involved in this process. Some basic tax planning caveats are then considered followed a tax planning summary table. The focus of the chapter is on the difference between income tax for the self employed and corporation tax for a small incorporated entity. This area of taxation has generated considerable interest over recent years, and as you will have seen from the sections on both income tax and corporation tax is subject to change on an annual basis.

What is tax planning?

2. Given a set of circumstances or a situation where a decision is to be made which involves the incidence of taxation, then tax planning is concerned with achieving the best result with respect to that decision from the taxation perspective. The 'best result' is usually taken to mean achieving the least amount of tax payable consistent with any cash flow advantages which are also often important.

There is no set body of knowledge called tax planning as it usually requires the application of threads of tax law and practice from across the whole spectrum of taxation and law. An exercise in tax planning therefore involves the following.

a)   Identification of the specific problem to be considered.

b)   Identification of the relevant parts of the tax statutes which have relevance to the problem.

c)   Application of the tax rules identified to the problem.

d)   Evaluation of the various options available in order to minimise the incidence of taxation.

e)   Identification and examination of any other factors of a legal, commercial or financial nature which should be taken into consideration.

Objectives of tax planning

3. Tax planning objectives for individuals may be summarised as follows.

a)   To reduce taxable income and/or chargeable gains falling to be assessed.

b)   To lower rate of tax which is applicable to taxable income or chargeable gains.

c)   To defer the date on which tax becomes payable, thereby gaining a cash flow/interest advantage.

For companies in general, similar objectives can be applied. However, for family companies with shareholder directors/employees, tax planning for the individual must inevitably be considered together with that for the family company. This arises because in many cases most of the income of the family director/employee shareholder is in fact derived from family company sources, in the form of remuneration, benefits in kind and dividends.

Tax planning caveats

4. The following points should be borne in mind when undertaking any tax planning exercise.

a) Tax planning, sometimes called tax avoidance, should not be confused with tax evasion. The latter, which is unlawful and may lead to criminal prosecution, is associated with fraudulent or dishonest plans to avoid taxation.

b) Commercial factors should not be ignored just for the sake of a business tax planning exercise. For example, there is no point in investing in additional capital expenditure to obtain capital allowances if the capital project itself shows negative returns on investment.

c) Future financial security should not be put at risk. The making of substantial gifts inter vivos to mitigate IHT on the death of the donor should be balanced against the possible shortfall in annual income which might ensue.

d) Possible changes in the law in the future may render current tax planning exercises less advantageous.

e) Tax plans should be flexible to accommodate, if possible, changes in circumstances. There is no permanent long-term relationship between capital and income which will meet all the requirements of all taxpayers.

f) W.e.f July 2005 tax avoidance schemes proffered by any organisation must be disclosed to the IR who will maintain a register of such schemes. Taxpayers utilising any such scheme must disclose this fact in their SATR.

Tax planning summary

5. Individuals

I	Income tax	Employees	Self-employed	Directors
1.	Claim expenses of employment	✓	–	✓
2.	Claim capital allowances for privately owned asset/Authorised M rates	✓	✓	✓
3.	Company pension scheme: consider AVC	✓		✓
4.	No company pension scheme: maximise contributions up to 100% of income	✓	✓	✓
5.	Inter-spouse transfer of assets to use PA's and MCAA where available	✓	✓	✓
6.	Car fuel benefit/payment business mileage	✓	–	✓
7.	Phase capital expenditure to save Class IV NIC income tax	–	✓	–
8.	Employ staff with earnings below NI thresholds	–	✓	–
9.	Consider ISA – tax-free	✓	✓	✓
10.	Consider Enterprise Investment scheme	✓	✓	✓
11.	Consider Venture Capital Trust	✓	✓	✓

II	Capital gains tax			
1.	Consider business and non business assets rate	✓	✓	✓
2.	Inter-spouse transfer of assets to minimise CGT	✓	✓	✓

		Employees	Self-employed	Directors
3.	Phase disposals between tax years to use Annual exemption	✓	✓	✓
4.	With takeover consider cash/shares to minimise CGT	✓	✓	✓

III Inheritance tax

				Employees	Self-employed	Directors
1.	Maximise use of general exemptions –	£250		✓	✓	✓
		£3,000		✓	✓	✓
	Normal expenditure –	for marriage		✓	✓	✓
		inter-spouse		✓	✓	✓
		charitable bequests		✓	✓	✓
2.	Consider gifts intervivos –	personal assets		✓	✓	✓
		business assets		–	✓	–
3.	Deeds of Variation to change distribution of estate			✓	✓	✓

IV VAT

		Employees	Self-employed	Directors
1.	Consider voluntary registration to claim input tax	–	✓	–
2.	Phase capital expenditure to benefit cash flow from input tax	–	✓	–
3.	Consider payment for private fuel rather than scale charge	–	✓	–
4.	Consider turnover levels as it approaches registration point	–	✓	–
5.	Consider Flat rate scheme – small firms		✓	

6. Companies

1. Extended account period, e.g. 18 months to 6 and 12.

2. Phasing capital expenditure to maximise AIA.

3. Consider payment of additional remuneration/dividend – NI saving for latter.

4. Consider dividends payments.

5. Maximise pension contributions.

7. Sole trader vs incorporation

This area of taxation has received a considerable amount of interest due to the number of changes that have been made in relation to the small business corporation tax rules. This section provides an example of a small business and the choice of whether to incorporate or not. It should be noted that there are many factors to consider depending on the circumstances and this section provides a basic comparison based on material previously studied in the income tax and corporation tax sections.

Example

Peter is a self employed electrical engineer and makes profits of £60,000 each year. He pays £8,000 net into an approved private pension scheme. He is considering whether he should incorporate his business and pay himself a minimal salary with the balance in dividends or continue as a sole trader.

A possible approach

Sole trader

				£
Profits				60,000
Total income				60,000
PA				6,475
Taxable income				53,525
	£37,400	@ 20%	7,480	
extend BR	£10,000	@ 20%	2,000	
	£6,125	@ 40%	2,450	
	£53,525			
Total income tax				11,930
NI				
Class 2		2.40 p/w		125
Class 4		5,715-43,875 @ 8%		3,053
excess		60,000-43,875 @ 1%		161
Total national insurance				3,339
Total income tax and NI				**15,269**

Disposable income	£
Profits	60,000
Less pension	8,000
less IT and NI	15,269
Disposable income	36,731

Incorporation

	£
Profit	60,000
Salary	6,475
employer NI 6,475-5,715 @ 12.8%	97
Pension (assuming non contributory)	10,000
PCTCT	43,428
CT @ 21%	9,120
Profit for distribution	34,308

Director earnings				
Salary				6,475
Dividends(34,308 x 100/90)				38,120
Total income				44,595
PA				6,475
Taxable income				38,120
	£37,400	@ 10%	3,740	
	£720	@ 32.5%	234	
Total income tax				3,974
NI – 6,475-5,715 @ 9.4%				71
Total income tax and NI				**4,045**

Disposable income - Director	
Salary	6,475
Dividends	34,308
less IT	4,045
less pension	NC
Disposable income	36,738

Total deductions

Director	4,045
Company (9,120 + 97)	9,217
Total	**13,262**

Sole trader	**15,269**

Notes

1. This example produces a saving of £2,007 (15,269 – 13,262)in total taxation for incorporation when compared with a sole trader.
2. This example assumes that under incorporation, Peter will make use of a non-contributory pension scheme and this will be paid by the company.
3. Disposable income is negligible due to several factors, such as the fact that the company has not been able to obtain tax relief on the pension contribution in the same way that Peter has as a sole trader.
4. The dividend is grossed up at the 10% rate as a notional tax credit and accounted for in Peter's self assessment return.
5. There are many other factors to consider especially in terms of personal preferences for the pension contribution, dividend and salary combination, this example provides a useful basic comparison of two approaches.

8.   Example 2 – dividend/remuneration

P is the 100% owner of Alpha Ltd, an unquoted trading company with a year end of 30th June 2009.

Trade profits of Alpha Ltd are £280,000 for the year ended 30th June 2009 after directors remuneration to P of £80,000. There were no dividend payments.

P would like to have available cash of about £25,000 by December 2009 and requests advice as to the tax costs of obtaining this sum from the company. Advise P.

Solution

Cash of £25,000 – Dividend Route			**Tax cost**
Net cash required		25,000	
$25,000 \times \dfrac{100}{75}$		8,333	8,333
Net dividend		33,333	
Gross dividend $33,333 \times \dfrac{100}{90}$		37,037	
Inc tax @ 32.5% × 7,037	12,037		
Less Inc tax @ 10% × 37,037	3,704	8,333	8,333

Cash of £25,000 – Salary Route			
Gross salary $25,000 \times \dfrac{100}{59}$		42,373	
Income tax @ 40% × 42,373	16,949		
Class I NIC 1% × 42,373	424	17,373	17,373
Net Cash		25,000	
Emp NIC 12.8% × 42,373	5,423		
C Tax saving (42,373 + 5,423) × 21%	(10,037)		(4,614)

Notes

i)   Income tax @ 32.5% – 10% of the gross dividend is equivalent to 25% of net dividend (100 × 22.5 is equivalent to (100 – 10) × 25).

ii)   The total tax cost is higher for the salary route than the dividend.

iii) C Tax saved. Gross Salary + Emp NIC = (42,373 + 5,423) × 21% = 10,037.

9.   Example 3

Mr Smith has a chain of shoe shops and trading profits of £200,000 for the year to 5th April 2010. He is currently operating as a sole trader and is considering whether he should incorporate his business or not. He informs you that he currently contributes £16,000 (net) each year into an approved personal pension plan. He also advises you that if he were to incorporate his business he would require a director's salary of £60,000 per year gross and that he would like the company to pay his pension for him with a non contributory arrangement.

Required:

Compute the total income tax and national insurance as a sole trader and the total income tax, corporation tax and national insurance as an incorporated entity for the year to 5th April 2010.

Sole trader			**£**
Profits			200,000
Total income			200,000
PA			6,475
Taxable income			193,525
37,400	@ 20%	7,480	
extend BR 20,000	@ 20%	4,000	
136,125	@ 40%	54,450	
193,525			
Total income tax			65,930
NI			
Class 2	2.40 per week		125
Class 4	5,715-43,875 @ 8%		3,053
excess	200,000-43,875 @ 1%		1,561
			4,739
Total income tax and NI			**70,669**

Incorporation		
Profit		200,000
Salary		60,000
Employer NI 60,000-5,715 @ 12.8%		6,948
Pension		20,000
PCTCT		113,052
CT @ 21%		23,741
Profit after tax		89,311

Director		
Salary		60,000
Total income		60,000
PA		6,475

Taxable income			53,525
37,400	@ 20%	7,480	
16,125	@ 40%	6,450	
53,525			
Total income tax			13,930
NI 43,875-5,715@9.4%			3,587
60,000-43,875 @ 1%			161
Total income tax and NI			**17,678**
Total deductions			
Director			17,678
Company			
(23,741 + 6,948)			30,689
Total			**48,367**
Sole trader			**70,669**

Notes:

i)   In this example, the owner is not extracting all the profits from the company, therefore a tax saving has arisen and incorporation results in an effective total tax saving of £22,302 (£70,669 - £48,367).

ii)   Mr Smith could extract additional funds out of the business either in the form of an increase in salary or dividends (or a combination of the two) if he required, this would impact upon the tax saved.

iii) Mr Smith could also consider increasing his pension provision if he wished.

iv)   It may be more efficient for Mr Smith to draw out a dividend payment instead of the salary of £60,000.

Question without answer

1. Mr Chapman, a single man, is about to start a business which will be engaged in the repair of domestic appliances. His starting date is 1 April 2009 and he will make up accounts to 31 March each year.

His business plan shows that he is likely to make a taxable profit in the first few years, before any salary for himself, of approximately £40,000 per annum.

He is uncertain whether he should set up the business as a sole trader or as a limited company and seeks your advice. He has advised you that, if the business is run as a company, he will require a gross salary of £25,000 per annum.

 Required:

 Draft a report for Mr Chapman, indicating the important differences from a tax and NIC point of view, of the two alternative methods of running the business. Your answer should contain, as an appendix, computations showing the overall tax and NIC burden which will arise in each case. Assume 2009/2010 rates apply throughout.

 (15 marks)

(CIMA Business Taxation November 1997)

Index

Tax rates 2009/10

Income tax

Starting rate 10%	Savings income £0 – £2,440 band	
Basic rate	Savings/Non savings 20%	Dividends 10%
Higher rate	Savings/Non savings 40%	Dividends 32.5%

Taxable income	Band	Basic rate	Tax payable on band
£0 – 37,400	£37,400	20%	£7,480

Personal reliefs 2009/10

		£
Personal allowance		6,475
Allowances: Aged 65–74		
Personal allowance		9,490
Married couple's allowance (65 before 6.4.2000) min £2,540	*	6,965
Abatement income level		22,900
Allowances: aged 75+		
Personal allowance		9,640
Married couple's allowance (65 before 6.4.2000) min £2,540	*	6,965
Abatement income level		22,900
Blind person's allowance		1,890
Relief only at 10%*		

National insurance 2009/10

Retirement pension – single person - based on adequate contributions from a 49 year working life £4,953

Self employed

Class 2 contributions		£2.40 per week
Class 4 contributions	8.0% of profits between	5,715 – 43,875
	1.0% above	43,875

Class 1 Employed earners from 6th April 2009

£ per week earnings	Not contracted-out	Contracted-out COSR	COMP
Employee			
Earnings up to £110 a week – ET	Nil	Nil	Nil
Earnings between £110 and £844 a week	11.0%	9.4%	9.4%
Earnings over £844 a week	1.0%	1.0%	1.0%
Employer			
Earnings up to £110 a week	Nil	Nil	Nil
Earnings between £110 and £844 a week	12.8%	9.1%	11.4%
Earnings over £844 a week	12.8%	12.8%	12.8%

Corporation tax

	Years to 31st March	
	2009	**2010**
Financial year	**FY08**	**FY09**
Full rate	28%	28%
Small companies rate	21%	21%
Small companies fraction	7/400	7/400
Small companies profit levels		
Lower relevant amount	£300,000	£300,000
Higher relevant amount	£1,500,000	£1,500,000

Small companies formula: $(M - P) \times \dfrac{I}{P} \times (\text{a fraction})$

Car Benefit	Car Fuel Benefit
List price × CO_2 emission% 15% for a car with up to 135g/km CO_2 emissions, increasing by 1% for every 5g/km to a maximum of 35% 3% supplement for diesels 10% rate for cars with up to 120g/km emissions	£16,900 × CO_2 emission %

Tax rates 2009/10

Capital allowances

Plant and machinery
Annual investment allowance 100% on £50,000 of expenditure
Enhanced capital allowances   100%

Low Emission Cars	100%
Enterprise zones initial allowance	100%

First year allowance (FYA)

1 April 2009 – 31 March 2010 companies	40%
6 April 2009 – 5 April 2010 unincorporated businesses	40%

Writing down allowance (WDA)

General pool of plant and machinery and cars with CO_2 emissions of 160 g/km or less	20% per year
Special rate pool features integral to a building, long life assets and cars with CO_2 emissions of more than 160 g/km or less	10% per year

Industrial/Agricultural buildings

Writing down allowance (WDA)	4% of cost x 50%
Business Premises Renovation Allowance	100%

Capital gains tax

	Rate %	Exempt amount
Individuals	18	10,100

Lease premium
Capital element of a premium received on a lease of less than 50 years

$$P \times 2\% \times (n-1)$$

where
P = premium
n = length of lease in years

Value added tax

Standard rate	17.5% (7/47 x gross) from 1 January 2010
Temporary standard rate	15% (3/23 x gross) until 31 December 2009
Lower rate	5%
Zero rate	0%
Registration limits (From 1 May 2009)	£68,000 taxable turnover in cumulative 12 month period £68,000 taxable turnover in next 30 days

Inheritance tax

IHT on transfers on death on or after 6th April 2009

Chargeable transfer bands £	Rate of IT %
0 – 325,000	Nil
325,001 –	40